Financial
Statements

Economic analysis
and interpretation

Chris Higson

RIVINGTON

RIVINGTON PUBLISHING LIMITED

51 Eastcheap, London EC3M 1JP
www.rivingtonbooks.com

For restricted permission to copy or reproduce any part of this book, and for all other enquiries, contact the publisher at www.rivingtonbooks.com.

FINANCIAL STATEMENTS
Economic analysis and interpretation
www.higsonfinancialstatements.com

First edition published 2006, © Rivington Publishing 2006
ISBN 1 84578 010 8

British Library Cataloguing-in-Publication Data
A CIP catalogue record of this book is available from the British Library.

Cover design by Benjamin Parton

Printed in the UK by Norwich Colour Print, Norwich, on paper derived from forests sustained with 'two-for-one' planting.

Preface

The aim of this book is to explain what financial statements mean, and how we can use them to understand firms in economic terms. Since we can't use financial statements without knowing how accounting works, this is also a book about accounting.

The reader will see that the approach of this book is quite different to that of previous books in a number of ways. Perhaps the most fundamental is its focus on the measurement of return on capital, and its resulting emphasis on the integrity of the balance sheet – on the completeness of the balance sheet and on the valuation of assets and liabilities. This provides the organising principle for much of the book. As we will see, it brings a remarkable amount of order to an apparently complex subject and, not least, it provides the framework for reviewing 'GAAP', which is the body of accounting rules that firms use.

The book is written equally for students and for finance practitioners; indeed the book is for anyone who uses financial statements. The book is international in its scope – the cases it uses cover a wide range of industrial and commercial firms drawn from around the world, and it reviews and compares what are now the two principal systems of accounting rules internationally, 'US GAAP', and International GAAP or 'IFRS'. The book website *www.higsonfinancialstatements.com* is a vital companion to the book. It contains case discussions and examples, supporting materials and literature.

Acknowledgements

My principal debt is to a generation of London Business School students and finance practitioners with whom I have worked. Their enormous enthusiasm for the ideas in this book has been a continuing source of inspiration.

Here is a, certainly incomplete, list of individuals who contributed to the book in some way: Eli Amir, Patrick Barwise, John Briginshaw, Martin Deboo, Jeremy Dent, Keith Freeman, Arabella Grant, Paul Griffin, Yanling Guan, Cag Guner, Christine Holly, Maria Holly, Xi Li, Andrew Likierman, Gilad Livne, Richard Logan, June McEnroe, Chris Noke, Christopher Nobes, Sachin Oza, Federico Perciavalle, Craig Pickering, Stelios Platis, Oliver Rivers, Andrew Ryan, Amir Sabeti, John Senouf, Maria Simatova, Andy Simmonds, Andrei Vykhristyouk, Rory Winston, Meng Wu, Li Zhang. I am very grateful to Bernadette Salas and Yvonne Nash at London Business School for their skilled help in production along the way. Tom Albrighton, for Rivington, has been a great companion in this project.

There is a small group of people who have displayed extreme heroism. Jochen Zimmermann, Brian Singleton-Green and Julie Conder each read the whole manuscript with a close but sympathetic eye. Julie Conder also worked on a number of the cases. Finally, I must thank my wife, Sarah. She contributed to the book in all its stages. Without her wise counsel and loving support the book would not have seen the light of day.

Chris Higson,
London Business School, 2006

About the author

Chris Higson is a professor at London Business School, where he served as chair of the accounting group. He has degrees in philosophy and economics from University College London, and a doctorate in finance from London Business School. He is a qualified chartered accountant and was with Deloitte and Touche. Chris Higson publishes extensively on the financial performance and valuation of firms and on accounting policy and financial governance, and he regularly comments on television, radio and in the international press on these issues. Chris Higson has worked with many of the world's leading industrial firms and financial institutions both as a consultant and in senior management development. He also advises a number of governmental and not-for-profit organisations.

Contents

Chapter 1

The main ideas

Overview

This book is about the economic analysis and interpretation of firm's financial statements. Because we cannot make sense of financial statements without understanding accounting, this is also a book about accounting, and about 'GAAP' or Generally Accepted Accounting Principles, which are the rules that determine what goes into financial statements. A firm's financial statements consist of a balance sheet, an income statement and cash flow statement, plus any subsidiary statements and supporting data. Even in the digital age of continuous data flow, firms still publish their main financial statements annually, and update them half-yearly or, maybe, quarterly. These financial statements provide our window into firms.

Using financial statements to get reliable economic insights about firms looks like a tough task. There is a rich variety of beasts in the corporate jungle, and GAAP adds its own challenge with its technical vocabulary and seemingly arcane rules and conventions. The way to bring order to this complexity is to use an economic model. Investment theory tells us how the accounting would need to be done for financial statements to give reliable measures of the return a firm is earning on its investors' capital. The balance sheet would need to be complete in terms of assets, and record all the claims that others have over the firm; and these assets and liabilities would need to be measured at their current values. This turns out to be a pretty stern test of accounting that is very hard to achieve in practice. But its emphasis on the *completeness* of the balance sheet and on the *valuation* of assets and liabilities gives a very clear structure for thinking about accounting. It provides the organising principle for this book.

The book is in four parts. The first part, *Introduction to accounting,* explains the logic of accounting and describes the content of a balance sheet and an income statement. The second part, *Return on capital*, shows how investors use the balance sheet and income statement to calculate the return a firm is earning on their capital. The third part, *Financial analysis*, explains how we do forensic analysis of the financial statements to reveal as much as possible about the economics of the firm. The final part, *Accounting analysis*, conducts a systematic review of GAAP to identify the issues that need our attention as users of financial statements. In the remainder of this chapter we describe what is coming.

Introduction to accounting

Chapter 2, *Basics of accounting*, uses the simplest of businesses to explain how accountants record transactions, then make adjustments to the data to produce financial statements. It introduces the basic idea in accounting, which is that the income of a business is the change in its assets over a period. The actual balance sheets and income statements firms publish are identical in principle to the simple examples in Chapter 2; they just contain more detail, and frequently use different words. Chapter 3 *Reading the balance sheet and income statement*, shows how to put published balance sheets and income statements into a common vocabulary and into the format we need for analysis. Essentially what we do in these two chapters is introduce the economic framework – categories of asset and claim, and income and expense – that accounting uses and that we need to calculate return on capital, and in financial analysis. We compare four international firms that are in very different businesses; that use different types of resources and make their money in quite different ways. We will be struck by how effective the accounting framework is in representing them so that they can be directly compared to one another in financial terms.

The fundamental idea in accounting is that a firm's income is the change in its assets or, strictly, its assets less its liabilities. So accounting income depends on how the balance sheet is prepared. The firm's 'accounting model' is the set of rules that determine what assets and liabilities go into the balance sheet and at what values. Chapter 4, *Accounting models*, describes the accounting model that firms would need to use for financial statements to yield reliable measures of return on capital, period by period. This 'investment' accounting model requires a balance sheet that is both complete and at current values. We compare this to the accounting model that GAAP actually uses, and this gives us a look ahead to the issues we encounter through the book.

Return on capital

Financial statements look perfectly set up for measuring return on capital. The balance sheet lists the firm's assets and liabilities, so it tells us how much of the investors' capital the firm is using, and the income statement describes how much income it has earned using that capital. Chapter 5, *Measures of return on capital*, use this data to construct the principal measures of return on capital: 'return on equity', which is the return the firm earns on the funds provided by equity shareholders, and 'return on capital employed', which is an 'entity-level' return on all of the finance raised from shareholders and by borrowing. Return on capital can then be compared to the investors' required return, which is the firm's cost of capital. This leads naturally to the idea of 'economic profit', which is widely used for performance measurement within firms. Economic profit simply internalises the cost of capital comparison by deducting a capital charge from profit.

In practice, people frequently do use financial statement data as a 'value metric'; that is, as a measure of investment return that is compared to the cost of capital. Investors do it when they use accounting data to rank and screen stocks. Regulators do it when they use return on capital to identify monopoly profits, or as the basis for controlling the prices charged by regulated firms. Firms themselves do it when they use accounting data to make investment decisions or to measure divisional performance, or as a factor in management remuneration. Chapter 6, *Value metrics*, discusses some of these applications and the accounting adjustments that practitioners make to get the data integrity needed for reliable measures of return. The chapter ends by comparing accounting returns and share price performance as measures of performance.

Financial analysis

Measuring investment return is an important task but, most of the time, we are wearing a different hat when we read financial statements. We are simply trying to get as rich an understanding as we can of the 'economics' of a firm – the drivers of its profitability and growth, its financial structure, and how cash flows into and out of the firm, and we are comparing firms in these terms. This requires us to understand the accounting, because profitability, financial structure and cash flow are all sensitive to how the accounting is done. We also need to understand the business the firm is in and the 'business model' it is using. The contractual sophistication of the modern world makes it easy for firms to change their business model, by outsourcing some activities or arranging for parts of the productive process to be undertaken by other firms. This can radically change the appearance of the financial statements.

Chapter 7, *Operating profitability*, shows how to use financial ratios to conduct a systematic decomposition of return on capital employed, first into margin and asset turn, then into their component costs, and assets and liabilities. Chapter 8, *Cash flow*, explains how to analyse the cash flow statement to get most insight into the way a firm is generating and using cash. Cash flow is a story, not a number, and we want the cash flow statement to present the story in a transparent and coherent way. We discuss how the appearance of the cash flow, like the other financial statements, is affected by the firm's business model, by growing and shrinking, and by the firm's accounting policies. Chapter 9, *Capital structure*, provides the tools for analysing the firm's financial structure, but from the perspective of the adequacy of the firm's assets to meet its liabilities, and to measure the extent to which the firm funds its capital employed using debt. Borrowing brings a fixed commitment to pay interest, and we show how this affects the level as well as the volatility of earnings. Chapter 10, *Growth*, explains how to analyse a firm's growth. It is easy enough to measure the firm's overall sales growth, year on year, and GAAP also requires firms to report sales growth at the segment level. But we will see that GAAP does not currently provide the disclosure to go much deeper than this.

Financial analysis is story telling – we are trying to tell the firm's economic story using financial statement data and any non-financial information that the firm has provided. Even when the firm is not using the accounting model we might want, if we know how the numbers were measured we can adjust the data, or use our experience to form a judgement. If financial statements do not give a clear window into the firm this is mainly because of the aggregate nature of financial statements and the lack of disclosure and transparency, rather than the way the numbers are measured. So the stories we tell are necessarily conjectures and we should constantly seek more data and look for alternative explanations, and keep asking ourselves just how much confidence we have in our judgements.

Accounting analysis

Until quite recently the accounting world was truly a 'Babel' where most countries required their firms to report using national rules. However, two systems now dominate – US GAAP and International GAAP, that for shorthand we call IFRS, and we review both systems in this book. The exhibit opposite, *GAAP history and institutions*, describe some of the institutional background. Though, viewed from close up, there remain many differences of detail, from the high-level perspective of this book IFRS and US GAAP are similar in most important respects. We explain the differences as we encounter them, but where the systems are effectively the same we talk generically about 'GAAP'.

GAAP is always controversial; people disagree with particular treatments, or just complain that GAAP is too complex. But, with one or two exceptions, it is the world that is the problem, not GAAP. Balance sheets are black and white, so assets and liabilities are either in the balance sheet, or out. But the world is complex and ambiguous. What assets and liabilities are worth, and whether they even exist, may be uncertain. Sometimes it is unclear whether or not a firm owns a particular asset, especially if it has written a complex contract that shares the risks and rewards of ownership with others. The only way GAAP can represent this complex world in the binary framework of the balance sheet is with a system of categories and thresholds, applied with a bias to conservatism. Systems like this always seem arbitrary at the margin.

In this part of the book, the focus remains the integrity of the balance sheet – its completeness, and how assets and liabilities are valued. Chapter 11, *Assets*, discusses asset recognition and, in particular, the treatment of intangible assets. For GAAP, a necessary condition for recognising an asset in the balance sheet is that the future benefits can be measured reliably. This turns out to be tough on home-grown intangible assets, such as brands, patents, organisational competencies and know-how, that may be the most valuable assets many firms have. But if an intangible asset was purchased rather than home-grown, as commonly happens in a takeover, GAAP requires it to be recognised in the balance sheet. So we also discuss the accounting treatment of takeovers at this point. Chapter 12, *Liabilities*, discusses the recognition of liabilities in the balance

Exhibit: GAAP history and institutions

The US Securities and Exchange Commission (SEC), which was formed in 1933-4 in the wake of the Great Crash, mandated the US accounting profession to set financial reporting rules and the body that does this is now called the Financial Accounting Standards Board (FASB). In countries such as the US where GAAP has evolved over a lengthy period and that have a legal system based on Common Law, GAAP is multi-source and need not even be written down so long as it represents accepted practice. The prime written sources of US GAAP are Statements of Financial Accounting Standards (SFAS) and also bulletins and interpretations issued by the FASB. Statements of Position (SOP) by the American Institute of Certified Public Accountants (AICPA), and opinions and discussions by the Emerging Issues Task Force (EITF) are also influential.

In 1973 a group of countries (Australia, Canada, France, Germany, Japan, Mexico, the Netherlands, the UK and the US) created the International Accounting Standards Committee (IASC) to develop a unified set of international accounting standards called International Accounting Standards (IAS). In 2001 the IASC became the International Accounting Standards Board (IASB), which issues International Financial Reporting Standards (IFRS). In this book we refer to 'International GAAP' as IFRS. IFRS is progressively replacing national GAAP in countries outside the US, and it became mandatory for stock market listed firms in the European Union from 1 January 2005.

IFRS and US GAAP are continuing to converge with each other and now develop their standards jointly. Of course, optimism about convergence has to be qualified because nationalism remains a powerful instinct. So far at least, countries have tended to maintain their own GAAP, even after they have accepted IFRS. For example, European countries still use their national GAAP for non-listed firms. But since IFRS and US GAAP usually represent best practice, there is a natural tendency for national GAAPs to evolve to look like them. A strong force for convergence is the actions of firms themselves. Firms that want to be seen as world class will endeavour to report to the highest standards, especially if they want to raise money on international capital markets. German firms are a good example of this. Even though IFRS was not mandatory until 2005, by 2003 67% of the largest German firms were already using IFRS and 23% US GAAP, leaving only 10% following German GAAP (see Chris Higson and Mark Sproul, *Coping with IFRS*, London Business School/Company Reporting, 2005).

sheet. Again, we discuss how GAAP deals with the indeterminacy of the world, and we examine some of the most important classes of liability for firms, including tax liabilities and pension liabilities. From a GAAP perspective, the other key issue for asset recognition is the property rights question: does the firm own the asset? We postpone the ownership question to Chapter 13, *Asset/liability netting*, where it is best discussed in tandem with the recognition of liabilities. We discuss techniques such as non-consolidation and operating leasing which permit firms to finance some assets in such a way that the asset and the corresponding debt finance can be netted and excluded from the balance sheet.

Chapter 14, *Balance sheet valuation*, discusses how assets and liabilities are valued in practice. GAAP strives for balance sheet completeness, but it doesn't give us balance sheets that are at current value. Revaluing assets and liabilities each year would be costly and would introduce significant subjectivity into accounting. So the value basis of balance sheets remains, fundamentally, historic cost – if assets become worth less than cost they are written down, but if they become worth more they are left at cost. IFRS permits fixed assets and intangibles to be revalued, while US GAAP insists on historic cost. Also GAAP requires 'fair valuation' of some financial assets and liabilities. The result is that financial statements give us a cocktail that has a base of historic costs with some current value mixed in.

Chapter 15, *Income*, examines the income statement. Through choices about when to recognise revenues and costs, accrual accounting gives firms some discretion in timing earnings. Here we focus on revenue recognition. How the income statement is presented can be as important as how income is measured. For example, firms may emphasise some components of income while classifying other components as extraordinary or exceptional and inviting the analyst to treat them as transitory. In recent years some firms have taken this even further by producing a so-called 'pro-forma' report alongside their GAAP numbers.

Using this book

Building an understanding is not like building a wall; it is usually best to start at the top and work down to the foundations. In this book, we begin with the idea of a balance sheet and of an income statement, and how they are used to measure return on capital. These are all very intuitive constructs – they make sense as ideas, without needing to know in great detail how accountants build them. We fill in that detail as the book proceeds.

We use a lot of cases and examples to illustrate the points along the way. *Cases* are based on the publicly available data of real firms. *Examples* are simple stories that are made-up; they have no connection at all to real-world businesses that might happen to share the same name! *Exhibits* are short narratives describing pieces of history or literatures that help put the ideas we are discussing into context. The book's website *www.higsonfinancialstatements.com* contains plenty more supporting materials: cases, examples and readings. We do not reproduce the financial statements of firms that we discuss because these are now invariably available from the firm's own website; in most cases the book's website contains links to them.

A significant barrier to entry to understanding financial statements is vocabulary. Accounting has a very powerful conceptual structure to describe firms in economic terms. But GAAP does not police the vocabulary and formats that firms use very tightly. Accountants can use different words for the same thing, and can mean different things by the same word. The vocabulary and formats that we use in this book are a mix of US GAAP and IFRS practice. We italicise terms the first time they are introduced and defined and, where there is a variety of vocabulary used in practice, we explain the main alternatives as we go along. The vocabulary is collected in a *Glossary* at the end of the book. Also at the end of the book are a *Glossary of financial ratios*, and an appendix on *Financial arithmetic* covering the financial arithmetic we use in accounting and financial analysis.

Part 1

Introduction to accounting

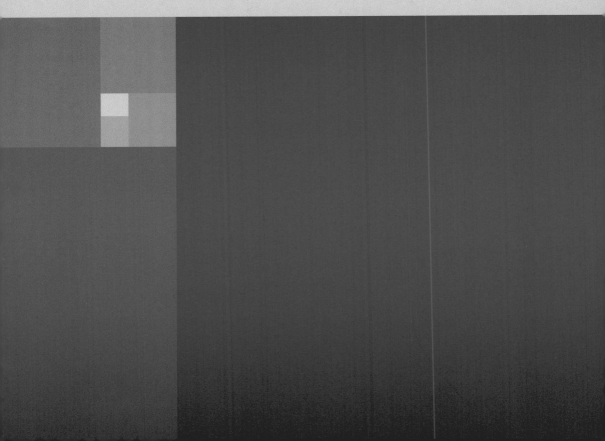

Chapter 2

Basics of accounting

This chapter introduces some of the basic ideas and vocabulary in accounting including the most basic idea of all, which is that the income of a business during a period is the change in its assets. The chapter explains the book-keeping process by which accountants record transactions, then make adjustments to the transactional data to produce financial statements. We use a spreadsheet approach to book-keeping that will be useful when we need to analyse the effect of particular accounting treatments later.

ASSETS AND INCOME

The basic principle in accounting is that the income of a business during a period is the change in its assets, adjusted for any withdrawals by its owners. Consider the simplest example of a business.

Example: The match-seller

A match-seller has $4 in her pocket when she arrives at the wholesaler. She uses it to buy 100 boxes of matches at 4¢ a box. For the rest of the day she stands in the town square selling the matches for 10¢ a box. By evening she has sold her last box and has $10 in her pocket.

The match-seller's profit for the day is $6. We could figure this out on a unit basis – her profit per box was 6¢ and she sold 100 of them. But, in general, we are going to measure her profit in total as the difference between her business assets at the beginning of the day and at the end of the day. She began with $4 cash to buy goods and ended with $10 cash from selling them – hence $6 profit.

From the second week, rather than go to the cash and carry every day, she decides to go just once a week. She buys 500 boxes on Monday morning and sells 100 during the day as before, so she has 400 boxes left over on Monday night. The rest of the week continues the same way, selling 100 boxes each day so all stock is used up by Friday night. How shall we measure the match-seller's *daily* profit now? We can't measure profit day by day simply by tracking the change in cash, because she has other assets as well as cash. Take Monday. She starts the day with 500 boxes costing (4¢ × 500 =) $20. She ends the day with assets of $26 in total, comprising $10 in cash and an inventory of 400 boxes that cost $16. We get the same answer as before: her profit on the day is $6, which is the increase in her assets.

Asset valuation – a look ahead

Accounting works out how much profit has been made in a period by making a tally of assets, less liabilities, at the beginning and at the end of each period. So profit measurement inevitability involves estimation and judgement because it depends on the value we attribute to these assets and liabilities. These issues cannot be avoided, even in the simplest of businesses.

In the case of the match-seller someone might challenge like this: *'In what sense are you putting a 'value' on the match-seller's assets on Monday night? Surely you just recorded them at what they cost?'* Even to record assets at cost is to make a judgement that they are worth at least what they cost, which is a judgement about what might happen in the future. In the match business, it is fairly safe to record the inventory of matches at cost, but not entirely safe. It all hinges on whether the match-seller will be able to recover at least 4¢ per box for the remaining stock on subsequent days. If you put your mind to it, you can think of several reasons why this might not happen.
– Fashions may change, so that everyone wants cigarette lighters from now on.

- A horde of competing match-sellers may appear in the square tomorrow, so that there is not enough business to go around.
- Some of the boxes were defective and she just sold the best ones on Monday.

All of these are possible; the question is how probable are they? If it seemed likely she will not be able to sell the remaining boxes for what they cost, we should value the inventory at what could be recovered. The match-seller's Monday profit would be correspondingly reduced.

Instead of valuing the inventory at cost, we might be tempted to record the boxes of matches at 10¢ a box on Monday night, since this is what the match-seller hopes to sell them for. The effect of that would be to anticipate all of the week's profit and attribute it to Monday, including the profit on the matches she has not sold yet. This is easy to see:

Monday morning's assets	*$500 \times 4¢ = 20*
Monday night's assets	*$10 cash plus $400 \times 10¢$ of inventory = $50*
So, Monday's profit	*$50 - $20 = $30*

Valuing inventory at selling price is one of many 'accounting models' that accountants could use for valuing assets. Even if there is a very high probability that the match-seller will sell her remaining matches at full price, accounting does not recognise the profit until it is earned, and accounting views profit as earned when it is realised rather than just because it is expected. Profit is 'realised' when a legally enforceable sale has taken place, that is, when an asset has been created in the form of cash or a claim on the customer. These issues of asset valuation will preoccupy us throughout this book. In the remainder of this chapter, though, we focus on basic book-keeping.

WHAT IS A FIRM?

The match-seller is simply a 'sole trader', but most economic activity is conducted through 'incorporated' firms that have been given a legal existence separate from their owners by *incorporation* (that comes from the Latin *corpus*, a body)[1]. The words *company* and *corporation* are commonly used for an incorporated firm; we simply refer to them as *firms*. Because incorporation gives a firm a separate legal existence this brings *limited liability*. In principle, the owners of a firm are not liable for its debts beyond the capital that they have contributed. In reality, the officers of a firm can find themselves personally liable if they have behaved negligently or criminally and, also, banks commonly require the owners of small firms to forfeit limited liability when they give a personal guarantee in order to secure a loan.

An incorporated firm is a legal construct, so every dollar of asset in the firm must be matched by a dollar claim on the firm from outside. The *balance sheet* describes this. It consists of two lists that must be equal in total, a list of the firm's assets and a list of the claims upon the firm. There are two sorts of claim on a firm: *liabilities*, which are

---

1   The alternative to incorporation is to use an unincorporated entity. A business that has not been incorporated is treated in law, and particularly by the tax authorities, as a *sole trader*, or if there is more than one owner, as a *partnership*. Partnerships are commonly used, for instance in professions such as law and accountancy. Many countries now allow hybrids such as the 'limited partnership' structure that gives limited liability but is taxed as a partnership. Much of what we discuss in this book would equally apply to partnerships, though we do not analyse any. It has always been possible to write the statutes of a business in a way that protects some of the partners. The 'en commendite' partnership structure that was developed in early 12th century Italy is an early example of this.

amounts the firm owes to third parties, and *shareholders' funds*, which is the ownership claim of the firm's shareholders.

Since shareholders own the firm, it is no surprise that the balance sheet balances – shareholders' funds are the balancing figure. The difference between the firm's assets and its liabilities measures the shareholders' wealth in balance-sheet terms. If the firm makes a profit, for example, by selling some goods for more than they cost, this increases the firm's assets, net of liabilities. So the firm's income is the increase in shareholders' funds in the balance sheet. The *income statement* is a stylised description of how the firm has earned its income over a period.

Shareholders' funds

There are two sources of shareholders' funds in the balance sheet. They own the firm, so as it makes profit and its assets grow this gets added to the shareholders' account. But also, when the firm is created and when it subsequently raises more share capital, shareholders contribute cash in exchange for shares. They withdraw wealth by being paid a *dividend* out of accumulated profits or by allowing the firm to repurchase their shares.

'Paid-in share capital' is the finance provided by shareholders when they buy shares. Ownership rights are denominated in shares that are issued to the shareholders. In most countries the shares of a firm are denominated in terms of a *par* value, which is sometimes called *nominal* value. When the firm makes an issue of shares it will do so at a price based on their market value at that time, which is usually above par. So the consequence of the par value convention is that accountants have to record the proceeds of issuing new shares on two lines: the par value, and the remainder, which is called the *share premium* or 'capital in excess of par'.

We start the Lucia example later by having her contribute $25,000 to get her business going and, to keep things simple, we just call this 'share capital'. Suppose, in fact, her accountant registers the business with an authorised share capital of 20,000 shares at a par value of 50¢ each. Lucia subscribes $5,000 for 10,000 of these shares 'at par'. She persuades her friends and relations to contribute the remaining $20,000, but at a valuation of $4 per share. That way she only has to issue them with another ($20,000/$4 =) 5,000 shares, which means she still has (20,000 -10,000 - 5,000 =) 5,000 unissued, in case she needs more capital later. More to the point, she keeps control of the firm since she now owns ⅔ of the issued shares. If this were what had happened, it would be recorded as:

	Lucia	Friends	Total
Share capital, at par	$5,000	$ 2,500	$ 7,500
Share premium		$17,500	$17,500
Paid-in share capital	**$5,000**	**$20,000**	**$25,000**

Par value is a hangover from earlier times when it was common for firms to issue 'partly-paid' shares. The firm might issue $1 par value shares but only require 20¢ to be subscribed initially, giving it the option to 'call up' the remaining 80¢ if and when it needed the funds. If the firm subsequently became bankrupt the creditors were entitled to require shareholders to 'pay up' the shares, in other words, to subscribe further capital up to the par value of the shares. The notion of par value is nowadays an oddity and it rarely has any economic significance. For financial analysis there is usually no economic insight in separating par value and share premium, so they can be added back together to give *paid-in share capital*. For simplicity, in the Lucia example in this chapter we just talk about 'share capital'.

THE ACCOUNTING PROCESS FOR A FIRM

When accountants do the book-keeping they are simply updating a firm's balance sheet to record the effects of transactions and, usually at the end of the period, to make adjustments to the transactional data.

Every transaction (or adjustment) has two equal and opposite effects on the balance sheet. The firm may exchange one asset for another, for example when it buys a machine for cash. It may exchange one claim for another, for example when it swaps shareholders' funds for a debt. The firm may simultaneously increase an asset and a claim, for example when it buys a machine on credit. It may simultaneously reduce an asset and a claim, for example when it uses cash to pay an amount it owes. Accountants use an extremely efficient vocabulary for describing these possibilities. An increase in an asset or a reduction in a claim is known as a *debit*, and a reduction in an asset or an increase in a claim is known as a *credit*. So every event must have one debit and one credit. The possible pairs of book-keeping entries are the horizontals and verticals in the following grid:

	Increase	Decrease
Asset	Debit (+)	Credit (-)
Claim	Credit (-)	Debit (+)

The rest of this section examines the book-keeping for some representative transactions and accounting adjustments. We use a spreadsheet as an active balance sheet. It has a row for each class of asset and claim, and each column records the effect of a transaction. At any stage, so long as we are doing our accounting properly and making two entries for each transaction, the totals of the asset and claim columns will balance and record the firm's balance sheet at that point. The spreadsheet method of keeping accounts would work perfectly well in practice. Commercial accounting packages use the same logic but are designed to handle lots of transactions and multiple users.

Recording transactions

A *transaction* is an exchange of assets and claims with third parties, including receipts and payments of cash. To start with, consider these common transactions: *financing the firm; buying and selling goods; buying services; buying assets.*

Example: Lucia's bookshop

Lucia decides to run a bookshop and she incorporates a business for the purpose. She puts $25,000 into the bank to start the business. To help us keep track of Lucia's transactions we will assign each one a letter. The spreadsheet would record that the firm had (a) raised $25,000 of shareholders' funds in the form of paid-in share capital, and received $25,000 of the asset, cash.

Table 1 Financing the firm

	Opening balance sheet (a)
Cash	25,000
TOTAL ASSETS	**25,000**
Shareholders' funds:	
Share capital	25,000
TOTAL L&SF*	**25,000**

* Total Liabilities and Shareholders' Funds

Lucia will need to lease a shop before she does anything else. But we will reverse the natural order and go straight to the heart of the business, which is buying things and selling them at a profit. Lucia finds a supplier who will supply her with books on credit. She (b) buys $30,000 of books, and subsequently (c) sells books for $10,000 in cash and sells another $15,000 on credit. The cost of the books she sold was (d) $18,000.

These transactions have the following effects. First, Lucia acquires $30,000 of the asset, 'inventory'. She generates a corresponding $30,000 liability, in the form of a payable to the supplier. Thus far she has simply acquired an asset. From an accounting perspective, the books become an expense when she sells them. If Lucia sells books for $25,000 that cost her $18,000, she has made a profit of $7,000.

Since shareholders own the profits that the firm makes, we insert another row under shareholders' funds to record profit because we want to keep this separate from share capital. Accounting records the earning of profit in two steps. First, it records the sale of $25,000 in the profit column. Correspondingly, assets increase by $25,000: $10,000 as cash and $15,000 as a receivable from customers. Second, it records the cost of the goods sold. Inventory is reduced by $18,000, which is shown as cost of goods sold in the profit column. She has increased her net assets by $7,000, and this is the measure of the profit in the transaction.

Table 2 Buying and selling goods

	Opening balance sheet	Buy books (b)	Sale of books (c)	Cost of books sold (d)	Closing balance sheet
Cash	25,000		10,000		35,000
Receivables			15,000		15,000
Inventory		30,000		-18,000	12,000
TOTAL ASSETS	**25,000**				**62,000**
Payables		30,000			30,000
Shareholders' funds:					
Share capital	25,000				25,000
Profit			25,000	-18,000	7,000
TOTAL L&SF	**25,000**				**62,000**

Lucia's spreadsheet now shows $35,000 in cash, $15,000 in receivables and $12,000 in inventory. Therefore she has $62,000 of assets in total. These assets are financed by $30,000 of payables and the rest by shareholders' funds, consisting of the $25,000 she originally invested plus the $7,000 profit to date.

Lucia has some bills to pay. She (e) pays $20,000 of the amount she owes to the supplier. She has $5,000 of business expenses (f) for utility bills, maintenance, travel and so forth. Lucia tops up her cash with a $10,000 bank loan (g), repayable in five years. Lucia also buys a five year lease on a shop for $15,000 cash, and office equipment for $2,100 on credit (h). The effects of these transactions are shown in Table 3.

Table 3 Lucia continued

	Opening balance sheet	Pay supplier (e)	General expenses (f)	Loan (g)	Lease and equipment (h)	Closing balance sheet
Cash	35,000	-20,000	-5,000	10,000	-15,000	5,000
Receivables	15,000					15,000
Inventory	12,000					12,000
Lease					15,000	15,000
Equipment					2,100	2,100
TOTAL ASSETS	**62,000**					**49,100**
Loan				10,000		10,000
Payables	30,000	-20,000			2,100	12,100
Shareholders' funds:						
Share capital	25,000					25,000
Profit	7,000		-5,000			2,000
TOTAL L&SF	**62,000**					**49,100**

Accounting adjustments

Recording transactions is fairly mechanical. However, accountants then review the book-keeping to see whether it has generated a balance sheet that fairly reflects the firm's assets and claims at the end of the period. They make some adjustments to the transactional record, reflecting judgements about whether debits should be treated as assets or charged as expenses against the profit of the year, and about the treatment of credits as revenues or as liabilities. These adjustments do not affect the cash row, which is a factual description of receipts and payment of cash, but they do involve shifts between assets and liabilities, and profit. Accounting adjustments are the essence of what accountants do; their effect is to shift costs, and therefore profit between periods.

Accruals and provisions

Lucia's spreadsheet is showing a profit of $2,000. The expenses that were charged to calculate Lucia's profit were simply the amounts billed. The accountant needs to check there are no bills outstanding that relate to this period. It turns out that there is a payment on the bank loan, due to be made just after the year end, that contains $500 for the interest relating to this period. So the accountant charges (i) $500 interest expense to this period's profit – profit is reduced by $500. The other side of the adjustment is to recognise a liability in the balance sheet as an *accrual* for interest. It could have run the other way, so that part of a payment that had been charged against profit this period actually relates to next period. In this case the accountant would make the opposite entry, reducing the expense this year and recognising an asset called a *prepayment*.

The accountant also has to consider if there are any other costs relating to the period in question that have not been taken into account in accruals for outstanding bills. If so, a *provision* needs to be made. The difference between a provision and an accrual is that whereas an accrual will be for a known amount, because a bill has been received after the year end for example, a provision is an estimate of a cost, the exact amount of which is uncertain. The tax charge is an example of a provision: an estimate is made of the tax payable on the current year's profits (it is often charged to the accounts as a round figure). The final figure will not be known until the tax computation has been prepared and agreed with the tax authorities. When the accountant has completed the adjustments it is becomes clear that Lucia has made a loss, so her tax provision is nil.

Lucia's advertising campaign has alerted a rival bookshop to her existence. The rival is claiming that the name of Lucia's bookshop is too similar to their own and will damage their trade, and is suing Lucia for compensation and damages. The outcome of this dispute is uncertain, but it seems likely that a settlement will have to be made so Lucia's accountant makes a provision (j) of $1,500 for the settlement and legal fees.

Depreciation and amortisation

The lease on the shop is currently sitting as an asset, but is only of five years' duration. So this year and each of the next four years should be charged with their share of the cost of the lease. Similarly, the office equipment is expected to last only three years before it is replaced. Accountants use the words *depreciation* for the consumption of a tangible asset and *amortisation* for the consumption of an intangible asset, or of a financial asset such as a lease. Lucia charges this year's profit with ($2,100/3 =) $700 for depreciating the equipment and ($15,000/5 =) $3,000 for amortisation on the lease (k). This assumes that, as is conventional, the cost is spread evenly over the years of the assets' lives; that is, depreciated or amortised *straight line*. This leaves things not looking so good – Lucia is now showing a loss for the period of $3,700. But this would not be uncommon in the first year of trading.

Table 4 The full picture, with adjustments

	Pre-adjustment balance sheet	Accrued expenses (i)	Provision for settlement (j)	Amortisation depreciation (k)	Closing balance sheet
Cash	5,000				5,000
Receivables	15,000				15,000
Inventory	12,000				12,000
Lease	15,000			-3,000	12,000
Office equipment	2,100			-700	1,400
TOTAL ASSETS	**49,100**				**45,400**
Accruals		500			500
Loan	10,000				10,000
Payables	12,100				12,100
Provisions			1,500		1,500
Shareholders' funds:					
Share capital	25,000				25,000
Profit (Loss)	2,000	-500	-1,500	-3,700	-3,700
TOTAL L&SF	**49,100**				**45,400**

THE FINANCIAL STATEMENTS

The spreadsheet contains a full financial record of Lucia's business. All that remains is to describe its contents in a systematic way by producing financial statements. The fruits of the book-keeping are the final column in Table 4, which measures the assets and claims of this business at the end of the period. The accountant will assemble these into a *balance sheet*.

Two rows in the spreadsheet are particularly important. One is the profit row, which records revenues and expenses and thus calculates the firm's profit or loss for the period. The other is the cash row, which that records the asset, cash. The *income statement* and the *cash flow statement* analyse these two rows to help understand what has happened. They describe how the firm got from the *stock* of assets and liabilities in its opening balance sheet to the *stock* of assets and liabilities in its closing balance sheet in terms of the *flow* of profit and the *flow* of cash. We present the income statement here, but defer talking about the cash flow until Chapter 8.

The balance sheet

Accountants classify assets into *current* and *long-term* or *non-current*, depending on whether they are expected to be liquidated, or turned into cash, within a year. In the same way, liabilities to third parties are *current* if they are expected to be discharged within the year, and are *long-term* otherwise. Since firms publish their primary financial statements annually, current assets and current liabilities are those that are expected to be turned into cash, or settled, by the next balance-sheet date. So a balance sheet looks like this:

CURRENT ASSETS
LONG-TERM ASSETS
TOTAL ASSETS

CURRENT LIABILITIES
LONG-TERM LIABILITIES
SHAREHOLDERS' FUNDS
TOTAL LIABILITIES and SHAREHOLDERS' FUNDS

Lucia's balance sheet is laid out in this way in Table 5. Note that because the provision for the legal case is expected to take a while to settle, it is included in long-term liabilities.

Table 5 Lucia's balance sheet

Cash	5,000
Receivables	15,000
Inventory	12,000
CURRENT ASSETS	**32,000**
Lease	12,000
Office equipment	1,400
LONG-TERM ASSETS	**13,400**
TOTAL ASSETS	**45,400**
Payables	12,100
Accruals	500
CURRENT LIABILITIES	**12,600**
Loan	10,000
Provisions	1,500
LONG-TERM LIABILITIES	**11,500**
Share capital	25,000
Profit	-3,700
SHAREHOLDERS' FUNDS	**21,300**
TOTAL L&SF	**45,400**

The income statement

The income statement is simply an analysis of the change in shareholders' funds. The income statement is commonly called the *profit and loss account*, and may be called by other names too. The income statement starts by showing the value of the *sales* – sometimes called *revenue* and *turnover* – made in the year. It then deducts the expenses incurred to achieve these sales, to give *operating profit*. Accountants use many names for operating profit in practice; a common one is *trading profit*. The term *cost of sales* or *cost of goods sold (COGS)* is used for the costs of bringing goods to a saleable condition – this includes the consumption of raw materials, and factory costs including labour, factory overhead and factory depreciation, or warehousing costs in a retail business. In Lucia's case, cost of goods sold is simply the purchase cost of the books she sold. The difference between sales and cost of sales is called the firm's *gross profit*. The remaining expenses are then deducted to get to operating profit. The firm may have *other income,* that is, income from non-operating sources. Lucia has none.

The firm will have to pay interest on its debt but will receive interest on any cash it holds. So the first claim on its income is for *net interest payments*. The income after interest is 'earnings before tax', and corporate tax is charged on this. What remains after these outside claims belongs to the equity shareholders, who own the firm and so are the residual claimants on its income. This is known as *earnings*. Here is Lucia's income statement.

Table 6 Lucia's income statement

SALES	**25,000**
Cost of sales	-18,000
GROSS PROFIT	**7,000**
General expenses	-5,000
Amortisation, depreciation	-3,700
Legal provision	-1,500
OPERATING LOSS	**-3,200**
Net interest payable	-500
EARNINGS BEFORE TAX	**-3,700**
Tax	0
EARNINGS	**-3,700**

Income vocabulary

In everyday language people use the words income, profit and earnings interchangeably; we have used them loosely in this chapter thus far. From now on we will use the words in the following way. *Income* is a general term for any flow that increases assets. *Profit* is income from trading or from operations, or gains on the sale of assets. Profits, together with income from other sources, comprise the *earnings* of the firm.

SOME FURTHER EVENTS

Example: Lucia's second year

In her second year of trading Lucia (l) pays the $10,000 outstanding balance with her book supplier from the first year; pays the $2,100 owing to the office equipment supplier; collects $15,000 of receivables from customers. So, net, cash increases by $2,900. She buys a further $40,000 books; $15,000 for cash and $25,000 on credit (m). She makes sales (n) of books for $35,000, $24,000 for cash and $11,000 for credit. These books had cost her $20,000 (o). She decides she can manage without the loan, so she repays it early. (p). The effect of these transactions is shown in Table 7:

Table 7 Second year transactions

	Opening balance sheet	Lucia pays suppliers, customers pay her (l)	Purchase books (m)	Sale of books (n)	Cost of books sold (o)	Loan repaid (p)	Provisional balance sheet
Cash	5,000	2,900	-15,000	24,000		-10,000	6,900
Receivables	15,000	-15,000		11,000			11,000
Inventory	12,000		40,000		-20,000		32,000
Lease	12,000						12,000
Office equipment	1,400						1,400
TOTAL ASSETS	**45,400**						**63,300**
Accruals	500						500
Loan	10,000					-10,000	
Payables	12,100	-12,100	25,000				25,000
Provisions	1,500						1,500
Shareholders' funds:							
Share capital	25,000						25,000
Profit (loss)	-3,700			35,000	-20,000		11,300
TOTAL L&SF	**45,400**						**63,300**

The effect of accruals and provisions

The legal dispute is bringing bad publicity and diverting Lucia's attention from the business of selling books, so she agrees to settle and pays $1,900 including legal fees. Her balance sheet at the end of the first year had a provision of $1,500 for this, so her accountant now 'releases' or uses this provision, and records an additional expense of $400 (q). The effect of having made the provision was to charge the first year's profit with the expense, or at least with $1,400 of it, since Lucia rather underestimated the settlement. This reduces the charge to profit in the year in which the payment was actually made to $400. The interest accrual had the same effect; the payment of $500 is absorbed by the accrual and does not touch this year's profit (r).

Lucia has made a profit this year, so she will have to pay tax. The tax will not be due until the next year, so her accountant creates a tax provision. Based on the best estimate of the amount payable, and taking into account the losses she made in the first year of trading, she provides $750 for tax (s). Table 8 shows the effects.

Table 8 The effect of accruals and provisions

	Provisional balance sheet	Settle legal claim (q)	Interest paid (r)	Tax provision (s)	Provisional balance sheet, cont
Cash	6,900	-1,900	-500		4,500
Receivables	11,000				11,000
Inventory	32,000				32,000
Lease	12,000				12,000
Office equipment	1,400				1,400
TOTAL ASSETS	**63,300**				**60,900**
Accruals	500		-500		
Payables	25,000				25,000
Provisions	1,500	-1,500		750	750
Shareholders' funds:					
Share capital	25,000				25,000
Profit (loss)	11,300	-400		-750	10,150
TOTAL L&SF	**63,300**				**60,900**

Profit or loss on disposal

Lucia finds that the office equipment she bought in the first year is not needed in the business, so she sells it for $800 cash. The equipment she sells was recorded in her books at a net book value of $1,400, which is the original cost of $2,100 less depreciation of $700. She has made a *loss on disposal* of ($1,400 - $800 =) $600 (t). If she had sold the equipment for more than $1,400 she would have made a *profit on disposal*. A profit or loss on disposal is effectively a final adjustment or catch-up to depreciation when the true final value of the asset is known.

Capitalisation and write off

The accrual and prepayment adjustments, and the depreciation and amortisation adjustments, are about matching costs to periods. Consider a more controversial adjustment of the same sort. Lucia spent $4,000 on business expenses in the second year, including $2,000 on redecorating the shop (u). Lucia argues that the refurbishment will last the next 3 years, which is the remaining life of the lease. So, rather than being an expense of the current period, ($2,000 × ¾ =) $1,500 of this expenditure should be viewed as creating an asset. Accountants use the word *capitalisation* when expenditure is treated as an asset, and more generally use the word *recognition* when any asset or liability is shown in the balance sheet.

Of course, as well as looking at expenses to see if they should properly be treated as assets, accountants must do the reverse, and review assets to see if they truly have value. Lucia discovers that one of her customers, who owes her $500, has gone bankrupt. Lucia writes off this asset (v).

Lucia has got rid of the loan, so does not have to accrue interest this year, and has sold the equipment. But she must still amortise the lease at $3,000 (w). The final position is shown in Table 9.

Table 9 Second year, continued

	Provisional balance sheet, cont	Sell equipment (t)	General expenses (u)	Write-off receivable (v)	Amortis- ation (w)	Closing balance sheet
Cash	4,500	800	-4,000			1,300
Receivables	11,000			-500		10,500
Inventory	32,000					32,000
Lease, improvements	12,000		1,500		-3,000	10,500
Office equipment	1,400	-1,400				
TOTAL ASSETS	**60,900**					**54,300**
Payables	25,000					25,000
Provisions	750					750
Shareholders' funds:						
Share capital	25,000					25,000
Profit (loss)	10,150	-600	-2,500	-500	-3,000	3,550
TOTAL L&SF	**60,900**					**54,300**

Financial Statements

The final outcome for Lucia's second year is recorded in the income statement and balance sheet as follows. The tax liability is expected to be settled in the following year so the provision is included in current liabilities in the balance sheet. Lucia's earnings are $7,250 this year, so retained earnings carried forward is (-3,700 + 7,250 =) $3,550.

Table 10 Lucia's balance sheet at the end of year two

Cash		1,300
Trade receivables		10,500
Inventories		32,000
CURRENT ASSETS		**43,800**
Lease, and improvements		10,500
LONG-TERM ASSETS		**10,500**
TOTAL ASSETS		**54,300**
Payables		25,000
Provision		750
CURRENT LIABILITIES		**25,750**
Common shares – paid-in capital		25,000
Retained earnings:		
Brought forward	-3,700	
Earnings of the year	7,250	3,550
SHAREHOLDERS' FUNDS		**28,550**
TOTAL L&SF		**54,300**

Table 11 Lucia's income statement for year two

SALES	**35,000**
Cost of sales	-20,000
GROSS PROFIT	**15,000**
General expenses	-2,500
Amortisation	-3,000
Bad debt	-500
Loss on disposal	-600
Law suit	-400
OPERATING PROFIT	**8,000**
Net interest payable	
EARNINGS BEFORE TAX	**8,000**
Tax	-750
EARNINGS	**7,250**

REVIEW

- The most basic idea in accounting is that the income of a business during a period is the increase in its assets adjusted for any withdrawals by the owners.

- A firm's balance sheet is a list of its assets, and the claims against those assets.

- There are two types of claim. Liabilities are amounts owed to third parties. Shareholders' funds are the residual claim on the firm, the difference between its assets and liabilities, and measure the shareholders' wealth in balance sheet terms.

- The change in shareholders' wealth over a period, adjusted for any capital flows, measures the firm's profit.

- The bookkeeping process updates the balance sheet to record the effect of each transaction. A transaction is an exchange of assets and claims, including cash, with a third party.

- The accountant then makes a number of adjustments to the transactional record to ensure the balance sheet fairly reflects the firm's assets and claims at the end of the period.

- Finally, the accountant produces the financial statements from the accounting records. The principal financial statements are the balance sheet and the income statement and cash flow statement explain why the stock of assets and liabilities in the balance sheet changed, in terms of the flow of income and the flow of cash respectively.

Chapter 3

Reading the balance sheet and income statement

The first step in analysing financial statements is to read them. This shows us what is there and gives us a feel for the shape of the firm. It indicates where we may need to reformat the data to reveal the magnitudes we need. This chapter describes the main categories of asset and claim, and income and expense we encounter in a published balance sheet and income statement. It shows how to put them into a format that identifies the key numbers we will need for calculating return on capital, and for financial analysis.

READING PUBLISHED FINANCIAL STATEMENTS

When we read financial statements we are usually wearing two different hats. For calculating return on capital, the key task is to separate the balance sheet and income statement into their 'operating' and 'financing' elements. For financial analysis, more broadly, we want to tell as rich an economic story about the firm as the data will permit. In this context we are hungry for detail, and the task is to make sure we identify and group all economically-similar items.

In the rest of this chapter we identify the elements we typically need for analysis, and consider the main issues that arise when formatting published balance sheets and income statements. We will argue against getting too fixated on a particular vocabulary and format; what matters is transparency and consistency. For example, while US balance sheets list assets and claims in decreasing order of liquidity, IFRS does exactly the opposite. Clearly, the ordering is of no consequence so long as the data we need is there.

In logic and structure, the balance sheets and income statements that firms actually publish are identical to the simple ones we built in Chapter 2; but they contain more items and, because GAAP is not very prescriptive about language, they vary in vocabulary. However, the international harmonisation that has taken place in GAAP means that balance sheets and income statements usually arrive in good shape, and there is not a lot of work to do in reformatting them. We examine four firms in this chapter: Tiffany, a high-end US jewellery retailer, Publicis, a French media services conglomerate, Odfjell, a Norwegian shipping and logistics business and Asahi, a Japanese brewer. These firms could hardly be more different in terms of what they do and how they do it, but we will be struck by just how effective accounting is in representing them so that they can be directly compared to one another in financial terms.

A group of firms

Before we go further, we need to distinguish between a 'group' and a 'firm' and to acquire some more vocabulary. When a firm effectively owns or controls another firm, that firm is its *subsidiary*. Most large firms operate through a network of subsidiaries – the *parent* or *holding company* has subsidiaries, they, in turn, have subsidiaries, and so on. So what may look like a single firm from the outside is actually a *group* of legally distinct firms. Some large multinationals have hundreds, even thousands of subsidiaries, all with a separate legal existence that may involve filing separate financial statements and filing separate tax returns.

There are many reasons why firms work this way. It may be a requirement of regulators in certain industries. It may be tax-efficient for multinational businesses. The separate legal structure may simply be a legacy of the past if the subsidiary was acquired in a takeover. The firm may hope to ring-fence losses by relying on the limited liability that comes with separate incorporation. The legal structure may facilitate internal reporting; and so forth. From an economic perspective, we are interested in the group, that is, the parent plus its subsidiaries. So when we talk about 'a firm' and its financial statements we are usually referring to the group and its 'consolidated' financial statements.

The GAAP treatment of groups is discussed in Chapter 13, but here is an overview. GAAP requires the parent to publish group or *consolidated* financial statements, either separately or alongside those of the parent. At the end of the year, the accountant adds together, line by line, all of the balance sheets and income statements of the parent and its subsidiaries, eliminating any double-counting where firms in the group have been selling to each other. Just to complicate matters, sometimes the parent owns less than 100% of the shares of a subsidiary; perhaps it owns 70%. GAAP says that, so long as the parent controls the other firm, then it is a subsidiary and it has to be fully consolidated. 100% of its assets and liabilities are taken into the group balance sheet, and 100% of its income into the income statement. To correct the overstatement, a *minority interest* or 'minorities' line is inserted into the liability side of the balance sheet, quantifying the proportion (30% in the current example) of the consolidated assets and liabilities, spread around the balance sheet, that belongs to third-party shareholders. A similar insertion is made in the income statement.

If a firm owns a relatively small proportion of the shares of another firm then it is carried as an investment in the balance sheet at cost, and any dividends received are shown as other income in the income statement. But, there is an important middle category of investment, that is sizeable but falls below the threshold for consolidation. This is called an *associate*, and is accounted for using the 'equity method' – the balance sheet shows the firm's share of the net assets of the associate, and the income statement shows its share of the associate's profit or loss.

THE ELEMENTS OF A BALANCE SHEET

Fixed assets and working capital

Though in practice accountants distinguish between current and long-term assets and liabilities on the basis of liquidity – whether or not they will be realised in cash, or settled, within the year – there is also a difference of purpose. Long-term assets, which are often called *fixed assets*, are the productive capacity of the business and are intended for *use* in the business. Current assets are intended for *sale,* and revolve as part of the trading cycle.

Inventory is the stock of raw materials, partly completed goods or 'work in progress', and finished goods. The firm buys some inventory and perhaps works on it, but in due course sells it. When it is sold, the inventory leaves the balance sheet and, assuming the firm allows its customer time to pay, it is replaced by a *trade receivable*, which is the amount owing from the customer, also known as *accounts receivable* or *trade debtors*. The customer eventually pays, so the receivable is then replaced by cash. This cash cycle is shortened if the firm itself receives credit from its supplier in the form of a *trade payable*. Inventory, plus trade receivables, less trade payables is known as *working capital*.

This distinction between fixed assets and working capital is an old one. Adam Smith devoted a chapter[1] of the *Wealth of Nations* to what he called 'fixed capital' and 'circulating capital'. His discussion of why different types of business need different amounts of fixed and circulating capital would still serve today and resembles the discussion we will have in Chapter 7 when we talk about the analysis of operating profitability.

In Adam Smith's day, fixed assets essentially meant the land, buildings and equipment used by the business. We refer to these as *property, plant and equipment* or *PP&E.* Nowadays these are referred to as the *tangible* fixed assets of the firm, which are assets that have physical substance. The contrast is with intangibles, and financial assets. *Intangibles,* which are fixed assets that are non-financial and that lack physical substance, are very important to the modern firm and we discuss their accounting treatment in Chapter 11. Of course intangibles – things like reputation, relationships, capabilities, human capital, know-how – have been key to business success since the beginning of time. But in Adam Smith's day they were probably not the focus of the accounting debate as they are now.

Operating and financing

Particularly in the context of valuation, GAAP distinguishes *financial* assets and liabilities from those that are 'non-financial'. A financial asset is cash, or a claim that is denominated in money terms, either in the form of a loan or an investment in a security, or a receivable. All of a firm's liabilities are financial, and assets such as receivables and investments in shares of other firms are financial assets. The main non-financial assets are tangible and intangible assets and inventories.

---

1   See Book II, Chapter I of *An Inquiry into the Nature and Causes of the Wealth of Nations*, first published in 1776.

GAAP asks firms to group cash and *cash equivalents* together. Cash equivalents are financial assets such as Treasury bills that are sufficiently liquid as to have negligible risk of changing in value. Typically these are assets with a maturity of less than three months. Under IFRS, firms net their *overdrafts*, which are negative balances on chequing accounts, against cash and cash equivalents, but under US GAAP, these are treated as short-term borrowing. For financial analysis we may want to take a wider view of cash, and include in 'cash' any other short-term investments the firm has. These are typically disclosed alongside cash and cash equivalents.

When calculating return on assets in the next chapter we will partition the balance sheet into its 'operating' and 'financing' elements. 'Financ*ing*' is not the same as 'financ*ial*' in a GAAP sense. Usually we will treat all of a firm's assets as operating, except for 'cash'. We group financing liabilities together under the label *debt*. Debt includes borrowing and also liabilities under leases and, since a firm that holds cash is essentially lending to the bank or to other firms, we usually deduct the firm's cash from its debt to find its 'net debt'. By default, operating liabilities are those that are not financing. So operating liabilities include trade and other payables, including current tax liabilities, and perhaps include provisions, which are amounts that the firm has provided for future liabilities that are expected but not contractual. In practice, significant provisions include 'deferred tax', that is, expected tax liabilities payable after a year, and provisions for pensions and healthcare liabilities.

Shareholders' funds

The word *equity* is used for the shareholders' funds provided by the *ordinary* or *common* shareholders[2]. They are the investors who own the firm and have the residual claim on its assets. Equity shareholders' funds comprise paid-in share capital, less 'treasury stock', plus reserves. Firms sometimes issue different classes of equity share capital with names such as 'A shares' and 'B shares', or 'founders' shares'. These shares tend to differ in terms of their voting rights. They may be non-voting shares, or on the other hand may give enhanced voting rights to the founders of the firm. From a financial analysis perspective, these are all 'equity'. The most common *non-equity shareholders' funds* are minorities and preference shares. This distinction is important because we involve non-equity shareholders' funds in the broad measure of external financing called 'capital employed', but exclude it when calculating return on equity shareholders' funds.

Firms repurchase their own shares and, rather than cancelling them, hold them in the balance sheet for reissue, perhaps to employees under share or option schemes. Repurchased shares are known as *treasury stock* and are deducted from equity in the balance sheet. For financial analysis, these shares should be treated as cancelled. The cost of repurchased shares should be deducted from equity in calculating capital employed, and the number of issued shares in earnings per share calculations should be adjusted to exclude repurchased shares.

---

2   In the US, the word 'stock' is used for shares and 'common stock' is used for equity shares; though note that elsewhere, inventory is also known as stock.

In summary, for analysis we want to identify the following components of the balance sheet. In practice, every firm has some idiosyncratic content to its balance sheet that will show up as 'other'.

Cash
Trade receivables
Inventory
Property, plant and equipment (PP&E)
Intangibles
Financial assets and investments
Other assets
TOTAL ASSETS

Debt
Trade payables
Provisions
Other liabilities

Equity shareholders' funds
Non-equity shareholders' funds
TOTAL LIABILITIES and SHAREHOLDERS' FUNDS (TOTAL L&SF)

GAAP: balance sheet formats

GAAP is not prescriptive about language and presentation and, as a result, firms use a variety of vocabulary and of layout in their financial statements. Though most firms report their balance sheets in the 'total assets' format some firms use a 'net assets' format with current and long-term liabilities netted against assets on one side of the balance sheet leaving shareholders' funds on the other side. This is not helpful, and such a balance sheet needs restating into the total asset format. GAAP allows most of the balance-sheet detail to be shown as notes, or in secondary statements such as the 'statement of movements in shareholders' equity', rather than on the face of the balance sheet. These are all an integral part of the balance sheet and we will find some of the data we need there.

Case: Tiffany & Co

Tiffany & Co was founded in 1837 by Charles Tiffany and John Young in New York City as a retailer of stationery and costume jewellery. Charles Tiffany took control in 1853 and renamed the firm after himself. Tiffany opened its first store in Japan in 1972, and in London in 1986. It has 123 retail stores in 16 countries, all of which are directly owned except for four in Japan. The company also sells online, through its catalogues, and business-to-business. Tiffany was listed on the New York Stock Exchange in 1987. In 1961, Tiffany's Fifth Avenue store was featured in the iconic film *Breakfast at Tiffany's* starring Audrey Hepburn, reinforcing its image as a retailer of luxury goods. Jewellery remains the core of the business, accounting for some 80% of sales.

Tiffany reports under US GAAP. The financial year-end is to January, so 2005 refers to the year ending 31 January 2005. In common with all of the cases in this book, we do not reproduce Tiffany's published financial statements here. They are readily available on Tiffany's web site and the book web site explains how to access them.

Table 1 shows Tiffany's balance sheet for 2005; the published version on the left and the formatted version on the right. There is not much work to be done in reformatting. A few categories are combined, for example 'short-term investments' and 'cash and cash equivalents' to give 'cash'. The breakdown of 'accounts payable and accrued liabilities' has to be identified from the notes to the accounts to extract the figure for trade payables.

Table 1 Tiffany's published and formatted balance sheets

Published	(figures in $000s)	Formatted	(figures in $m)
Cash and cash equivalents	187,681		
Short-term investments	139,200	Cash	326.9
Accounts receivable, less allowances	133,545	Trade receivables	133.5
Inventories, net	1,057,245	Inventories	1,057.2
Deferred income taxes	64,790		
Prepaid expenses and other current assets	25,428	Other	90.2
Total current assets	**1,607,889**	**CURRENT ASSETS**	**1,607.9**
Property, plant and equipment, net	917,853	PP&E	917.9
Other assets, net	140,376	Other	140.4
		LONG-TERM ASSETS	**1,058.2**
	2,666,118	**TOTAL ASSETS**	**2,666.1**
Short-term borrowings	42,957	Debt	43.0
Accounts payable and accrued liabilities	186,013	Trade payables	74.5
Income taxes payable	118,536		
Merchandise and other customer credits	52,315	Other	282.4
Total current liabilities	**399,821**	**CURRENT LIABILITIES**	**399.8**
Long-term debt	397,606	Debt	397.6
Postretirement/employment benefit obligations	40,220		
Deferred income taxes	33,175	Provisions	73.4
Other long-term liabilities	94,136	Other	94.1
		LONG-TERM LIABILITIES	**565.1**
Common stock, $0.01 par value, authorized 240,000			
Shares, issued and outstanding, 144,548	1,445		
Additional paid-in capital	426,308	Paid-in share capital	427.8
Retained earnings	1,246,331	Retained earnings	1,246.3
Accumulated other comprehensive gain (loss), net of tax:			
Foreign currency translation adjustments	29,045		
Deferred hedging loss	-2,118		
Unrealized gain on marketable securities	149	Other reserves	27.1
Total stockholders' equity	**1,701,160**	**SHAREHOLDERS' FUNDS**	**1,701.2**
	2,666,118	**TOTAL L&SF**	**2,666.1**

BALANCE SHEETS IN DIFFERENT BUSINESSES

The accounting system of classifying assets and claims is very powerful and fits all firms. But the nature of the assets and liabilities that a firm needs will depend very much on the business it is in and the business model it is using. To see this, compare the balance sheet of Tiffany with three other firms in quite different businesses: Odfjell, Asahi and Publicis.

Case: Tiffany, Odfjell, Asahi and Publicis compared

Odfjell ASA is a Norwegian firm specialising in the global transportation and storage of chemicals and other bulk liquids. It owns tank terminals and has a fleet of ships operating worldwide. Odfjell reports its figures under both IFRS and Norwegian GAAP. Asahi Breweries Ltd is a Japanese firm that produces beer and other alcoholic and soft drinks in Asia and worldwide. Asahi reports under Japanese GAAP, nevertheless the presentation is similar to that of IFRS. Publicis Groupe SA is a French firm offering global services for advertising, marketing, PR and communications. It has expanded internationally through a strategy of acquisitions to rank fourth in communications worldwide (by sales) in 2005. Publicis reports under IFRS for the first time in 2005, as does Odfjell. Table 2 presents their four balance sheets side by side. It calculates for each line in the balance sheet, the percentage this represents of total assets, to highlight how the nature of the businesses of these companies has an impact on their balance sheets. For ease of presentation we have re-ordered the lines in the balance sheets to align with Tiffany, which happens to be in US order[3].

Both Tiffany and Publicis have balance sheets that are weighted towards current assets. For Tiffany this reflects the large inventory it carries of raw materials and finished goods, of both precious metals and gemstones. For Publicis the largest item is accounts receivable. Publicis is a service company, so its inventory consists primarily of work-in-progress, being advertising work carried out but not yet billed to clients. It does not have large amounts of fixed assets, because the principal asset it uses to generate income is the human capital of its employees.

Odfjell carries 84% of its assets in the form of PP&E. Out of this, $1,219m is for ships, and the remaining $425m for tank terminals, new building contracts, and a small amount of real estate. Odfjell's 'fleet overview' as at 3 March 2006, discloses that Odfjell also has a large number of ships on operating leases, which are not reflected in the balance sheet; it operates a total of 92 ships, of which it owns 56. Asahi also has a lot of PP&E (52%), which consists of land, buildings, and machinery and equipment – largely the production facilities for its alcoholic beverages and soft drinks. Like Publicis, and unlike Tiffany and Odfjell, it has a high proportion of trade receivables (20%), reflecting the fact that it sells to the wholesale rather than retail markets. Tiffany, as a retailer, receives much of its income at the time of sale and does not have a large balance of outstanding receivables.

---

3 The spreadsheets that reformat their published balance sheets, equivalent to Tiffany in Table 1, are available on the website for the reader who wants to trace the numbers back.

Table 2 Four balance sheets compared

	Tiffany		Odfjell		Asahi		Publicis	
Balance sheet date	31 Jan 05		31 Dec 05		31 Dec 05		31 Dec 05	
	US$m	%	US$m	%	¥bn	%	€m	%
Cash	327	12.3	190	9.7	15	1.2	1,980	16.9
Trade receivables	134	5.0	94	4.8	244	20.0	4,014	34.2
Inventories	1,057	39.6	16	0.8	87	7.1	580	4.9
Other	90	3.4			39	3.2	577	4.9
CURRENT ASSETS	**1,608**	**60.3**	**300**	**15.3**	**385**	**31.6**	**7,151**	**60.9**
PP&E	918	34.4	1,644	84.0	635	52.1	580	4.9
Intangibles			9	0.5			3,646	31.0
Investments			1	0.1	128	10.5	33	0.3
Other	140	5.3	2	0.1	70	5.8	334	2.8
LONG-TERM ASSETS	**1,058**	**39.7**	**1,656**	**84.7**	**833**	**68.4**	**4,593**	**39.1**
TOTAL ASSETS	**2,666**	**100.0**	**1,956**	**100.0**	**1,218**	**100.0**	**11,744**	**100.0**
Debt	43	1.6	96	4.9	121	9.9	224	1.9
Trade payables	75	2.8	20	1.0	93	7.6	4,605	39.2
Other	282	10.6	140	7.2	286	23.5	2,138	18.2
CURRENT LIABILITIES	**400**	**15.0**	**256**	**13.1**	**500**	**41.1**	**6,967**	**59.3**
Debt	398	14.9	942	48.2	168	13.8	1,913	16.3
Provisions	73	2.7	48	2.5	29	2.4	759	6.5
Other	94	3.5	18	0.9	39	3.2		
LONG-TERM LIABILITIES	**565**	**21.2**	**1,008**	**51.5**	**236**	**19.4**	**2,672**	**22.8**
Minority shareholders' funds					**27**	**2.2**	**20**	**0.2**
Paid-in share capital	428	16.1	139	7.1	329	27.0	2,663	22.7
Other reserves	27	1.0	-4	-0.2	20	1.6		
Retained earnings	1,246	46.7	557	28.5	106	8.7	-578	-4.9
Equity shareholders' funds	**1,701**		**692**		**455**	**37.4**	**2,085**	**17.8**
SHAREHOLDERS' FUNDS	**1,701**	**63.8**	**692**	**35.4**	**482**	**39.6**	**2,105**	**17.9**
TOTAL L&SF	**2,666**	**100.0**	**1,956**	**100.0**	**1,218**	**100.0**	**11,744**	**100.0**

Just one of these companies, Publicis, has significant intangibles (31%), which includes both goodwill and other intangible assets that mainly result from acquisitions of other firms. For example, its net goodwill balance of €2,883m includes €1,895m relating to the acquisition of Bcom3 in 2002. Other intangible assets, total €763m, consist of client relationships, software and tradenames and also arise from its acquisition of other companies. Asahi has sizeable non-current investments of ¥128.3bn, of which ¥48.0bn relates to investments in unconsolidated subsidiaries and affiliated companies.

Both Asahi and Publicis have a high proportion of current liabilities (41% and 59% respectively). In Asahi's case this is partly because of substantial amounts of short-term debt. (Asahi has plenty of long-term debt too.) But Asahi also has a large amount of other current liabilities, of which half relates to tax. Most of this is for alcohol tax, which is obviously peculiar to its own business. Publicis' current liabilities include advances it has received from clients, purchases of media space it has made as an agent, and liabilities to its personnel.

Odfjell has far more debt than the other companies – 53%, taking short-term and long-term amounts together. On the other hand Tiffany funds nearly 64% of its total assets with shareholders' funds – 16% from paid-in share capital and 48% from retained earnings and reserves. Publicis's reformatted balance sheet reveals something that was not apparent: it has a deficit on its retained earnings and reserves. Its published balance sheet combines 'Additional paid-in capital and retained earnings' into one line to give a net positive figure of €2,006m. In the previous years' financial statements, we discover that it wrote off direct to shareholders' equity a total of €447m in 2000 and 2001 relating to its acquisition of Saatchi and Saatchi. The company explained that it applied the 'derogatory' method of accounting for this acquisition, meaning that no goodwill was recognised in the balance sheet and instead there was a reduction in shareholders' equity. Another item affecting shareholders' equity was the unusually large charge of €366m for 'translation adjustments' in 2003. This is an accounting adjustment made direct to reserves that arises on the consolidation of subsidiaries whose financial statements are denominated in currencies other than the euro.

THE ELEMENTS OF AN INCOME STATEMENT

The income statement starts by showing the value of the sales made in the year. It then deducts the expenses incurred to achieve these sales to give the 'operating profit'. If a business involves buying-in significant inputs from other firms and adding further value to these by manufacturing, or by providing a service such as retailing, it is common to identify two levels of cost and to report an intermediate 'gross profit' number. The 'cost of sales' is the cost incurred in acquiring the goods and bringing them to a saleable condition, and gross profit is the difference between sales and cost of sales. Our label for all the remaining costs is *sales, general and administration* costs *(SG&A)*. For financial analysis, we need to use all the detail the firm provides about its costs, but for now we simply partition costs into cost of sales and SG&A.

Alongside operating profit, there may be *exceptionals,* which are items of income or expense that, whilst arising in the normal course of business, are material enough in size to merit separate disclosure. For example, firms usually disclose separately within operating profit (or just below it), items such as reorganisation costs, gains or losses on sale of assets or businesses, and so forth. *Extraordinary items,* by contrast, are costs or revenues that do not arise in the ordinary course of business of the firm. The firm may have *other income,* that is, income from non-operating sources. Examples are dividends received on investments in other firms, the firm's share of the income of associated firms, and rental income. Firms now partition their operating results into 'continuing' operations and 'discontinued' operations, the latter being the results of activities that were sold or abandoned during the year.

GAAP: Income statement formats

GAAP is not particularly prescriptive about the format of the income statement. US GAAP permits either the gross profit format or that the income statement simply lists the firm's revenues and expenses classified by nature or type. IFRS is silent on formats. Where the gross-profit format is used, the issue of which costs are included in cost of sales and in SG&A is not policed by GAAP, so we have to be careful when comparing firms on this basis. GAAP requires firms to identify separately any material items of cost or of income when it is needed to understand operating performance, but GAAP does not use the term 'exceptional' as such. US GAAP is now very restrictive as to what may be treated as an extraordinary item, while IFRS no longer permits extraordinaries.

EBIT

An income statement is best thought of in two halves. The top half explains how the firm earned its income in the period. The bottom half of the income statement explains who gets the income; how it is shared amongst the people with a claim on the firm. We call the sum of profit from operations and income from all other sources that the firm has earned during the period and that is available for claimants, *earnings before interest and tax (EBIT)*. EBIT is used as the numerator in return-on-asset measures, so it is a pivotal number in financial analysis. EBIT is not normally flagged in income statements so once you have figured it out you need to draw (at least mentally) a thick line across the page.

Note that although EBIT was described as income from all sources, it does not include interest received. Consistent with treating a firm's cash as part of its financing, essentially as negative debt, the interest received on cash is netted from interest paid as a claim on EBIT. There is no reason to be doctrinaire about what goes into EBIT. When we are doing financial analysis it is sometimes appropriate to view exceptionals, other income, and even extraordinaries as part of EBIT, and other times not. It depends entirely on the context. At this stage, what matter is to ensure that they are clearly identified in the income statement.

Earnings and comprehensive income

From EBIT, the income statement deducts the interest and tax claims on the firm's income and, if there are any, minorities and preference dividends. After meeting other claims, what remains belongs to the equity shareholders, who own the firm and so are the residual claimants on its income. This is earnings after tax, minorities and preference dividends but before extraordinary items and is simply known as earnings. The firm's *earnings per share (EPS)* is its earnings divided by the average number of ordinary shares outstanding in the year. This is an important number for capital markets – the earnings per share is compared to the share price to give the price earnings ratio. The interpretation of earnings per share will be affected by stock options that the firm has issued. A stock option gives someone the right to buy further shares in the firm. Stock options are frequently issued to employees as part of their remuneration. If the firm has options outstanding at the end of the year it is required to report a 'fully diluted' EPS, as though all outstanding options were exercised. Another implication of stock options is that, since the number of shares in issue can change almost daily in companies with active employee stock option schemes, the firm has to report its own calculation of its average number of shares in issue during the year.

In principle, the shareholders' accounting income in a period is the increase in the shareholders' funds in the balance sheet, excluding any contributions of capital by shareholders but adding back dividends paid. Shareholders' income, measured this way, is called 'comprehensive income'. Not all changes in shareholders' funds pass through the income statement and get included in earnings. So the final step is to identify such balance-sheet changes and add them to earnings as 'other comprehensive income', to get the comprehensive income number. We can use the balance sheet notes to find the data to calculate comprehensive income. In addition, to help the reader do this, GAAP now requires firms to publish a reconciliation of earnings to the change in shareholders' funds.

Case: Tiffany's formatted income statement

Table 3 shows Tiffany's income statement as published, and rearranged into the format and vocabulary we use in this book.

One thing that always requires great care is firms' quixotic use of pluses, minuses and brackets in published financial statements. Tiffany is no exception – for example, 'other (income) expense' is shown as negative, whereas 'gain on sale of equity investment' on the line below, which is also an item of income, is shown as positive. In a formatted income statement we impose the simple rule that income (a credit) is shown as positive and cost (a debit) as negative.

There is little work needed to put Tiffany's income statement into our format, but we need more detail. For example, Tiffany does not tell us what makes up 'interest expense and financing costs' although we learn that the company does capitalise some of its interest costs, and the figure of $22m is net of capitalisation. 'Other income' of $6m includes interest income, gains and losses on investment activities and foreign currency transactions, and minority interest income and expense. This information is supplied in the narrative disclosure, 'Management's Discussion and Analysis of Financial Condition and Results of Operations' which is part of the company's SEC filing. No detailed analysis is given and so we are unable to strip out the interest income for incorporation with interest expense in the formatted income statement. So we leave 'other income' as it is, and treat 'interest expense and financing costs' as if it is net interest. In Note G to the accounts the company declares its cash interest paid figure, net of capitalisation, to be $19m, so this gives us some comfort that our solution is not too far from the true picture. The 'gain on sale of equity investment' of $193m arises from the sale of Tiffany's 14.7% stake in Aber Diamond Corporation which it acquired in 1999. In the formatted income statement we include this in 'exceptionals' and show this category after arriving at operating profit, on the grounds that this is a 'one-off'. As we discuss in Chapter 7, we should always be completely pragmatic about whether we treat particular items of 'other income' or 'exceptionals' as operating.

The reported income statement stops at the line 'net earnings', so we conclude by adding any elements that are accounted for directly in reserves, in order to get to comprehensive income. A detailed analysis is given in the 'Consolidated Statement of Stockholders' Equity and Comprehensive Earnings'. Tiffany's other comprehensive income mainly consists of foreign currency translation gains of 13.2 in 2005.

Table 3 Tiffany's published and formatted income statement (year end 31 January 2005)

Published	(figures in $000s)	Formatted	(figures in $m)
Net sales	2,204,831	**SALES**	**2,205**
Cost of sales	974,258	Cost of sales	-974
Gross profit	1,230,573	**GROSS PROFIT**	**1,231**
Selling, general & administrative expenses	936,044	SG&A	-936
Earnings from operations	294,529	**OPERATING PROFIT**	**295**
		Other income	6
		Exceptionals	193
		EBIT	**494**
Interest expense and financing costs	22,003	Interest	-22
Other (income) expenses, net	-6,025		
Gain on sale of equity investment	193,597		
Earnings before income taxes	472,148	**EARNINGS BEFORE TAX**	**472**
Provision for income taxes	167,849	Tax	-168
Net earnings	304,299	**EARNINGS AFTER TAX**	**304**
		Minorities	0
		Preference dividend	0
		EARNINGS	**304**
		Other comprehensive income	14
		COMPREHENSIVE INCOME	**318**

Some issues in finding EBIT

Our cases, Asahi, Odfjell, and Publicis demonstrate the process of formatting the income statement, and the issues that arise in finding EBIT, in particular. We always encounter a variety of vocabulary. Frequently, some of the detail we need to categorise an aggregate number will be found in a footnote. Firms sometimes bundle other income in with financing elements, that is, with interest received and paid. Asahi do this. None of these presents a problem in practice. More troublesome is when an EBIT component is shown further down the page, below the tax line, as is the case in Odfjell and Publicis. Firms show 'extraordinary' items net of tax at the bottom of the income statement, below earnings. Also, both US GAAP and IFRS require the firm's share of the income of associates and joint ventures to be included in the income statement, net of tax. Any item reported below the tax line is shown net of tax. So if we think something belongs in EBIT we need to take a view on the appropriate tax rate, gross it up for tax, and add the corresponding tax to the tax charge. Finally, EBIT is an analytical construct, not a GAAP-required number. Some firms, like Asahi, try to be helpful and report an EBIT number. We do not use this, and should calculate our own; the firm's definition of EBIT may not coincide with ours.

Asahi Breweries Ltd

Asahi's income statement, under Japanese GAAP, shows a lot of detail so the main task is to group this into the categories we want. In its published income statement Asahi groups interest and dividend income, 1,352. However on its website an unaudited version of its statement shows the 1,352 split between interest, 569, and dividends, 783, so we have used this to get the net interest figure (569-4069 =) 3,500. Dividends, the share of the income and losses of unconsolidated companies and 'other-net' are included in other income, and the rest of its non-operating items in exceptionals. Other comprehensive income is derived from the 'Consolidated Statements of Shareholders' Equity', and is significant at Asahi. Its main components are an 11,816 increase in the market value of investments, and a 2,880 translation gain.

Table 4 Asahi Breweries Ltd's income statement (figures in ¥m, 31 December 2005)

Published		Formatted	
Net sales	**1,430,027**	**SALES**	**1,430,027**
Costs and expenses:			
Cost of sales	440,220		
Alcohol tax	513,776	Cost of sales	-953,996
		GROSS PROFIT	**476,031**
Selling, general & administrative expenses	385,782	SG&A	-385,782
Operating income	**90,249**	**OPERATING PROFIT**	**90,249**
Other income (expenses):			
Interest and dividend income	1,352		
Interest expenses	-4,069		
Equity in net income (loss) of unconsolidated subsidiaries and affiliated companies	4,426	Other income	5,850
Compensation for transfer of plant	695		
Gain (loss) on sale of securities - net	-736		
Loss on sale and disposal of property, plant and equipment - net	-9,717		
Loss on devaluation of investment securities	-337		
Restructuring charges	-3,598		
Loss on write-down of land	-3,181	Exceptionals	-16,874
Other - net	641		
		EBIT	**79,225**
		Interest	-3,500
Income before income taxes and minority interests	**75,725**	**EARNINGS BEFORE TAX**	**75,725**
Income taxes:			
Current	18,542		
Deferred	15,479	Tax	-34,021
Income before minority interests	**41,704**	**EARNINGS AFTER TAX**	**41,704**
Minority interests in net gain of consolidated subsidiaries	-1,834	Minorities	-1,834
Net income	**39,870**	**EARNINGS**	**39,870**
		Other comprehensive income	14,478
		COMPREHENSIVE INCOME	**54,348**

Odfjell ASA

Odfjell reports EBITDA and EBIT numbers. At the moment we are not interested in EBITDA, so we add the depreciation and capital gains and losses to SG&A to give (-64,449 - 107,449 + 14,210 =) -157,688. Also, we need to check Odfjell's calculation of EBIT to ensure it includes all items apart from interest and tax. We need to add 'other financial items' and 'currency gains and losses' as a net 411 of 'other income' and include this in EBIT. The 'Net result discontinued operations' is the gain made by Odfjell on the disposal of its 50% share in a joint venture. It is reported lower down the income statement, net of tax. We want to include the gross amount in 'exceptionals' within EBIT, and the tax element as part of the overall tax charge. We do not know the actual tax payable on this gain, so we have used the firm's reported effective tax rate of 13.1% to gross it up for inclusion in EBIT. If 4,376 is net of tax at 13.1%, the gross, pre tax, is (4,376/(1-13.1%) =) 5,036, and the tax is (5,036 × 13.1% =) 660. The tax line in the formatted version becomes (-18,628 - 660 =) -19,288. Other comprehensive income is derived from the published 'Statement of Changes in Equity'. Its main components are cash flow hedges transferred to the profit and loss account, -27,975, and foreign exchange translation differences, -13,298.

Table 5 Odfjell's income statement (figures in $000s, 31 December 2005)

Published		Formatted	
Gross revenue	1,044,847	**SALES**	**1,044,847**
Net income from associates	101		
Voyage expenses	-340,905		
Time-charter expenses	-156,354		
Operating expenses	-219,577	Cost of sales	-716,735
Gross result	**328,112**	**GROSS PROFIT**	**328,112**
General and administrative expenses	-64,449	SG&A	-157,688
Operating result before depreciation and capital gain (loss) on non-current assets (EBITDA)	**263,663**		
Depreciation and gains on non-current assets	-107,449		
Capital gain (loss) on non-current assets	14,210		
Operating result (EBIT)	**170,424**	**OPERATING PROFIT**	**170,424**
		Other income	411
		Exceptionals	5,036
		EBIT	**175,871**
Interest income	7,892		
Interest expenses	-36,206	Interest	-28,314
Other financial items	-1,372		
Currency gains (losses)	1,783		
Result before taxes	**142,521**	**EARNINGS BEFORE TAX**	**147,557**
Taxes on result before extraordinary items	-18,628	Tax	-19,288
Net result from continuing operations	**123,893**	**EARNINGS AFTER TAX**	**128,269**
Net result discontinued operations	4,376		
Allocated to: Minority interests	-777	Minorities	-777
Shareholders	127,492	**EARNINGS**	**127,492**
		Other comprehensive income	-41,331
		COMPREHENSIVE INCOME	**86,161**

Publicis Groupe SA

Because of the nature of its business Publicis does not record a 'cost of sales'. Instead it shows 'personnel expenses' as this is the main component of its 'direct costs'. Its published accounts record separately various items of depreciation and amortisation. We have added all these items together into 'operating expenses'. 'Cost of net financial debt' represents interest receivable and payable. 'Other financial expense' includes foreign exchange gains and losses, changes in the value of derivatives, and other financial items, so has been included in 'other income'. The 'share of net income of non-consolidated companies' has to be grossed up for tax using the firm's effective rate of 32% (as disclosed in the notes to the financial statements). It is then added to 'Other income' for inclusion in EBIT as (11 + tax 5 =) 16. 'Other income' is therefore (-14+16 =) 2. Total tax is (-157 - 5 =) -162. Publicis has significant other comprehensive income, containing 116 of translation gains, 9 arising on the fair value of hedges, and -16 from revaluation of available-for-sale investments.

Table 6 Publicis Groupe SA's income statement (figures in €m, 31 December 2005)

Published		Formatted	
Revenues	**4,127**	**SALES**	**4,127**
Personnel expenses	-2,454		
Other operating expenses	-908		
Operating margin before depreciation and amortization			
Depreciation and amortisation expense (excluding intangibles arising on acquisition)	-116		
Operating margin	**649**		
Amortisation of intangibles arising on acquisition	-23		
Impairment	-33	Operating expenses	-3,534
		OPERATING PROFIT	**593**
		Other income	2
Non-current income (expense)	59	Exceptionals	59
Operating income	**652**	**EBIT**	**654**
Cost of net financial debt	-78	Interest	-78
Other financial income (expense)	-14		
Income of consolidated companies before taxes	**560**	**EARNINGS BEFORE TAX**	**576**
Income taxes	-157	Tax	-162
Net income of consolidated companies	**403**		
Share of net income of non-consolidated companies	11		
Net income	**414**	**EARNINGS AFTER TAX**	**414**
Net income attributable to minority interests	-28	Minorities	-28
Net income attributable to equity holders of the parent	386	**EARNINGS**	**386**
		Other comprehensive income	109
		COMPREHENSIVE INCOME	**495**

REVIEW

- The first step in financial analysis is to read the financial statements carefully to see what is there, and to understand the nature of the firm and its business model. We then put the balance sheet and income statement into a format and vocabulary that makes it easy to pull out the numbers needed for analysis.

- The conceptual structure of accounting – its way of categorising assets and claims, and income and expense – is extremely powerful in representing very different businesses in a single economic framework that enables us directly to compare them in financial terms.

- Because GAAP is not very prescriptive, published balance sheets and income statements vary in vocabulary and format. But, nowadays, balance sheets and income statements prepared under US GAAP, IFRS, and other GAAPs that are converging with these, usually arrive in pretty good shape. Though they may look superficially different in terms of layout and vocabulary, there is not usually a lot of work to do in reformatting them.

- For financial analysis, we simply want to group items that are similar in economic terms. For calculating return on capital, our main concern is to separate the financial statements into their operating and financial elements.

ANNEX Tiffany's balance sheets and income statements

We use Tiffany as a case for financial analysis later, so in this Annex we show its formatted balance sheets and income statements for 2003 to 2005, and some underlying detail.

Tiffany's cash in 2005 includes $139.2 ($27.5 in 2004) of short-term investments in the form of auction rate securities, which are short-term variable rate notes whose margin is determined by a Dutch auction. Other current assets include a deferred tax asset of 64.8 (45.0 in 2004) and prepayments and other current assets of 25.4 (23.7 in 2004). Like most high-end jewellers, Tiffany carries a lot of inventory (Note H in 2005; Note F in 2004), principally as finished goods stock, as Table A1 shows.

Table A1 Tiffany's inventory

	2003	2004	2005
Finished goods	615.2	659.6	771.2
Raw materials	91.5	165.8	236.8
Work in progress	29.7	50.5	54.0
	736.4	**875.8**	**1062.0**
Provisions	-4.4	-4.6	-4.7
Total	**732.1**	**871.3**	**1,057.2**

'Property, plant and equipment' form the main component of Tiffany's long-term assets and are further analysed in the notes (Note I in 2005; Note G in 2004) as shown in Table A2. Other long-term assets includes some intangibles: goodwill ($19.9 in 2005) and trademark and product rights ($14.2). In 2003 and 2004 'other' also included an investment in the Aber Diamond Corporation which was sold in December 2004.

Table A2 Tiffany's PP&E

	2003	2004	2005
Land	78.8	233.3	238.3
Buildings	171.6	188.3	188.8
Leasehold improvements	302.2	400.3	454.4
Construction in progress	92.1	16.5	27.2
Office equipment	275.1	292.3	335.6
Machinery and equipment	61.7	97.1	107.9
	981.4	**1,227.9**	**1,352.2**
Accumulated depreciation	-303.8	-342.8	-434.4
Total	**677.6**	**885.1**	**917.9**

Other current liabilities in 2005 includes accrued compensation and commissions 31.1, income taxes, 118.5, other taxes, 40.6, customer credits, 52.3, and 'other', 39.8. Provisions includes post-retirement and employment benefit obligations, and deferred tax. Long-term debt consists of borrowings in both dollars and yen, the latter being used to finance the purchase of Tiffany's flagship store in Japan. In 2005, these comprised dollar loans and notes, 204.2, and a yen loan and bond, 193.4. Par value of Tiffany's shares is $0.01. Tiffany has issued no preference shares, nor are there any minority interests. Other reserves derive principally from the adjustments needed to translate the assets, liabilities, income and expenses of overseas subsidiaries into US dollars for inclusion in the consolidated financial statements, and from the hedging activities the company undertakes to manage its currency and interest-rate exposure.

Table A3 Tiffany's formatted balance sheet for 2003 to 2005 (figures in US$m)

	2003	2004	2005
Cash	156.2	276.1	326.9
Trade receivables	113.1	132.0	133.5
Inventories	732.1	871.3	1057.2
Other current assets	69.0	68.7	90.2
CURRENT ASSETS	**1,070.4**	**1,348.1**	**1,607.9**
Property, plant & equipment	677.6	885.1	917.9
Other long-term assets	175.6	157.9	140.4
LONG-TERM ASSETS	**853.2**	**1,043.0**	**1,058.2**
TOTAL ASSETS	**1,923.6**	**2,391.1**	**2,666.1**
Debt, current	52.6	93.9	43.0
Trade payables	67.2	91.0	74.5
Other current liabilities	180.2	210.3	282.4
CURRENT LIABILITIES	**299.9**	**395.2**	**399.8**
Debt, long-term	297.1	393.0	397.6
Provisions	33.1	59.1	73.4
Other long-term liabilities	85.4	75.6	94.1
LONG-TERM LIABILITIES	**415.6**	**527.7**	**565.1**
Paid-in share capital	352.8	396.6	427.8
Other reserves	-19.5	13.3	27.1
Retained earnings	874.7	1,058.2	1,246.3
SHAREHOLDERS' FUNDS	**1,208.0**	**1,468.2**	**1,701.2**
TOTAL L&SF	**1,923.6**	**2,391.1**	**2,666.1**

Table A4 Tiffany's formatted income statement for 2003 to 2005 (figures in US$m)

Years ended 31 January	2003	2004	2005
SALES	**1,706.6**	**2,000.0**	**2,204.8**
Cost of sales	-695.2	-842.7	-974.3
GROSS PROFIT	**1,011.4**	**1,157.4**	**1,230.6**
Sales, general & administration costs	-692.3	-801.9	-936.0
Exceptionals	0	0	193.6
OPERATING PROFIT	**319.2**	**355.5**	**488.1**
Other income	-4.4	2.1	6.0
EBIT	**314.8**	**357.6**	**494.2**
Net interest paid	-15.1	-14.9	-22.0
EARNINGS BEFORE TAX	**299.6**	**342.7**	**472.1**
Tax	-115.0	-118.4	-191.3
Deferred tax	5.2	-8.8	23.5
EARNINGS AFTER TAX	**189.9**	**215.5**	**304.3**
Minorities	0	0	0
Preference dividend	0	0	0
EARNINGS	**189.9**	**215.5**	**304.3**
Other comprehensive income	19.3	32.8	13.7
COMPREHENSIVE INCOME	209.2	248.4	318.0

Chapter 4

Accounting models

This chapter goes back to the basic logic of accounting to understand just what the numbers in a balance sheet and an income statement mean. The firm's 'accounting model' is the set of rules that determine what assets and liabilities go into the balance sheet and at what values. We outline the accounting model that firms would need to use for financial statements to yield reliable measures of return on capital, period by period. This 'investment' accounting model requires a balance sheet that is both complete in terms of property rights, and is at current values. We identify the main ways in which GAAP departs from this model in practice, and this provides a look ahead to the issues we will have to deal with later in the book. The investment accounting model is a theoretical ideal, but its requirements in terms of balance-sheet completeness and valuation provide an invaluable framework for thinking about accounting.

THE ACCOUNTING IDENTITY

A business's profit during a period is the change in its assets, adjusted for any withdrawals by its owners. Applying this concept to a firm the accounting income is the increase in shareholders' funds in the balance sheet, plus any dividend shareholders have received during the period, less any capital they have contributed. This relationship between accounting income, dividends and the balance sheet is called the *accounting identity:*

Accounting income = Dividend + Increase in shareholders' funds

The accounting identity measures income in terms of the change in shareholders' funds because shareholders' funds are the difference between the firm's assets and its liabilities, so measuring the shareholders' wealth in balance-sheet terms. 'Dividend' measures their consumption of the firm's assets. In the accounting identity, it is shorthand for all exchanges of cash between the firm and its shareholders, including cash they have taken out as dividend or as a result of share repurchases during the period, offset by cash they have contributed by subscribing to new issues of shares. The exhibit *Hicksian income* describes the work of the economist John Hicks. Hicks defined an individual's income in a period as his or her consumption plus the increase in their wealth. The accounting identity is this insight applied to a firm.

The accounting model

The accounting identity is correct by definition; it is not an equation that measures an economic magnitude. Strictly, we should be using the mathematical sign '≡' not '='. So on its own the accounting identity is not telling us much; it just describes the logic of a balance sheet in which assets and claims must always be equal.

The accounting identity explains how accounting works. It says that constructing a balance sheet and measuring income are the same thing. Accounting income is determined by what assets and liabilities are recognised in the balance sheet, and at what values. We call the set of rules that determine what assets and liabilities go into a balance sheet and at what values the *accounting model*. The following example illustrates how the choice of accounting model allocates income to periods but also how, over the whole life of a business, income is unaffected by the accounting model.

Example: Manuel

Manuel is a hair stylist. He has spent his career working for someone else, but he wants to retire at 50 so he needs to make some serious money in his last five years. He takes a five-year lease on a salon for €300,000 and spends another €100,000 fitting it out. Manuel is a great stylist, very popular with his clients, so he reckons he should be able to take €200,000 from the business each year, even after paying the running costs of the salon and the wages of his assistants.

What is Manuel's income each year? That depends how we draw up his balance sheet. As accounting models, we will contrast two versions of the GAAP accounting model, and also cash accounting.

Under GAAP accounting, the balance sheet records the firm's assets at depreciated cost. Manuel makes an initial 400 investment in assets (in €000) but he reckons he should be able to recover 50 by selling the fittings at the end of five years. So the value of the assets ends up at zero for the lease when it expires at the end of year 5, and 50 for the residual value of the fittings. In the intervening years accountants would depreciate the assets down to their residual values, typically on a straight-line basis; in this case, 60 a year for the lease, and 10 a year to write down the fittings down to 50 after 5 years. Panel A of Table 1 shows the result. Manuel's income each year is the 200 of net takings less (60 + 10 =) 70 for depreciation. This gives a level income of 130 a year, which is probably a fair description of the economics of Manuel's business.

Table 1 Manuel's income (figures in €000s)

	Year 1 Start	Year 1 End	Year 2	Year 3	Year 4	Year 5	TOTALS
A GAAP accounting							
Lease	300	240	180	120	60	0	
Fittings	100	90	80	70	60	50	
Accounting assets	400	330	260	190	120	50	
Depreciation (= change in assets)		-70	-70	-70	-70	-70	
Net takings		200	200	200	200	200	
Income		**130**	**130**	**130**	**130**	**130**	**650**
B GAAP accounting, conservative depreciation							
Lease	300	225	150	75	0	0	
Fittings	100	75	50	25	0	0	
Accounting assets	400	300	200	100	0	50	
Depreciation (= change in assets)		-100	-100	-100	-100		
Profit on disposal						50	
Net takings		200	200	200	200	200	
Income		**100**	**100**	**100**	**100**	**250**	**650**
C Cash accounting							
Cost of assets (expense)	-400						
Sale of assets						50	
Net takings		200	200	200	200	200	
Income		**-200**	**200**	**200**	**200**	**250**	**650**

Depreciation requires judgements about the future; about the useful life of the assets, and whether they will have any value at the end. Suppose Manuel is more conservative, and thinks it prudent to plan for four years, and to assume that the fittings won't have any residual value. So he depreciates the 400 of assets in full over 4 years; that is, he charges 100 a year of depreciation. Panel B of Table 1 shows that Manuel's income is now 100 a year for the first 4 years. In the event, he does have a fifth year and the income in year 5 is 250. There is no depreciation because the assets are fully depreciated down to zero by the end of year 4. When he finally sells the fittings for 50, this will be recorded as a 'profit on disposal', though in reality it is better seen as the reversal of excess depreciation in earlier years.

Under *cash accounting* (Panel C), the only asset recorded in the balance sheet is the stock of cash. In Manuel's case, this means showing nothing at all in the balance sheet since he either contributes the cash the business needs each year or he takes out any surplus. For a business that uses assets, cash accounting is the most conservative accounting model in terms of income recognition, because the cost of the assets is an expense as they are acquired. The 400 cost of Manuel's lease and fittings now become expenses offsetting his takings of 200; his year 1 income is -200. Thereafter his income is the takings of 200 a year, plus, in year 5, the proceeds of selling the fittings, 50. In total Manuel's income over the five years is 650, under all three models.

In the end, it's just timing

There are two important messages in the Manuel example. One is that income results from how the balance sheet is constructed. The other is that, over the whole life of a firm, all accounting models generate the same income. Just to nail these home, consider another model.

Suppose Manuel is doing sensible GAAP accounting as in panel A of Table 1, but after a couple of years he goes crazy. In year 3 he decides to value the assets in the balance sheet, once and for all, at 369. He gets this number by multiplying a number he saw in the phone book, 123, by the age of his cat, who is 3 years old. Table 2 shows the effect. In years 1 and 2 income is 130, as before. In year 3, income is 329, which is takings of 200 plus the *increase* in assets from 260 at the end of year 2 to 369. Let's believe, for the sake of the story, that his accountant would allow Manuel both to revalue in this way and to show the increase as income rather than as comprehensive income! In year 4, since Manuel neither revalues nor depreciates his assets, they stay at 369, so income is just the takings of 200. In year 5 he suffers a 'loss on disposal' of 319 when he gets 50 for assets that were being carried in the balance sheet at 369. This, with the final takings of 200, gives him a loss for the final year of -119. The revaluation boosted his income in year 3, but it eventually caught up with him in year 5.

Table 2 Manuel's income, with crazy accounting (figures in €000s)

	Year 1 Start	Year 1 End	Year 2	Year 3	Year 4	Year 5	TOTALS
Accounting assets	*400*	*330*	*260*	*369*	*369*	*50*	
Change in assets		-70	-70	109	-	-319	
Net takings		200	200	200	200	200	
Income		**130**	**130**	**309**	**200**	**-119**	**650**

In total, Manuel's income is 650 over the life of the business. There is no magic in this. It just follows from the logic of the accounting identity, which is also the logic of double-entry book-keeping. Firms are born as cash and die as cash – the opening balance sheet contains the cash contributed by investors, and the closing balance sheet contains the cash remaining after liquidating the assets. Over the whole life of a business, its income is purely determined by external transactions: the initial purchase and ultimate sales of its assets, and the purchase and sale of goods and services to third parties along the way. The accounting model determines how that income is recognised period by period. Viewed over the whole life of a firm, the accounting model the firm uses along the way does not matter at all. Should we be consoled by this? Not really. We just about never look at a firm over its whole life and, year by year, the accounting model matters a lot.

Does the balance sheet *actually* drive income?

The key idea in this chapter, in fact a core idea in the whole book, is that it is the way that the items in the balance sheet are measured that determines income. This follows from applying the fundamental economic idea of 'income' to the context of a business. Historically, people used to measure the income of a business by looking at the balance sheet. Income statements are quite a new thing, as the exhibit, *History of the income statement*, recounts. However, this balance-sheet driven view is exactly the opposite to how most people think about accounting, as reflected in the language of *matching*. The accountant figures out the sales in the period, then matches the costs that were needed to generate the sales. Any costs left over from the matching process become assets, so assets are simply unused costs carried forward to a later period. Of course, the accounting identity is neutral on all of this; it works either way round. If the accounting process has income as the residual then, as we described it:

$$Accounting\ income = Dividend + Increase\ in\ shareholders'funds$$

If income measurement comes first then the closing balance sheet is the residual:

$$Closing\ shareholders'funds = Opening\ shareholders'funds + Accounting\ income - Dividend$$

Exhibit: Hicksian income

The classic economic analyses of income were published by Irving Fisher in 1930 and John Hicks in 1946. They were both writing about the income of individuals, rather than businesses. Indeed, for Fisher, only individuals could have income because he equated income with consumption and enjoyment. This consumption-based view of income led Fisher to conclude that an individual's savings were not part of his or her income in a period. On the other hand, if the individual consumed part of their capital, that was income.

Hicks, who became one of the earliest Nobel Laureates in economics, provided what is now the accepted definition of an individual's income. He defined income as the maximum value a person could consume during the week and still expect to be as well off at the end of the week as he was at the beginning. So for Hicks, in contrast to Fisher, an individual's income is the amount they actually consume during a period plus the increase in the money value of their wealth; it is their consumption plus their capital accumulation. Put differently, income is the amount an individual could have consumed after maintaining their capital. Hence:

$$Income = Consumption + Closing\ wealth - Opening\ wealth$$

References: I. Fisher, *The Theory of Interest*, Macmillan, 1930; J.R. Hicks, *Value and Capital*, Oxford University Press, 1939.

The danger with the income-driven view of accounting is that when assets and liabilities are left over as a residual they might not correctly measure property rights. Indeed there may be no asset, or liability, there at all in any meaningful sense. GAAP is now clear about this, and has become increasingly insistent that accounting should be 'asset-driven' rather than 'income-driven'.

Example: Doris

Doris spent $3m advertising the launch of her new online dating business. She argued that only $1m of this generated sales in the current year, but the rest will generate sales in the future. In consequence, she argued, $1m should be charged as an expense in the current year, and the remaining $2m should be carried forward as an asset in the balance sheet. Doris's accountant replied '*I agree about the $1m, but if we're going to carry the $2m forward you will have to convince me that it represents an asset. Just where is the assurance that we are going to generate at least $2m of additional future income as a result of that expenditure?*' Doris could not produce a convincing response, and her accountant insisted on expensing the whole of the $3m in the current year.

In practice accountants work both ways at the same time. They start with an accruals approach to income measurement, then they test whether the resulting assets and claims represent property rights. Much of the popular discussion about accounting is income-focused. It focuses on ways in which firms smooth their income through time or aggressively boost current earnings. This is not necessarily inconsistent with the balance sheet-driven view of accounting. When it determines what assets and liabilities should

Exhibit: History of the income statement

Historically, income statements are quite a new thing. Previously, owners of businesses looked to the balance sheet to see how much profit had been made. In the early days the business was often a trading venture. For example, a group of individuals joined together to buy a ship and they each stocked it with goods, which is the origin of the phrase 'joint-stock' business. They took a tally of these assets to compare with the tally of assets on the ship's return, which might be years later. The profit was the difference between the opening and closing balance sheets. Probably no more was needed – the owners were close to the business and in economic terms the venture was fairly simple. For a trading venture the accounting period was the length of the voyage, which was also the life of the venture. In due course trading companies emerged that had a continuing existence beyond a single voyage, and the manufacturing businesses that grew in importance after the industrial revolution were also continuing entities rather than single ventures. For continuing businesses it became the norm to draw up a balance sheet and measure profit annually.

The early industrial enterprises were usually privately owned and were frequently highly profitable, so their growth could be funded out of profits. The practice of financing business by listing a firm's shares on a public stock market developed in the early or mid-1800s, initially to finance railways and utility firms. Railways, for example, needed a large amount of investment and could not be financed from profits since there would be none until the whole line was built. This was the origin of the modern firm with a diffuse and potentially large group of shareholders, remote from management. Nonetheless, it was well into the 20th century that firms started regularly to produce an income statement. It was in the UK in 1928 that company law first required an income statement to be given to shareholders. For an excellent introduction to accounting history see John R. Edwards, *A History of Financial Accounting*, Routledge, 1989.

be recognised, and at what values, GAAP leaves room for discretion. This same wiggle-room enables firms to manage their income, to an extent, as we see in Chapter 15.

The investment accounting model

A firm's income is determined by what assets and liabilities go into a balance sheet and at what values, that is, by its accounting model. So what is the 'right' accounting model for firms to use?

The appropriate accounting model partly depends on the context. Different balance sheets may be needed for different purposes. For instance, we normally assume the firm is a *going concern*, that is, it is solvent and is expected to survive for at least another year. So the firm's long-term assets are recorded on the basis that they will be kept and used, and they are valued by depreciating or amortising their cost over their expected useful life. But if the firm is not a going concern it may be more relevant for the balance sheet to show the firm's break-up value – what assets can be sold and at what price? This balance sheet will probably look radically different to the going-concern balance sheet.

Take another example. We will see that the full GAAP accounting model is quite costly to implement. It requires the firm to collect a lot of information, particularly about the value of its assets and liabilities. This might be reasonable to demand from large firms with lots of outside investors and other stakeholders. But small firms are often '*closely held*', that is, the managers and owners are largely the same people. For them, the costs of collecting this information may exceed the benefits. So for small firms it might be appropriate to use a simpler accounting model.

One accounting model is particularly important and is our touchstone throughout this book. Suppose we want to use income statement and balance sheet data to measure the return the firm is earning on investors' capital. For the financial statements to generate reliable measures of return on capital, period by period, they need to have the data integrity of a carefully constructed investment analysis. This is achieved when the following two requirements are met:
- The balance sheet would need to be *complete*, that is, to contain all of the assets over which the firm has *property rights*, and to recognise as liabilities all of the claims that outsiders have over the firm.
- The balance sheet would need to be valued at current values. It would measure what investors forego by allowing the firm to use the assets and liabilities this year; that is, their *opportunity cost*.

This *investment accounting model* is a theoretical construct that is hard to achieve in practice. But the ideas of balance-sheet completeness and of current value provide us with a powerful framework for describing and assessing the GAAP accounting model that firms actually use. We will see that GAAP strives for balance-sheet completeness, but faces challenges in implementing it. For various reasons, GAAP does not require balance sheets to be at current value and the default remains valuation at historic cost.

BALANCE SHEET COMPLETENESS

The fundamental role of balance sheets in a capitalist economy is to record property rights: to record the assets the firm owns, and the claims outsiders have against those assets. In the exhibit *The role of the balance sheet* we tell two stories. One describes organisations that traditionally have not kept balance sheets, even though they may have vast asset holdings: governments. Governments of Western economies have only very recently started to produce balance sheets, and for those that have now done so, the effect is that they can see what assets they have and what they are worth. They can assess how efficiently they are using their assets, sell redundant assets to fund new investment, and borrow more easily against assets.

The other story describes the work of Hernando de Soto, which tries to explain the relative economic underdevelopment of the third world. De Soto puts it down to a lack of settled legal systems for enforcing and representing property rights. Without this, the incentive to invest in assets is reduced, and the ability to leverage the assets, that is, to use the capital stock to secure funding for further investment, is very limited. There has been pressure to recognise intangible assets in balance sheets, and the arguments are much the same as de Soto's: the inability to protect assets such as intellectual property may lead to underinvestment, and the inability to leverage these assets may limit the growth of the firm.

Accountants do not normally describe what they do in terms of property rights. They use the language of 'accruals' – accountants record transactions, which are exchanges of assets and claims with third parties. But this is another way of saying that accounting records property rights. The test for what should go into the balance sheet is enforceable contractual claims. As a simple example, recall the way accounting records a sale.

Example: Ivana

A customer has agreed to buy a rug from Ivana for $1,000. The rug costs $500 and is sitting as inventory in Ivana's warehouse. At present Ivana owns the rug, and this remains the case even though the customer has agreed to buy it. But once delivery has taken place Ivana exchanges the inventory for a legally enforceable claim over the customer, who is now bound to pay the selling price of $1,000, containing, as it does, Ivana's profit. By recognising the receivable of $1,000 in the balance sheet, Ivana records the profit as soon as the property rights are established. An alternative accounting model might be 'cash accounting', where the sale is recognised only when the $1,000 of cash is received in the bank account. Cash accounting mis-states the assets of the firm before payment is received, and it postpones the recognition of profit until after it has been realised. This is why GAAP uses accrual accounting.

Exhibit: The role of the balance sheet

Systems of property rights

Hernando de Soto is a Peruvian development economist whose professional life has been devoted to seeking solutions to the economic underdevelopment of the third world. In his classic book *The Mystery of Capital,* Bantam Press, London, 2000, he explains the success of the developed world in terms of property rights. The West possesses settled and robust legal systems that record assets, embody them in a defensible legal title, and provide a system for classifying them. For a firm, its balance sheet is an account of those property rights. "The reason capitalism has triumphed in the West and faltered in the rest of the world is because most of the assets in Western nations have been integrated into one formal representational system."

De Soto argues that the third world contains an enormous stock of assets but that these remain largely 'extra-legal', that is, outside the legal system. Without the ability to enforce property rights, the incentive to invest in assets is reduced, and the ability to leverage the assets, that is to use the capital stock to secure funding for further investment, is very limited. He reminds us how recently a settled property system has arrived in some parts of the West. For example, in California after the 1849 gold rush there were some 800 competing and separate property jurisdictions. It took most of the 19th century to achieve a unified system of title to property in the US. Arguably, this was the necessary precondition for the explosion of economic growth that followed in the US.

De Soto's preoccupation is with the institutional reforms needed to create a world where people can establish and record property rights over their tangible and financial assets. There is an active debate about whether de Soto's prescriptions are sufficient to deliver economic growth; but they are surely necessary. In fact, the project is also still continuing in the West, but now in the context of intangible assets. A lot of effort is going into strengthening the legal protection of certain types of intangible asset, and into harmonising property rights internationally. As we will see in Chapter 11, there has been corresponding pressure to recognise intangible assets in the balance sheet. The arguments are much the same as de Soto's; the inability to protect assets such as intellectual property leads to underinvestment, and the inability to leverage these assets may limit the growth of the firm.

National balance sheets

In most countries the state owns a vast portfolio of assets: holdings of land and buildings accumulated over centuries, of plant and equipment, and of inventories and receivables. The government is frequently the country's largest employer, and its employees need the same infrastructure to support them as in any business. Consider the asset holdings of one function in particular, defence. The defence department typically has large holdings of real estate in the form of training grounds, ports and airbases. It uses military hardware, including weaponry and communications systems, that may have cost billions or trillions.

Extraordinarily, most governments still do not maintain a central balance sheet, or even an asset register to provide a complete record of the state's assets. Without an asset register they do not know what assets they have got, and without a balance sheet would be unlikely to have the basis to calculate what they are worth. In the absence of such information, they cannot assess asset efficiency; whether resources are being used efficiently or wastefully. Instead they use a traditional cash accounting system that records receipts and payments. The informational focus is to ensure that receipts from taxes and borrowing cover planned expenditure, year by year. A small number of countries – Australia, New Zealand and the UK– have now introduced accrual-based accounting for central government. In the UK, this has measured government assets at opportunity cost, using 'deprival value' principles that we describe later. This is, historically, very recent – for example since 2001 in the UK – and it is transforming the public finances of countries that have done this. Countries using accrual-based accounts have far better information to sell redundant or underperforming assets to fund new investment. Should they wish to do so, their ability to borrow directly against assets – to use the sort of 'asset financing' that private firms use – is greatly increased.

The challenge of a complete balance sheet

GAAP is fully signed up to the principle that balance sheets should be complete. However, the complexities and ambiguities of the real world make this hard to deliver. GAAP faces challenges from two directions.

— *Uncertainty* A balance sheet is black and white and assets and liabilities are either in the balance sheet or out of it. But the value, and even the existence, of some assets and liabilities is *uncertain*. In an uncertain world it would sometimes be fairer to say 'if this happens, the asset or liability will be x, whereas if that happens, the asset or liability will be y.'

— *Ownership* A complete balance sheet records all the assets that the firm owns. However *ownership* may be ambiguous. Firms may share ownership of assets, or they can write complex contracts that enable them to use assets they do not own, or confer ownership on one party in certain states of the world, and on the other party in other states of the world.

GAAP conservatism

GAAP's way of accommodating the ambiguities of the real world in the binary world of the balance sheet is to apply the accounting model with *conservatism*. Its preoccupation is to stop firms overstating their assets while trying to ensure they recognise all their liabilities. So GAAP only allows firms to recognise assets in the balance sheet if they can be reliably measured. Establishing that an intangible asset exists, and demonstrating its value reliably, requires an active market in similar assets. This is usually possible for tangible assets and financial assets, but not for intangibles. On the liabilities side, GAAP's challenge is to make an appropriate provision for liabilities such as pensions and deferred tax whose eventual size is highly uncertain.

Accounting is based on transactions, and this roots financial statements in property rights. But this also brings a bias to conservatism because accounting *only* records an asset if it was acquired in a transaction or because of some identifiable event. Accountants do not sit chewing their pens in front of a blank sheet of paper, saying 'what are our assets and liabilities?' An asset that in effect arrived as a windfall will not get into the balance sheet. Intangible assets are, again, the main victims because there is often no identifiable transaction or cost associated with assets such as brands, intellectual property, and organisational capabilities that may be built over many years.

Here is a look ahead at the main balance sheet completeness issues we will encounter:

— *Intangibles* Intangible assets are the main source of asset incompleteness. GAAP conservatism turns out to be tough on internally generated intangible assets such as brands, intellectual property and know how. But when a firm acquires another firm, GAAP requires the acquired intangibles and the 'goodwill', which is the difference between the consideration paid and the identifiable assets, to be carried in the balance sheet. Hence the balance sheets of firms that grow organically are likely to be less complete than those that grow by acquisition. These issues are discussed in Chapter 11.

— *Off-balance-sheet financing* The firm may have written complex contracts so that assets and their related liabilities are excluded from the balance sheet, using what is known as 'off-balance sheet financing'. For instance, firms write operating lease contracts to shift tangible fixed assets and the corresponding debt off the balance sheet. Factoring receivables, and consigned inventory may achieve the same effect for current assets. Structuring the firm or the group so that subsidiaries are not consolidated has a similar effect. We discuss off-balance sheet financing in Chapter 13.

- *Pensions* Though GAAP strives to ensure firms record all their liabilities, in the past it overlooked some. The most significant source of liability incompleteness by far was pension liabilities. GAAP has now broadly corrected this omission, as we see in Chapter 12, though given the size of the liabilities the user of financial statements still needs to be careful in interpreting the data.
- *Reserves and provisions* If a firm is actively seeking to report lower earnings it may overstate its liabilities and understate assets by over-providing for depreciation and amortisation of long-term assets, for doubtful receivables and for slow-moving inventory.
- *Contingencies* Some liabilities are highly uncertain. Liabilities that are insufficiently likely to crystallise for them to be included in the balance sheet are known as 'contingencies'. We need to be alert to these.

Cases: Tiffany, Odfjell, Asahi and Publicis

When we formatted the balance sheets for these four firms in Chapter 3 we got some preliminary insights into the completeness of their balance sheets. Tiffany and Publicis are two firms that clearly possess valuable intangibles. Tiffany itself is an iconic brand name, and a number of Publicis' subsidiaries are global brands in their industries. Moreover human capital is a key resource in a business like Publicis. Tiffany's brand is not in its balance sheet. But when you acquire subsidiaries their intangibles are recognised in the balance sheet, either specifically or as residual goodwill. €3.6bn, which is 31% of Publicis' total assets, are intangibles. These were mostly acquired but Publicis also took advantage of the IFRS standard that allows some internally generated development expenditure to be capitalised. On the other hand Odfjell is a firm that mainly uses tangible long-term assets. PP&E account for around 85% of Odfjell's total assets. But Odfjell tells us that 36 of the 92 ships it uses are on operating leases, and so are off the balance sheet.

BALANCE SHEET VALUATION

GAAP wants balance sheets to be complete but faces some problems in implementation. However, GAAP does not accept that balance sheets should be at current values. We will defer a full discussion of how balance sheets are valued until Chapter 14, but here we sketch the theoretical background and give an overview of practice.

Some theory

When we make an investment decision, if we are being rational we should cost the resources that we commit to the project at their *opportunity cost*, which is what we will forego by not using them elsewhere. In the same way, for a balance sheet to have the data integrity of a carefully constructed investment appraisal it would need to measure the opportunity cost of the firm's assets and liabilities; that is, it should measure what investors forego by allowing them to be used in the firm. When a firm is analysing a specific investment project the true cost of the necessary assets is normally pretty obvious, in context. But conceptually, finding a general rule for identifying opportunity cost for balance sheets is not straightforward.

The question 'what is the current value of an asset?' has at least three answers, each describing a different aspect of the asset's value. The 'replacement cost' of an asset is the current cost of acquiring the asset in the market place. The 'realisable value' of the asset is the expected proceeds from selling the asset. The 'economic value' is the present value of the expected stream of income from the asset. We need all three of these measures of value. Opportunity cost is best quantified by asking what the loss would be if the asset, or liability, was taken away; which is known as 'deprival value'. The deprival value of an asset is generally its replacement cost, because if the firm loses the asset it would replace it, and 'replacement cost' is what it costs to do that. But if the firm is deprived of an unprofitable asset that is not worth replacing, then the firm's loss is either the asset's economic value, which is the value of the income it would have earned, or its realisable value, which is what it could have been sold for. In an important contribution to economic theory, John Kay and Colin Mayer demonstrated that if firms valued their assets and liabilities in the balance sheet at opportunity cost using the deprival value rule, then the accounting return on capital would correctly measure the economic return or 'internal rate of return' of the firm[1].

Revaluation in practice

In practice, GAAP does not require balance sheets to be kept at current value. The subjectivity in estimating current costs, and the cost of the exercise, have been the most influential factors in GAAP's thinking; also concern about the nature of the resulting income number. Cost considerations also lie behind the apparent reluctance of firms themselves to keep assets at current values in the balance sheet.

Essentially, balance sheets are a cocktail containing a base of historic cost with some current values mixed in. GAAP does not generally require upward revaluation of long-

---

1   See John Kay and Colin Mayer *On the Application of Accounting Rates of Return*, Economic Journal 96 (1986) pp 199-207, and Jeremy Edwards. John Kay and Colin Mayer *The Economic Analysis of Accounting Profitability*, Oxford University Press, 1987. Internal rate of return is defined and explained in the Financial arithmetic appendix at the end of the book.

term assets to current values, but downward revaluation is required if the value is 'impaired'. The GAAP accounting model is moving towards current value for available-for-sale financial assets and liabilities, but historic cost remains the default for long-term financial assets. We describe the GAAP approach to balance sheet valuation in Chapter 14. Here is a look ahead at some of the balance sheet valuation issues we will encounter:

– *Valuation of long-term assets* By default, transaction-based accounting records an asset at its 'historic cost' which is the original transaction price. US GAAP does not permit revaluation. IFRS allows long-term assets to be revalued to current values, though most firms do not take advantage of it. In consequence, when there is inflation, balance sheets are likely to understate the value of long-term assets.

– *LIFO (last in, first out) inventory valuation* US GAAP permits the use of the last-in, first-out rule (LIFO) for inventory valuation. This has the effect of valuing inventories in the balance sheet at out of date prices.

Cases: Tiffany, Odfjell, Asahi and Publicis

When we reviewed the balance sheets of these firms we saw that their long-term assets are mainly carried at historic cost. They have chosen not to revalue or, in the case of Tiffany because it reports under US GAAP, could not revalue. This raises the possibility that their balance sheets are significantly undervalued. Tiffany, for example, has a global portfolio of prime real estate that it has been building for decades. A partial exception, which demonstrates the potential for misvaluation is Publicis. IFRS permits revaluation, and when it adopted IFRS in 2005 Publicis took the opportunity to revalue one of its properties, which had been carried at €5m, to €156m. Also, to the extent that a firm's growth is recent, this tends to reduce the potential historic cost bias. Again, a large part of Publicis' intangibles were recently acquired. Tiffany demonstrates the potential under US GAAP to value inventory at 'LIFO' and return to this in Chapter 14.

INCOME

An accounting model – that is, a set of rules about what goes into the balance sheet and at what values – yields an accounting income number. GAAP's accounting model is a conservative version of the investment accounting model. But the GAAP concept of 'realised' income is slightly more conservative still. GAAP *realised income* is income that is realised in the form of cash or of assets, whose ultimate cash realisation can be assessed with reasonable certainty. Realised income is the accounting income that can be reported in the income statement, so realised income equates to earnings.

We have been calling the income yielded by an accounting model, 'accounting income'. GAAP calls this *comprehensive income*[2], and this has two components:
– **Earnings** Realised income, recognised in the income statement.
– **Other comprehensive income** The components of income that GAAP says are unrealised. These are *reserve accounted*, that is, dealt with as movements in shareholders' funds in the balance sheet.

The distinction between realised income and accounting income, that is, the distinction between earnings and comprehensive income, gives GAAP a handy buffer. It allows GAAP to detach the property rights aspect of assets from the valuation aspect. As an example, IFRS allows firms to revalue upwards long-term assets such as property. But IFRS will not allow firms to treat this surplus as realised income until the assets are sold. Initially the surplus on revaluation is recorded as a revaluation reserve within shareholders' funds in the balance sheet. The surplus is 'realised' when the asset is sold and at that point it is passed through the income statement as a 'profit on disposal'. GAAP is saying that, at the time the revaluation takes place, the surplus is not far enough down the road to being cash. The firm has property rights over the long-term asset but probably does not have an enforceable contract to sell it at the revalued amount.

The components of income that GAAP treats as unrealised are relatively few in number and we list them in Chapter 15. For many firms, the earnings in the income statement are pretty close to measuring comprehensive income. But we need to beware because, sometimes, an important component of income can bypass the income statement altogether. GAAP is aware of the importance of comprehensive income, and both US GAAP and IFRS now require firms to provide a clear statement of other comprehensive income so that the analyst can assemble the comprehensive income figure.

Cases: Tiffany, Odfjell, Asahi and Publicis

The list of potential candidates for reserve accounting as 'other comprehensive income' is quite short. It includes the effects of foreign exchange gains and losses, and of fair valuation of hedges and available-for-sale investments. In practice, when we reviewed our four firms we found that for three of them, other comprehensive income was significant. Odfjell had earnings of $127.5m and other comprehensive income of -$41.3m, Asahi ¥39.9bn and ¥14.5bn, Publicis €386m and €109m.

---

2 Comprehensive income is also variously known as *clean-surplus* income, *complete* income, *all-inclusive* income or *total recognised gains and losses*.

A DIVISION OF LABOUR

To see what accounting is, and is not, trying to do, suppose, as people sometimes propose, that balance sheets recorded the economic value of the firm[3]. The *economic value* of an asset to its owner is the value of the expected stream of cash flows it will generate, found by discounting the expected cash flows to get their present value.

Example: Manuel, revisited

Manuel's cost of capital is 10%. During year 1 Manuel got an income of 200 but had to invest 400 at the beginning of the year to achieve it. His cash flow in the first year was therefore -200. Thereafter, Manuel expects takings of 200 each year for the next four years plus 50 in the final year from selling the fittings. The present value of that stream of cash flow is 668, which is the economic value of the business at the end of year 1. We could conduct a similar exercise at the end of each year. So at the end of year 3, for example, there remains future cash flow of 200 in year 4, and 250 in year 5 which is the takings of 200 plus the 50 from disposing of the assets. The present value of these is 388 at the end of year 3.

Suppose Manuel's balance sheet simply records the economic value of his business each year. So income is the change in economic value plus the cash flow over the period. In year 1 Manuel's income is 468 because he creates a business from nothing with an economic value of 668[4] at the end of the year, but it costs him (200 - 400 =) -200 of cash flow to achieve it. During year 2 the economic value of Manuel's business falls from 668 to 535, a decline of 133, but he receives 200 cash so income is 67 (to be slightly more precise, it is 66.8), and so forth through to the end of year 5. Table 3 shows all this.

Table 3 Economic value as Manuel's accounting model (figures in €000s)

	Year 1 Start	Year 1 End	Year 2	Year 3	Year 4	Year 5	TOTALS
Investment	-400					50	
Net takings		200	200	200	200	200	
Cash flow	-400	200	200	200	200	250	
Economic value		668	535	388	227	0	
Change in economic value		668	-133	-147	-161	-227	
Income (rounded)		**468**	**67**	**53**	**39**	**23**	**650**

Realisation versus expectation

Economic value is a valuation rule with a very particular outcome. It allocates income so that all the expected surplus is taken as income in the first year, leaving just enough to give a fair return each year, thereafter. When you discount a series of cash flows to find a present value using a discount rate, in this case 10%, you are saying 'what is the capital sum today, on which subsequent cash flows will just give a 10% return?' So Manuel's income in year 2 was 66.8, which is precisely 10% of the economic value of 668 at the beginning of that year.

---

3   If the language of this section is unfamiliar, refer to the Financial Arithmetic appendix at the end of the book.

4   The present value of 200 received in one year's time is 200/(1+10%) = 200/1.1 =181.8, in two year's, 200/1.1^2 =165.3, in three year's, 200/1.1^3 =150.3, 250 in four year's is worth 250/1.1^4 =170.8, in total, 668.

Manuel's series of income numbers in Table 3 looks completely different to the series in Table 1. As always, the difference is simply timing because in total his income for the five years is also 650. Manuel has a very profitable business and, using economic value as the accounting model, this superior performance gets recognised as income as soon as it is *expected*, which in this case is all in the first year. This is not what accounting does. The GAAP accounting model recognises income when it is *realised* in terms of property rights.

Economic value is precisely what is measured by share prices, or more precisely, by the firm's market capitalisation, which is its share capital times the number of shares in issue. If Manuel's business had been listed on the stock market then, rationally valued, its market capitalisation would have been 668 at the end of the first year, 535 at the end of year 2, and so forth.

Opportunity cost valuation

When the stock market measures the market capitalisation of a firm it is measuring the value of the expected stream of income the firm will generate, which is the economic value of the entity as a whole. Economic performance measurement is about comparing the performance of an asset in its current use with its performance in its next best use. This is the logic for valuing balance sheets at opportunity cost. It permits a useful division of labour between stock markets and accountants. If the balance sheet measures the opportunity cost of the firm's assets, then a comparison of the balance-sheet value to the market capitalisation tells us how much value the firm is creating. Here is another reason why we do not want balance sheets to measure economic value; if they did, they would lose their vital role in performance measurement. A balance sheet that measures economic value has no value, because stock markets do that already.

We can measure Manuel's value creation this way. At the end of year 1 he is using 330 of assets (Table 1, first panel), but has created a business worth 668 (Table 3). So he has created (668 - 330 =) 338 of value. Similarly, when we are comparing the firm's return on capital to the cost of capital we are relying on the balance sheet to measure the opportunity cost of the capital stock in just the same way.

In reality, valuation at opportunity cost represents an unattainable ideal. The idea of a neat separation of tasks, with the balance sheet measuring the opportunity cost of the capital stock, works well for a cotton mill, where all the inputs are in competitive supply. But in many modern firms the key assets are frequently intangible assets and it is hard or impossible to measure their opportunity cost. Economic value is usually the only way to value these assets. This is another reason why GAAP is reluctant to recognise intangibles, unless they were acquired and there is a transaction price.

REVIEW

- Accountants measure the income of a firm in a period by measuring its assets and liabilities at the start and the end. The firm's accounting income over a period is then the change in shareholders' funds in the balance sheet, adjusted for any dividends. So income is a function of what assets and liabilities are included in the balance sheet, and at what values. Constructing a balance sheet and measuring income are essentially the same thing.

- The choice of accounting model – the set of rules that determine what assets and liabilities go into the balance sheet, and at what values – is therefore crucial in determining income.

- There are many accounting models a firm could use, but one is particularly important. It is the accounting model needed for financial statements to provide reliable measures of return on investors' capital. The 'investment' accounting model requires a balance sheet that is complete in property rights and valued at current values.

- GAAP strives for a complete balance sheet that records the assets over which the firm has property rights, and records as liabilities the property rights that others have over the firm. GAAP faces a number of challenges in the quest for a complete balance sheet, most significantly the problems of uncertainty over the value or existence of assets, particularly intangibles, and lack of clarity over who owns them. In response, GAAP errs on the side of caution, or conservatism, to prevent firms from overstating their assets and/or underestimating their liabilities.

- Though we would like the balance sheet to measure the opportunity cost of a firm's assets, in practice historic cost is used as the base for valuing assets, with some revaluation upwards and downwards from cost for certain classes of asset, and in certain situations.

- The firm's accounting income in a period is the change in its shareholders' funds, adjusted for contributions and withdrawals of capital. This is known as 'comprehensive income'. In practice most of this income is recognised in the income statement as earnings, but some elements of income may be 'reserve accounted' and recorded directly in the balance sheet.

Part 2

Return on capital

Chapter 5

Measures of return on capital

The principal measures of return on capital are return on equity, which is the return the firm earns on the funds provided by equity shareholders, and return on capital employed, which is an entity-level return on all of the finance raised from shareholders and by borrowing. This chapter shows how to use balance sheet and income statement data to calculate these return on capital measures.

We measure return on capital employed pre tax and after tax. Pre-tax return on capital employed is the best basis for analysing the firm's operating performance. But we need an after-tax return to compare to the firm's cost of capital. Comparing return on capital to the cost of capital leads naturally to the idea of economic profit, which is widely used for performance measurement within firms. Economic profit simply internalises the cost of capital comparison by deducting a capital charge from profit.

RETURN ON EQUITY

The financial ratio that measures the return on the capital provided by the firm's shareholders is *return on equity (ROE)*. The numerator is earnings. The denominator is equity shareholders' funds from the balance sheet; it excludes non-equity shareholders such as preference shares and minorities.

$$Return\ on\ equity = \frac{Earnings}{Average\ equity\ shareholders'funds}.$$

Note that the ratio uses the average of the equity shareholders' funds in the 'opening' and 'closing' balance sheets, that is, the balance sheet at the end of the previous year and at the end of the current year. Measures of return on capital relate a *flow* of income that arose throughout a period to a *stock* of capital that is measured periodically when the balance sheet is drawn up. Since assets are unlikely to grow smoothly through the year, the denominator of the return on capital measure should perhaps be an average of the daily capital. This is impractical: outsiders do not have this data, and even firms themselves rarely bother to do this when they calculate return on capital for internal performance measurement. Using the average of the opening and closing balance sheets is a reasonable compromise. In practice, many analysts do not even bother to do this and simply use the closing balance sheet to provide the denominator of return on capital.

Return on equity is normally calculated using earnings. But if we want to compare return on equity to the cost of equity capital then, strictly, comprehensive income should be used in the numerator. In practice, it is wise to calculate ROE both ways.

Case: Return on equity at Tiffany

Using the formatted financial statements in Chapter 3, Tiffany's equity shareholders' funds at the end of 2005 were (all figures in $m) 1,701.2, and at the end of the previous year were 1,468.2, so average equity during 2005 was 1,584.7. Tiffany's earnings in 2005 were 304.3 so return on equity in this year was (304.3/1,584.7 =) 19.2%. Tiffany's equity shareholders' funds at the end of 2004 were 1,468.2 and at the end of the previous year were 1,208.0, so average equity was 1,338.1 during 2004. Tiffany's earnings were 215.5 in 2003. Tiffany's return on equity in 2004 was (215.5/1,338.1 =) 16.1%. In the year to 31 January 2005, Tiffany's comprehensive income was 318.0, so the comprehensive return on equity is (318.0/1,584.7 =) 20.1%. In 2004, the comprehensive return on equity was (248.4/1,338.1 =) 18.6%.

RETURN ON CAPITAL EMPLOYED

Return on equity measures the performance of the firm from the perspective of its shareholders, but frequently we want to measure the return on capital of the whole business, that is, we want an *entity* return on capital that measures the profitability of the firm's assets, independent of how they are financed. When firms use a return on capital measure for internal performance measurement they typically use an entity return on capital and many external analysts use entity return on capital too. As we see in Chapter 7, an entity measure is also the best starting point for the analysis of profitability, where the aim is to drill down into the numbers to understand as much as possible about the economics of the business. 'Entity-level', in the context of a measure of return on capital, is also commonly known as *enterprise-level*, *firm-level* or *capital employed-level*.

Defining the denominator

The firm's *net operating assets* is its total assets (but excluding cash) less its short and long-term operating liabilities. For short, we like to call net operating assets *net assets*. Correspondingly, *capital employed* is shareholders' funds plus net debt. The first step in measuring an entity return on capital is to rearrange the published balance sheet into its operating and its financing components, as shown in Figure 1. Some of the financing that the firm needs arises as a natural by-product of operations: for example, suppliers give credit; the tax authorities allow some time to pay taxes, and so forth. The remainder has to be raised from investors and is the 'capital employed' by the firm. A well-run firm should make best use of the financing potential of accounts payable, tax liabilities, etc. These all serve to reduce the bundle of net operating assets that the firm needs to finance from investors. Capital employed measures this financing from investors.

Figure 1 Finding capital employed and net assets

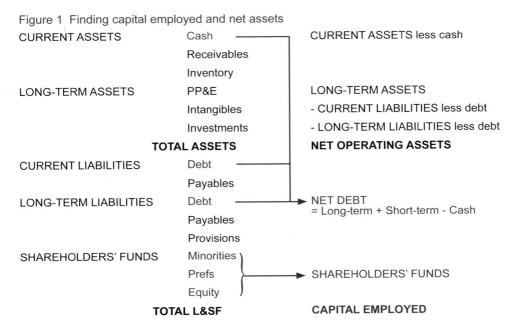

Return on capital employed (ROCE) measures the return that the firm has earned on the capital raised from all its investors. Capital employed is an inclusive measure; it measures funds from all sources. Shareholders' funds include the equity shareholders' funds used in the return on equity measure, but also non-equity shareholders' funds such as preference shares and minorities. Debt includes both short-term or 'current' debt, and long-term debt, less cash. Since capital employed comprises the funds provided both by net debt and by shareholders, the corresponding income measure is *Earnings before interest and tax (EBIT)*.

$$\text{Return on capital employed (ROCE)} = \frac{EBIT}{Average\ capital\ employed}$$

Alternative measures of return

In this book we use ROCE as the entity-level return. But net operating assets is logically identical to capital employed. So return on capital employed can be, and frequently is, called *return on net operating assets*, or just *return on net assets (RONA)*. There is ambiguity around the term 'net assets' in finance. Confusingly, 'net assets' is frequently encountered as a synonym for 'shareholders' funds'.

$$\text{Return on net assets (RONA)} = \frac{EBIT}{Average\ net\ operating\ assets}$$

So long as they all use EBIT as their numerator they are the same measure. The choice of measure is purely a matter of taste. ROCE is commonly used by outsiders to the firm; it emphasises the link to investors, which is helpful if we are to compare the ratio to the cost of capital. RONA tends to be the label when the ratio is used inside the firm for performance measurement and control purposes; it emphasises the underlying operating assets and liabilities. Pragmatically, it is usually quickest and easiest to take the capital employed route, but you can get at just the same number by coming from the asset side of the balance sheet. Either way, the same distinction has to be made between the liabilities that arise from operating the business and the finance provided by investors.

In practice, there are many, many names for what we call ROCE, and many ways of defining it. It is never worth getting fixated on labels. What matters is to be crystal clear about how the measure you are looking at is constructed.

Case: Return on capital employed at Tiffany

Using the data from Chapter 3, we calculate Tiffany's 2005 capital employed following the format of Figure 1:

Table 1 Tiffany's 2005 capital employed (figures in $m)

Original balance sheet		Rearranged balance sheet	
Cash	326.9		
Trade receivables	133.5	Trade receivables	133.5
Inventories	1,057.2	Inventories	1,057.2
Other current assets	90.2	Other current assets	90.2
PP&E	917.9	PP&E	917.9
Other long-term assets	140.4	Other long-term assets	140.4
TOTAL ASSETS	**2,666.1**	*Trade payables*	*-74.5*
		Other current liabilities	*-282.4*
Debt, current	43.0	*Provisions*	*-73.4*
Trade payables	74.5	*Other long-term liabilities*	*-94.1*
Other current liabilities	282.4	**NET OPERATING ASSETS**	**1,814.8**
Debt, long-term	397.6	*Cash*	*-326.9*
Provisions	73.4	Debt, current	43.0
Other long-term liabilities	94.1	Debt, long-term	397.6
SHAREHOLDERS' FUNDS	1,701.2	SHAREHOLDERS' FUNDS	1,701.2
TOTAL L&SF	**2,666.1**	**CAPITAL EMPLOYED**	**1,814.8**

Table 2 summarises Tiffany's capital employed from 2003 to 2005.

Table 2 Tiffany's summary capital employed (figures in $m)

	2003	2004	2005
Shareholders' funds	**1,208.0**	**1,468.2**	**1,701.2**
Debt (current and long-term)	349.7	486.9	440.6
Less cash	-156.2	-276.1	-326.9
Net debt	**193.5**	**210.7**	**113.7**
Capital employed	**1,401.5**	**1,678.9**	**1,814.8**

Capital employed was 1,814.8 at year end 2005 and 1,678.9 at 2004, so its average capital employed during 2005 was 1,746.9. Tiffany's EBIT was 494.2 in 2005, so ROCE was (494.2/1,746.9 =) 28.3%. Capital employed was 1,678.9 at year-end 2004 and 1,401.5 at 2003; average capital employed in 2004 was 1,540.2 and EBIT was 357.6 so Tiffany's 2004 ROCE was (357.6/1,540.2 =) 23.2%.

Issues in measuring capital employed

Two tests help to distinguish liabilities that are part of capital employed from liabilities that reduce net assets.

- A rule of thumb for identifying a financing claim asks, is the claim interest or dividend-bearing? Though this works in almost all cases, it is not entirely reliable. For example, debt instruments such as zero-coupon bonds and bills of exchange have no explicit servicing cost. The interest is rolled up into the discount on the issue, or premium on redemption, of the instrument.
- The more robust test concerns motive. Did the claim arise primarily with a financing motive, rather than as a by-product of some other transaction? For example, the tax authorities may allow firms to pay part of their corporate taxes with a lag of months or even years. This tax deferment provides valuable financing, but no-one would volunteer to pay tax simply in order to take advantage of the financing. So tax liabilities are not normally included in capital employed.

Separating the operating elements from the financing elements of a balance sheet is not a precise science, and there will be times when we are unsure which side of the boundary to put some item. Sometimes the costs of collecting the data needed for further precision exceed the benefits. Consider the following example.

Example: Maria and Helpful

Helpful&Co supply components, and their normal credit term is 30 days. Currently, Maria is buying €4.0m of materials from Helpful, but she will have difficulty paying in 30 days. She agrees to pay €4.1m for the same goods on three months' credit. Effectively, she is borrowing €4.0m for another two months for an additional €0.1m. This represents a (rather high!) borrowing cost of (.1/4.0 =) 2.5% for two months, which is roughly (2.5% × 6 =) 15% a year. In current liabilities, Maria will show a payable of €4.1m for three months. But, strictly, this is a €4.0m trade payable for one month that becomes a loan (debt) for the next two months, with €0.1m of accrued interest liability that is strictly 'other liabilities' throughout the three months. When the material is used, Maria will show €4.1m as cost of goods sold, but strictly €0.1m of this should be treated as interest paid.

Even if the analyst had the energy to separate the loan from the payable in Maria's balance sheet and the interest element from the cost of sales in the income statement, they would rarely have enough information to do it.

Netting cash and debt

We define capital employed in terms of net debt: the firm's debt less its balances of cash and the debt element of liquid investments. The logic of using net debt is that when a firm holds cash in the bank it is essentially lending to the banking system, so cash is really negative debt. Return on capital employed seeks to measure the return on the operations of the business, independent of financing, and holding cash is a financing rather than an operating activity.

Though netting cash against debt is the dominant practice amongst financial analysts, there are some countervailing arguments. We are implicitly treating all of a firm's cash as surplus to the operational needs of the business. Arguably, this is unrealistic because the firm will need an inventory of cash to run the business and to cover the payments cycle. Some analysts like to make an allowance – perhaps 2% of sales – for 'operational' cash and only deduct the remainder, the 'surplus' cash, from capital employed. In this case, since the operational cash will be earning interest, for consistency a proportion of interest received should be included in EBIT. Though it is hard to fault this logic, the simplicity of netting all the cash is very attractive. This is one of the many occasions where the costs of, (possibly spurious,) precision may exceed the benefits.

There is a stronger argument not to net cash against debt at all. Whenever we net two numbers we lose sight of some information, and we imply some equivalence between the two numbers that were netted. So in the present case, are we indifferent between one firm with $1bn of debt and with $0.9bn sitting as cash on the other side of the balance sheet, and another firm with $0.1bn of debt and no cash? Though they both have net debt of $0.1bn they may be very different firms, especially when the financial system in which the firm operates is illiquid. Though netting debt is the default treatment, sometimes it makes sense to unpack net debt when analysing a firm with a large cash pile.

The consistency test

People often struggle with the idea of capital employed when they first meet it. They find it counter-intuitive. A common reaction is: *'Why are we only including debt and shareholders' funds in capital employed? Surely all liabilities finance the firm in some way, so why not include accounts payable or tax liabilities in capital employed? Indeed, why not use total assets as capital employed because total assets equal total claims, which is the finance provided by shareholders' funds and by all third-party liabilities?'* In any return-on-capital measure, consistency between the numerator and the denominator is vital.

Some people use *return on total assets* – defined as EBIT/Total assets – as a measure of return on capital. This may work fine if total assets is simply being used as a measure of size and the need is just for a measure of scaled income across firms of different sizes. But even used this way, return on total assets is unreliable if there are differences between firms in their ability to use operating liabilities to finance their assets. Return on total assets does not provide a measure of economic return that can be compared directly with the cost of capital. It fails the consistency test. Though EBIT might measure the income the firm has generated for investors, 'total assets' does not measure the investment they have made to get it.

Some analysts include only long-term debt in capital employed on the grounds that short-term debt is transitory. This is hard to justify in practice since some firms do appear to include short-term debt in their planned capital structure, and persist in using short-term debt for lengthy periods. But, again consistency is key, and a pragmatic reason to include both short and long-term debt is that in calculating the corresponding EBIT it may be difficult to split the reported interest payment into its long- and short-term components.

AFTER-TAX RETURN ON CAPITAL EMPLOYED

EBIT is earnings *before* interest and tax, so ROCE is a pre-tax entity-level return. Sometimes, and particularly for comparing to the cost of capital, an after-tax entity return on capital is what we need. The after-tax version of EBIT is *earnings before interest and after tax (EBIAT)*, which is EBIT less the tax on EBIT.

$$EBIAT = EBIT - Tax\ on\ EBIT$$

giving
$$After\text{-}tax\ ROCE = \frac{EBIAT}{Average\ capital\ employed}$$

EBIAT is also known as *net operating profit after tax (NOPAT)*, or *net operating profit less adjusted taxes (NOPLAT)*. A common name for after-tax ROCE is *return on invested capital (ROIC)*.

Separating tax into operating and financing

The logic of an entity-level return such as ROCE hinges on separating the firm's 'real' or operating activities from its financing activities. To get after-tax ROCE we need to split the firm's tax charge in the same way. This turns out to be problematic because 'before interest but after tax' is not the natural order of things in the income statement. In income statements, tax is reported after interest. As a result firms just report a single tax figure. This contains the tax the firm pays on its EBIT, but it also contains the tax the firm pays on its interest received and saves on its interest paid, in other words, the tax saved on net interest paid. The tax that the firm saves on net interest paid is commonly known as the *interest tax shelter*.

$$Reported\ tax = Tax\ on\ EBIT - Interest\ tax\ shelter$$
so,
$$Tax\ on\ EBIT = Reported\ tax + Interest\ tax\ shelter$$

To get to the tax on EBIT, we need to unpack the reported tax charge, but this requires information the outsider does not usually have. Two approaches are used in practice, involving different assumptions about the effective tax rate on EBIT and the effective tax rate on net interest paid.

Using the statutory corporate tax rate

The 'classical' approach to unpacking the reported tax charge is to assume that interest is deductible for tax at the statutory tax rate, and get to the tax on EBIT by elimination. So in this case the interest tax shelter is the net interest paid times the statutory tax rate.

$$Tax\ on\ EBIT = Reported\ tax + Net\ interest\ paid \times Statutory\ tax\ rate$$

so,
$$EBIAT = EBIT - (Reported\ tax + Net\ interest\ paid \times Statutory\ tax\ rate)$$

The reason there is a '+' in this equation is that if the firm is a net payer of interest this saves tax; interest is providing a tax shelter. So we add the tax shelter on net interest paid to the reported tax to get back to the tax on EBIT. Another way of doing the same thing is bottom up, by working from earnings after tax. Starting from earnings after tax we need to add back the interest less the tax shelter on the interest, that is, add back the after-tax net interest paid:

$$EBIAT = Earnings\ after\ tax + Net\ interest\ paid \times (1 - Statutory\ tax\ rate)$$

The effective tax rate on EBIT, that is, the percentage of tax the firm actually pays on its EBIT, will rarely equal the statutory rate. When the tax authorities are doing a firm's tax computation they start from EBIT, but they make a number of adjustments. For example they disallow certain expenditure for tax; entertainment is a common example. For some other items the tax treatment may be more generous than the accounting treatment; depreciation is a common example. By assuming that interest paid and received are taxed at the statutory tax rate, the classical EBIAT tax calculation allocates all the firm's tax idiosyncrasies to operating profit, which is where they usually belong. The lazy way to get EBIAT, by simply applying the statutory tax rate to EBIT, would have the opposite effect.

Using the average effective corporate tax rate

Unfortunately, and especially for a multinational firm, it may not be safe to assume that the statutory rate is the appropriate rate for taxing interest. If the firm has international operations it will have structured its financing for tax efficiency and may have located its borrowing in the highest-tax jurisdiction to get the best tax shelter. It would be too simplistic to assume that net interest is taxed at the statutory tax rate of the home country in which the firm reports. For this reason it is common practice amongst analysts to adopt a compromise and assume the firm's average effective tax rate applies to everything and so apply that average rate directly to EBIT to get EBIAT.

$$Average\ effective\ corporate\ tax\ rate\ =\ \frac{Reported\ tax}{Earnings\ before\ tax}$$

which yields, $EBIAT = EBIT \times (1 - Average\ effective\ corporate\ tax\ rate)$

Example: Brigand & Co

Brigand & Co has average capital employed of 500 and has the income statement described below. The corporate tax rate is 35%.

Table 3 Brigand & Co's income statement

EBIT	**100**
Interest received	10
Interest paid	-30
Earnings before tax	**80**
Tax	-15
Earnings	**65**

Brigand's EBIT is 100, so its ROCE is (100/500 =) 20%. To find EBIAT, we need to know the tax on EBIT. The actual tax paid is 15, but on its net interest payments of (30 - 10 =) 20 the firm would have got a tax deduction (20 × 35% =) 7. So tax on EBIT must have been (15 + 7 =) 22, and EBIAT is (100 - 22 =) 78. Brigand's after-tax ROCE is thus (78/500 =) 15.6%. Working from the bottom up, Brigand's net interest paid, net of tax, is (20 - 7 =) 13, again giving EBIAT (65 + 13 =) 78. Brigand's EBIT is 100 and the statutory tax rate is 35%, so it is tempting to calculate EBIAT as (100 × (1 - 35%) =) 65. This understates EBIAT because it ignores tax shelters from which Brigand clearly benefits, since Brigand's overall average effective tax rate is only (15/80 =) 18.75%. If we apply Brigand's average effective tax rate of 18.75%, EBIAT would be (100 × (1 - 18.75%) =) 81.25. After-tax ROCE is now (81.25/500 =) 16.25%.

ECONOMIC PROFIT

Arguably, income statements are incomplete; there is a line missing. They contain a charge for using net debt finance, which is net interest paid, but there is no charge for using equity finance. This is understandable – interest payments are clear and contractual, but the cost of equity is nowhere written down and does not reflect a contractual liability of the firm.

The cost of capital

In this chapter we are actively starting to talk about the 'cost of capital', and this requires some explanation. The cost of capital is a key concept in financial analysis. We use it as a discount rate when finding present values, and we use it as the benchmark for assessing the firm's return on capital. At the centre of corporate finance and financial reporting is the investor, who provides the capital that firms use to buy the assets they need. By providing capital to the firm, investors are prevented from investing it somewhere else, so they require the firm to earn a return that is at least as good as they could have got elsewhere. The investors' required return becomes the firm's cost of capital. Equity and debt investors will have different costs of capital, reflecting the different risks they experience, and their different tax treatments. The average dollar of capital employed uses a mix of debt and equity finance, and so has a cost of capital that is an average of the cost of debt capital and the cost of equity capital, weighted by their contributions to financing. This is known as the firm's weighted average cost of capital (WACC). There is a fuller discussion of how to calculate the cost of capital, using Tiffany as an example, in Chapter 9.

The cost of equity is an opportunity-cost concept and requires estimation. People sometimes confuse dividend payments with the cost of equity capital. But many firms do not pay dividends, and even when a firm does pay a dividend this usually provides only a small part of the shareholders' required return. In any case, dividends are viewed in law as a distribution of profit rather than as an expense in earning it, and so are not charged against earnings in the income statement.

If the cost of using equity capital is not included, accounting earnings do not measure the true surplus earned by the firm. Earnings measured after charging for all of the capital the firm is using are called *economic profit*. To calculate economic profit we go back to EBIAT; to a pre-interest measure, then make a charge for using the whole of the capital employed in the year, calculated by applying the WACC to the average capital employed during the period:

$$Capital\ charge = Average\ capital\ employed \times WACC$$

so, $$Economic\ profit = EBIAT - Capital\ charge$$

The term 'economic profit' is used quite loosely in finance; for instance, it is sometimes applied to the per cent 'spread' between the return on capital and the cost of capital. Early pioneers of economic profit called it *residual income*. *Economic value added* is a more recent name coined by consulting firms.

Case: Tiffany's economic profit and after-tax ROCE

Tiffany's EBIT for 2005 was 494.2, and its average capital employed was 1,746.9 (all figures in US$m). Tiffany report an average statutory corporate tax rate of 35%, which is close to their effective tax rate at 36.6%, 37.1% and 35.6% for 2003, 2004 and 2005. Using the statutory rate to calculate the tax shelter on interest, Tiffany paid net interest of 22.0, and this gave a tax shelter of (22.0 × 35% =) 7.7. Tiffany's tax charge was 167.8, so we calculate the tax on EBIT as (167.8 + 7.7 =) 175.6, giving an EBIAT of (494.2 - 175.6 =) 318.6 and after-tax ROCE of (318.6/1,746.9 =) 18.2%. In 2004 the numbers were EBIT 357.6, average capital employed 1,540.2, tax charge 127.2, net interest 14.9. So the tax shelter was (14.9 × 35% =) 5.2 and EBIAT was (357.6 - 127.2 - 5.2 =) 225.2. After-tax ROCE for 2004 was (225.2/1,540.2 =) 14.6%.

For working out Tiffany's economic profit we need Tiffany's WACC. We calculate this in Chapter 9 as 9.6%. In 2005 average capital was 1,746.9, so the capital charge was (1,746.9 × 9.6% =) 168.1. EBIAT was 318.6, so economic profit was (318.6 - 168.1 =) 150.5. In 2004, economic profit was (225.2 - (1,540.2 × 9.6%) =) 77.3.

REVIEW

- The formatted balance sheet and income statement provide us with the data we need to construct the main measures of return on capital. Return on equity measures the return on the capital provided by equity shareholders. But for many purposes we prefer to work at the 'entity level' and measure the return on the firm's capital employed, which is the capital provided by both shareholders and debt investors.

- We need both a pre-tax and an after-tax version of ROCE. The pre-tax ROCE is the best starting point for a forensic decomposition of the firm's operating return. But if we want to compare ROCE to the cost of capital, the after-tax ROCE is what we need.

- Economic profit is an attractive way of presenting the relationship between return on capital and the cost of capital, which is sometimes very helpful, especially for internal management control purposes.

- Conceptually, the calculation of capital employed is a critical exercise in which the analyst separates the operating activities of the firm from its financing activities.

- But the operating/financing distinction is not always an easy one in practice. We will need to use judgement in deciding whether all of a firm's financial assets should be netted against debt, or whether some be treated as operating. Judgement is also needed in splitting the tax charge into its operating and financing components.

Chapter 6

Value metrics

We are using accounting numbers as *value metrics* when we compare the return on capital to the cost of capital to signal whether a firm is creating or destroying value for investors. Chapter 4 used this to provide the framework for thinking about how financial statements are constructed and what they mean. But this is not just a theoretical exercise; in practice, people frequently use financial statement data to calculate value metrics. Investors do it when they use accounting data to rank and screen stocks. Regulators do it when they use return on capital to identify monopoly profits, or as the basis for controlling the prices charged by regulated firms. Firms themselves do it when they use accounting data to make investment decisions or to measure divisional performance, or as a factor in management remuneration.

The chapter starts by examining the financial concept of 'value creation'. It then discusses the use of value metrics in practice, focusing on the accounting adjustments that practitioners make to try and get the data integrity needed for a reliable comparison with the cost of capital. The chapter ends by discussing the use of share price performance to measure value creation. It argues that accounting returns may be a more reliable basis for measuring value creation than share returns, because they are based on realised income, not expected income.

VALUE CREATION

We start this chapter by recalling some basic principles from investment theory. In the language of finance, a firm *creates value* when it uses investors' capital to earn a better return than the cost of capital, which is the return that investors could get elsewhere on their capital. The more capital a firm invests in this way the more value it creates. So value creation is a function of return and growth.

Suppose a firm is thinking about making an investment in a new project and wants to know if the investment will create value. It collects the relevant data, which means finding out the cost of the assets required to undertake the project and predicting the cash flows the project will generate, including the value of the assets that will remain at the end. There are then two ways to do the arithmetic[1].

– The economic value of the investment is the present value of the expected cash flows from the project, discounted at the firm's cost of capital. The *net present value (NPV)* of the investment is its economic value less the cost of the assets, that is, 'net' of the required investment in assets.

– The alternative is to calculate the *internal rate of return (IRR)*, which is the average annual return on the investment, and to compare this to the cost of capital.

Using NPV, the decision rule is *invest when NPV is positive*. Using IRR, the decision rule is *invest when the IRR is greater than the cost of capital*. The difference between the IRR and the cost of capital is also known as the *return spread*. So the decision rule becomes *invest when the spread is positive*.

Return spread = Internal rate of return - Cost of capital

NPV has a very direct interpretation: it measures the amount of value created by a project, that is, the increase in investors' wealth as a result of making the investment. For our purposes NPV and IRR can be viewed as equivalent. In practice, like any measure of return, IRR has to be treated with care. As investment textbooks like to emphasise, the comparison with the cost of capital becomes ambiguous when a project switches from being cash positive to cash negative at different points in its life because, mathematically, the cashflow will have multiple IRRs.

Example: Wonderful Hotels

It costs Wonderful Hotels $100 million to build a new hotel. Wonderful is entirely financed by equity shareholders who require a return of 8%, and every time a new hotel is to be built they inject $100m. Wonderful lives in a simple world where, once built, a hotel produces the same earnings every year for ever, after charging the costs of maintaining the hotel as new. So we do not need to worry about the value of the assets at the end of the project because it continues for ever. The earnings are distributed in full to the shareholders as dividend. Suppose a hotel earns $10m per year. On either the NPV or the IRR test, investing in a hotel creates value:

---

1 At this point, readers who are unfamiliar with NPV and IRR should read the Financial Arithmetic appendix at the end of the book.

- If earnings are $10m per annum in perpetuity on an investment of $100m, the IRR is easy to calculate as 10%. This beats the 8% cost of capital.
- If earnings are $10m per annum, the economic value of a Wonderful hotel is ($10m/8% =) $125m[2], so its NPV is a positive ($125m - $100m =) $25m.

The table below shows the same calculus applied to some other earnings levels from a hotel.

Table 1 Different assumptions about hotel economies

Investment	100	100	100	100
Earnings	6	8	10	12
Return	**6%**	**8%**	**10%**	**12%**
Economic value	75	100	125	150
NPV	**-25**	**0**	**25**	**50**

A hotel breaks even if it earns $8m a year; that is, if it earns a return of 8% when the cost of capital is 8%. An investment in a hotel that is expected to earn $6m a year destroys $25m of value – it makes investors $25m poorer because it takes $100m of their money and uses it to earn a stream of income worth $75m. If building one hotel that earns a return of 10% creates $25 million of value then building ten of them creates $250 million of value. Assuming the case where hotels earn a 10% return, these are the rewards to growth:

Table 2 Value of Wonderful if it grows

	Value	Value created
A firm with 1 hotel	125	25
A firm with 10 hotels	1,250	250

The purpose of the Wonderful example is to demonstrate the basic principle that a firm makes its investors richer when it earns a return greater than their required return *and* it grows. This basic truth is universal but it is most easily envisaged in a business like Wonderful that invests in a series of discrete productive units such as hotels, restaurants or power stations. Of course, reality is more complicated than this in all sorts of ways. On the one hand Wonderful might expect to learn as it grows and capture some economies of scale, so the return on each additional hotel increases. On the other hand, if it were so easy to create value from building hotels everyone would do it. Competition would be attracted and drive down the return on all hotels.

Value creation is easy to describe but hard to achieve. Firms will be able to create value only if they can create and sustain competitive advantage in the markets in which they work, for example by the innovation and successful exploitation of some intellectual property, or by developing a valuable brand. In competitive markets where there is intense rivalry other firms will be striving to compete their advantage away.

Figure 1 shows a firm's options in terms of creating and destroying value. The firm wants to be in the top right hand-corner, growing while investing in projects that earn a return

---

2   Using the rule for the present value of a perpetuity: the value of an amount, C, received each year forever when the required return is r, is C/r. See the Financial Arithmetic appendix.

greater than the cost of capital. The bottom left-hand corner is also a value-creating quadrant though it should perhaps be called the 'value-releasing' quadrant; if the firm has projects that irredeemably earn a return less than the cost capital it should divest them to release the capital.

Figure 1 Creating and destroying value

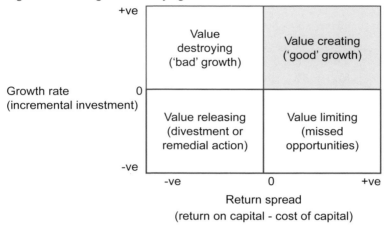

Value added and value retention

In the language of finance, value creation has the precise meaning described above – a firm creates value when it makes its investors richer by earning a superior return while growing. But the phrase 'value creation' is sometimes used rather differently. Take the situation where a firm is excellent at innovation but rivals copy its ideas. Some writers would then distinguish value creation and *value retention* – this firm created value, but was not able to retain it.

Another similar sounding phrase to value creation is 'value added'. *Value added* is the difference between the value of sales and the cost of the material inputs used to produce the sales. Value added is an idea with a long pedigree. For Classical economists, economic activity brought together three fundamental factors of production: labour, land, and capital. The surplus generated – the value added – was then shared between the factors as wages, rent and profit. In a modern context, just as EBIT is essentially the stream of income before the claims of interest and tax, one can back further up the income statement to get a value added measure:

Value added = EBIT + Labour and salary costs + Rental payments

Some writers find this a useful measure. But the complex contracting of the modern economy makes value added hard to define unambiguously and it is not a concept we use in this book.

Value added should not be confused with 'economic value added', as economic profit is known commercially. As we saw in Chapter 4, to calculate economic profit or EVA we need to head in exactly the opposite direction. EVA is EBIT less tax and less a fair return on capital. In other words EVA just measures the surplus earned for one factor, shareholders' capital, beyond the shareholders' required return.

ACCOUNTING RETURN AS A MEASURE OF IRR

Some theory

Economic theory has shown the exact relationship between a series of accounting returns on capital and the IRR measured over a number of years. The key insight was by John Kay[3]. Making this connection was a major breakthrough because previously it was always assumed that accounting lived in a different universe to economic truth and that accounting measures of return were inherently unreliable.

Think of a single year in the life of a firm as an investment project. The shareholders' investment is the bundle of assets less liabilities measured by their funds in the starting balance sheet. The firm trades for a year and delivers back to its shareholders some dividends plus the bundle of assets less liabilities measured by the shareholders' funds in the balance sheet at the end of the year. The IRR of this one-year project is easy to calculate. It is the shareholders' income for the year which is the increase in the shareholders' funds plus any dividend paid out in the year, divided by the investment which is the opening shareholders' funds. But we know from the accounting identity that shareholders' income is earnings:

Earnings = Dividend + Closing shareholders' funds - Opening shareholders' funds

So the IRR is measured by earnings/shareholders' funds, which is return on equity[4]. Though this discussion is in terms of the return to equity shareholders the argument could equally be made at the entity level in terms of return on capital employed.

Return on capital is an annual measure whereas IRR is usually measured as an average return over a number of years. Measured over a number of years, the IRR from a firm is equal to the weighted average of its annual accounting return on capital plus an error term.

IRR = Weighted average of annual return on capital + Error term

The error term reflects the extent to which the balance sheet mismeasures the firm's assets and liabilities at the beginning of the starting year and at the end of the final year. This is the same insight we got from the Manuel example in Chapter 4. The relationship holds true whichever way the accounting is done – you could pick the accounting numbers

---

3   Several people have shown the mathematical relation between a series of accounting rates of return and a firm's internal rate of return, notably John Kay '*Accountants, Too Could Be Happy in a Golden Age: The Accountant's Rate of Profit and the Internal Rate of Return*,' Oxford Economic Papers, 1976, and Ken Peasnell, '*Some formal connections between economic values and yields and accounting numbers.*', Journal of Business Finance and Accounting, 1982.

4   To show the link to IRR we measured return on equity on opening shareholders' funds, not the average shareholders' funds or capital employed that we normally use in financial analysis. In investment analysis it is often convenient to assume that all the cash flows occur at discrete, usually annual, intervals. In reality, investment flows occur continuously through time and calculating return on capital using the average of opening and closing shareholders' funds or capital employed gives a better approximation to this.

from the telephone book with a pin and still get the correct IRR. All that matters is the way the opening and closing balance sheets are measured.

Tax consistency

The income that a firm delivers to its investors has borne corporate taxes, so the cost of capital, which is their required return, is set in terms of income after corporate taxes. If return on capital is to be compared to the cost of capital, this also needs to be measured after tax. The two basic measures of return on capital are an equity-level measure, return on equity, and an entity-level measure, return on capital employed. Since earnings are after tax, return on equity is an after-tax measure of return and it can be benchmarked against the cost of equity capital. The entity-level cost of capital is WACC, the weighted average cost of capital. For tax consistency, it is after-tax ROCE that must be compared with the WACC. We saw in Chapter 5 that it can be difficult to get the tax precisely right when calculating EBIAT. But this should not get in the way of the important insight that it makes no sense to compare a pre-tax return on capital to an after-tax cost of capital.

Using a pre-tax cost of capital

So long as it is done with care, an alternative to calculating an after-tax ROCE is to calculate a *pre-tax* WACC and compare this to the basic (i.e. pre-tax) ROCE. Since we got after-tax ROCE by applying a corporate tax rate to EBIT, we should get the same insight about value creation by grossing up the cost of capital at the corporate tax rate. The pre-tax WACC would be WACC/(1-tax rate), and the intuition is that this is the return the firm would have to earn before tax just to meet the investors' required return. Instead of saying, *is ROCE × (1 - tax rate) > WACC*, we are saying, *is ROCE > WACC/(1 - tax rate)?*

Example: Brigand

We used Brigand as an example in the last chapter. Brigand's WACC is 8%, and its effective corporate tax rate is 18.75%. So the pre-tax cost of capital is (8%/(1 - 18.75%) =) 9.85%. ROCE was 20%, so the return spread is now (20% - 9.85% =) 10.15%, compared to a spread of 8.25% calculated on the basis of post-tax figures and a tax rate of 18.75%. (After-tax ROCE 16.25% - WACC 8% = 8.25%). The difference is tax. If we do a pre-tax comparison we get a pre-tax spread, 8.25% = 10.15% × (1 - 18.25%). A pre-tax spread is an odd concept in economic terms, but works fine for comparative analysis.

The pre-tax approach has a lot to recommend it to firms who are using return on capital for internal performance measurement. First, it prevents operating managers having to think about tax. Most firms sensibly treat tax as a black art that is best handled at the corporate level and best left to the specialists in the tax department. This way the tax department can give its judgement on an appropriate pre-tax hurdle rate or cost of capital that reflects the tax position of the firm, and maybe the particular circumstances of different divisions. This can be disseminated by head office. Secondly, the pre-tax cost of capital is operationally simpler. It reduces the number of concepts managers need to deal with and it preserves (pre-tax) ROCE as the prime performance measure.

ACCOUNTING BIASES

We outlined in Chapter 4 how GAAP accounting diverges from the accounting model that would be needed for return on capital measures to give reliable value metrics, year on year. We need a complete balance sheet valued at current prices, but a firm's balance sheet is likely to diverge from this ideal in many ways, large and small.

The general effect of GAAP conservatism is to understate assets and overstate liabilities, and so to recognise losses early, but postpone gains. Omission of intangibles; use of historic costs for assets; overstatement of liabilities; and conservatism in the form of over-provision for the consumption of assets all yield understated equity, which is commonly known as *hidden reserves*. Other things being equal, understated equity means capital employed is also understated. Accounting conservatism correspondingly depresses income too, for example when R&D expenditure is expensed, when assets are over-depreciated, etc.. Later in the book we conduct some simulations and show that the balance-sheet effect almost always outweighs the income effect in return-on-capital measures. So, though there will be exceptions, the working hypothesis is that GAAP accounting *overstates* return on capital. The effect will be significant for firms with a lot of intangible assets, and for firms that deploy a lot of old tangible assets carried at historic cost.

The effect of arrangements that net off assets and liabilities, such as operating leases, factoring and unconsolidated subsidiaries is rather different. They have no effect on return on equity because assets and liabilities are reduced equally, though they will impact ROCE. Their principal effect is on gearing measures.

A strategy for adjusting the accounting

If we are going to use return on capital as a value metric we need a strategy for dealing with accounting biases. Should we attempt to adjust the data fully to get the data integrity of the investment accounting model, just make a partial adjustment to correct the major biases or, indeed, make no adjustments but rely on judgement to interpret the data? The strategy will depend on the context. A utilities regulator, say, who requires regulated firms to set their prices so that they just achieve a return on capital equal to their cost of capital, really needs to ensure that the accounting has complete data integrity. In this context, return on capital is being used as a value metric and benchmarked against a hard, externally derived cost of capital. The Ofwat and Ofgem case describes how regulators deal with this.

Case: Ofwat and Ofgem

Ofwat, the UK water industry regulator, and Ofgem, the UK gas and electricity distribution regulator, were pioneers in the price control of private, but potentially monopolistic, utility businesses. Both use a complex pricing formula, but one goal of the formula is to allow firms to earn a return on capital that covers the cost of capital. To do this requires a complete, and fairly valued, balance sheet measure of capital. The regulators use GAAP accounting. The regulated business is likely to be part of a larger firm, but it is ring-fenced and inter-firm transactions that might deflate income or inflate capital are tightly policed. On its own, the regulated firm is unlikely to have significant intangibles. However, the regulatory capital or assets are valued at current value. This is done by setting the base value of the assets to equal the market capitalisation of the firms when they were initially privatised. Subsequent asset additions are accounted at cost, but the assets are then inflated each year using the retail price index.

On the other hand, using return on capital as the basis for financial analysis or to compare a group of firms is a less demanding task. The degree of accounting bias differs significantly from industry to industry and firm to firm. So the first step is to conduct a thorough review of the firm's accounting, and to think hard about the nature of the firm and the business it is in, so as to develop an understanding of where the problem areas are likely to be found. Especially for firms that do not have many old tangible assets and do not deploy significant intangibles, it can be possible to approximate a reliable value metric without too much adjustment.

Intangible assets are the biggest challenge. Recreating a complete balance sheet will probably remain an unattainable ideal for firms that deploy a lot of valuable intangible assets – sadly, many interesting firms fall into that group. The most dangerous strategy is tokenism. The analyst uses easily available data to make a few adjustments – operating-lease capitalisation and R&D capitalisation are current favourites – then claims to have a perfect value metric.

Case: The pharmaceutical industry

In Chapter 11 we undertake the exercise of capitalising the R&D expenditure of a pharmaceutical firm. This is easy to do because R&D expenditure is separately disclosed under GAAP. It is also informative: proprietary drug companies spend a large proportion of their sales revenue on R&D and it helps to see to what extent the data are biased by expensing those costs. Are we tempted to conclude that we have made the drug company's balance sheet complete? Not at all; brands, IT, and human capital are also very important intangible assets for these firms. But GAAP does not require separate disclosure of these costs, so there is not much the external analyst can do. Should we generally capitalise R&D in this industry when the task is comparative analysis? For comparing proprietary drug firms that spend a similar percentage on R&D and have similar growth rates, there will be little extra insight. When comparing with generics, who typically spend much less on R&D, then it will be useful to see to what extent accounting is biasing the comparison.

The most commonly used proprietary value metrics are economic profit measures such as EVA, which are widely used within firms for performance measurement, and adjusted return on capital measures such as *cash flow return on capital (CFROI)*, which are widely use by investors and equity analysts. Both EVA and CFROI providers typically make a lot of accounting adjustments, but tend to be realistic about the precision of the resulting metric.

Usually, accounting flatters return on capital

Even without making any accounting adjustments, it is frequently possible to draw quite strong conclusions about value destruction. Mostly, the biases in accounting work in the same direction; accounting flatters return on capital. So if we see a firm earning a return on equity of, say, 25% we need to do further work before feeling confident that it is creating value. But if we see a company with a return on equity of 10%, there is a strong presumption that it is not creating value. This insight is very important in practice because, in the highly competitive modern economy, many firms struggle to earn their cost of capital. A case where it would have been fruitfully applied was Enron.

Case: Enron

In the late 1990s, the management of Enron developed a reputation for managerial brilliance, and Enron was regularly described as the world's most admired firm. Enron management were busy turning an old-economy gas pipeline and utilities business into what was intended to be predominantly a trading and a market-making 'new economy' business. Over the five years 1996 to 2000, Enron reported impressive growth in sales, with 149% sales growth in 2000 alone. The share price rose from $20 in January 1999 to $87 by mid-2000. It was perhaps no coincidence the share price followed the same trajectory as sales. This was the era of the dot-com bubble when, though without apparent logic, investors got into the habit of pricing new-economy stocks on a multiple of sales.

Enron established a reputation for delivering earnings growth to investors. In their own words 'Enron is laser focused on earnings per share growth'. In fact, Enron's earnings growth was erratic, and though the compound earnings growth rate was 12.1% between 1996 and 2000, it had been 18.8% from 1992 to 1996. Enron's change in business model involved selling off asset-heavy businesses and replacing them with businesses requiring a lighter balance sheet. So investors might have expected to see an increasing return on capital. Instead, return on capital fell during the second half of the 1990s.

What is striking about Enron is that just as investors were marking up Enron's stock in 2000, they would have had in front of them financial statements suggesting that, thus far at least, Enron was not creating value. It was growing wholesale revenues rapidly, but at lower and lower margins, and as a result it was failing to earn an adequate return on capital. Assuming a 5% equity risk premium on the market as a whole then, in happier, pre-scandal days, Enron's investors were perhaps expecting a return on equity of 9%–10%. Enron's WACC was perhaps one or two percentage points lower than the cost of equity. Enron had a reported after-tax ROCE of 7.5% in 1999 and 5.6% in 2000, and a return on equity of 10.8% in 1999 and 9.5% in 2000. Economic profit told a similar story.

Table 3 Enron's value metrics (figures in $bn)

	2000	1999	1998	1997	1996	1995	1994	1993	1992
Sales	100.9	40.4	31.4	20.5	13.5	9.3	9.1	8.1	6.4
Sales growth	150%	29%	53%	52%	46%	2%	13%	26%	
After-tax ROCE	**5.6%**	**7.5%**	**5.9%**	**3.9%**	**8.9%**	**9.7%**	**8.0%**	**7.2%**	**6.1%**
Estimated WACC	*7.9%*	*8.6%*	*6.6%*	*7.0%*	*8.1%*	*6.9%*	*8.5%*	*6.8%*	*7.2%*
Return on equity	**9.5%**	**10.8%**	**11.1%**	**1.9%**	**17.2%**	**17.5%**	**16.8%**	**13.1%**	**14.0%**
Estimated cost of equity	*9.0%*	*10.4%*	*8.6%*	*9.7%*	*10.3%*	*8.9%*	*11.1%*	*9.1%*	*10.0%*
Economic profit $m	**-604**	**-246**	**-125**	**-439**	**90**	**265**	**-45**	**35**	**-88**

Of course, the stock price of $80 in 2000, and the poor fundamental performance to date were not *necessarily* inconsistent. But the analyst would need to develop a powerful transformational story in which Enron would sustain much higher margins in the future, while maintaining the growth. Alternatively, the analyst would need to develop a convincing evidence-based argument that Enron's margins were currently depressed because of heavy current investments in IT and in other intangibles.

The extent of accounting fraud at Enron was not revealed until afterwards. It turned out that between 1998 and 2000 earnings were overstated by a factor of 2 to 3 times, while capital employed was understated by a massive concealment of debt. So return on capital was biased upwards, to an extreme degree. But even using the data as published, Enron's return on capital did not signal value creation.

ECONOMIC PROFIT AND EVA

We saw in Chapter 5 that conventionally measured income is incomplete because interest is charged, but there is no charge for using equity capital. Economic profit is profit less a capital charge for using *all* of the firm's capital employed, both debt and equity. Calculating economic profit is logically equivalent to comparing the after-tax ROCE to the WACC. This is easy to see. Value is created when after-tax ROCE is greater than WACC, that is:

$$\frac{EBIAT}{Average\ capital\ employed} > WACC$$

Multiplying both sides of this inequality by 'average capital employed'

$$EBIAT > Average\ capital\ employed \times WACC$$

Moving the right-hand side over to the left tells us that value is created when economic profit is positive:

$$EBIAT - Average\ capital\ employed \times WACC > 0$$

By making a capital charge, economic profit effectively internalises the cost-of - comparison. In terms of signalling value creation or value destruction, economic profit and the spread between after-tax return on capital and the cost of capital are logically identical.

Example: Xinc and Zinc

Xinc and Zinc are two manufacturing firms in the same line of business and with the same WACC, 14%. Their numbers are in the table below. Xinc has EBIAT of 200 and uses 1,000 of assets; Zinc has EBIAT of 380 and 3,000 of assets. To calculate economic profit, if the WACC is 14% we deduct a capital charge of (1,000 × 14% =) 140 from EBIAT. So Xinc's economic profit is (200 - 140 =) 60, while Zinc's is -40 on the same basis. Evidently Xinc is creating value and Zinc is destroying value. But we would have got the same insight from calculating after-tax ROCE. Xinc's after-tax ROCE is (200/1,000 =) 20% and Zinc's is (380/3,000 =) 12.7%. Their return spreads are (20% - 14% =) +6% and (12.7% - 14% =) -1.3% respectively.

Performance measurement within the firm

Where economic profit really comes into its own is for performance measurement and control within the firm, which is the context in which it was originally developed. Robert Lewis credits General Electric with first using economic profit in the 1930s, calling it *residual income*. General Electric was one of the pioneering multidivisional US corporations that contributed so much to management science in the first half of the 20th century. One problem that they were grappling with was how to set incentives to divisional managers that were compatible with the goals of the firm as a whole. Economic profit is a safer way to measure divisional performance than return on capital on its own because it counters the human tendency to try and maximise return.

The 'maximise return' fallacy

Comparing IRR to the cost of capital signals whether or not an investment will create value, but it is dangerous to over-interpret the absolute level of the IRR. For instance, you cannot conclude which of two projects is creating *more* value simply by comparing their IRRs because they may require different quantities of capital. The way to maximise the return on capital from a business is simply to shrink its activities back to the one project with the highest return. So in a real sense, maximising return on capital is the antithesis to maximising value (or, as it is commonly known, maximising profit). Firms create value by earning a return on capital that is greater than the cost of capital, and they create more value the more capital they can invest at a positive spread, in other words the more they grow. The problem with rewarding managers just on the basis of return on capital is that their incentives are not aligned with the objectives of the shareholders, who want return *and* growth. By combining growth and return, economic profit solves the 'maximise return' problem, which is why it is so widely used in managerial incentive and reward systems.

Example: Smith & Co

Smith & Co has a cost of capital of 10% and its divisional managers have three investment projects available to them, A, B and C. Each project requires 1,000 of investment and will generate income in perpetuity of 400 for project A, 300 for B, and 200 for C.

Table 4 Smith & Co's projects

	Assets	Profit	Return
A	1,000	400	40%
B	1,000	300	30%
C	1,000	200	20%

Managers can invest in any or all of these three projects. If their bonuses are based on their divisional return on capital then managers will just choose A. Even if return on capital is not the explicit goal of the organisation but managers feel that maximising return on capital sounds right and that it is 'virtuous', they will be tempted to choose A and report a return of 40%. Investing in A and B or in A, B and C dilutes the overall return to 35% and 30% respectively. Unfortunately, investing just in A is the opposite of what Smith wants managers to do. Since all three projects earn a return well above the cost of capital, managers maximise value by doing them all. The economic profit of project A is (400 - 1,000 × 10% =) 300, for B it is 200 and for C, 100. If managers are rewarded on the basis of the economic profit that they create then they will undertake all three projects, and indeed they will go hunting for other projects that might yield less than 20% so long as they yield more than the cost of capital. This is presumably what the firm would want them to do.

Accounting adjustments

Economic profit is potentially vulnerable to accounting in just the same way as return on capital. Consider one pervasive problem, which is the use of out-of-date valuations in the balance sheet.

Example: Xinc and Zinc continued

Suppose Zinc bought its assets years ago and still carries them in the balance sheet at their cost of 1,500 rather than at 3,000. Now, the capital charge will only be (1,500 × 14% =) 210, giving an apparently positive economic profit of (380 - 210 =) 170. Zinc's after-tax ROCE will be flattered in just the same way. Now it is (380/1,500 =) 25.3% giving Zinc an apparent return spread of 11.3%.

When used commercially in performance measurement systems, economic profit is commonly known as *economic value added (EVA)*. The name 'EVA' was coined and registered as a trademark by the consulting firm, Stern Stewart & Co, who popularised the measure. EVA measures usually incorporate a number of accounting adjustments designed to correct shortcomings of GAAP accounting, principally:
- capitalisation of R&D expenditure
- capitalisation of operating leases
- treating provisions, particularly deferred tax provisions, as equity
- replacing LIFO by FIFO for inventories

Purely used as a value metric to signal value creation or destruction, and assuming the same accounting is used, economic profit cannot tell us anything that traditional return on capital measures do not. For financial analysis, many people argue that measures like return on capital employed may provide a clearer starting point because they can be more easily and transparently decomposed in forensic analysis to understand the drivers of the firm's return. Nonetheless, economic profit is a useful presentational tool in the analyst's toolkit.

The reason that economic profit dominates return on capital as a target for managers is that it bundles both a positive return spread and growth into one measure. However, a feasible alternative to economic profit that is used by some firms is to set managers both a return target and a growth target separately.

STOCK RETURNS AND ACCOUNTING RETURN ON CAPITAL

We can apply Hicks' concept of income, that we introduced in Chapter 3, to the income a shareholder gets. If the asset is shares in a firm, the cash flow that investors expect is a stream of dividends. Even if a firm is liquidated and the assets are sold, the shareholders receive what remains as a final liquidating dividend. If the firm's shares are traded on a stock market, the share price – which in aggregate is the firm's 'market capitalisation' – measures the value that shareholders put on the stream of dividends they expect to receive in the future. So the market capitalisation measures the firm's economic value, that is, the shareholders' wealth in the firm. The shareholders' economic income from a firm in a period is the dividend they receive plus the change in the firm's market capitalisation over the period.

Shareholders' economic income from the firm = Dividend + Change in market capitalisation

Compare this expression for economic income to the accounting identity that defines accounting income. They have the same shape because they are both income measures, but in the shareholders' economic income the underlying asset is the firm's market capitalisation, whereas for accounting income the underlying asset is the assets less liabilities in the firm's balance sheet.

The stock return is the shareholders' income expressed as a return on the shareholders' initial investment, that is, the opening market capitalisation.

$$Stock\ return = \frac{Dividend + Change\ in\ market\ capitalisation}{Opening\ market\ capitalisation}$$

Capital market practitioners frequently call the stock return the *total shareholder return (TSR)*. Financial markets strive to anticipate the future and immediately capitalise expectations into stock prices. As a result, the profile of stock returns from a firm looks very different to the profile of its return on capital. We can see this if we go back to the Wonderful example and think about the returns it generates from its hotels.

Example: Wonderful – scenario 1

We can imagine many different sequences of events, but one might be as follows:
- Investors give Wonderful $1bn of cash at the beginning of year 1 and they assume that Wonderful will simply keep it in the bank.
- During year 1, Wonderful announces that it can build 10 hotels that will earn $10m each, and it builds them.
- From the beginning of year 2 and in each subsequent year Wonderful runs the hotels, earns $100m and distributes it as dividend.

These events will generate the following stock returns.
- At the beginning Wonderful is valued as a pile of cash so its market capitalisation is $1bn.

- By the end of year 1, Wonderful's market capitalisation is $1,250m, which is the economic value of Wonderful with hotels instead of cash. This gives shareholders a stock return of 25% in year 1.
- Thereafter, Wonderful's market capitalisation remains $1,250m, which is the present value of the expected dividend stream in perpetuity, the sum upon which the $100m dividend just yields the investors required return of 8%. So from year 2 onwards investors receive a stock return of 8% each year, which is the $100m of dividend and zero capital gain divided by the opening market capitalisation of $1,250m. This is the operation of an efficient market – the asset is priced at the level at which it just yields the investors' 8% required return.

In terms of return on capital, assuming for convenience that it did not receive any interest while its money was in the bank, Wonderful makes a zero return on capital in year 1 then 10% return per annum thereafter.

Market capitalisation is a mix of assets and expectations

The return on capital and the stock return both describe the same underlying performance but the return on capital records it as it is realised while the stock return records it as expectations are formed. There are two sorts of expectation capitalised into stock prices:
- There is an expectation about the return the existing assets will earn; that is, an expectation about the economic value of the *existing assets*. This is sometimes called the *value of assets in place*.
- There is also an expectation about the ability of the firm to create value by earning a superior return when it invests in *new assets*; that is, the value of the option to grow. This is sometimes called the *value of growth opportunities*.

Because the investors have already supplied the assets, the value of assets in place is a pure measure of economic value; it is the value of an expected income stream. But the value of growth opportunities is a *net* present value. It is the value of expected income less the future cost of buying the assets needed to achieve that income.

Example: Wonderful – scenario 2

Consider another scenario for Wonderful; a slightly more realistic one in which it takes a year or two to build the ten hotels.
- Investors give Wonderful $400m of cash at the beginning of year 1.
- During year 1 Wonderful announces that it can build 10 hotels and will require another $600m from investors. It builds the first four.
- In year 2 Wonderful runs the first four hotels and builds the remaining six hotels, which come into operation from year 3.

Wonderful's profile of return on capital remains the same as before: zero in the first year and 10% thereafter, although in year 2 this is achieved on the smaller asset base of just four hotels.

Wonderful's market capitalisation develops as follows:
- It is $400m at the beginning of year 1, which is the value of the cash.

- At the end of year 1 Wonderful is part-way through its investment process – it has assets that cost 400 in the form of the four hotels already built, and it is expected to build another six. Its market capitalisation comprises the economic value of the four existing hotels and the expected *value added* from the remaining six. Each of the hotels-to-be has an economic value of 125, but investors will have to contribute the 100 needed to build it. Therefore the expected value added from each hotel is 25, which is essentially the value of an option to build another hotel. So the market capitalisation at the end of year 1 contains, *the value of assets in place, the economic value of the existing hotels,* which is *(4 × 125 =) 500* plus *the value of growth opportunities, the value added of the remaining six,* which is *(6 × 25 =) 150.* That is 650 in total.
- At the end of year 2, the investors have contributed another 600 and the remaining six hotels have been built, so the market capitalisation is the economic value of the ten hotels, which is $1,250m.

As a result, the profile of stock returns is as follows:
- In year 1 the stock return is the increase in market capitalisation of (650 - 400 =) 250 divided by the opening value of 400, which is 62.5%.
- In year 2 the shareholders' economic income is the dividend of 40 on the first four hotels; market capitalisation increases by 600 but shareholders subscribe 600, so their capital gain is zero. Stock return in year 2 is therefore 40 divided by the opening market capitalisation of 650, which is 6.15%.
- Thereafter stock return is 8% a year as before.

This variability in Wonderful's stock return simply reflects the market's capitalisation of expectations before the investment has been made. In reality investors will be unsure how many more hotels Wonderful would build and at what return, so the actual profile of stock returns year by year would depend entirely on how the market's expectations of Wonderful's growth and return evolves.

Stock return as a signal of value creation

Because accounting returns are based on realised earnings, rather than expectations (assuming the accounting is done properly), it is accounting returns, not stock returns, that provide the appropriate measure of value creation period by period, and the safest basis for managerial rewards and compensation. In competitive markets, even well-managed firms suffer reversals from time to time. Well-managed businesses then set about a process of recovery, or implement a new strategy. The story usually maps well into accounting return on capital. Nike provides an example.

Nike

Nike, which went public in 1980, is the largest seller of athletic footwear and apparel in the world. This statement by Phil Knight, the co-founder, partly explains their business model, *'There is no value in making things anymore. The value is added by careful research, by innovation and by marketing.'* Figure 2 plots their after-tax ROCE and TSR from 1992 to 2005. Here, in the broadest of outline, is what happened to the fundamental performance. Nike's after-tax ROCE dipped from 27% in 1992, to 21% in 1994, before recovering to 27% in 1997. But in 1998 after-tax ROCE plunged to 12 %, mainly due to a drop in EBIT margin and some reduction in asset turnover. Customer spending fell sharply in that year and a large restructuring program lead to a \$129.9m charge in the fourth quarter. Over the period 1999 to 2005 Nike succeeded in restoring EBIT margins, while improving asset turn through tight working capital management. In 2005, after-tax ROCE was once again 27%.

Figure 2 NIKE's performance from 1992 to 2005

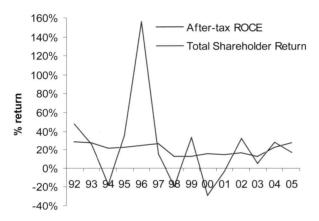

The danger of basing rewards, particularly for top managers, on sustaining superior stock returns is clear. If stock markets are doing their job properly, today's stock return already captures future excellent performance, so what does management do to deliver superior stock returns next year? The more efficient the stock market, the greater the pressure to change strategy. Furthermore, shifts in expectations mean that the stock returns may become hard to relate to underlying performance.

Price to book as a measure of NPV

The *price to book* ratio is the ratio of the firm's market capitalisation (the value of the equity shareholders' claim on the business), to the book equity (the capital provided by equity shareholders as measured by equity shareholders' funds in the balance sheet).

$$Price\ to\ book = \frac{Market\ capitalisation}{Equity\ shareholders'\ funds}$$

Price to book is also known as *market to book* or *market to net asset value (NAV)*, and as the *valuation ratio*.

Price to book can be measured at the entity level, rather than at the equity level. The denominator of this ratio is capital employed, which is equity plus net debt finance, rather than just equity. The numerator is known as *enterprise value*, which is the value of outstanding debt less cash plus the market capitalisation of equity. So the price to book ratio is now:

$$Enterprise\ price\ to\ book = \frac{Enterprise\ value}{Capital\ employed}$$

We discuss the measurement of enterprise value in Chapter 9. The entity price-to-book ratio may fit more naturally into the story if the rest of the financial analysis is being undertaken at the entity level.

Since market capitalisation measures economic value, and book equity measures the cost of the shareholders' investment, price to book is effectively a measure of net present value, but expressed as a ratio rather than as a difference. Some consultants use a firm-level measure that has the same structure as NPV by calculating the difference between market capitalisation and book equity and calling it *market value added (MVA)*. So while NPV is the difference between value and cost, and the threshold for value creation is 0, price to book is the ratio of value to cost, so the break-even threshold is 1. A firm or an asset is creating value when it has a price to book ratio greater than unity. But because market capitalisation is a mix of assets in place and expectations we have to be careful when interpreting price to book as a proxy for net present value.

Example: Wonderful's price to book

Consider Wonderful in scenario 2, part-way through its investment process at the end of year 1. It has built four hotels and is expected to build another six. Wonderful's price to book is calculated as follows. Its balance sheet contains 400 of assets for the four hotels already built. Its market capitalisation is 650, reflecting the economic value of those hotels (125 × 4 =) 500 and the value to be created by the remaining six (25 × 6 =) 150. This gives a price to book of (650/400 =) 1.63.

Table 5 Components of Wonderful's price to book

	Actual, in place				Expected					
	1	2	3	4	5	6	7	8	9	10
Value	125	125	125	125	125	125	125	125	125	125
Asset	100	100	100	100	100	100	100	100	100	100
Value created	25	25	25	25	25	25	25	25	25	25

REVIEW

- A firm creates value when it uses investors' capital to earn a better return than the cost of capital, which is the return that investors could get elsewhere on their capital. We are using accounting numbers as value metrics when we compare the return on capital to the cost of capital to signal whether a firm is creating or destroying value for investors.

- Our two basic measures of return on capital are an equity-level measure, return on equity, and an entity-level measure, return on capital employed. Since earnings are after tax, return on equity is an after-tax measure of return and it can be benchmarked against the cost of equity capital. The entity-level cost of capital is WACC, the weighted average cost of capital. For tax consistency, it is after-tax ROCE that must be compared with the WACC.

- Economic profit is profit less a charge for using capital. Measuring economic profit effectively internalises the cost-of-capital comparison. This is useful as a way to measure performance within a firm because it bundles both positive return spread and growth into one measure.

- Just as accounting return on capital is a proxy for IRR in investment analysis, we can view the price-to-book ratio as a proxy for NPV. The implication is that a firm or an asset is creating value when it has a price to book ratio greater than unity. But because market capitalisation is a mix of assets in place and expectations we have to be careful when interpreting price to book in this way.

- The reliability of return on capital and price to book as value metrics depends on the integrity of the data. GAAP accounting, usually, overstates return on capital. The effect will be significant for firms with a lot of unrecognised intangible assets, and for firms that deploy a lot of old tangible assets carried at historic cost. The challenge, when we need to use accounting data to calculate value metrics, is how to adjust the data to control for accounting bias.

- Stock returns are frequently used as measures of value creation, but this can be misleading. The profile of stock returns from a publicly traded investment in a firm can look very different to the profile of returns on capital.

Part 3

Financial analysis

Chapter 7

Operating profitability

The aim in analysing operating profitability is to learn as much as possible about the way in which the firm earns its return on capital. We do this by deconstucting return on capital employed. We first separate ROCE into margin and asset turn, that is, the ratio of profit to sales, and the ratio of sales to net assets. We then analyse margin in terms of costs, and asset turn in terms of its component assets and liabilities, as far as the data permits. Since accounting data is highly aggregated, we need to use any non-financial performance data the firm has provided. As well as analysing ROCE horizontally in terms of costs, assets and liabilities, we want to do the same analysis vertically for each of the distinct businesses that make up the firm. Unfortunately, the scope for segment analysis is often limited by lack of disclosure.

The way a firm earns its return depends on the business it is in and the business model it is using. Other things equal, a more capital- intensive business requires a higher margin. But there may be different ways of achieving the same business goal, involving different patterns of ownership of assets that give a very different look in terms of margin and asset turn. In the final part of the chapter we think about how the firm's business model affects its profitability equation.

THE PROFITABILITY EQUATION

The first step in analysing operating performance is to take ROCE and split it into two parts. Broadly speaking, any measure of return on capital is the ratio of a profit number to an asset number. If we relate each of these to sales, the return on capital is the profit to sales ratio (call this *margin*) times the sales to assets ratio (call this *asset turn*). If ROCE is the measure of return on capital we are using, then we have:

$$\frac{EBIT}{Average\ capital\ employed} = \frac{EBIT}{Sales} \times \frac{Sales}{Average\ capital\ employed}$$

or,   ROCE   =   'EBIT margin'   ×   'Asset turn'

We call this relationship the *profitability equation*. As a bit of arithmetic the profitability equation is trivial, but splitting return on capital into margin and asset turn proves extraordinarily useful in forensic analysis. It is very revealing in explaining the trend in a firm's profitability or in pinpointing why one firm is more profitable than another. It is also very helpful in focusing management's attention on areas where action is needed.

The idea behind the profitability equation is that a firm earns a return for its investors in two parts. 'Margin' measures the amount of profit in each dollar of sales. This is a measure that operating managers live with day by day. It describes the firm's terms of trade in the markets in which it buys its inputs and sells its outputs. Other things equal we want margin to be as high as possible. But just as important for delivering a return on investors' capital is the relationship between sales and assets. The firm uses investors' capital to buy its assets and this capital has a cost so, other things equal, we want the firm to use as few assets as possible to support each dollar of sales.

Of course, in practice, margin and asset turn are not independent of each other and strategies that improve one can worsen the other. For instance, customers may be only willing to pay more for the firm's product – thus improving margin – if the firm offers speedier delivery by holding more inventory, or if it gives them longer to pay thus increasing receivables – both of which depress asset turn. Again, shifting assets out of the balance sheet by leasing them under an operating lease, rather than owning them, improves asset turn. But operating leasing forces the firm to take financing charges in operating costs, thus reducing margin.

People use many different words for margin. To some extent, the vocabulary reflects the return on capital measure being used. If we are using ROCE, then we talk about *EBIT margin*. If we are measuring on the return on net operating assets, then *operating margin*. Other general terms for margin are *return on sales* and *profit margin*. The term *net margin* is sometimes also used to describe the ratio of after-tax earnings to sales.

The drivers of margin and asset turn

The next step is to see what is driving the EBIT margin and the asset turn. EBIT is operating profit plus other income and exceptionals, and operating profit is gross profit less SG&A, which is the catch-all term we use for the firm's overhead costs. We decompose the EBIT margin to see how much the firm is spending per dollar of sales in each cost category. These numbers can then be tracked through time and compared between firms. Differences in cost ratios can help identify efficiency differences between firms, though, as we see later, they may simply reflect different business models.

Asset turn is the ratio of sales to capital employed. Since capital employed equals net assets, asset turn is analysed by decomposing capital employed into its component assets and liabilities, relating each to sales in this way: PP&E/sales, inventory/sales, payables/sales, and so forth. Average capital employed was used in the denominator of ROCE and of asset turn, so for consistency we should continue to use average balance sheet amounts in this decomposition. Notice that asset turn is inverted in order to analyse it – there is most insight in putting sales on the bottom and showing each balance sheet component as a percentage of sales. This has the added advantage that the component asset and liability to sales ratios can more easily be summed.

The drivers of return on capital employed are summarised in Figure 1. Finally, note that we are using ROCE, rather than after-tax ROCE, in this chapter. After-tax ROCE is the number we want when we need a value metric, to compare to the cost of capital. But for the forensic analysis of operating performance it is usually best to work pre-tax. As always, this is not compulsory – some analysts might prefer to work with EBIAT, and identify tax as an element when decomposing it.

Figure 1 The drivers of ROCE

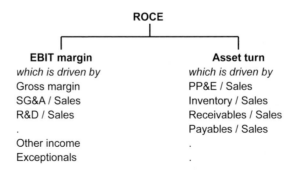

Case: Tiffany's operating performance

Table 1 shows Tiffany's ROCE from 2000 to 2005, its component EBIT margin and asset turn, and their drivers[1]. As a start point, it is good practice to calculate basic ROCE comprehensively, with nothing excluded from EBIT or net assets. On this basis Tiffany's ROCE appears to decline from 36.8% in 2000, but to pick up strongly in 2005, when ROCE was 28.3% and EBIT margin was 22.4%. But, casting our eye over the data, we see there was a large exceptional in 2005. This was the income of $193.6m generated by the sale of the Aber Diamond Corporation investment; it added 8.8% to margin and, without it, EBIT is $300.6m, EBIT margin is 13.6% and ROCE is 17.4%.

Table 1 Tiffany's operating ratios, 2000-2005

	2000	2001	2002	2003	2004	2005
Sales	1,471.7	1,668.1	1,606.5	1,706.6	2,000.0	2,204.8
Sales growth	25.87%	13.34%	-3.69%	6.23%	17.19%	10.24%
ROCE	36.8%	36.1%	28.4%	24.8%	23.2%	28.3%
ROCE ex. exceptional						17.4%
EBIT margin	17.9%	20.0%	19.2%	18.4%	17.9%	22.4%
margin ex. exceptional						13.6%
Gross margin	55.8%	56.9%	58.7%	59.3%	57.9%	55.8%
SG&A, % of sales	-38.4%	-37.2%	-39.4%	-40.6%	-40.1%	-42.5%
Exceptionals,% of sales	0.0%	0.0%	0.0%	0.0%	0.0%	8.8%
Non-operating, % of sales	0.4%	0.4%	0.0%	-0.3%	0.1%	0.3%
Asset turn	2.06	1.80	1.48	1.35	1.30	1.26
PP&E/sales	17.4%	22.4%	29.5%	35.3%	39.1%	40.9%
Intangibles/sales	0.7%	0.6%	0.7%	1.0%	1.4%	1.6%
Inventory/sales	33.5%	34.7%	39.3%	39.4%	40.1%	43.7%
Inventory days on COS	277	293	348	353	347	361
Trade receivables/sales	7.7%	6.8%	6.4%	6.2%	6.1%	6.0%
Trade payables/sales	-6.6%	-4.9%	-4.2%	-3.9%	-5.7%	-3.8%
Other net assets/sales	-6.6%	-4.9%	-4.2%	-3.9%	-5.7%	-9.2%

Tiffany's deteriorating ROCE comes both from EBIT margin and asset turn. EBIT margin initially reached 20%, then declined to 13.6% by 2005. Asset turn has declined over the six years under review, from 2.06 in 2000, to 1.26 in 2005. With the exception of 2002, which was affected by 11 September 2001, sales have been increasing year on year, but the capital used to generate these sales has been growing much faster.

The next step is to explore the drivers of margin and asset turn. The declining EBIT margin is the result of the interplay between gross margin and SG&A; gradually increasing SG&A was offset by gross margin until 2003, but gross margin itself worsened in 2004 and 2005, from 59.3% to 55.8%. Our next step would be to collect what additional data we can, perhaps from the firm itself, to understand these changes. We show some more information on Tiffany in the Annex to the chapter. As we see there, Tiffany do not give a lot of detail on the components of SG&A, but they do profess a long-term goal to get the SG&A/sales ratio down.

1 It is useful to check how these numbers hang together arithmetically. For instance in 2003 Tiffany's ROCE is 24.8%, which is the EBIT margin times the asset turn, 18.4% × 1.35 = 24.8%. Because we are careful to maintain the integrity of the data in terms of positives and negatives, the components of margin and asset turn should sum, though there will occasionally be small rounding discrepancies. So gross margin less SG&A, plus Exceptionals and non-operating gives the EBIT margin; 59.3% - 40.6% + 0.0% - 0.3% = 18.4%. For asset turn, the elements that are separately identified are PP&E, intangibles, inventory, trade receivables, trade payables, and 'other', which is the net of all the remaining assets and liabilities. In 2003 these sum to (35.3% + 1.0% + 39.4% + 6.2% - 3.9% + 3.9% =) 74.1%. The reciprocal of this is (1/74.1% =) 1.35, which is the asset turn.

The principal drivers of the falling asset turn are PP&E and inventory. (The Annex contains more detail on Tiffany's inventory and PP&E). Tiffany has always maintained very high levels of inventory, but inventory/sales rose from 33.5% in 2000 to 43.7% in 2005, or 361 days on a cost of sales basis almost enough inventory for a whole year's sales. This would be extraordinarily high for a retailer, but is typical for a high-end jeweller. Raw diamond stocks, in particular, have grown very rapidly to around $237m in 2005, evidently out of a desire to protect supply. PP&E/sales rose steeply from 17.4% in 2000 to 40.9% in 2005. Tiffany is vertically integrating – it is investing heavily in its estate of retail stores, and in its manufacturing capabilities.

Disclosure and data

We could take the disaggregation of the profitability equation to any level of detail, but the problem is data. The disclosure of the detail of costs and of assets and liabilities in financial statements is limited and varies from firm to firm. However, firms frequently disclose valuable additional data elsewhere and we should hunt this information down and use it. Some firms carry additional disclosures on their web sites, and presentations to brokers are available online. US listed firms that are governed by Securities and Exchange Commission (SEC) filing requirements disclose significant detail in their SEC 10K filing, which is available online.

Non-financial data, which is quantitative data not recorded in the accounting system, can be a useful companion to the financials. For example, firms disclose their number of employees, permitting us to calculate a sales-per-employee measure that may give additional insight into labour costs and productive efficiency. Beyond this, the nature and quantity of non-financial disclosure varies widely from sector to sector. Its principal use is in giving extra insight into asset utilisation. The airline industry and the hotel industry have very similar economics. The demand for travel is cyclical, and most of their costs are fixed. As a result, profitability in both industries is very sensitive to the extent to which firms are using their capacity. Firms report this in terms of occupancy, in the case of hotels, and load factors in the case of airlines.

GAAP: Narrative disclosure

GAAP is increasingly asking for *narrative* disclosures in which firms themselves provide the sort of analysis we are doing in this chapter. US GAAP requires firms to provide a rounded discussion of the firm's performance, looking at the firm through the eyes of management in the Management Discussion and Analysis (MDA). Other countries either have or are planning something similar; they include Australia, Canada, Germany and the UK. In 2006, IFRS was also considering the requirement for a Management Commentary, which would disclose information on: the nature of the business; its objectives and strategy; its resources, risks and relationships; its results and prospects; its performance measures and indicators.
[References: SEC regulation S-K, and updates]

WORKING CAPITAL

When analysing the components of working capital – that is, receivables, inventory and payables – it can add intuition to think in terms of 'days', which is the asset-to-sales ratio multiplied by 365. For example, in the case of receivables, the ratio of average receivables to sales tells us what proportion of the year's sales is waiting to be collected at any point. Multiplying by 365 expresses this in terms of how many days of credit the firm's customers are taking, on average.

$$Receivable\ days\ =\ \frac{Average\ receivables\ \times\ 365}{Sales}$$

'Days' measures – *receivable days, payable days, inventory days* – are intuitive, but cannot be interpreted too literally. For instance, in the case of receivables days, problems of interpretation include the following:
- In the income statement, sales excludes sales taxes and value-added taxes, but in the balance sheet, receivables includes these taxes.
- Strictly, to assess the current receivables policy, receivables would have to be related to annualised sales for the last month or two, but that is not visible to the outsider.
- If the relationship between sales and receivables is going to tell us anything about credit policy, sales need to be credit sales. But in sectors like retailing and fast food, a significant proportion of sales are cash sales. Income statements do not disclose cash and credit sales separately.
- If the firm has factored some of its receivables by selling them to a bank (see Chapter 13), they disappear from the balance sheet and it becomes hard to interpret receivables days, or to compare them between firms.

However, 'days' usually work fine as indicators of trends and for revealing differences between firms for further analysis. For instance, if a firm with significant cash sales is being analysed, but the overall (cash and credit) sales figure is used in the receivables ratio, there will be no distortion for comparative purposes so long as the proportion of cash sales is fairly constant through time or between comparator firms.

Unlike receivables, inventory and payables are carried in the balance sheet at cost – that is, at input prices excluding profit. Arguably, for inventory days and payables days, cost of sales should be used as the denominator for the working capital ratio. But if these ratios are being used for comparisons rather than as absolute measures, using sales is not usually problematic. The use of sales rather than cost of sales will only cause bias when the relationship between purchases and sales differs across firms or through time; in other words, if the gross margin is not constant.

Some analysts use the following as an overall measure of working capital efficiency:

$$Net\ credit\ given = (Receivables\ \text{-}\ Payables)\ \times\ 365/sales$$

$$Working\ capital\ days = (Receivables + Inventory\ \text{-}\ Payables)\ \times\ 365/sales$$

SEGMENT ANALYSIS

Most firms of any size are made up of activities that may be quite different from one another in terms of return on capital and in terms of profitability equation. Ideally, we would like to do a full forensic ratio analysis for each economically distinct operating segment of a firm. In other words, we want to be able to analyse the firm 'vertically' in terms of business segments, as well as 'horizontally' in terms of the detail of costs and assets. Unfortunately, the scope for segment analysis is limited. The firm may not segment the business in the same way, or down to the level of disaggregation, that we would have chosen. Also, firms disclose less information at the segment level than at the firm level. GAAP requires firms to disclose sales, profit and assets for each segment; in other words, enough data to calculate a return on capital, a margin and an asset turn. But firms do not usually provide the data to go much deeper. And while 'sales' is unambiguous, there is no guarantee that the firm will report segment profit and segment assets in the way we want. For instance, firms commonly report total assets rather than net assets at the segment level. In practice, we may not need to worry too much about this. Significant differences in performance between segments will usually show up in the segment ratios, however defined.

Another problem concerns the impact of transfer pricing, especially on geographic sector performance. Despite the best efforts of tax authorities, multinational firms may succeed in shifting profits to lower-tax jurisdictions to minimise global tax. There is not much we can do to judge the scale of this, but we can exercise caution, especially when a tendency is observed for low returns to be earned in high tax jurisdictions.

GAAP: Segment disclosure

GAAP requires firms to report key financial data at the business segment level. IFRS requires segment disclosure both in terms of the nature of operations and geographically; one is nominated as primary and the other, requiring less disclosure, as secondary. IFRS provides a set of factors to determine the segments; whether operations may be aggregated and what geographical segments may be aggregated. US GAAP requires firms to report the same operating segments that the CEO uses internally for performance measurement and asset allocation. Broadly, GAAP requires separate disclosure of any segment that comprises 10% or more of the total in terms of sales, profit or assets. IFRS puts no limit on the number of segments there may be, while US GAAP suggests a maximum of 10 be used.

GAAP requires sales, a measure of profit, and a measure of assets to be reported for each segment. US GAAP does not require liabilities to be reported, but IFRS requires it for the primary segment. Beyond this, IFRS requires disclosure, inter alia, of depreciation and non-cash expenses, and accrued capital expenditure. US GAAP requires these and other disclosures including interest, tax, exceptionals and extraordinaries – but only where this forms part of the firm's internal reporting.
[References: IAS14, FAS131]

Non-operating and transitory income

Firms sometimes carry assets in their balance sheet that are not used in the core activities of the firm. These assets arrive in the balance sheet in various ways. They may be legacy assets that are the residue from some earlier strategy or were left over after a programme of divestment. They may reflect the passions of the chief executive: the corporate art collection for instance. But usually they fall into one of two categories:
– Surplus cash
– Unconsolidated investments in other firms

Because we use net debt to calculate capital employed, holdings of cash, and the income on that cash, are already excluded from ROCE. So it is only unconsolidated investments in other firms that need concern us here.

The income from associates and other investments shows up as 'other income' rather than operating income; so it is tempting to exclude it from EBIT, and to exclude the corresponding investments from capital employed. But trying to argue for excluding unconsolidated investments as 'non-operating' on philosophical grounds is difficult. These strategic investments are usually 'operating' in the sense that they directly or indirectly support the operations of the firm. Had the ownership stake been high enough to give control they would, after all, have been consolidated, and the only issue for analysis would have been, do they constitute an economically distinct segment?

However, there is a strong pragmatic reason for analysing unconsolidated investments separately, which is to do with lack of data on sales. Though the income statement includes income from associates and the balance sheet includes the associates' net assets, the associates' sales are not included in the consolidated sales figure. Although including unconsolidated investments generates an overall return on capital measure that is reliable, the absence of the corresponding sales figure means margin and asset turn will be biased; if the investment in associates is significant these numbers will become meaningless.

GAAP: Transitory components of income

Extraordinary items are profits and losses that relate to events that are significant but are infrequent and unusual. They are traditionally shown net of tax, at the bottom of the income statement. The logic of this was to allow firms to exclude items that are non-recurring and non-sustainable from the earnings figure. IFRS has now prohibited the use of extraordinary items altogether, and they can only be used rarely under US GAAP. In consequence the pressure has moved up the income statement to exceptionals. GAAP does not use the term *exceptional* as such, but both IFRS and US GAAP require separate disclosure of items of sufficient size or nature where this is necessary to explain performance. GAAP requires firms to disclose exceptionals as part of, or alongside, operating profit for items such as reorganisation costs, or gains or losses on sale of assets or businesses.
[References: FAS101, APB30, APB18]

Frequently firms disclose exceptionals below the operating profit line. It is tempting for the reader to conclude that if something is treated by the firm as exceptional it must be either non-operating, or transitory, or both. As a result, many analysts *exclude* exceptionals when calculating financial ratios in the belief that this gives a fairer view of the underlying economics of the firm. Our view is that these items should be *included* in EBIT, accepting that this will give a 'noisier', more variable, returns series. Including exceptionals in return on capital measures is a good discipline – these items are real and excluding them may tend to mislead by flattering the firm's return. But the decision whether to include or exclude them depends on the context. Including them may damage comparability and, especially if they are non-operating in nature, margin and asset turn will start to become meaningless as there is no corresponding figure in sales. On the other hand, if we are calculating a value metric they must be included, otherwise income is not comprehensive.

Both investments in other firms and transitory components of income are best thought of as segments. They can be excluded from operating returns if they have different 'economics' to the core business, but they must be kept in the picture if we are to tell a complete story about how the firm earns its return. So the structure of segment analysis is described in Figure 2.

Figure 2 Structure of segment analysis

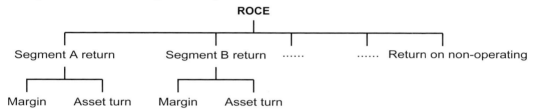

THE EFFECT OF OPERATING LEVERAGE

The way in which a firm's costs respond to an unplanned change or 'shock' to sales is a function of its 'operating leverage'. Costs are described as *variable, semi-fixed* and *fixed* depending on the extent to which they vary with sales in the short run – fully, partly or not at all. We use the phrase *operating leverage* to describe the proportion of fixed to total cost. Analysing costs in this way is important for understanding the volatility of a firm's EBIT and for forecasting profitability around the business cycle.

In reality, most firms have costs that are semi-fixed. Industries such as airlines and hotels have a notoriously high operating leverage – the costs of flying a plane or running a hotel are not much different if there is only one customer instead of one hundred. At the other extreme, to find a business whose costs are almost entirely variable we would have to look at activities like commodity trading.

Example: André, Bharat and Chan

André, Bharat and Chan all have sales of 1,000 and costs of 920 giving them EBIT of 80. However André's costs are all variable, Chan's are all fixed and Bharat's are semi-fixed, it has 400 of fixed cost. Table 2 shows what happens when there is a 10% shock to sales. If sales fall or rise by 10%, André's costs change in proportion to sales, so André's EBIT falls or rises by 10% too. On the other hand Chan's costs are fixed, so a 10% drop in sales comes straight off EBIT and pushes him into loss: EBIT is -20. Even for Bharat, with semi-fixed costs, a 10% drop in sales translates into a 60% drop in EBIT.

Table 2 The effects of operating leverage

	André (variable)			Bharat (semi-fixed)			Chan (fixed)		
Sales	1,000	900	1,100	1,000	900	1,100	1,000	900	1,100
% change		-10%	+10%		-10%	+10%		-10%	+10%
Variable	920	828	1012	520	468	572	0	0	0
Fixed	0	0	0	400	400	400	920	920	920
Costs	920	828	1,012	920	868	972	920	920	920
EBIT	**80**	**72**	**88**	**80**	**32**	**128**	**80**	**-20**	**180**
% change		-10%	10%		-60%	60%		-125%	125%

It is clear that high operating leverage is not all bad news – on the upside, firms with high operating leverage experience a disproportionate improvement in profits when sales increase. But firms with higher operating leverage have more volatile profits and will show more variation in profits around the business cycle. These days, managers try to reduce operating leverage where they can. For example, they might arrange to rent some part of the long-term assets they need on short-term contracts. Airlines use operating leases for this. In a similar spirit, many firms have tried to make their labour costs more variable by shifting people from full- to part-time contracts and by increasing the proportion of bonus or 'performance pay' in the pay packet. The effect is to shift some of the profit volatility to labour.

Operating leverage is an important concept, and we know it when we see it – for instance when we see the profits of firms that we believe to have high fixed costs, such as hotels and airlines, tumbling in an economic downturn. But the firm's operating leverage is not easy to measure from financial statements because costs are not classified on the basis of whether they are fixed or variable in the short run.

The root cause of the problem is that the distinction between 'fixed' and 'variable' cost is complex and elusive: it depends on time horizon; it reflects contractual detail that is not visible to the outsider; it is determined by managerial behaviour. Take labour costs as an example. What happens to the wage bill when there is a fall in demand depends on the nature of the firm's contracts with its workers. At one extreme they may be casual workers hired by the day, on the other hand they may be on long-term contracts and have accumulated hefty redundancy entitlements. But what the contracts say is not the whole story. Even if it could, a firm may well choose not to lay people off in a downturn. It may care about their welfare and its responsibility for them. It will also be conscious that their human capital may be costly to replace when there is an upturn.

Gross margin in cost analysis

Gross margin (= gross profit/sales) is often used as a measure of fundamental profitability with which to compare firms. This can be very useful, but care is required when comparing firms using gross margin because there is no guidance in GAAP as to what expenses should be included in the cost of sales. Also it is tempting to interpret cost of sales as variable costs and SG&A as fixed cost. Though it would be nice if this were the case, it is not so. Firms have fixed and semi-fixed elements in their cost of sales – such as factory overhead and labour – and have purely variable costs in SG&A, such as salespersons' commission.

Economies of scale and learning

Operating leverage describes the effect on EBIT of an unplanned shock to sales, and the language of variable and fixed cost relates to short-term variability in costs. In the long term, all costs are variable as the firm undertakes planned growth or contraction. The issue then becomes the relationship between sales and costs through time. If a firm has better cost ratios than similar-sized firms, assuming the business model and the accounting model are the same, this suggests *learning* or *experience* effects. If larger firms enjoy lower costs per dollar of sales than smaller firms in certain cost categories, this suggests the presence of *economies of scale*. In either case the starting point for analysis is to get as detailed a cost breakdown as possible for the firm and for its peers.

When we are trying to find potential scale economies, the issue is the extent to which costs will remain proportionate to sales as the firm grows. This is an area where gross margins can be helpful. A starting hypothesis could be that the direct costs of the business that are reflected in the gross margin – the costs of manufacturing, for example – are per-unit costs, so will grow in proportion as sales grow. On the other hand, some elements of SG&A – for example the costs of running the central administration – may be quite invariant to the level of activity over a wide range of growth. Some costs may even fall in absolute terms as time goes on – for example, initial expenditure on intangibles.

Start-ups are a particular instance of the scale economy issue. Start-ups tend to make big losses in their early years when they do not have enough sales revenue to cover their costs. Obviously, the hope is that as they grow they will reach break-even, then become profitable. When trying to forecast the future performance of a start-up, forming a view about the way costs will change as the firm grows or matures is crucial. The task is made more difficult because start-ups often have little history, few comparators, and may well be using an untried technology and business model. Amazon.com provides a good case.

Case: Amazon cost analysis

Many 'dot-com' businesses that listed on the stock market during the technology boom of the late nineties shared certain characteristics: they were new-born, and they were using new technology and new business models. Almost all of them were loss-making, and some of them had barely any revenues. Thus they posed a challenge. Were they loss-making because their businesses were just innately unattractive and would never be profitable? Or was it because they were at the start-up stage? Naturally, the dot-coms themselves wanted to encourage the second theory, and this led some of them to be quite creative in their income statement accounting. The game was to show as much revenue as possible and, even if EBIT was negative, to try to report a positive gross margin. That way, investors might calculate that as sales grew in the future the gross profit would grow and, in due course, provide sufficient contribution to cover the firm's overheads.

Amazon.com was founded by Jeff Bezos in 1994. By the end of 1999 it had sales of $1.64bn, which was a 170% increase on the previous year. But Amazon's losses were growing faster and Amazon made an operating loss of -$690m in 1999, representing a margin of –42.1% on sales. Nonetheless, Amazon remained in favour with investors. Its stock price in early 2000 was $64, giving a market capitalisation of some $22bn. To reach this valuation, investors had to make some difficult judgement calls: that the relatively untried technology of internet retailing would find a market; that Amazon would be able to retain its share of that market against new entrants; and that Amazon could turn its costs round. We will focus on the cost issue.

Table 3 shows Amazon's income statements from 1996 to 2005 and Table 4 calculates the gross margin and the SG&A/sales ratio on a reported and an adjusted basis. The investor valuing Amazon in early 2000 would have had data up to 1999. Though Amazon reported an operating loss of -$690m in 1999, its reported gross profit was $291m, which represented a gross margin of 17.7% of sales. However Amazon had included some of its fulfilment costs in marketing expense. In the adjusted ratios we include these costs in cost of sales, and also some fulfilment-related stock-based compensation costs. On this basis, Amazon's gross margin was just 3.2% in 1999, and its SG&A/sales was correspondingly lower (SG&A 2 in Table 4). On the other hand, when projecting SG&A forward it is appropriate to exclude transitory costs, and also amortisation and impairment of goodwill and intangibles, which are legacy effects of earlier acquisitions. In 1999, and for the next two years, Amazon had large amortisation and impairment charges of around $0.75bn in total, writing down investments it made in recent years. Many acquisitive firms were forced to take large write-downs at this time. Excluding these (SG&A 3 in Table 4) reduces Amazon's SG&A to sales from 45.3% to 31.8% in 1999.

So in early 2000 the investor would have to take a view on Amazon's ability to get its gross margin up, through learning and efficiency, and perhaps through price increases. They would need to assess the components of Amazon's SG&A and take a view on whether these would grow in absolute terms. Some components of SG&A might even fall in absolute terms; for example, a business like this might require higher expenditure on promotion and IT at the beginning than in later years.

The data shows what actually happened after 2000. Amazon's gross margin rose quite sharply in the next couple of years and settled at around 15%. Amazon managed to hold its SG&A expenditure in absolute terms at more or less 1999 levels over the next five years despite a five-fold increase in sales. In 2004, Amazon reported a positive operating profit of $440m.

Table 3 Amazon income statements (figures in $m, year end 31 December)

	1996	1997	1998	1999	2000	2001	2002	2003	2004	2005
Sales	**16**	**148**	**610**	**1,640**	**2,762**	**3,122**	**3,933**	**5,264**	**6,921**	**8,490**
Cost of sales	12	119	476	1,349	2,106	2,324	2,940	4,007	5,319	6,451
Gross profit	**3**	**29**	**134**	**291**	**656**	**799**	**993**	**1,257**	**1,602**	**2,039**
Fulfillment	0	0	0	237	415	374	392	477	590	745
Marketing	6	40	133	260	180	138	125	123	158	198
Technology, content	2	13	46	160	269	241	216	208	251	451
General & administration	1	7	16	70	109	90	79	88	112	166
Stock-based compensation	0	1	2	31	25	5	69	88	58	
Amort, goodwill and intangibles	0	0	43	215	322	181	5	3	1	5
Restructuring	0	0	4	8	200	182	42	0	-9	42
Total expense (SG&A 1)	**-9**	**-61**	**-243**	**-981**	**-1,520**	**-1,211**	**-928**	**-987**	**-1,162**	**-1,607**
Income from operations	**-6**	**-33**	**-109**	**-690**	**-864**	**-412**	**64**	**271**	**440**	**432**

note: some totals do not tally due to rounding

Table 4 Amazon analysis

	1996	1997	1998	1999	2000	2001	2002	2003	2004	2005
Gross margin, reported	**22.0%**	**19.5%**	**21.9%**	**17.7%**	**23.7%**	**25.6%**	**25.2%**	**23.9%**	**23.1%**	**24.0%**
Cost of sales, reported	*12*	*119*	*476*	*1,349*	*2,106*	*2,324*	*2,940*	*4,007*	*5,319*	*6,451*
Fulfilment				237	415	374	392	477	590	745
Stock comp (fulfilment portion)				0	-2	0	12	18	10	
Cost of sales, adjusted				*1,587*	*2,519*	*2,699*	*3,345*	*4,502*	*5,920*	*7,196*
Gross margin, adjusted				**3.2%**	**8.8%**	**13.6%**	**15.0%**	**14.5%**	**14.5%**	**15.2%**
SG&A 2 (1. less CofS adjust)	9	61	243	744	1,107	836	524	492	561	862
SG&A 2, % sales	**59.9%**	**41.6%**	**39.8%**	**45.3%**	**40.1%**	**26.8%**	**13.3%**	**9.3%**	**8.1%**	**10.2%**
SG&A 3 (also less amortisation)	9	61	197	521	585	473	477	489	569	815
SG&A 3, % sales	**59.9%**	**41.6%**	**32.2%**	**31.8%**	**21.2%**	**15.2%**	**12.1%**	**9.3%**	**8.2%**	**9.6%**

THE EFFECT OF BUSINESS MODEL

The place to start in thinking about the shape of a firm's profitability equation is the idealised world of perfect competition. In a competitive market place there is convergence in returns on capital. High returns signal to competitors that the market is attractive, so they enter and compete away the excess profits, while managers seek to reverse low returns for fear of disciplinary action by investors or because of the threat of a hostile takeover bid. As a result, in a perfectly competitive world each firm would just earn its cost of capital, and since differences in the cost of capital due to risk are frequently quite small, in that world all firms would earn much the same return on capital.

Even in a competitive world what *may* differ between firms in different businesses is the asset turn. Asset turn measures the amount of sales a firm achieves by using $1 of net assets. This is a function of technology. More capital-intensive activities will have lower asset turns – you need a lot more capital to support $1 of sales in construction and in aerospace than you do in advertising, for example. In that world a firm's asset turn is a 'given' and is determined by the technology of the industry in which it operates. So margin must be the balancing figure: the lower the asset turn, the higher the margin needed to earn a given return on capital.

In summary, our basic model of how the profitability equation works in a competitive market is as follows: *competitive markets allow a firm to earn the margin it needs to achieve a return on capital equal to its cost of capital, given the net assets it requires to operate in its business.* But a number of factors make the world more complex than this, and the challenge for the analyst is to form judgements about the performance of firms in the presence of these confounding factors. Even if a market is fundamentally competitive, it might take some time for firms to adjust and reach equilibrium. So at any time, we will see firms earning different returns. Markets may not be fully competitive. Some firms succeed in creating competitive advantage and sustaining it, at least for a while. These firms will earn higher returns than their competitors. Systematic biases in accounting will affect the numbers we observe. So some firms may appear to be earning superior returns in accounting terms, even when they are not.

Business models

Even within the same industry, firms can adopt different business models that require different balance sheets and look very different in financial terms. Firms can choose whether to own the assets that they use, or to access the resources of other firms through formal contracts or informal networks.

A firm's strategy determines what business it is in, what products and services it offers, the way in which it provides them, and what markets it trades in, domestically and internationally. People often use the term 'business model' broadly to refer to a firm's strategy or some aspect of its strategy. In this book we use *business model* more narrowly to describe a particular way of configuring resources, given the choice of business. A firm's business model reflects the choices it makes about the *value chain*[2]. Productive activity can be seen as a sequence of *primary activities*, with *support functions* that service all parts of the chain of primary activities. For example, the value chain for a computer manufacturer might contain the following:

– *Primary activities* Research and development, purchasing and logistics, manufacturing and assembly, distribution, sales and marketing, after-sales service.
– *Support functions* Finance, human resources, security, transport…

Once a firm has decided to operate in a particular business, which of the primary activities and support functions it undertakes itself, and which it leaves to other firms, defines its business model. So there are two aspects to a firm's choice of business model: vertical integration and outsourcing.

The extent to which a sequence of primary activities is undertaken within a single firm measures the degree of *vertical integration*. The firm has to decide which primary activities it undertakes in-house, and which it leaves to other firms. The unpretty term *deverticalising* is used to describe a firm that is becoming less vertically integrated by exiting from some primary activities. We use the less precise but more appealing term *unbundling* for this.

Using other firms to provide support activities is known as *outsourcing*. For instance, many firms need a fleet of vehicles but they do not have, or want to have, the capabilities needed to manage it themselves – these include fleet management skills, insurance and repair, good access to second-hand vehicle markets and so forth. So they lease their fleet by writing a contract with a firm that possesses those skills. Firms have no shortage of suitors in the form of service providers encouraging them to outsource their support functions. Outsourcing fleet management, security and catering is long established, but firms are now also able to outsource core support functions like IT, accounting and HR, and resources such as property.

Vertical integration

A simple numerical example will show us how vertical integration affects the profitability equation and running the same logic backwards shows the effect of unbundling a vertically integrated firm.

Example: Castor and Pollux

Castor is a computer manufacturer and Pollux is a computer dealer. The first two columns of Table 2 show how these firms look as standalone entities. Castor takes over Pollux, which becomes a division of the new Castor Group. Table 2 now shows how the consolidated accounts of the new group look.

First, assume the two firms had no dealings with each other. Imagine this is a 'horizontal' merger and two similar firms have just been brought under one roof and, moreover, there were no efficiency gains. In this case the group accounts are a straight addition of Castor and Pollux, line by line. Column 3 shows this; it provides a useful benchmark.

2 The value chain was popularised by Harvard economist Michael Porter in his *Competitive Advantage*, New York, Free Press, 1984.

In fact, Castor only sells through Pollux, and Pollux only buys from Castor, so when Castor acquires Pollux, this is classic vertical integration. These firms *do* trade with each other, and it is the effect of internalising this inter-firm trading that changes the shape of the profitability equation. Column 4 shows the group accounts of Castor Group. Assuming there are still no efficiency gains, EBIT and capital employed are additive but sales are not, so ROCE is unchanged. To make this easy to see we have fixed it so that both firms had the same ROCE of 15% and so the ROCE of Castor Group is 15% too. The sales do not sum because the sales of one activity become the costs of sales for the next stage in the value chain; Pollux's cost of sales, 60, is Castor's sales. In this extreme case, where Castor only sells to Pollux, Pollux's sales now become the sales of the group as a whole because they are the sales to the external market. EBIT and capital employed are additive, but sales are not. So ROCE is unchanged, but EBIT margin is increased and asset turn reduced, all compared to the benchmark (column 3).

Other things equal, a vertically integrated firm has a higher gross margin. By buying Pollux, Castor internalises Pollux's gross margin, but also takes on its SG&A and its assets. Though the net assets/capital employed are additive, their composition changes because Castor's current asset of 70 is the receivable from Pollux, which shows up as a current liability of -70 in Pollux's balance sheet. These cancel out on consolidation.

Table 5 Castor and Pollux

	Castor	Pollux	Additive	Castor Group	Outsourcing
	(1)	(2)	(3)	(4)	(5)
Sales	60	80	140	80	80
Cost of sales	-20	-60	-80	-20	-20
Gross profit	40	20	60	60	60
SG&A	-25	-17	-42	-42	-52
EBIT	15	3	18	18	8
Current assets	70	70	140	70	70
Long-term assets	130	20	150	150	50
(Current liabilities)	-30	-70	-100	-30	-30
(Long-term liabilities)	-70		-70	-70	-70
Net assets,capital employed	100	20	120	120	20
Gross margin	66.7%	25.0%	42.9%	75.0%	75.0%
EBIT margin	25.0%	3.8%	12.9%	22.5%	10.0%
Asset turn	0.6	4.0	1.2	0.7	4.0
ROCE	15.0%	15.0%	15.0%	15.0%	40.0%

Outsourcing

We can also use Castor and Pollux to see the effect of outsourcing on the profitability equation. Suppose Castor Group decides it no longer needs to own its headquarters building. It sells the building to a property company and leases it back. The proceeds of sale are 100, which Castor Group gives back to the shareholders. Castor Group has been able to structure the arrangement as an operating lease, so the asset is 'off' Castor's balance sheet and, instead, Castor pays an annual lease rental of 10 which is part of SG&A. Column 5 of Table 2 shows the result. On the assumptions we made about Castor and Pollux, vertical integration changed the structure of costs and assets, but left EBIT and capital employed unchanged. So the impact on the shape of the profitability equation was through sales. By contrast, the property outsourcing has not touched sales, but changed EBIT and capital employed, so transforms the shape of the profitability equation in a different way.

We discuss operating leasing in some detail in Chapter 13. There is a view amongst some analysts and GAAP regulators that operating leasing is just ownership in disguise. This may be, but in terms of its impact on the financial statements it is a classic business model choice; the firm is outsourcing the provision of long-term assets. As a form of outsourcing, operating leasing has an extremely high impact on the balance sheet. Other types of outsourcing, for instance of accounting services or HR, will principally impact costs, since these activities do not require much balance sheet. IT and logistics outsourcing usually have elements of both; there may be cost savings, but assets – perhaps a data-centre or a fleet of vehicles – are typically also removed from the balance sheet.

Business model innovation

Business model innovation is one of the principal ways in which firms strive to create competitive advantage these days. The firm's choice of business model should be based on an analysis of competences, costs and risks. The firm looks at its value chain and focuses on those activities where it believes it can sustain some competitive advantage. If it has no special skills in undertaking an activity and others can do it better or cheaper, then it exits the activity by outsourcing or unbundling. Information technology now makes it easier for a network of independent entities to achieve some of the logistical efficiencies of an integrated firm. For instance, it permits the franchiser to have real-time access to sales information from the franchisee's till, or the supplier from the supermarket's till. It permits the component supplier to observe directly the state of the car manufacturer's production line. Medion AG provides a good example from the computer industry.

Case: Medion AG

In its early years, in the 1980s, the PC industry was quite vertically integrated, with the major firms doing everything from R&D through to selling through owned distributors and dealers. Since then, competitive pressure and business-model innovation have transformed the shape of the industry.

Medion AG produces consumer electronics products, mainly PCs and multimedia devices. It was listed on the Frankfurt market in 1999, since when it has pursued an international growth strategy. Most of its sales are within Europe, where Germany remains its largest market, though it is now starting to expand into the United States and the Asia-Pacific region. Medion works on a project basis and its products are built to order. The products are marketed principally through one-off sales campaigns in partnership with some of the world's largest retailers. It aims to provide these retailers with a single source for all consumer electronics products. Medion has a distinctive business model. It co-ordinates, monitors and manages the entire value chain from initial product idea through to after-sales service. It performs some of these functions in-house: product conceptualisation and design, quality management and after-sales service. It uses a global network of partner firms for manufacturing, logistics and forwarding, and sales and distribution. So its partners fund all the sections of the value chain that are capital-intensive, including production, logistics, and retail distribution.

On the other hand, it is potentially costly to relinquish control of strategic resources, including tangible assets, but especially organisational competences and knowledge, that may be scarce and valuable now or in the future. For example, some firms have regretted outsourcing their IT, having become locked into a costly long-term contract and passed a potentially important source of organisational learning and competitive advantage to outsiders. In some industries business-model innovation has been successful, and in others not. But the concern for the reader of the financial statements is to understand the impact of the choice of business model on the shape of the income statement and balance sheet.

The lighter-than-air balance sheet

Some firms have re-engineered their business models so effectively that their net operating assets are negative. What few operating assets are required are more than covered by liabilities. This often involves using other people's tangible assets, by renting them or leasing them under off-balance sheet operating leases. It usually involves highly efficient working capital management, with intensive use of IT to minimise inventory and optimise the balance between receivables and payables. Dell Computer is the exemplar of this. Many other firms are experimenting with similar structures.

One response to these balance sheets is to dismiss them as 'smoke and mirrors'. 'It's to do with balance sheet incompleteness,' it is argued, 'and if the balance sheet was made complete, perhaps by capitalising operating leases, or recognising missing intangibles, then it would look more like an old-fashioned heavier-than-air balance sheet.' This may or may not be the case; we discuss such balance-sheet-completeness adjustments elsewhere in the book. For now, we take these balance sheets on their own terms. They have some important implications for the way we understand financial performance.

If a firm reduces its net operating assets, and thus its capital employed, to zero, then its asset turn becomes infinite. As a result, however modest its EBIT margin, its return on capital employed will be infinite too. Is this sensible? Yes and no. It is literally true that such a firm has a return greater than its cost of capital. It isn't using capital, so if it has positive EBIAT, this must be so. To use another vocabulary, the firm has a positive economic profit because it has positive EBIAT and no capital charge. There are good reasons why light-balance-sheet strategies may be real rather than merely the result of creative accounting. These firms have worked hard to improve asset efficiency, and have found a position in the value chain that requires little investment in balance sheet assets. Indeed, given the challenging nature of industries like the computer industry, 're-engineering the balance sheet' became a prerequisite for survival for many firms.

But the idea that its return on capital is infinite for these firms is not helpful. The problem is that we are also using capital simply to scale profit, and using capital this way lets us down as capital approaches zero. The ratio becomes meaningless. Economic profit comes into its own as a value metric in situations such as this. And for forensic analysis, the focus is on the margin side of the profitability equation.

Case: Dell Computer

Michael Dell founded PC's Limited, later to become Dell Computer in 1984, while he was still a student. Its business model was to sell IBM-compatible computers built from stock components directly to customers. Dell believed that the direct-selling model offered the best way to understand and meet consumers' computing needs. In a market still largely populated by enthusiasts – hobbyists and those who might be termed 'early adopters' today – Dell's model provided an attractive half-way house between buying your own parts and assembling them and buying a ready-made machine in a shop. Table 6 shows Dell's financial ratios – ROCE and its components using the structure outlined earlier in the chapter – from 1989 to 2001. (We omitted 2002 onwards for clarity; they tell a consistent story).

Table 6 Dell's financial ratios

	1989	1990	1991	1992	1993	1994	1995	1996	1997	1998	1999	2000	2001
ROCE	34%	13%	50%	51%	58%	-15%	81%	99%	∞	∞	∞	337%	252%
ROCE ex. investments	34%	13%	50%	51%	58%	-15%	81%	99%	496%	∞	∞	∞	∞
EBIT margin	9%	3%	8%	7%	7%	-1%	6%	7%	9%	10%	11%	9%	9%
Gross margin	31%	28%	33%	32%	22%	18%	21%	20%	21%	22%	23%	21%	20%
R&D/sales	-3%	-4%	-4%	-3%	-2%	-1%	-1%	-1%	-1%	-1%	-1%	-2%	-2%
Exceptionals/sales	-0%	-0%	-0%	-1%	0%	-3%	-2%	-0%	-0%	-0%	-0%	-1%	1%
Other SG&A/sales	-20%	-20%	-21%	-21%	-14%	-14%	-13%	-12%	-11%	-10%	-10%	-9%	-10%
Asset turn	4	4	6	7	8	10	15	14	∞	∞	∞	38	27
PP&E/sales	4%	6%	5%	4%	3%	3%	3%	3%	3%	2%	2%	3%	3%
Investments/sales	0%	0%	0%	0%	0%	0%	0%	0%	0%	0%	0%	5%	8%
Other Fixed/sales	0%	0%	0%	0%	0%	0%	0%	0%	0%	0%	0%	0%	0%
Intangibles/sales	0%	0%	0%	0%	0%	0%	0%	0%	0%	0%	0%	1%	1%
Inventory/sales	25%	22%	14%	12%	11%	9%	7%	7%	4%	2%	1%	1%	1%
Receivable/sales	10%	12%	14%	14%	13%	14%	14%	12%	10%	10%	11%	10%	9%
Payable/sales	-9%	-11%	-12%	-10%	-10%	-10%	-10%	-9%	-10%	-11%	-11%	-12%	-12%
Other net ass/sales	-5%	-4%	-5%	-7%	-5%	-6%	-7%	-6%	-8%	-7%	-6%	-6%	-6%

The 1990s was an extremely challenging period in the PC industry, with tumbling prices and many firms exiting the industry. In 1994 Dell suffered losses. This proved to be a turning point for Dell. In the same year Dell's gross margin slumped to 18% and, though it recovered slightly, was to remain at around 10% below the gross margins of over 30% that Dell enjoyed in the early-nineties. Despite this loss of gross margin, Dell managed to both improve EBIT margin and stabilise it in the years after 1994. It did this by radically reducing its overheads. Dell halved both its SG&A to sales and its R&D to sales through the nineties.

The most striking transformation is in Dell's asset turn, which rose from 4, in 1989 and 1990, to infinite, by 1997. This simply reflects the fact that Dell's net operating assets were negative by 1997 – operating liabilities exceeded operating costs. Dell had always been an energetic user of operating leasing. The change was in inventory management. Energetic use of internet selling, and of IT to manage a network of suppliers, gave Dell negligible inventory and negative net trade credit. The only confounding factor, weighing on Dell's balance sheet, was the effect of its growing investments in other firms after 2000. These show up as 'investments' in Dell's balance sheet, so we calculate ROCE with, and without, investments to show their impact.

REVIEW

- In this chapter we looked at tools for analysing a firm's profitability, and considered some of the issues we may encounter.

- The first step in analysing profitability is to split ROCE into EBIT margin and asset turn. We then decompose margin into component costs, and capital employed into its component assets and liabilities, calculating ratios, based on costs, assets and liabilities as a proportion of sales.

- Additional information can be got by using non-financial data and narrative disclosure in the accounts. As well as analysing a firm horizontally in terms of its costs and assets, we need to analyse it vertically in terms of business segments. Segment analysis is important, but in practice firms rarely disclose as much segment data as we want.

- Exceptional and transitory components of income are often excluded by analysts, but this can flatter a firm's return. A better approach is to include them when calculating value metrics, since they represent real events, but exclude them when comparability might be damaged through their inclusion.

- The way in which a firm's costs respond to an unplanned change to sales is a function of its 'operating leverage', that is, the proportion of fixed to total costs. A firm's operating leverage has a strong impact on the volatility of its operating profits, but is hard to model because the income statement does not identify costs in terms of 'fixed' and 'variable'. Examining gross margins can be helpful when looking for potential economies of scale and the effects of learning, particularly in a start-up situation.

- A firm's business model reflects the choices the firm makes about the value chain: the degree to which it is vertically integrated across a sequence of primary activities, and the extent to which it outsources the support functions. The profitability equation can be significantly affected by the choice of business model. Some firms even achieve negative net operating assets and, as a result, asset turn becomes infinite and ROCE ceases to be useful as a metric. In this situation, margin, and economic profit, come into their own.

ANNEX Tiffany's operating drivers

Based on the analysis earlier, the three drivers of Tiffany's ROCE over the period under review were the levels of its inventory and PP&E, and also Tiffany's SG&A. Here is some more analysis of those, based on the data they disclose in the financial statements.

Inventory

Table A1 is compiled from the notes to the financial statements:

Table A1 Tiffany's inventory

	2000	2001	2002	2003	2004	2005
Finished goods	438.5	51 .9	528.7	615.2	659.6	771.2
Raw materials	43.3	87.2	67.8	91.5	165.8	236.8
Work-in-progress	25.6	56.6	18.7	29.7	5 .5	54.
	507.4	**654.7**	**615.2**	**736.5**	**875.8**	**1,062.0**
Reserves	-2.6	-3.	-3.5	-4.4	-4.6	-4.7
Net Inventory	**504.8**	**651.7**	**611.7**	**732.1**	**871.3**	**1,057.2**

Management explain that they increased inventory to support the opening of new stores and the introduction of new product ranges. In 2003, specifically, they argue that part of the increase was due to the weak dollar; the 20% increase in inventory over the previous year would have been only 14% on a constant-exchange-rate basis. In the latter part of 2000 the firm made extra purchases of high-quality diamonds to ensure they had adequate supplies, leading to the jump from $43.3m to $87.2m in raw materials inventory.

This concern to safeguard future supplies of diamonds was reflected in the purchase of the Aber Diamond Corporation in 1999. Aber had an interest in a gem-quality diamond mining project in Canada. This acquisition cost $70m, and accounted for a significant increase in other long-term assets with no direct sales increase; this is a prime example of how vertical integration affects the profitability equation discussed. Although the investment was sold in 2004, Tiffany maintained its purchase agreement with Aber to acquire a minimum of $50m of rough diamonds every year through to 2013. Tiffany's holding of raw materials (primarily rough diamonds) increases year by year at a far greater rate than its inventory of finished goods. In 2000 raw materials was 10% of finished goods; in 2005 the proportion was 31%.

PP&E

Table A2 contains a breakdown of Tiffany's PP&E. Tiffany explains that it is expanding its retail and office space, its distribution facilities and its internal jewellery manufacturing operations. The construction of a new shipment and distribution centre in New Jersey is reflected in the 2002 to 2004 figures. The firm began a project in 2000 to renovate its New York flagship store and relocate various support functions; it anticipates spending $110m on this project, due for completion in 2007. It acquired the land and buildings housing its London flagship store in the year to 31 January 2003 for $43m (budgeting $24m for renovations), and its Tokyo store in the following year for $140.4m. Again, Tiffany is vertically integrating.

Table A2 Tiffany's PP&E

	2000	2001	2002	2003	2004	2005
Land	39.0	39.0	55.5	78.8	233.3	238.3
Buildings	62.0	63.5	119.3	171.6	188.3	188.8
Leasehold improvements	184.4	216.1	255.2	302.2	400.3	454.4
Capital leases	0	42.0	0	0	0	0
Construction-in-progress	7.4	33.7	55.7	92.1	16.5	27.2
Office equipment	158.6	186.8	229.6	275.1	292.3	335.6
Machinery and equipment	23.1	34.7	49.4	61.7	97.1	107.9
	474.5	**615.8**	**764.7**	**981.4**	**1,227.9**	**1,352.2**
Accumulated depreciation	-152.1	-192.6	-239.2	-303.8	-342.8	-434.4
Net PP&E	**322.4**	**423.2**	**525.6**	**677.6**	**885.1**	**917.9**

SG&A

Detail on the component parts of Tiffany's sales, general and administrative expenses is limited in its financial statements. The narrative explains that these costs include store payroll and benefits, rent and store operating expenses (including depreciation), advertising and marketing and corporate-level administrative costs. Instead of a numerical breakdown, the firm merely gives an indication of reasons for the large increases in SG&A. These reasons include: 'incremental depreciation, staffing and occupancy expenses related to the firm's expansion', 'higher insurance and marketing expenses', 'the translation effect of a generally weaker US dollar increased SG&A by 3% in 2003'. Meanwhile, the firm promises that its 'long-term objective is to reduce the ratio of SG&A expenses to net sales'. In 2005, it provided the following disclosures, perhaps to explain the increase in SG&A as a percentage of sales from 40.1% in 2004 to 42.5% in 2005.

Contribution to Tiffany & Co Foundation	25.0
Early adoption of SFAS 123R [share-based payments]	19.0
Impairment charge	12.2
Exit costs re discontinued speciality retail concept	2.9
Subtotal	**59.1**
Advertising	135.0
Unanalysed costs	742.0
Total SG&A	**936.0**

The only component for which comparative figures are given year by year is advertising. This includes media, production, catalogues and promotional events:

	2003	2004	2005
Advertising	101.9	122.4	135.0

Chapter 8

Cash flow

Cash flow is a story, not a number, and we want the cash flow statement to present the story in a transparent and coherent way. It should group economically similar items, and separate operating from financing elements to identify operating free cash flow. The chapter starts by explaining the logic and language of a cash flow statement. It then turns to interpretation, and discusses how the appearance of cash flow is affected by the firm's business model, by growing and shrinking, and by the firm's accounting policies.

The final section discusses how to reformat published cash flow statements. This can be challenging, and always involves some work because GAAP cash flow statements are an unhelpful mix of operating and financial elements. This section is fairly advanced and some readers will want to omit it.

FORMAT OF A CASH FLOW STATEMENT

Profitable trading is the main source of cash for most established firms. But profit is not cash; if you make €1,000 of profit it does not mean you will have €1,000 more cash in the bank. Accountants record transactions, irrespective of when the cash was spent or received, and a cash flow statement undoes these accruals to get back to the cash effects. The cash flow statement is derived from the other financial statements so, in principle, if you have the opening and closing balance sheets and you have the income statement then you know the cash flow. The *cash flow identity* describes this relationship[1].

Cash flow = Income - Change in balance sheet

Specifically:

Sales cash flow = Sales - increase in receivables

Expense cash flow = Expense - Increase in payables

Example: Youssef

Suppose Youssef owes the tax authorities 100 at the beginning of the year. His tax charge on this year's profit is 120. During the year he actually pays the tax authorities 80. So at the end of the year he must owe them 140. We can also work this out the other way round. If we know the opening and closing amounts owed and know the expense for the year, we can figure out what he paid: Youssef's cash tax paid = tax expense (120) - increase in liability (140 - 100) = 80.

Direct versus indirect cash flow

There is debate amongst accountants about whether cash flow statements should be presented using the 'direct' or the 'indirect' method. Under the *direct method*, the cash flow statement lists the net cash effect of an item directly (the left-hand side of the cash flow identity). The alternative is to show its two components instead (the right-hand side of the cash flow identity), which is known as the *indirect method*. In Youssef's case, in his cash flow statement prepared by the direct method we would show:

Tax paid	80

If the indirect method was used, the cash flow statement would show:

Tax charge	120
Change in taxes payable	-40

Many accountants argue passionately that the direct method makes it clear what the cash flow actually was. The counter argument, which we favour, is that the indirect method is more informative. In general, netting two numbers always loses information. Our

---

1 For simplicity, we use the equality sign (=) rather than the identity sign (≡) in these identities.

preferred cash flow format contains a mix of direct and indirect. For items like tax, investment in long-term assets, and interest paid, the direct cash flow is adequate – there is no real advantage to having more detail. But elsewhere the extra information in the indirect presentation is important. For example, it is wise to unpack the components of operating cash flow in order to show EBIT separately from the working capital changes, or 'accruals', for receivables, payables and inventories. Changes in working capital can be very large – positive or negative – year on year. They can signal significant shifts in the firm's trading conditions, and they sometimes signal significant accounting manipulation.

The goal is a cash flow statement that is transparent and comparable, both over time and between firms, enabling us readily to identify where the story is. The cash flow should group economically similar items and, ideally, should separate the operating from the financing activities of the firm. Though most of the data we need is visible in GAAP cash flow statements, published cash flows have one major shortcoming – they mix operating and financing elements. As a result, they do not identify 'operating free cash flow', which is a pivotal number for financial analysis, and in corporate finance. Reformatting published cash flow statements is challenging, and we defer it until the end of the chapter.

Our preferred format for a cash flow statement is as follows:

	EBIT
	Non-cash charges
=	**EBITDA**
	Tax on EBIT
	Investment in working capital
=	**Cash from operations**
	Investment in long-term assets (Capex)
=	**Operating free cash flow**
	Interest and dividends
	Tax shelter on interest
=	**Cash flow before financing**
	Equity financing
	Debt financing
=	**Change in cash and financial assets**

EBITDA

We start the cash flow with EBIT, which is also the cornerstone for the financial analysis of profitability. The first step in preparing a cash flow statement is to add back to EBIT the *non-cash charges* that accountants make in measuring income:

- Some of the expenses that accountants charge in calculating EBIT are allocations of cash costs incurred in earlier periods, such as the depreciation and amortisation of long-term assets.
- Profits and losses on disposal of assets are close relations to depreciation - a *loss on disposal* is essentially final catch-up depreciation, and a *profit on disposal* reverses excess depreciation charged in earlier periods.
- Some of the expenses that accountants charge are in anticipation of cash costs expected to be incurred in the future, notably increases in provisions.

Because depreciation and amortisation are usually the largest non-cash charges, the resulting figure is usually known as *earnings before interest, tax, depreciation and amortisation* or *EBITDA*.

Cash from operations

The next step is to deduct from EBITDA the cash taxes paid on EBIT in the year, which we will talk about later, and investment in working capital. The step from EBIT to EBITDA reversed any *long-term accruals* like depreciation and provisions that the accountant made in measuring profit. But there is another important class of ways in which profit and cash differ. The accountant estimates revenues and expenses by accruing the amounts receivable or payable, but not necessarily paid in cash, in the year. Deducting from EBITDA the changes in the components of working capital – receivables, payables and inventory – reverses those *short-term accruals*. The resulting measure of cash flow is usually known as operating cash flow or *cash from operations*.

Operating free cash flow

Cash from operations is an important part of the story – it tells us how much cash the firm has generated internally from operating and from other income. In many firms a large part of this cash is reinvested in long-term assets – particularly in PP&E – and in investments in other firms. In a rapidly growing firm, investment in long-term assets can easily exceed the internally generated funds measured by cash from operations. Investment in long-term assets is commonly known as *capital expenditure* or *capex*.

Cash flow after investment in long-term assets is known as *operating free cash flow*. Free cash flow is a pivotal number. In a cash flow statement, free cash flow is the frontier between the firm's operating activities and its financing activities. It is the cash that the firm has generated from trading profitably less the cash used to pay tax and the cash used to build the balance sheet. It is the flow of cash that the firm has generated for its investors, that is available to service the interest and repayments of principal to lenders and to distribute to shareholders.

Some analysts argue that free cash flow should be measured after 'maintenance' or 'replacement' capex, rather than all capex, as a better measure of the cash flow available to managers for discretionary expenditure. *Maintenance capex* is the capex required to maintain the capital stock at its current level. Because long-term assets depreciate, there is still a need for investment to maintain capacity in a no-growth world. So maintenance capex is perhaps best interpreted as maintaining zero growth – the remainder becomes 'growth capex'.

The problem with 'maintenance capex' is that it can require the analyst to make quite arbitrary judgements about what constitutes maintenance of capacity, typically involving some rule of thumb. This becomes especially conjectural when technology is changing. Analysts commonly use accounting depreciation as a proxy for maintenance capex. Working capital does not depreciate, so for consistency the analyst should set working capital investment to zero in a no-growth model. In practice this is often ignored.

Cash flow before financing and change in cash

The final call on a firm's cash flow is the cash needed for servicing the claims of investors: interest paid less interest received, less the tax shelter on this interest, less dividends paid to equity and non-equity shareholders. What remains is *cash flow before financing*. If the firm is in surplus at this stage, this cash flow can be used to repay borrowings or repurchase equity. But if cash flow before financing is negative, the firm may raise additional finance from outside investors by borrowing or by issuing new equity.

If the cash flow after financing is positive, the surplus is stored as cash in the bank or invested in 'cash equivalents'. But if cash flow after financing is negative, this is the amount that will have to be taken from the bank. GAAP requires the company to disclose what is included in cash equivalents and to disclose their policy. Consequently, there are some short-term investments that are classified as cash equivalents by GAAP, while others are classed as 'investments in financial assets'. We include all of these as 'cash', from a financial analysis point of view.

Example: CashCow Co

These are CashCow's financial statements in its fourth year of operation:

Table 1 CashCow's balance sheets (figures in €m)

	Year 3			Year 4
Cash	163			8
Trade receivables	175			256
Inventory	92			107
CURRENT ASSETS	**430**			**371**
PP&E	255			358
LONG-TERM ASSETS	**255**			**358**
TOTAL ASSETS	**685**			**729**
Trade payables	172			93
Taxation	30			41
CURRENT LIABILITIES	**202**			**134**
Loan stock	75			100
LONG-TERM LIABILITIES	**75**			**100**
Paid-in share capital	300			300
Retained earnings at end of Year 3	108	108		
Cash dividends paid		-8		
Earnings after tax Year 4		95		
Retained earnings at end of Year 4		195		195
SHAREHOLDERS' FUNDS	**408**			**495**
TOTAL L&SF	**685**			**729**

CashCow's PP&E note discloses:

	Year 3	Additions	Disposals	Deprec'n	Year 4
Land and buildings – cost	130				130
Accumulated depreciation	-15			-5	-20
Net book value	**115**				**110**
Equipment – cost	146	195	-15		326
Accumulated depreciation	-36		5	-67	-98
Net book value	**110**				**228**
Vehicles – cost	40				40
Accumulated depreciation	-10			-10	-20
Net book value	**30**				**20**
TOTALS	**255**	**195**	**-10**	**-82**	**358**

Table 2 CashCow's income statement for year 4 (figures in €m)

SALES	**703**
Cost of sales	-456
GROSS PROFIT	**247**
SG&A	-105
EBIT	**142**
Interest payable	-6
EARNINGS BEFORE TAX	**136**
Taxation	-41
EARNINGS AFTER TAX	**95**

SG&A includes a loss on disposal of equipment of €7m. This relates to equipment that originally cost €15m, had a net book value of €10m, and was sold for €3m in cash. There was no interest income in the year, and cash interest paid was €6m. Cash tax paid was €30m.

These are the steps in preparing CashCow's cash flow statement:
a Adjust EBIT for non-cash charges to arrive at EBITDA.
   CashCow's non-cash charges are for depreciation, and the loss on disposal of equipment. Depreciation is not shown separately in the income statement, but the balance sheet note discloses that €82m was charged for depreciation. The loss on disposal of equipment on was €7m.
b Adjust cash tax paid by the tax shelter on cash net interest to get cash tax on EBIT. Cash tax paid was €30m. Net interest paid was €6m so, at a tax rate of 30%, the tax shelter was (€6m × 0.3 =) €2m. So cash tax on EBIT was (€30m + €2m =) €32m.
c Calculate the movement in working capital.
   Recall that an increase in working capital represents a use of cash. EBITDA less cash tax paid on EBIT and investment in working capital gives cash from operations.

	Year 3	Change	Year 4
Inventory	92	15	107
Receivables	175	81	256
Payables	-172	79	-93
Net increase		175	

d Deduct net capital expenditure to give operating free cash flow.
Using the balance sheet PP&E note, capex is the cost of additions, €195m, less the cash received on disposal, €3m, (€195m - €3m =) €192m.

e Deduct after-tax cash net interest paid.
Cash net interest paid was €6m and the cash tax shelter on interest calculated in step **b**, was €2m.

f Deduct cash dividends paid to give cash flow before financing.
Cash dividends paid were €8m.

g Record equity and debt financing to give change in cash.
CashCow did not issue any shares, however it increased its loan stock by (€100m - €75m =) €25m. Cash decreased by (€8m - €163m =) -€155m

Table 3 CashCow's cash flow for year 4 (figures in €m)

		€m	Steps
EBIT		**142**	
Depreciation charge	82		
Loss on disposal of equipment	7		
Non-cash charges		89	a
EBITDA		**231**	
Cash tax paid	-30		
Tax shelter on interest	-2		
Cash tax on EBIT		-32	b
Investment in working capital		-175	c
CASH FROM OPERATIONS		**24**	
Capital expenditure		-192	d
OPERATING FREE CASH FLOW		**-168**	
Cash net interest paid	-6		
Tax shelter on interest	2		
After-tax cash net interest paid		-4	e
Cash dividends paid		-8	f
CASH FLOW BEFORE FINANCING		**-180**	
Increase in long-term borrowing		25	g
CHANGE IN CASH		**-155**	

Equity free cash flow

The top half of the formatted cash flow statement describes how the firm generates its operating free cash flow. An alternative format for the bottom half of the statement starts from operating free cash flow then deducts after-tax net interest and contractual or scheduled debt repayments – call these *debt servicing* – to give *equity free cash flow*. So long as the format is consistent and informative, the ordering of the bottom half of the cash flow statement is pretty much a matter of taste.

	Operating free cash flow
	Interest
	Tax shelter on interest
	Scheduled debt repayments
=	**Equity free cash flow**
	Dividends paid
	Equity financing
	Other debt financing flows
=	**Change in cash**

Some people argue for using equity free cash flow on the grounds that interest payments and scheduled debt repayments are contractual, so should be deducted to measure the surplus that is truly 'free' or discretionary surplus. Bankers like to cut the data in this way because equity free cash flow tells them the amount of cash flow available to service further debt. Current practice in valuation tends to be to value the entity as a whole on the basis of projected operating free cash flow, then to deduct debt claims to get to an equity valuation. But analysts who wish to model the value of the equity directly may prefer to focus on equity free cash flow.

One issue in measuring equity free cash flow using published financial data is whether the analyst can actually identify the firm's scheduled repayments of debt in the period. Bank analysts may have this data, but other outsiders will not usually be able to separate out scheduled repayment from other movements in debt. Some analysts just include interest paid and received in debt servicing. At the other extreme, many analysts measure equity free cash flow after *all* debt financing. This is a pragmatic solution, but it no longer catches the idea of a discretionary flow that is available to equity. It reflects a debt financing decision, so it is not, strictly speaking, a measure of free cash flow.

Case: Schindler

Schindler Group was founded in Switzerland in 1874. Their first hydraulic freight elevator was delivered in 1890, followed by the first electric belt-drive model in 1892 and the firm's first electric passenger lift with automatic push-button controls in 1902. Today, the Schindler Group employs around 40,000 people worldwide and is listed on the SWX Swiss Exchange. In addition to lifts of all types it also produces escalators and moving walkways. The group comprises two core businesses: elevators and escalators, which contributed 78% of sales in 2005, and also, a European IT distributor in which Schindler holds a majority stake. We use Schindler Group to provide an example of a formatted cash flow. The steps in formatting its cash flow are described at the end of the chapter.

A review of Schindler's formatted cash flow statement reveals the following. Schindler's net income increased by 22% from 329 in 2004 to 401 in 2005, an increase of 72. The first step in reformatting the cash flow is to trace this back to EBIT. Net interest income, tax and non-cash charges were much the same in 2005 as they were in 2004, hence the underlying increase in Schindler's EBIT of 82, from 510 to 592, is much the same as that in net income. EBITDA was 653 in 2005, as against 654 the year before. Tax consumed 143 of cash in 2005, a small increase from 126 the year before. But working capital investment consumed 142 of cash in 2005, compared to 35 in 2004, leaving cash from operations sharply down at 361. Nonetheless Schindler remained cash-positive. Cash from operations was more than sufficient to fund capex, leaving free cash flow of 182 and cash before financing of 68. The cash outflow for financial debt of 185 reflects primarily a reduction in bank loans.

Table 4 Schindler, formatted cash flow (figures in €m)

	2005	2004	2003
NET INCOME	**401**	**329**	**202**
Interest received per income statement	*-32*	*-25*	*-19*
Interest paid per income statement	*52*	*52*	*66*
Tax paid per income statement	*171*	*154*	*142*
EBIT	**592**	**510**	**391**
Depreciation and amortisation	*117*	*135*	*160*
Provisions and other	*-56*	*9*	*57*
Non cash charges	61	144	217
EBITDA	**653**	**654**	**608**
Cash tax paid	*-143*	*-126*	*-118*
Tax shelter on interest	*-7*	*-9*	*-15*
Tax on operations	-150	-135	-133
Investment in working capital	-142	-35	11
CASH FROM OPERATIONS	**361**	**484**	**486**
Purchase of PP&E, intangibles, other	*-71*	*-100*	*-62*
Investments in associates/subsidiaries/minorities	*-108*	*-45*	*-41*
Investment in long term assets	-179	-145	-103
OPERATING FREE CASH FLOW	**182**	**339**	**383**
Cash interest received	*30*	*25*	*19*
Cash interest paid	*-51*	*-51*	*-65*
Tax shelter on interest	*7*	*9*	*15*
Cash dividends	*-100*	*-87*	*-14*
Servicing of financing	-114	-104	-45
CASH FLOW BEFORE FINANCING	**68**	**235**	**338**
Change of financial debt	*-185*	*-82*	*-71*
Common and preferred issued, repurchased	*-11*	*4*	*-73*
Financing	-196	-78	-144
Foreign exchange translation differences	**35**	**-35**	**5**
CHANGE IN CASH AND FINANCIAL ASSETS	**-93**	**122**	**199**

INTERPRETING THE CASH FLOW STATEMENT

Cash flow is a story, not a number

People often want to be told the 'right' measure of cash flow. They want a single number, like earnings, that can have a multiple applied to it to value the firm, but that is more reliable than earnings. However earnings has a unique status as an economic measure. So long as it is measured comprehensively, earnings measures the increment in shareholders' wealth in balance-sheet terms. The quest for a cash flow magic bullet reflects the common view that, while profit numbers are created by accountants, cash flow numbers are hard, factual and trustworthy. EBITDA has been a popular candidate for this. In fact, cash flow measures are also vulnerable to accounting policy, with EBITDA particularly so.

The goal should be to use a cash flow statement to tell as rich a story as possible about the way a firm generates and uses cash. The cash flow statement contains five or six subtotals. EBITDA is one, and cash from operations is another. But these are not the only numbers we are interested in and they may not be the most important. As with the analysis of profitability we need to understand what *drives* cash flow: the effect of growth on cash flow; the effect of a firm's choice of business model on cash flow; the effect of a firm's accounting policies on cash flow.

The effect of growth on cash flow

Chapter 7 used the 'profitability equation' to discuss the relationship between profit, sales and assets. The profitability equation also helps us understand how growth affects free cash flow.

Example: Omni Stores

Omni is a retailer with a conventional profitability equation; Omni makes profits, but uses assets. To keep things simple, there is no depreciation in Omni's world, tax is paid immediately in cash at a rate of 30%, and the firm is all equity-financed. In year 1 Omni has an EBIT margin of 10% and, since working capital is 20% of sales and PP&E is 30% of sales, Omni has an asset turn of 2. So ROCE is (2 × 10%) 20% and after-tax ROCE is the same as return on equity, which is 14%. Let us assume margin, asset turn, and return on capital stay constant as Omni grows at different rates in year 2, at +10%, and +20%.

Suppose Omni grows by +10% (column 2). Because we are assuming no depreciation, EBITDA equals EBIT, which is 110. With an asset turn of 2, increasing sales by 100 requires an extra 50 of net assets, 20 of working capital and 30 of PP&E, which consumes a large part of Omni's cash flow. Cash from operations is 57 and free cash flow is 27. If growth were 20% (column 3), free cash flow would be negative, -16. 16 is the amount of additional finance that Omni would have to provide in order to fund next year's growth.

Table 5 Omni Stores: different assumptions about growth

	1	2	3	4	5
	Year 1	Year 2	Year 2	*Year 3 ->*	Year 2
Growth rate		10%	20%	*0%*	-10%
Income statement					
Sales	1,000	1,100	1,200	*1,200*	900
EBIT, 10% margin	100	110	120	*120*	90
Tax, at 30%	-30	-33	-36	*-36*	-27
Earnings	70	77	84	*84*	**63**
Balance sheet					
Working capital, 20% of sales	200	220	240	*240*	180
PP&E, 30% of sales	300	330	360	*360*	270
Net assets	500	550	600	*600*	**450**
Cash flow					
EBITDA (=EBIT)		**110**	**120**	*120*	**90**
Cash tax		-33	-36	*-36*	-27
Change in working capital		-20	-40	*0*	20
Cash from operations		**57**	**44**	*84*	**83**
Capex		-30	-60	*0*	30
Operating free cash flow		***27***	***-16***	*84*	***113***

Growth results in negative free cash flow because it requires an additional investment in working capital and in long-term assets that exceed the firm's internally generated cash flow. There is nothing inherently wrong with this and investors should be happy to provide additional finance for profitable growth. The sacrifice of free cash flow associated with reinvesting creates a bigger firm that, assuming it can maintain the same return, will have a larger stream of EBITDA thereafter. For instance, if Omni does not grow at all after its year of 20% growth (column 4), then there will be no need for further investment in working capital or capex, so free cash flow will be 84 in subsequent years.

For simplicity, we assumed Omni's margin and asset turn stayed constant as the business grew. In reality, growth may have to be bought at the price of reduced profit margins; this may be offset by improved asset turn if there are some economies of scale in using assets, and so forth.

The effect of shrinking

Growth consumes cash, but the corollary is that shrinking firms throw off cash. Collapsing sales brings the pleasant side effect (for a while at least) of improving free cash flow as the firm shrinks its working capital and sells off unneeded long-term assets. Column 5 of Table 5 shows the effect on Omni of shrinking by 10% in year 2, instead of growing. EBITDA is 90 compared to the base year of 100, which is 63 (= 90 - 27) after tax. But this is boosted by a release of 50 of assets, in the form of 20 of working capital and 30 of long-term assets, to give free cash flow of 113.

The effect of business model

The choices that firms make about their business model are primarily choices about ownership of assets. As the previous chapter showed, business-model innovation frequently involves outsourcing and unbundling, which may or may not improve the firm's growth rate and return on capital, but usually involves a movement of assets out of the balance sheet and a radical increase in asset turn. To see the effect of a change in business model on cash flow we can revisit Omni.

Assume, now, that Omni is growing at 10% per annum. In year 2, Omni continues with its existing business model, with an EBIT margin of 10% and an asset turn of 2. The year 2 column in Table 6 is the same as column 2 in Table 5. In year 3 Omni implements a new model – it unbundles and sheds assets but gives away some of its margin too. The result is that its ROCE is still 20% but the underlying profitability equation is now EBIT margin 2%, asset turn 10. So in year 3 for example, EBIT is 2% of sales, $(1{,}210 \times 2\% =)$ 24.2. Net assets are 1/10 of sales, $(1{,}210/10 =)$ 121.0. ROCE is $(24.2/121.0 =)$ 20%.

The example contains two important general messages about the impact of the business model on free cash flow:

- **Continuing free cash flow** In general, free cash flow is lower under a high-asset-turn model at zero or low growth rates, *assuming*, as we are doing, that ROCE is unchanged. This is because the loss of EBITDA that results from the reduced EBIT margin is more than the reduced cash investment in working capital and PP&E. Column 4 shows that Omni's free cash flow is 6.5 in year 4 under the new business model compared to 27 in year 2.
- **Transitional free cash flow** The analyst needs to be particularly vigilant for the flattering effects of business-model transition. During the period of transition to a high-asset-turn model, year 3 in Omni's case, free cash flow is flattered by the sell-off of working capital and PP&E. Column 3 shows that in the year it is in transition to a less capital-intensive model, Omni's free cash flow is a spectacular +445.9.

Of course there are many different assumptions we could make about Omni. For clarity, in separating the 'transitional' from the 'continuing' effects on Omni's free cash flow it was essential to assume that Omni's increased asset turn would be exactly offset by reduced margin, so as to be ROCE-neutral. This may be unreasonable. In practice, firms hope to improve their ROCE by shifting to a high-asset-turn model and, at least in the short term, many succeed. If a firm can radically improve its asset turn without an offsetting loss of margin this is win-win in terms of cash flow too. For example, suppose that Omni can increase its asset turn to 10, but manages to maintain its margin at 10%, giving a ROCE of 100%. The reader can confirm that the transitional free cash flow will be 513.7 in year 3, and continuing cash flow will be 81.1 in year 4 compared to 27 in year 2.

Table 6 Omni Stores: changing the business model

	Year 1	Year 2	Year 3	Year 4
Growth rates		10%	10%	10%
Income statement				
Sales	1000	1100	1210	1331
EBIT	100	110	24.2	26.6
Tax at 30%	-30	-33	-7.3	-8.0
Earnings	70	77	16.9	18.6
Balance sheet				
Working capital	200	220	48.4	53.2
PP&E	300	330	72.6	79.9
Net assets	500	550	121.0	133.1
Cash flow				
EBITDA (=EBIT)	**100**	**110**	**24.2**	**26.6**
Cash tax	-30	-33	-7.3	-8.0
Change in working capital		-20	171.6	-4.8
Cash from operations		**57**	**188.5**	**13.8**
Capex		-30	257.4	-7.3
Operating free cash flow		***27***	***445.9***	***6.5***

Case: Apple Computer

Apple Computer is one of the survivors of the personal computer industry. Apple's golden age, financially, was in the late 1980s, when its return on capital was well in excess of 100%. The early 1990s were challenging for all firms in this industry, with intense competition and tumbling prices. Apple's operating performance from 1994 to 2005 is shown below. Apple had made a loss in 1993, but profits recovered in 1994 when it delivered a ROCE of 27% from an EBIT margin of 5.4% and an asset turn of 5.0. Sales that year were (all figures in $m) 11,062, up 20% on 1994. However, Apple's sales would not return to this level until 2005, when they were 13,931. Apple reported losses in three of the next six years, from 1996 to 2001. By 2001 the value of Apple's sales had more than halved, to 5,363.

Table 7 Apple's performance (figures in $m)

	1994	1995	1996	1997	1998	1999	2000	2001	2002	2003	2004	2005
Sales	9,189	11,062	9,833	7,081	5,941	6,134	7,983	5,363	5,742	6,207	8,279	13,931
Sales growth	*15%*	*20%*	*-11%*	*-28%*	*-16%*	*3%*	*30%*	*-33%*	*7%*	*8%*	*33%*	*68%*
ROCE	27%	28%	-62%	-98%	57%	244%	324%	-181%	∞	∞	∞	∞
EBIT margin	5.4%	5.6%	-13.2%	-14.9%	4.9%	9.4%	11.3%	-4.7%	-0.3%	0.5%	3.9%	11.7%
Asset turn	5.0	5.0	4.7	6.5	11.7	25.9	28.6	38.2	∞	∞	∞	∞
PP&E/sales	7%	6%	7%	8%	7%	5%	4%	8%	10%	10%	8%	5%
Investments/sales	0%	0%	0%	0%	0%	3%	7%	9%	1%	0%	0%	0%
Other Fixed sales	2%	2%	3%	4%	5%	4%	3%	4%	2%	2%	2%	2%
Intangibles/sales	0%	0%	0%	0%	0%	0%	0%	1%	2%	2%	1%	1%
Inventory/sales	14%	13%	12%	8%	4%	1%	0%	0%	0%	1%	1%	1%
Receivable/sales	16%	16%	17%	18%	17%	13%	10%	13%	9%	11%	9%	6%
Payable/sales	-9%	-9%	-10%	-10%	-12%	-12%	-12%	-18%	-15%	-17%	-16%	-12%
Other net sales	-10%	-8%	-8%	-12%	-13%	-10%	-9%	-14%	-10%	-10%	-10%	-10%

What happened to cash flow? As we saw earlier, from a cash-flow perspective, shrinking can be good, at least for a while. Compare Apple's cash from operations to its EBITDA from 1996 to 2001. It is higher in all years, as Apple releases cash from working capital. From 1998 to 2001 Apple also reported positive capex – they were selling more fixed assets than they were buying. The high negative capex of -497 in 1997 is rather misleading; Steve Jobs was returning to Apple, and around -400 of this was the cost of buying NeXT, his business. So, during this period of apparent meltdown, with sales tumbling, and with losses in many years, Apple's free cash flow was strongly positive in all years, except for the year of the NeXT purchase.

Chapter 8 Cash flow

Despite Apple's style success with attractive and strikingly designed products, its EBIT margin was a modest -4.7%, -0.3%, 0.5% and 3.7% in the years 2001 to 2004. Moreover, Apple was now growing again, so we might expect this to take its toll on cash flow. However, Apple was shifting its business model to a Dell-style lighter-than-air balance sheet. The principal impact was on working capital. Compare Apple's performance in 1995 and 2004. At the 1995 year end, Apple's inventory was 13% of sales and its receivables 16%, offset by payables of 9%. So working capital was (13% + 16% - 9% =) 20% of sales, which on sales of $11bn meant over $2bn invested in working capital. In 2004, Apple's inventory was 1% of sales, its receivables 9% and its payables -16%. So sales of 8,279 gave negative working capital of (8,279 × (1% + 9% - 16%) = approximately) -$0.5bn. Overall, Apple's asset turn has been infinite in recent years – it has negative net operating assets. Though Apple has been loss-making or only marginally profitable in some years, its cash flow has been strong: first it enjoyed the cash flow benefits of shrinking, then when growth returned it did so with a lighter-than-air balance sheet so that growth consumed no cash.

Table 8 Apple's cash flow

	1994	1995	1996	1997	1998	1999	2000	2001	2002	2003	2004	2005
EBIT	497	622	-1,295	-1,056	291	579	903	-254	-20	31	322	1,632
Depreciation and other	-71	86	343	626	-29	-143	-307	47	161	106	190	230
EBITDA	427	708	-952	-430	262	436	596	-207	141	137	512	1,862
Tax on operations	-42	-168	-29	19	31	1	33	37	28	-25	29	56
Inventories	*418*	*-687*	*1,113*	*225*	*359*	*58*	*-13*	*22*	*-34*	*-11*	*-45*	*-64*
Accounts receivable	*-199*	*-350*	*435*	*469*	*72*	*274*	*-272*	*487*	*-99*	*-201*	*-8*	*-121*
Accounts payable	*139*	*283*	*-374*	*-107*	*34*	*93*	*345*	*-356*	*110*	*243*	*297*	*328*
Adjustments and other	*-11*	*-57*	*319*	*-1*	*-8*	*-116*	*17*	*83*	*-116*	*117*	*-117*	*364*
Investment in working capital	347	-811	1,493	586	457	309	77	236	-139	148	361	507
CASH FROM OPERATIONS	732	-271	512	175	750	746	706	66	30	260	902	2,425
Capex, other long-term assets	-163	-261	-122	-497	47	117	6	71	-208	-86	-160	-281
OPERATING FREE CASH	568	-532	390	-322	797	863	712	137	-178	174	742	2,144
Cash interest received	*43*	*100*	*60*	*82*	*100*	*144*	*210*	*218*	*118*	*69*	*64*	*183*
Cash interest paid	*-34*	*-49*	*-49*	*-61*	*-59*	*-58*	*-10*	*-20*	*-20*	*-20*	*-10*	*0*
Tax shelter on interest	*-3*	*-20*	*-4*	*-8*	*-16*	*-34*	*-80*	*-79*	*-39*	*-20*	*-22*	*-73*
Cash dividends	*-57*	*-58*	*-14*	*0*	*0*	*0*	*0*	*0*	*0*	*0*	*0*	*0*
Servicing of financing	-51	-27	-7	13	25	52	120	119	59	29	32	110
CASH BEFORE FINANCING	517	-559	383	-309	822	915	832	256	-119	203	774	2,254
Borrowing	-234	167	371	-161	-22						-300	
Stock issue, less repurchase	82	86	39	184	41	11	-31	42	105	-27	427	543
Financing	-152	253	410	23	19	11	-31	42	105	27	127	543
CHANGE IN CASH	366	-306	793	-286	841	926	801	298	-14	230	901	2,797

The effect of accounting

There is a view on the street as follows: *'Cash flow measures are reliable because, unlike profit measures, they are not vulnerable to accounting. After all, taking the raw transactional data and pushing it around between periods using judgements about accruals is what accountants do. The cash flow statement simply undoes these accruals.'* A popular version of this view then says, *'Depreciation and amortisation are pretty soft accounting numbers, so let's add them and other long-term accruals back to EBIT to give us EBITDA, a hard number that will measure cash flow.'* Unfortunately, the general view that cash flow is robust to accounting choices is, at best, only partly true. The specific view about EBITDA is wrong.

Chapters 11 to 15 focus on GAAP and on firms' accounting policy choices. These accounting policy choices, when abused, provide the tools for creative accounting. We will sketch some of them here to see just how they affect the cash flow statement.

- **Depreciation and provisions** Long-term accruals such as depreciation and provisions are reversed in the calculation of EBITDA at the top of the cash flow statement, so do not affect EBITDA or any subsequent measures of cash flow.
- **Revaluations** Asset revaluations have no impact on cash flow. Revaluation involves an increase in other comprehensive income in the balance sheet, which bypasses EBIT. Investment in long-term assets excludes the corresponding increase in assets.
- **Revenue recognition** If a firm recognises revenue early this increases EBIT and creates a receivable in the balance sheet (*credit* income, *debit* receivables). So EBITDA is increased, but the effect is reversed at the *cash from operations* stage since the receivable shows up as increased investment in working capital.
- **Capitalising costs** If a firm capitalises costs, this increases EBIT and creates a long-term asset in the balance sheet (*credit* or reduce expenses and thus income, *debit* long-term assets). So EBITDA and cash from operations are both increased by this amount, but the effect is reversed at the free cash flow stage since the asset shows up as capex.

Asset/liability netting is viewed by some people as a business model choice and by other people as creative accounting. Receivables factoring and operating leasing are examples.

- **Factoring** If the firm factors some of its receivables it is effectively selling them for cash (*credit* receivables, *debit* cash). As a result, net investment in working capital is reduced in the year of the sale, flattering cash from operations and free cash flow. If the cash is simply stored in the bank, then the countervailing effect is an increase in the bottom line of the cash flow statement. Typically, though, firms use the proceeds of factoring to pay down debt, so the effect is to reduce apparent borrowing in the period.
- **Operating leasing** If the firm acquires assets under operating leases that it would otherwise have bought with borrowed funds, this has a number of effects. In the balance sheet, where there would have been both an asset and a debt liability, there is neither. So in the cash flow statement, capex and debt financing are correspondingly reduced. In the income statement, instead of an interest charge for the borrowed funds, there is a correspondingly larger lease charge against EBIT, so in the cash flow statement EBIT – and thus EBITDA – is reduced, but interest paid is reduced also.

Accrual accounting gets reversed at different points through the cash flow statement so, in general, cash flow statements get more robust to the effects of accounting policy choices the further down you go. For example, cost capitalisation is reversed in capex, and revenue recognition is reversed in working capital investment. As a result, free cash flow is *relatively* robust to accounting policy. But free cash flow can be radically affected by arrangements such as factoring and operating leasing. The final number in the cash flow statement – change in cash – should be factual. (This is always assuming the accounts are not fraudulent, as was the case with Parmalat!) EBITDA is at the top of the cash flow statement and it is the cash flow measure that is most vulnerable to accounting. Analysts developed an increasing enthusiasm for EBITDA in the late nineties. So flattering EBITDA became an easy option for a firm in financial difficulties such as WorldCom.

Case: WorldCom

WorldCom was formed in 1985 as a discount long-distance telecoms provider called LDDS. It grew by acquisition, and its 1998 merger with MCI Communications was the largest in history at that time. In mid-2002 CEO Bernard Ebbers resigned and the CFO was fired for accounting irregularities, and on 22 July, WorldCom filed for Chapter 11 bankruptcy protection. WorldCom said that $3.2bn in 2001 and $0.9bn in first quarter 2002 of 'line cost' expenses had been misrecorded as capital expenditures. Without these transfers, reported EBITDA would have been reduced to $6.54bn for 2001 and $1.4bn for first quarter 2002, and the company would have reported negative earnings in each period. Six weeks later, the firm discovered another $3.3bn of capitalised line costs and another $0.5bn of non-EBITDA related accounting fraud, bringing the total to $7.2bn.

Case: Parmalat

The Italian dairy products group, Parmalat, was founded in 1961 by Calisto Tanzi and by 2000 had become a global business with operations in thirty countries. Parmalat's failure to repay a $400 bond in December 2003 was puzzling since its balance sheet showed, *inter alia*, €3.95bn in a Cayman Island account with the Bank of America. However, it turned out that this account did not exist, a fact that the auditors had omitted to check. Fortunately such cases of governance failure and audit failure are rare!

FORMATTING PUBLISHED CASH FLOW STATEMENTS

In this final section of the chapter we discuss how to put published cash flow statements into the shape we described earlier, using Schindler as a case. This section is quite advanced, and some readers may prefer to stop at this point.

GAAP: Cash flow formats

Formatted as described earlier, the cash flow statement groups similar sources and uses of cash, and it makes a clear separation between the operating and the financing side of the business around free cash flow. The problem is that GAAP cash flow statements mix some operating and financing elements and do not attempt to identify free cash flow. Both US GAAP and IFRS adopt much the same format, asking firms to report cash flows under three headings:

> Earnings
> Non-cash charges
> Investment in working capital
> **Cash from operations**
>
> Investment in long-term assets (Capex)
> Investment in financial assets
> **Cash from investing activities**
>
> Dividends paid
> Equity financing
> Debt financing
> **Cash from financing activities**

These three elements sum to
> **Change in cash**

GAAP 'cash from operations' and GAAP 'cash from investing activities' contain financing elements. GAAP cash from operations starts from earnings, rather than EBIT; it is earnings before minorities, plus non-cash charges, less investment in working capital. But earnings is EBIT, less net interest paid, less tax. So GAAP cash from operations contains both net interest and the tax shelter on interest. GAAP cash from investing activities contains payments and receipts of cash from buying and selling operating assets, but it also includes the purchase and sale of financial assets[2].

The following three steps are needed to format the GAAP cash flow.

---

2   Actually, the reality is slightly more complex than this. US GAAP requires interest, taxes, and dividends received to be shown in operating, and dividends paid in financing. But IFRS also allows firms to show interest paid and dividends paid in financing, and interest received and dividends received in investing, with their associated tax.

1 Unpack earnings and adjust working capital

GAAP cash flow statements start like this:

	Earnings
+	Non-cash charges
-	(GAAP) Investment in working capital
=	**(GAAP) Cash from operations**

The income statement charges for net interest and tax are already deducted from earnings. Equally the (GAAP) investment in working capital figure is an overall figure that includes all the individual increases and decreases in net assets for working capital, including those that relate to interest and tax. In other words, interest and tax are already *implicitly* dealt with in the GAAP cash flow statement and are recorded 'indirectly'. In the reformatted cash flow statement we want to unpack them and show them *explicitly* and 'directly'.

Firms should disclose cash tax and cash interest as footnotes to their GAAP cash flow statements. The income statement expenses for tax and interest are, of course, disclosed in the income statement or in notes to the income statement.

If we are using cash tax and interest instead of the expense from the income statement we must remove the component of working capital investment, the balance sheet 'accruals', related to tax and interest from (GAAP) investment in working capital. Rearranging the cash flow identity, using tax as the example, we know that

Increase in tax payable = Tax expense - Cash tax payable

The adjustment to (GAAP) investment in working capital is therefore the difference between these two. So:

(Adjusted) Investment in working capital =
(GAAP) Investment in working capital + Increase in tax and interest payable

Although IFRS requires the disclosure of cash interest received, US GAAP does not, and while many firms reporting under US GAAP disclose this anyway, some do not. In this case an acceptable compromise is to proxy cash interest received by income statement interest received – to add the income statement interest receivable number to cash interest payable.

2 Split the cash tax

The next step is to separate the cash tax paid into cash tax on EBIT and the cash tax shelter on interest. This is exactly the same separation we made to calculate EBIAT, except that this time we are working on cash taxes, rather than on the tax expense in the income statement. As outsiders, we have to estimate the split. The reader should revisit Chapter 5, where two methods were described. The classical method is to calculate the tax shelter on interest by applying the statutory corporate tax rate to net interest, then treat the remainder as tax on EBIT. The alternative is to assume the firm's average effective tax rate applies to both elements.

3 Rearrange the data

The final step is to rearrange the data into the desired format. Figure 1 describes these three steps.

Disclosure issues

In principle we could check a particular cash flow number, or indeed reconstruct the whole of the cash flow statement, from the income statement and balance sheet using the 'cash flow equation', as we did with the CashCow example earlier. In practice reconciling a published cash flow statement to the other financial statements is frustrating because firms may not categorise the components of the cash flow in the way we want, or provide enough detail. It is not always clear quite what the elements of a firm's published cash flow contain. So we are always very reliant on the firm's disclosure when we are formatting and analysing cash flow statements. For instance:

– The 'cash net interest paid' number could be checked by adjusting the net interest paid charge in the income statement by the change in the balance sheet payable for interest. But firms do not generally disclose an interest liability separately from 'other payables' in the balance sheet.

– 'Cash tax' looks more promising since firms do separately disclose current and deferred tax liabilities in the balance sheet. However, the current tax payable may include taxes other than corporate tax, such as employee income taxes collected at source.

In practice, the components of a cash flow statement may vary from firm to firm and year on year, and the analyst will encounter items not included in the examples in this chapter. It will be obvious where most should go, but others will require some judgement. The impact of these items will only be significant if they are large, and if we incorrectly include them as elements of operating cash flow when they are truly financing cash flows, or vice versa.

Figure 1 Formatting GAAP cash flow

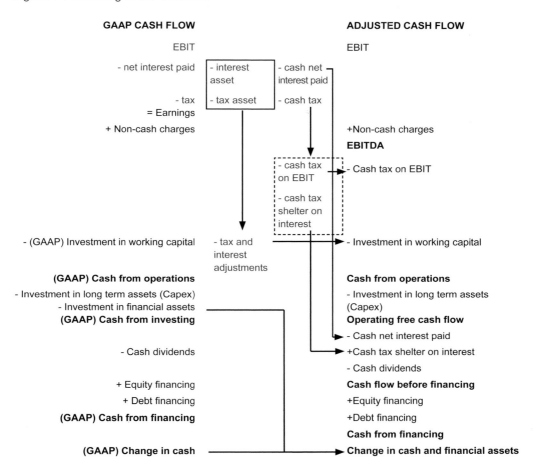

Case: Schindler

The formatted cash flow uses Schindler's published cash flow statement and supplementary cash flow disclosures, plus data from the income statement and notes. We use a consistent sign convention for inflows (+) and outflows (-) of cash that is easy to follow. Unfortunately, published financial statements do not always do this, especially in the supplementary information, so we need to take care. Apart from merely rearranging the data, the following adjustments deserve comment.

- The GAAP starting point is reported net income. We adjust for interest received, 32, and paid, -52, and tax, -171, from the income statement to arrive at EBIT.
- To EBIT we add non-cash charges of 61, comprising depreciation and amortisation, 117, and provisions and other, -56.
- To find 'tax on operations' the analyst adds back to GAAP cash tax paid the calculated tax shelter on net interest. In 2005, cash interest received was 30, and paid, -51. Schindler report that they face an average statutory tax rate of 33%. Using this rate, the tax shelter is ((30 - 51 =) 21 × 33% =) 7.
- Investment in working capital must be adjusted to exclude changes in tax payable and interest receivable and payable, which are now already reflected in the formatted cash flow as a result of moving from an accrual to a cash basis for these items. They are not usually separately disclosed. They were calculated as:

	Interest received	Interest paid	Tax
Per income statement	32	-52	-171
Per cash flow statement	30	-51	-143
Adjustment to working capital	-2	1	28

- Long term assets includes additions of PP&E and investment properties, -98 and -2, disposals of PP&E and investment properties, +47 and +5, and investments in intangibles -23; -71 in total. Investments in associates, subsidiaries, and minority interests are -7, -95, -6; -108 in total.
- Servicing of finance includes cash interest paid/received adjusted for the calculated tax shelter added back to tax on operations above.
- The formatted cash flow statement closes with 'cash and financial assets', which comprise GAAP cash and cash equivalents, but also sales of investments in financial assets deemed not to be cash equivalents under GAAP and hence included in 'cash from investing', 190.

Figure 2 Formatting Schindler's 2005 cash flow

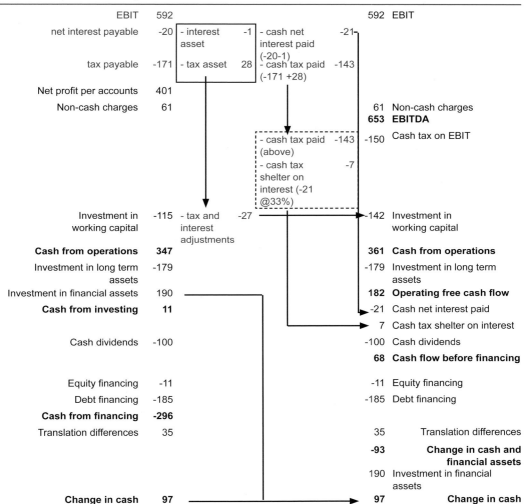

REVIEW

- Since the cash flow is simply a rearrangement of the balance sheet and income statement it might be expected have little additional contribution to financial analysis. In fact, cash flow analysis is a powerful tool in the analyst's kit. Because it uses the actual numbers that underlie the financial ratios, the cash flow statement adds a lot of insight to the analysis of operating performance.

- We should see cash flow as a narrative, rather than a single number or 'magic bullet'. The cash flow statement should group together economically-similar groups and, in particular, separate operating activities from financing activities. GAAP cash flow statements require rather more work to reformat than did the balance sheet and income statement – they are an unhelpful mix of operating and financing elements.

- To interpret cash flow statements successfully, we need to understand the effects on cash flow of growth, of business model choice, and of accounting.

- Growth usually involves the sacrifice of current operating free cash flow to reinvest in the balance sheet. On the other hand, falling sales brings the pleasant, but short-term, side effect of improving free cash flow as the firm shrinks its working capital and sells off unneeded long-term assets.

- Changes in the business model, particularly those involving outsourcing or moving to an 'asset-light' balance sheet, can result in dramatic short-term fluctuations in operating free cash flow.

- Counter to the popular view, the cash flow statement is quite vulnerable to accounting choices. Although change in cash, at the bottom of the statement, is a factual number, EBITDA is particularly vulnerable to accounting manipulation.

Chapter 9

Capital structure

One of the prime goals of financial analysis is to understand how a firm is financed, and to assess whether it is financially weak or strong. This chapter reviews the financial ratios that are commonly used to describe a firm's financial structure. 'Credit analysis' looks at the firm from the perspective of lenders and other creditors and assesses the probability that the firm will default on its liabilities to them. Asset-cover ratios describe the overall structure of the balance sheet from the perspective of the adequacy of the firm's assets to meet its liabilities. Gearing ratios focus on the claims of debt investors and measure the extent to which the firm funds its capital employed using debt. We also see how to calculate the firm's weighted average cost of capital, which is closely related to the gearing calculation.

Borrowing brings a fixed commitment to pay interest, so it has a leverage effect that amplifies the effect of operating leverage. We end the chapter by showing how EBIT is shared between interest, tax and earnings, and how financial leverage affects the level as well as the volatility of earnings and return on equity.

ASSET COVER

We spend most of this chapter on the analysis of financial leverage, that is, the degree to which the firm uses debt to fund its capital employed. But from the perspective of *credit risk*, which is the risk that creditors will not recover their money, the distinction between financing liabilities, that comprise capital employed, and operating liabilities, that reduce net assets, is not important. If the firm defaults and is liquidated, the pecking order for creditors will depend on the nature of the contract between the creditor and the firm, on whether creditors have secured their claim on the firm's assets, and on the provisions of bankruptcy law. All creditors are interested in the sufficiency of the assets available to meet their claims. Traditionally, they have used ratios that describe the nature and quantity of the firm's assets relative to its liabilities to shed light on this.

Equity to total assets

The *equity to total assets* ratio reveals the proportion of the firm's assets that are funded by equity.

$$Equity\ to\ total\ assets\ ratio\ =\ \frac{Equity}{Total\ assets}\ =\ 1 - \frac{Total\ liabilities}{Total\ assets}$$

Equity have the residual claim on the firm's assets; they come at the end of the queue in a liquidation. So the equity to total assets ratio measures the proportion of the assets on the balance sheet that could be lost before creditors' claims would not be met in full.

The relationship between the equity and the total assets of firms is an important one. Most business is conducted by incorporated firms that confer limited liability on their owners. In exchange for this privilege, corporate law has demanded since the early days that the equity capital provided by the owners of a firm be permanent capital that cannot be withdrawn. The aim is to provide a cushion to protect creditors against the carelessness or misfortune of management. Creditors would like this cushion to be as thick as possible. They want the firm to be 'well capitalised', that is, to have a high ratio of equity to assets. Correspondingly, one economic argument predicts that owners will try to reduce the equity capital to a minimum. They will just want to risk as little capital as possible and take a call option on the firm by capturing any upside but dumping any losses on creditors by allowing the firm to default.

In reality the equity cushion in most firms is quite thick. Here is the equity to total assets ratio for a few of the firms we discuss in this book:

Tiffany, 2005	64%
Schindler, 2004	26%
Apple, 2005	65%
Singapore Air, 2005	66%

The industry that plays by entirely different rules is banking. Internationally, many banks have an equity to total assets ratio around 5%. The extremely thin capitalisation of banks compared to other firms is just the consequence of their key economic role in creating credit. Society is telling banks they can leverage each $1 of equity capital to support $20 of loans. But this makes banks extremely risky structures. The bank only needs to lose around 5% of its assets, through loss-making or fraud, before the equity capital is consumed. This is why they have to be so closely regulated[1].

GAAP asks firms to treat preference shares as debt or equity depending on their attributes. Where debt or preference shares have an equity component – for example they are convertible into equity – IFRS requires firms to estimate its value, and detach it and include it in equity.
[Reference: IAS32, FAS150]

Solvency ratios

Another widely used class of balance sheet structure ratios is *solvency ratios* or *liquidity ratios*. These measure the ability of the firm to meet its most immediate liabilities from its liquid assets. The *current ratio* describes the relationship between the current assets of the firm and its current liabilities.

$$Current\ ratio\ =\ \frac{Current\ assets}{Current\ liabilities}$$

The *acid test ratio,* sometimes known as the *quick ratio,* excludes inventory from the numerator. In that it is the first step in the working capital cycle, inventory is the least liquid of the current assets, the furthest away from becoming cash.

$$Acid\ test\ ratio\ =\ \frac{Current\ assets\ less\ inventory}{Current\ liabilities}$$

Interpreting solvency ratios

Solvency ratios are widely used, but they have to be treated with care. It is sometimes asserted that 2 is the desirable level for the current ratio, and 1 for the acid test. But the level of the ratio will depend very much on technology, and the payment culture in the industry or country in question. The trend in the ratio may be more informative – other things equal, a failing firm will display falling solvency ratios. But the reverse does not follow. Falling solvency ratios may simply signal that the company is getting smarter at managing its working capital.

There is a traditional view that a firm should match the term of its financing to the life of its assets, so that its long-term finance should be at least as great as its fixed or long-term assets. This principle is the equivalent of the old banking adage 'never borrow short and lend long'. The idea is that if the firm were financing long-term assets with short-term funds and these were withdrawn, it might not be able to repay without selling off fixed assets and thus dismantling the fixed capital of the firm. But if finance is withdrawn there should be no more reason to consider a loss of fixed assets more significant than a loss of current assets; if a firm is not carrying redundant assets, both are vital.

---

1   In 1988 a committee of banking supervisors of the major developed economies, meeting under the auspices of the Bank of International Settlements (BIS) in Basel, Switzerland, published the Basel Accord. 'Basel I' described a capital adequacy regime for internationally active banks in the G10 countries, though it has been adopted by around 100 other countries. It required banks to maintain at least 4% of 'tier 1' capital, essentially equity, as a proportion of their 'risk' assets, which are their total assets weighted for risk. Basel I is in the process of being replaced by Basel II.

GEARING

The technology of the business the firm is in, and the firm's choice of business model, determine the net assets that it needs to support its operations. Investors fund these net assets by providing capital employed, either as net debt or shareholders' funds, and the firm's fundamental financing decision is whether to use debt or equity to fund its capital employed. The degree to which the firm is debt-financed is described as its *financial leverage*. There are several ways to measure financial leverage.

Book gearing

The most commonly used measure of financial leverage is *book gearing*, which measures the proportion of debt in capital employed in balance sheet terms. This is easy to find once ROCE has been calculated because it uses the same data. Note that the denominator is year-end capital employed – because a gearing ratio compares two balance sheet numbers, there is no need to use average capital employed in the denominator as we do with profitability measures. The gearing ratio goes by many names in practice, including the *leverage ratio* and the *debt ratio*. Also, in connection with measures such as gearing, the word *book* simply means 'using balance sheet data'.

$$Book\ gearing\ =\ \frac{Net\ debt}{Capital\ employed}$$

Book gearing uses 'net debt' in the numerator for consistency with the definition of capital employed. But we can lose information by netting cash against debt, especially when analysing a cash-rich firm. For instance, there is unlikely to be any right of legal set-off between cash and debt. So a useful companion measure of leverage, which uses gross debt rather than net debt, is the *debt to equity ratio*:

$$Debt\ to\ equity\ ratio\ =\ \frac{Debt}{Equity}$$

Hybrid securities

The distinction between debt and equity is not always clear-cut. Preference shares are a commonly encountered security that fall in the middle. They are treated as equity for tax and accounting and they use equity vocabulary – they are called 'shares' and they pay a 'dividend' – but they have debt-like risk properties. The investor receives a fixed rate of dividend, and has priority over equity for dividends and in winding-up. Typically preference shares are of fixed term or are redeemable. By default, in financial analysis, preference shares are treated as debt, but we may be persuaded that preference shares are at the equity end of the spectrum when they have some or all of the following equity-like features:

– They are *non-cumulative*, so that if the firm misses a dividend the dividend is not carried forward as a liability to future periods.
– They are *participating*, so that in addition to the contractual preference dividend the investor gets to share in any profits which are above a certain level.
– They are *irredeemable*, so that they are not repaid early.

Interest cover

Book gearing measures the impact of financial leverage on the balance sheet. We can also measure the impact of leverage in terms of its impact on the income statement. *Interest cover* measures the relationship between EBIT and net interest paid. In other words it measures the degree to which interest is 'covered' by EBIT.

$$Interest\ cover\ =\ \frac{EBIT}{Net\ interest\ payable}$$

Some analysts argue that in an interest-cover ratio, cash flow is a more relevant numerator than EBIT as a measure of ability to pay. In this context cash flow is commonly proxied by EBITDA and cash net interest paid is used in the denominator, so:

$$Cash\ interest\ cover\ =\ \frac{EBITDA}{Cash\ net\ interest\ paid}$$

As always when constructing financial ratios, common sense is the dominant virtue, along with clarity about what the ratio to trying to achieve. Clearly, a firm's ability to pay its interest depends on it finding sufficient cash on the day. This will depend on many factors – how much cash and liquid assets it has in the balance sheet, the willingness of the banks to lend more, the forbearance of other creditors, and so forth. A coverage ratio like interest cover, however measured, will not measure the firm's ability to meet the interest bill on the day. The aim of interest cover is rather different. Interest cover relates what a firm is *earning* to its interest commitments. As a measure of the trend in this relationship through time or for a comparison between firms, EBIT is probably as good as EBITDA. A more direct link between interest cover and financial distress is the role of interest cover in contracting. Loan covenants often specify a minimum interest cover that the firm must maintain, and if that limit is breached, this triggers legal default. Again, in practice, these covenants are as likely to be set in terms of EBIT as EBITDA.

Vulnerability of book gearing to accounting

Because they compare book debt to book equity, book-gearing measures are highly sensitive to balance sheet accounting: to whether the balance sheet is complete in assets and liabilities, and to how the assets and liabilities are valued. The absence of intangibles from the balance sheet, or the use of out-of-date historic costs, reduces equity. The sale of receivables, or operating leasing of long-term assets, reduces debt.

The vulnerability of book gearing to balance-sheet accounting is one reason for the popularity of interest-cover measures. But care is still needed to control for income-statement accounting:

- The analyst is on the lookout for capitalisation of interest. Whether or not interest was appropriately capitalised, capitalised interest should be added back in the interest cover calculation, since the interest still had to be paid, however it was subsequently accounted.

- The use of discounted, or zero-coupon, debt would potentially understate the interest payable figure. However GAAP now requires firms to smooth lumpy debt-service costs by amortising any issue discount or premium.
- If the firm has preference shares that are being treated as debt for the gearing calculation, preference dividends should correspondingly be included with interest paid in calculating interest cover.

Market gearing

Book gearing measures the relative claims of lenders and shareholders in balance-sheet terms. For some purposes, for example when calculating the firm's weighted average cost of capital, the analyst needs to measure the relative claims of lenders and of equity investors on the *value* of the firm, rather than in book terms. In this case the gearing ratio is reworked using the market values of debt and of equity instead of book figures to give *market gearing*. Capital employed measured using market values is known as 'enterprise value'. *Enterprise value* is the value of equity and non-equity shareholders' funds plus the value of net debt.

$$Market\ gearing\ =\ \frac{Value\ of\ net\ debt}{Enterprise\ value}$$

For a quoted firm, the value of equity is the market capitalisation, found by multiplying the number of shares in issue by the current share price. If the firm is unlisted, the value of equity needs to be estimated.

In the absence of a disclosure by the firm, the current value of debt can be found by capitalising interest paid at the current interest rate. In symbols, if c is the 'coupon' on the debt, that is, the amount of interest the firm is committed to pay, and r_d is the interest rate, then the value[2], v, of the debt, $v = c/r_d$

Example: Markus

Markus issued a $10m long-term bond with a coupon of $1m per annum when interest rates were 10%. Interest rates in the market have subsequently fallen to 5%. Markus is still committed to pay $1m in interest, so the bond is now worth $20m, which is what people are willing to pay for the right to receive $1m per annum when interest rates are 5%. $c = $1m$, and $r_d = 5\%$ so $v = $1m/0.05 = $20m$.

GAAP: Disclosure of market value of debt

GAAP now requires firms to report, in a footnote, the market value of their debt and financial assets, and state whether this is significantly different from book. Prior to this disclosure being available, because relatively few firms have market-traded debt, the analyst traditionally had to value the firm's debt to get enterprise value and, in practice, many analysts simply used book debt to proxy the value of debt.
[References: IAS 32, 39, FAS 107]

---

2   We are simplifying rather. This is the value of a perpetuity; in this case, of a bond with a long time to run. As debt approaches maturity, its value will be increasingly influenced by the terms of its redemption.

Case: Tiffany's capital structure

The work we did in Chapter 3 gives us the data we need to find its book gearing. We had already calculated its capital employed, as shown below. Tiffany's net debt in the year to 31 January 2005 was 113.7 (in $m) and its capital employed 1,814.8, so its book gearing was 6.3%.

Table 1 Tiffany's capital employed (figures in $m)

	2003	2004	2005
SHAREHOLDERS' FUNDS	**1,208.0**	**1,468.2**	**1,701.2**
Debt (current and long-term)	349.7	486.9	440.6
Less cash	156.2	276.1	326.9
Net debt	**193.5**	**210.7**	**113.7**
Capital employed	**1,401.5**	**1,678.9**	**1,814.8**
Book gearing	**13.8%**	**12.6%**	**6.3%**

To find market gearing we need to rework the data using values, where appropriate, instead of book amounts. For instance, Tiffany's share price at its 2005 financial year end was $31.4 and it had 144.548m shares in issue, so its market capitalisation was $4,543.1m. In a footnote it discloses that the value of its debt is 472.0 compared to book of 440.6. We deduct cash to get net debt, and it is possible that this may also need revaluing because under GAAP, cash includes marketable securities, and for financial analysis we also include other short-term investments. Tiffany's 'cash' does include marketable securities but these are already at market value in the balance sheet, so no adjustment is needed. Hence, net debt is (472.0 - 326.9 =) 145.2, and enterprise value is (4,543.1 + 145.2 =) 4,688.3. Tiffany's gearing is negligible: 6.3% in book terms and 3.1% in market value terms.

Table 2 Tiffany's gearing (figures in $m)

	2003	2004	2005
MARKET CAPITALISATION	**3,368.1**	**5,816.6**	**4,543.1**
Value of debt	371.0	520.8	472.0
Less cash	156.2	276.1	326.9
Value of net debt	**214.8**	**244.7**	**145.1**
Enterprise value	**3,582.9**	**6,061.3**	**4,688.3**
Market gearing	**6.0%**	**4.0%**	**3.1%**

Its capital employed was 1,814.8 at the year end and 1,678.9 a year earlier, so its average capital employed during 2005 was 1,746.9. Therefore Tiffany's ROCE is 494.2/1,746.9 = 28.3%. In 2004, Tiffany's EBIT was 357.6. Its capital employed was 1,678.9 at the end of 2004 and 1,401.5 a year earlier, so its average capital employed during 2004 was 1,540.2. So Tiffany's ROCE is 357.6/1,540.2 = 23.2%.

THE WEIGHTED AVERAGE COST OF CAPITAL

The firm's cost of capital is the link between the firm's financing and its investment decisions. It provides the benchmark for the return the firm is generating on its existing assets, and the discount rate for valuing future investments and for valuing the firm as a whole.

Once the firm has chosen the mix of debt and equity capital in its capital employed, the cost to the firm of using $1 of capital employed is simply the average of the cost of debt capital and the cost of equity capital, blended in the proportions described by the market gearing ratio. This is called the *weighted average cost of capital,* or *WACC.* If r_e is the cost of equity capital, g is the market gearing ratio, and T is the corporate tax rate:

$$WACC = r_d(1 - T) \times g + r_e \times (1 - g)$$

Market gearing rather than book gearing is used as weights for the cost of debt and cost of equity in the WACC. This is because the cost of capital is an opportunity cost – we want to know what it would cost to finance the firm today, maintaining today's capital structure and using today's costs of capital. It may be that the firm has not yet reached its target capital structure, in which case the logic of opportunity cost would dictate using target rather than actual gearing. However, the outsider is rarely in a position to make that judgement, so actual market gearing is almost always used.

Investors have the opportunity to invest in government securities at no risk. The purest riskless interest rate is the government bill rate, that is, the short-term rate. In practice, analysts commonly use a longer-term rate such as the yield on ten-year Treasuries or longer-dated Treasuries. The argument is that a longer-term bond embodies current expectations about the short-term rates that will prevail over the investment horizon.

When they invest in a firm by lending to it or by becoming shareholders investors, require a risk premium over the riskless interest rate to compensate them for the risk. Lenders assess this by assigning a credit score to a firm, or to a particular bond or tranche of borrowing by the firm. So the interest rate that the firm pays on its debt finance, r_d, will be the riskless interest rate, call this r_i, plus a *credit spread* reflecting the firm's probability of default. So for a particular firm,

$$r_d = r_i + credit\ spread$$

Listed firms now frequently disclose their marginal cost of borrowing, but this is straightforward to approximate as the firm's current interest payments divided by the *value* of its debt. The result can be sense-checked in terms of the firm's credit rating if one is publicly available, or by comparing the firm to similar firms that do have a rating.

The WACC formula describes a simple 'classical' tax system in which interest payments can be deducted for tax at the corporation tax rate, T, but where, by contrast, equity does not get a tax shelter. In some countries the tax authorities have sought to counter this extreme classical bias toward debt by giving a tax break to equity. They do this in various ways. For instance, 'imputation' tax systems allow dividend payments to generate a tax credit that either the firm or its shareholders can offset against their tax bills. Alternatively, a different rate of corporation tax may be set for retained and distributed earnings. So the WACC formula might need to be adjusted for local conditions.

The cost of debt is contractual and observable, but finding the cost of equity is not so easy. The equity risk premium has to be estimated, and its appropriate measurement has generated an enormous literature in financial economics. The debate is out of scope for this book, but the Exhibit *The equity premium* gives a flavour of the issues and some suggestions for further reading.

The formula that is very widely used to find the cost of equity capital is the *capital asset pricing model* or *CAPM* formula, which says that a firm's equity risk premium is simply the average equity risk premium for the market as a whole, scaled by the firm's 'beta', β, to give an equity risk premium appropriate to the firm. The equity risk premium for the market as a whole is the difference between the expected return on the market, r_m, and the riskless interest rate. So,

$$r_e = r_i + \beta \, (r_m - r_f)$$

Case: Tiffany's cost of capital

To find Tiffany's WACC, we need to estimate its cost of debt and cost of equity capital. The US 30-year government bond rate in early 2005 was 4.22%. We will simply assume Tiffany pays 1% over this on net borrowing, giving a pretax cost of debt of 5.22%. Interest is tax deductible at, we assume, a statutory tax rate of 35%. So the after-tax cost of debt is (5.22 × (1 -.35) =) 3.38%. Tiffany's equity beta is apparently 1.4. Assuming an equity risk premium of 4.0% over bonds, Tiffany's cost of equity capital would be (4.22 + 1.4 × 4.0 =) 9.82%. Tiffany's market gearing was 3.1% in 2005 and 4.0% in 2004; it had very little debt. So we calculate Tiffany's WACC in 2005 to be (3.38% × 3.1% + 9.82% × (1 - 3.1%) =) 9.6%. It was similar in 2004.

Credit scores

The premium over the riskless rate that a firm pays on its debt finance is a function of its *credit rating*. Credit rating agencies such as Standard & Poor's and Moody's classify firms in terms of their probability of default, based on financial indicators and on the judgement of their credit analysts. Firms are not automatically rated; they pay a fee to receive a credit rating, just as a fee must be paid to list shares on a stock exchange.

The credit rating agencies allocate firms to classes. In the S&P framework, AAA and AA indicate 'very high quality' and A and BBB, high quality. The equivalent Moody's ratings are Aaa and Aa, and A and Baa. Firms or bonds with ratings of at least BBB or Baa are known as *investment-grade*. Many investment funds are restricted by their statutes to invest only in 'investment grade' securities. Debt that is BB and B (Moody's Ba and B) is viewed as vulnerable to economic conditions or as 'speculative'. CCC (Caa) means 'currently vulnerable to default', and D (C) means that the firm is currently in default.

S&P report that, globally over the 25 years to January 2005, 0.44% of AAA firms defaulted during the 10 years after rating, while for the lowest investment grade (BBB) firms this figure was 5.82%. However for BB, B, and CCC firms the 10 year probabilities of default were 18.29%, 32.38% and 53.05%. So at one extreme, AAA firms have negligible default risk, while CCC firms have a high probability of default.

These probabilities of default translate into the debt risk premium or credit spread. A study by Caouette and others[3] provides some data on this. In 1997, AAA-rated US firms were paying a credit spread of just 1/4% over the 30-year US Treasury bond rate; firms rated A, just over 1/2%, and BBB firms, 0.83%. So investment-grade firms paid less than a 1% premium on their debt, over the riskless bond rate. B-rated firms paid a 3.3% spread, and CCC, a 7.3% spread.

THE EFFECT OF FINANCIAL LEVERAGE

In the last chapter we called the proportion of a firm's operating costs that were fixed its 'operating leverage', and we saw how operating leverage affects the volatility of EBIT. Debt finance brings a commitment to pay interest that is fixed in the sense that it does not vary with EBIT. So using debt in capital employed also has a leverage effect, and this amplifies the volatility of EBIT.

Example: André and Bharat

Recall André and Bharat from Chapter 7. André has sales of 1000 and costs of 920 giving him an EBIT of 80. His costs are all variable, so when sales fall or rise by 10%, EBIT falls or rises 10% too. Suppose now that André is also committed to pay 27 of interest a year, which is initially covered a reasonable (80/27 = approx.) 3.0 times by EBIT. Though André's operating costs are variable, his interest commitments are fixed, so when sales and EBIT fall or rise by 10%, earnings fall or rise by approximately 15%. This is the effect of financial leverage.

Financial leverage compounds the effect of operating leverage. Bharat's costs are semi-fixed because he has 400 of fixed cost, so a 10% drop or increase in sales translates into a 60% change in EBIT for him. But if Bharat also has 27 of interest payments, a 10% change in sales causes his interest cover to swing between 1.2 and 4.7, and his earnings to change by 91%.

---

3   John Caouette, Edward Altman, Paul Narayanan, *Managing Credit Risk: The Next Great Financial Challenge*, Wiley, New York, 1998

Exhibit: The equity premium

Shareholders own the firm, and they bought its shares in hope and expectation, but they have no legal entitlement to receive any particular return, or indeed, to receive a dividend. In contrast to debt finance, there is no piece of paper in the CFO's desk promising a particular return to equity investors, so finding the cost of equity capital requires 'opportunity cost' thinking. The question is, what return will equity investors be able to get elsewhere, on investments of similar risk, in the future? This is what they are foregoing by investing in the firm, and to protect their wealth the firm should treat this as the minimum return it will earn on its own activities.

The landmark economic theory was the 'capital asset pricing model', the CAPM, that was developed in the early 1960s, particularly in the work of Harry Markowitz, William Sharpe and John Lintner, two of whom became Nobel laureates. The beauty of the CAPM is its extraordinary simplicity. It says that the required return on any asset is a determined by just one factor, and that factor is measured by a simple linear coefficient called the asset's 'beta', β. The CAPM says that for any individual asset, the risk premium, which is the excess of an asset's return over the riskless interest rate, is simply a proportion β of the risk premium on the portfolio of all assets. In the case of a shares in a firm, the portfolio of all assets is usually measured by the stock market index. The firm's 'equity' β reflects the covariance between the return on the share and the return on the market.

The return to a share in a firm will be subject to specific risks associated with the business the firm is in, and enhanced by its operating and financial leverage. Equally, each individual investor has different risk preferences and a different appetite for risk. But in the CAPM world, none of this matters. The source of this simplicity is the idea of the fully-diversified investor. Rational, risk averse investors will have immunised themselves against the specific risk of individual assets by holding a diversified portfolio. The only risk that cannot be diversified away is the risk that all assets have in common, as they rise or fall, albeit to different degrees, with the market as a whole. This risk is what β measures. In the CAPM, this single risk factor is all investors care about, and thus price into their required return.

Some economists have argued that the single-factor CAPM is too simplistic and that there may be multiple risk factors that are priced by the market; some perhaps more important than β. Richard Brealey and Stewart Myers, *Principles of Corporate Finance*, 7th Edition, McGraw-Hill, 2003. provide a good review of this debate. Though people argue about its merits, the CAPM remains a widely used piece of theory, due, in large part to its great simplicity. All it requires is estimates of β, which are widely available for listed firms from providers such as Bloomberg, and a view about the market risk premium.

Researchers have taken two approaches to figuring out the market risk premium. One approach is to *induce* it by taking the population of quoted firms and, by relating consensus forecasts of their earnings to their share prices today, backing out the implied discount rate. Some large investment banks and fund managers do this on a daily basis. The alternative is to observe what premium equity investors have actually received over long recorded history, then use this as a guide to the future. The most extensive and thorough work in this area is by Elroy Dimson, Paul Marsh and Mike Staunton, who have collected stock returns for 17 markets, back to the year 1900. (See their, *Triumph of the Optimists: 101 Years of Global Investment Returns*, Princeton University Press, 2002. This data is updated annually in the *Global Investment Returns Yearbook*, published by ABN Amro.) They find that, globally, equities returned on average 4.7% per annum more than treasury bills and 4.0% more than long-dated government bonds measured as the geometric mean return in each case. These are historic returns, averaged over a period in which investors' ability to diversify and reduce equity risk has continuously improved. On this basis, looking forward, they argue for using a risk premium of 3.0% relative to bills on a geometric mean basis and 5.0% on an arithmetic mean basis.

Table 3 The effect of financial leverage

	André (variable)			Bharat (semi-fixed)		
Sales	**1,000**	**900**	**1,100**	**1,000**	**900**	**1,100**
Variable	920	828	1,012	520	468	572
Fixed	0	0	0	400	400	400
Costs, total	-920	-828	-1012	-920	-868	-972
EBIT	**80**	**72**	**88**	**80**	**32**	**128**
Interest	-27	-27	-27	-27	-27	-27
Earnings	**53**	**45**	**61**	**53**	**5**	**101**
Interest cover	3.0	2.7	3.3	3.0	1.2	4.7
% change in sales		-10%	+10%		-10%	+10%
% change in EBIT		-10%	+10%		-60%	+60%
% change in earnings		-15%	+15%		-91%	+91%

The effect of tax

The André and Bharat example ignored taxes. But in reality the tax authorities also have a claim on EBIT; a firm will have to pay tax on its EBIT but will save tax on its interest. While interest is fixed relative to EBIT, tax is in principle proportionate to EBIT and to interest, the proportion being the tax rate. We say 'in principle' because there are all sorts of asymmetries and non-linearities in taxation in practice, but the underlying principle is proportionality. So tax works like a purely variable cost. Table 4 takes Bharat and assumes he pays tax at 30%. The tax system does *not* increase the volatility to EBIT and to earnings that is caused by shocks to sales and that is amplified by leverage.

Table 4 The effect of tax and financial leverage

	Bharat taxed			Bharat untaxed		
Sales	**1,000**	**900**	**1,100**	**1,000**	**900**	**1,100**
EBIT	**80**	**32**	**128**	**80**	**32**	**128**
Tax on EBIT @ 30%	-24	-9.6	-38.4			
EBIAT	**56**	**22.4**	**89.6**	**80**	**32**	**128**
Interest	-27	-27	-27	-27	-27	-27
Tax shelter @ 30%	8.1	8.1	8.1			
Earnings	**37.1**	**3.5**	**70.7**	**53**	**5**	**101**
% change in sales		-10%	+10%		-10%	+10%
% change in EBIAT		-60%	+60%		-60%	+60%
% change in earnings		-91%	+91%		-91%	+91%

The drivers of return on equity

There are three principal claimants on EBIT: the tax authorities, and the two investor groups, debt and equity. To see how a given return on capital employed translates into return on equity, it is going to be most efficient to continue using symbols. Suppose a firm has D of (net) debt and E of equity, so its capital employed is D + E. EBIT is the stream of income that the firm generates by using its capital employed. The tax rate is T% so tax takes the proportion T of EBIT. Interest payments, which are the firm's debt, D, times its cost of debt, r_d, are also reduced by tax. Equity take what is left, as earnings. So:

$$Return\ on\ equity = After\text{-}tax\ ROCE + (D/E)\ (After\text{-}tax\ ROCE - r_d(1 - T))$$

This formula (see the Annex to the chapter for a derivation) explains the relationship between return on capital employed and return on equity. If the firm has no debt (D = 0) the return on equity is the after-tax ROCE. But if the firm can borrow at an after-tax cost of debt that is below the after-tax ROCE, this boosts return on equity and the higher the debt to equity ratio, D/E, the greater the uplift. Of course the reverse applies. If ROCE is below the cost of debt, gearing depresses the return on equity even further.

The love-hate relationship with debt

There is an ambivalence towards debt finance in the psyche of many firms – borrowing is nice to have, but they would rather not appear to have any. One reason debt is nice is its favourable tax treatment. In most tax systems there is an apparently large subsidy from the tax authorities on borrowing compared to equity finance, because interest is tax deductable but dividends are not or, at least, not to the same extent. But you would rather not appear to be borrowing because, while financial leverage usually increases the return on equity, it also increases the volatility of earnings. This increases the likelihood of breaching debt covenants based on interest cover that, in turn, may lead to bankruptcy. There may also be a more primitive emotion at work: a traditional moralistic view that equity financing is virtuous, and individuals, and firms only borrow because they have to.

As a result, firms have always been keen to present their financial statements in a way that de-emphasises debt, or debt-like finance. Firms would sometimes use hybrids like preference shares, or convertible bonds with a high probability of conversion, in the hope that analysts would class them as equity when calculating gearing ratios, and in order to reduce the interest charge in the income statement. They might issue deeply discounted bonds with a low or zero coupon in order to reduce apparent interest payments. GAAP has been successful in policing these mechanisms in recent years. The off-balance sheet financing arrangements – operating leasing, factoring, and unconsolidated subsidiaries – also conceal debt and permit firms to get the benefits of debt without appearing to borrow. GAAP is still struggling to police some of these arrangements.

If the firm is hoping that arrangements like operating leasing will reduce earnings volatility, this is illusory. The effect is simply to record an operating cost instead of a financing charge; in other words to swap higher financial leverage for higher operating leverage. Using available mechanisms to borrow without appearing to borrow is one thing. The challenge is for GAAP to police these mechanisms, and for readers of financial statements to be alert to them. But it is another thing if the firm actually starts to believe debt is bad. Then shareholders miss out on the tax benefits of borrowing and the risk is increased of a, possibly hostile, leveraged buy-out, exploiting the firm's unused debt capacity.

REVIEW

- In this chapter we analysed the firm's financial structure, and the relationship between debt and equity finance.

- The first issue is what proportion of the firm's assets are financed by equity. Creditors want a thick equity cushion, but owners want to reduce the proportion of equity capital. The equity to total assets ratio measures this cushion in broad terms. Solvency ratios – the current ratio and the acid test ratio – try to examine more closely the firm's ability to meet its liabilities from liquid assets.

- Gearing ratios, such as book gearing and the debt to equity ratio, examine the impact of financial leverage, which is the degree to which the firm funds its capital employed using debt finance.

- Book gearing can be vulnerable to balance sheet accounting. By contrast, interest cover looks at the impact of financial leverage on the income statement. Interest cover can also be vulnerable to accounting, for example to the capitalisation of interest and to the treatment of preference dividends

- Market gearing is a re-working of book gearing measures, using values rather than book measures. It provides the weights for the calculation of the firm's weighted average cost of capital that measures the blended cost of the firm's debt and equity capital.

- There are three principal claimants on EBIT: the tax authorities, and debt and equity finance. Interest is a fixed cost in that it does not vary with EBIT, while tax is, in principle, proportionate. Therefore, financial leverage compounds the effect of operating leverage, in increasing the volatility of earnings.

- Though tax systems favour debt, the effect of leverage on the volatility of earnings may be one reason firms are wary of debt finance. This makes off-balance sheet financing look attractive to firms, enabling them to enjoy the tax benefits of debt while not appearing to be borrowing. But, in terms of volatility, these benefits are illusory.

ANNEX Derivation of the return on equity expression

Earnings = EBIT (1 - T) - D r_d (1 - T)

A little rearranging of this expression gives

Earnings = EBIT (1 - T) - D r_d (1 - T) = EBIAT - D r_d (1 - T)

After-tax ROCE = EBIAT/(D + E)

so, EBIAT = (D + E) after-tax ROCE

Substitute this into the first equation, to give

Earnings = (D + E) after-tax ROCE - D r_d (1 - T)

Divide both sides by E:

Earnings/E = (D + E/E) after-tax ROCE - (D/E) r_d (1 - T)

Note that *Earnings/E* is return on equity.

Also, rearranging the right-hand side, gives

Return on equity = After-tax ROCE + (D/E) (After-tax ROCE - r_d(1 - T))

Chapter 10

Growth

Value creation is a function of growth and return. So we want to understand how the firm earns its return on capital and how it grows. It is easy enough to measure the firm's overall sales growth, year on year, and GAAP also requires firms to report sales growth at the segment level. The challenge when analysing growth is to get the necessary data to go any deeper than this. One important concern is to separate the firm's organic growth from the growth that is due to acquisitions. Another is to understand the extent to which growth came from volume or from price, or was merely inflationary. GAAP does not currently require disclosure on these issues, and we depend on voluntary disclosure by firms.

THE ANALYSIS OF GROWTH

Growth is key to value creation, and the analyst needs to understand as much as possible about the source and nature of a firm's growth[1]. Depending on the context, capital employed, total assets or number of employees can be the appropriate measure of size, but for most purposes we use sales as the indicator of the size of a firm, and sales growth as a measure of its overall growth. The 'headline' growth rate, which is the growth in reported sales, is easy to measure. The average sales growth rate over a number of periods is calculated as the compound growth rate, or 'geometric mean', g, where n is the number of observations:

$$Sales\ in\ the\ final\ period = Sales\ in\ the\ beginning\ period \times (1 + g)^{\,n-1}$$

Case: CTC Ltd

CTC (Cyprus Trading Corporation) is Cyprus's largest trading company. It imports, distributes and retails a wide range of goods, from consumer goods and tobacco to machinery and building products. These are its sales from 1997 to 2004.

Table 1 CTC Ltd's sales (figures in cy£m)

	1997	1998	1999	2000	2001	2002	2003	2004
Sales	**55.7**	**63.9**	**71.5**	**84.0**	**100.0**	**109.3**	**115.0**	**122.9**
Year-on-year growth		11.9%	17.5%	19.2%	9.3%	5.2%	6.9%	12.1%

There are eight sales numbers, so seven annual growth rates. The simple arithmetic mean of these rates is 12.1%. CTC's compound growth rate is similar. It is (122.9/55.7) ^ (1/7), which is 12.0%.

Once we have calculated the firm's overall rate of growth we need to analyse it. First we want to see where the growth is coming from, in terms of activities and markets, so we need to calculate growth at the segment level. Then we want to understand the nature of that growth and what is driving it; whether it is volume or price-driven, or merely inflationary, and whether it is organic or acquired growth.

GAAP: Growth disclosures

GAAP has significantly improved segment disclosure in recent years and, while we would always like more, the segment disclosure of sales data by firms that comply with GAAP can now be deemed satisfactory. But, otherwise, there is no direct requirement in GAAP for firms to disclose key data on the nature of sales growth, namely the organic/acquired split, price and volume components, and the inflation context and particularly overseas inflation.

Disclosure on the nature of growth is currently voluntary and is made principally by larger firms. Many large firms do disclose an organic growth measure, but few firms explain volume/price relationships or guide users to understand the impact of inflation.

---

1   I am grateful to Martin Deboo for his collaboration in writing this chapter.

Smaller firms typically will not disclose any of this. The case describes the growth data provided by Unilever and Procter & Gamble, who are two of the best disclosers of the components of growth. Even when there is disclosure, its interpretation requires care. When disclosure is voluntary it might be inconsistent between firms and it may not, in any case, give us what we want. In this chapter we focus on two broad sets of issues: identifying volume, price and inflation effects, and separating organic and acquisition growth.

ORGANIC GROWTH

'Organic' growth is a widely used concept in the discussion of financial performance. As a working definition, we will define *organic growth* as the growth that arises naturally from existing activities and, perhaps, from using existing capacity. People have strong views about organic growth. There is a common view that strong organic growth signals health and is likely to be valuable. The contrast is 'acquisition' growth, which comes from buying other businesses. The story goes that while acquisition growth may be quick and easy to achieve, it is much less likely to be valuable because you are likely to pay a full price for those businesses, and frequently will overpay. Studies of acquisitions suggest that they destroy shareholder value for the acquirer in most cases, either because the hoped for synergies do not emerge, or because the acquirer overpays.

Firms that do report an organic growth number find it by elimination: they exclude from reported, 'headline' sales the sales of businesses acquired and divested during the year. But the measure that results from this covers a wide range of possibilities, some of which do not align with the idea of organic growth as growth from existing capacity, or even from existing activities. Organic growth is an elusive concept and is quite hard to operationalise. The retail industry is a good example.

Cases: Unilever and Procter & Gamble, best practice in disclosure
Unilever and Procter & Gamble are two of the world's leading consumer goods firms. Their disclosure about the drivers of their sales growth goes well beyond what GAAP requires.

Unilever discloses its organic growth performance at both region and product category level in its quarterly earnings releases. This style of presentation is clear and typical of good practice in the consumer goods sector. The example shows product category data, but Unilever also repeats this presentation at the geographic region level.

Unilever 2005

Table 2 Extract from 2005 fourth quarter earnings release; continuing operations, full year (figures in €m)

	Savoury and dressings	Spreads and cooking products	Beverages	Ice cream and frozen foods	Foods total	Personal care	Home care and other	Home and personal care total	Group total
Turnover:									
2004	8,172	4,494	3,012	6,286	21,964	9,780	6,822	16,602	38,566
2005	8,369	4,364	3,054	6,373	22,160	10,485	7,027	17,512	39,672
Change	2.4%	-2.9%	1.4%	1.4%	0.9%	7.2%	3.0%	5.5%	2.9%
Impact of:									
Exchange rates	1.6%	1.1%	1.3%	0.7%	1.2%	1.3%	1.8%	1.5%	1.3%
Acquisitions	0.0%	0.0%	0.1%	0.4%	0.1%	0.0%	0.0%	0.0%	0.1%
Disposals	-2.1%	-4.6%	-1.1%	-1.4%	-2.3%	-0.5%	-1.2%	-0.8%	-1.6%
Underlying sales growth	**2.9%**	**0.7%**	**1.1%**	**1.7%**	**1.9%**	**6.3%**	**2.4%**	**4.7%**	**3.1%**

Procter & Gamble go a step further than Unilever and decompose organic or underlying sales growth into its component elements of unit price growth, mix growth and volume growth. 'Mix growth' refers to changes in the sales mix in terms of products with higher or lower unit prices.

Procter & Gamble 2005

Table 3 Extract from 2005 fourth quarter earnings release, net sales information, percentage change versus year ago

	Volume with acquisitions/ divestitures	Volume without acquisitions/ divestitures	FX	Price	Mix/Other	Total impact	Total impact ex. FX
P&G beauty	**12%**	**8%**	**3%**	**0%**	**-1%**	**14%**	**11%**
P&G family health							
Health care	10%	8%	2%	1%	-2%	11%	9%
Baby and family care	7%	7%	3%	1%	0%	11%	8%
P&G household care							
Fabric and home care	9%	7%	2%	0%	-1%	10%	8%
Snacks and coffee	3%	3%	2%	4%	-1%	8%	6%
Total company	**8%**	**8%**	**2%**	**1%**	**-1%**	**10%**	**8%**

P&G qualify this data by noting 'these sales percentage changes are approximations based on quantitative formulas that are consistently applied.' Perhaps because of this, P&G do not consider it meaningful to quote these numbers beyond whole percentage points.

Like-for-like growth in retail

Organic growth has a natural interpretation in the retail industry as the growth in sales achieved through a firm's existing stores. Retailers call this *like-for-like* (LFL) growth. LFL sales are relatively easy to define: consistently available space is easy to isolate and measure year on year, store locations and formats tend to evolve only slowly, and most firms are national operations or multinationals operating in a relatively small and slowly changing number of countries. The most rigorous definition of LFL sales growth uses a retail outlet as the unit, and a consistent square-metreage of space in that unit.

However, LFL growth based on operating units may well involve incremental investment. There may be investment in physical capacity, in enhancing and expanding the capacity of existing stores. Some retailers might see knocking through into the building next door as an 'existing store' operation. Even if physical capacity is untouched, there may be investment in intangibles such as brand and IT to drive growth. On the other hand, retailers may enlarge the number of outlets by leasing them, in which case there may be no incremental investment in physical capacity. If the retailer does invest, it may buy empty buildings, or it may buy existing operational outlets that already have sales. The extent of the subsequent investment in tangible and intangible assets will depend on just how much repositioning is required, though if the acquisition is of a successful business in a new area, not even rebranding may be required. Finally, the retailer may buy a portfolio of existing operating outlets by buying another firm. Clearly there are many ways of growing; each requiring different types and quantities of investment, and the organic/acquisition dichotomy can appear rather arbitrary.

In other industries, for example consumer goods, there is not an easily identifiable unit such as 'sales outlet' on which to anchor the organic growth measure. Large firms are highly diversified in terms of their brand and category portfolios and geographic spread. So the concept of what is and is not organic growth is harder to define. One could, for example, adopt a conservative definition and look only at sales growth in 'core' brands and in a constant set of territories. One could look at core brands in any territory, or one could look at growth in any brands anywhere. If organic growth is defined as any growth that is not acquisition growth, development of new brands and roll-out of existing brands into new territories is implicitly included in most measures of organic growth, even though the risk profile may be very different to the cultivation of existing brands in existing territories.

Acquisitions anyhow influence organic growth performance in subsequent periods, when acquisitions and divestments executed in a prior year become incorporated implicitly into the organic growth measure in subsequent years. Thus a company can increase its organic growth performance by buying businesses with higher growth rates than its average. The converse strategy is to exit slower-growing businesses with the intent of concentrating the residual top line. The positive implication of this is that maximising 'organic' growth reflects smart acquisition and divestment strategies, but the negative aspect may be a slavish focus on the top line that can lead to overpaying for high-growth businesses or, conversely, exiting low-growth businesses at fire-sale prices.

VOLUME, PRICE AND INFLATION

Volume and price

Both price and volume increases can deliver growth. At least in the short term, and if it can be achieved, an increase in price is an attractive source of growth. Price increases sales but requires no extra capital employed and thus enhances margin and asset turn. Volume also increases sales, but will not improve margin unless there are scale economies. Also if the firm is close to full capacity volume increases will require extra capital employed.

In reality, there are many routes to salvation in terms of value creation. In retail, some highly successful luxury goods firms pursue a strategy of limiting supply to maintain a premium margin. Equally, highly successful volume retailers like Tesco and Wal-Mart trade volume growth off against margin. They consistently pass cost reductions on to customers in order to put pressure on competitors and to gain market share.

So, depending on the firm's strategy and its context, we would like to be able to decompose growth into its volume and price components, especially when comparing similar firms. In reality, firms rarely give us the data to do this. Procter & Gamble's disclosure, discussed earlier, is exceptional.

Nominal growth and real growth

Though increasing prices may be a valuable source of growth, price increases due to *inflation*, that is, generalised increases in prices across the economy, are a different matter. Inflationary price increases are not valuable if costs inflate at the same rate. Profits will also inflate, but will be no more valuable to investors because their purchasing power will not have changed. So you cannot make much sense of growth without knowing what the rate of inflation was at the time.

When reviewing sales growth rates it is usually adequate just to run them alongside inflation rates for the same periods as a comparison. Alternatively, inflation rates can be subtracted from sales growth to show real growth. But sometimes it helps to convert the data from the *nominal* terms in which sales are reported, in which each observation is measured using the price of the day, to *real* terms, when the data are put into constant, inflation-adjusted prices by indexing them. Indexation or a comparison with inflation rates is only needed when comparing values – either in different years or between firms with different reporting dates. It is not necessary to index data that are already real such as 'number of employees'. Remember that the ratio of two values is a real figure, while the ratio of a value and a real is a value. So if you are tracking the Receivables/Sales ratio you do not need to worry about inflation, but if you are looking at sales per employee, you need to worry.

The specific price index relevant to the particular goods and services that the firm produces and consumes may move very differently to general economy-wide price indices such as the retail price index (RPI), the consumer price index (CPI), or the GDP (gross domestic product) deflator. But a general index has practical advantages. Specific indices may not be readily available. In a multi-product firm an appropriate composite index would have to be calculated, which would require information about the composition of the published figures that the outsider does not usually have. Also, when a firm has a dominant share of a local market, using the relevant category price index introduces circularity into the growth calculation. For example, SAB Miller has 90% of the South African beer market, so the local alcoholic beverages price index is essentially a SAB Miller price index. Even in less extreme cases, the local category leader may well behave as the price setter in the market, with the same result. Nonetheless conclusions about volume growth derived from indexing sales using a general price index have to be interpreted with care.

Case: CTC, continued

CTC sells consumer goods and industrial goods. To get a benchmark inflation rate we could seek segment data from CTC to establish the proportion of sales in different categories, and use this to create an appropriate weighted index of consumer and industrial prices. For most purposes something simpler will suffice. We show below the Cyprus consumer price index, CPI, and the Cyprus GDP deflator in annual % and in index terms, where 31.12.1996 = 100. The GDP deflator reflects a broader basket of goods and services and we use that to benchmark CTC's sales growth. We can also use the price index to 'deflate' the sales data, putting them into constant prices or 'real terms'. Essentially we are restating each number in the prices of another year, so we multiply each observation by *desired year index/actual year index*. In this case we have decided to restate the data at 2000 prices, so, for example, the 2003 sales of 114,953 becomes 114,953 × 111.7/123.4 = 103,999. This gives us a series of 'real' sales data from which we can calculate a real sales growth rate.

Table 4 CTC's real growth

	1997	1998	1999	2000	2001	2002	2003	2004
Reported sales	55.7	63.9	71.5	84.0	100.0	109.3	115.0	122.9
Annual growth		14.6%	11.9%	17.5%	19.2%	9.3%	5.2%	6.9%
CPI	3.6%	2.2%	1.7%	4.1%	2.0%	2.8%	4.1%	2.3%
GDP deflator	2.8%	2.4%	2.3%	3.7%	3.2%	2.2%	4.8%	2.2%
GDP index	102.8	105.3	107.7	111.7	115.2	117.8	123.4	126.2
Sales at 2000 prices	60.5	67.7	74.1	83.9	96.9	103.6	104.0	108.8
Real growth		1.9%	9.4%	13.3%	15.5%	6.9%	0.3%	4.6%

International differences in inflation

If a firm is operating in more than one country, local inflation rates may differ from the rate in the home economy. The international firm may simply be one that manufactures at home and exports, or it may be a multinational with subsidiaries in different countries, manufacturing in some and selling in others. In either case, in the theoretical world of 'purchasing power parity', currency markets and/or consolidated accounting should automatically correct the inflation differentials.

Example: Smith

Smith Inc is a US firm that manufactures generating sets. First we will imagine Smith manufactures the sets in the US and exports them; second, that Smith manufactures them locally.

Smith is an exporter. Smith Inc exports sets to Ruritania, where the local currency is the Ruritanian dollar, R$. Last year Smith sold 10,000 sets with a value of R$10m. This year unit sales are static but because Ruritanian inflation is running at 12.5% the value of those sales is R$11.25m. On the other hand, US inflation was only 2.5% during the year so Smith's manufacturing costs only rise by this amount.

Should Smith be happy? Not really. If currency markets are working efficiently, the currency of an economy with higher inflation will depreciate against the currency of the lower inflation economy to preserve relative *purchasing power parity* (PPP), which describes a world in which $100 converted to local currency will buy the same bundle of goods and services anywhere. This is an effect of supply and demand. Unless currency rates change, no-one is going to buy generator sets in Ruritania in the presence of higher R$ inflation. They will buy them in the US and ship them back, and the resulting demand for US$ and lack of demand for R$ will realign exchange rates. Last year, the R$/US$ exchange rate was 1. To restore purchasing power parity, the R$ must depreciate to 1/1.1US$ = .91US$, that is, depreciate by the difference in inflation rates. If so, when Smith collects its Ruritanian sales proceeds and converts them to US$ it will receive US$11.25/1.1, which is approximately US$10.25. So, Smith's sales expressed in the home currency will have inflated at the home country rate of inflation.

Smith is a multinational. Instead of exporting, Smith has a Ruritanian subsidiary that manufactures and sells generator sets. Smith may or may not remit the profits from this subsidiary back to the US, but when it prepares its consolidated income statement in the US it must convert the income statement of the foreign subsidiary each year at the average exchange rate ruling in the year (.91 this year and 1 in the previous year). This procedure, of converting the foreign subsidiaries' accounts at the ruling exchange rate, has the effect of eliminating the overseas inflation differential, just as though the cash had actually been remitted.

The investors' expectation in term of rates of return, which is the firm's cost of capital, is set in nominal terms, that is, it includes inflation. It embodies the expected rate of inflation in the home country. If PPP holds, exchange rates automatically immunise differences in inflation and prices, either when cash is remitted or through consolidated accounting. The reported sales, after exchange rate movements, would reflect home country inflation and would be consistent whatever the geographical mix of the underlying operations. They would give rates of organic growth that could be reliably compared between firms reporting in the same currency. They would give rates of return on capital that can be reliably compared to the firm's cost of capital.

Case: InBev's organic growth performance

If firms report segment results before currency effects they are effectively reporting in local currency, so the results need benchmarking against local inflation. A practical barrier to doing this is that few companies report their sales at a local, as opposed to regional level. An exception is the global brewing firm InBev. The impact of local market inflation on InBev's organic growth rates has been estimated by weighting local consumer price inflation by local market volume. While this method is not as accurate as weighting by local market revenue, it is reasonably fit for purpose. The analysis suggests that the impact of local market inflation on InBev's organic growth rate in 2004 was c. 5% – in excess of InBev's reported organic growth rate in 2004 of 4.3%.

Table 5 InBev's inflation exposure in 2004

	Local sales volumes (m HL)[1]	Local market consumer price inflation (%)[2]
Canada	9.4	1.8%
USA	6.8	2.7%
Cuba	0.8	4.2%
Brazil[3]	36.4	6.6%
Dominican Republic	0.5	51.5%
Ecuador	0.1	2.7%
Guatemala	0.1	7.6%
Peru	0.8	3.7%
Venezuela	0.8	21.7%
UK	12.6	1.3%
Belgium	6.4	1.9%
Netherlands	2.6	1.4%
France	2.4	2.3%
Luxembourg	0.2	3.2%
Germany	10.4	1.8%
Italy	1.0	2.3%
Export	3.7	3.0%[4]
Hungary	2.3	6.8%
Bulgaria	1.4	6.1%
Croatia	1.6	2.1%
Romania	2.2	11.9%
Serbia-Montenegro	3.6	9.5%
Bosnia-Herzegovina	0.1	0.4%
Czech Republic	2.6	2.8%
Russia	13.0	10.9%
Ukraine	7.5	9.0%
South Korea	7.5	2.7%
China	14.7	3.9%
Global exports	2.2	3.0%[4]
Total/weighted average	153.7	5.1%

1   Source: InBev Report & Accounts 2004
2   Source: IMF and European Central Bank
3   Total of beer, soft drinks and Quinsa
4   Assumed

How international firms report inflation effects

Because currencies are relatively costless to trade, currency markets are highly efficient in arbitrating differences in interest rates, so that *interest rate parity* holds – expected changes in exchange rates accurately reflect differences in interest rates. Purchasing power parity is a much tougher requirement and clearly does not hold. Goods and services are more costly to trade and some are untradeable. In the long term, demand and supply will drive exchange rates to reflect national differences in inflation, but short term they do not, and yearly movements in exchange rates do not capture the year's changes in relative prices in a timely way[2].

Because exchange rate movements are an unreliable measure of relative price changes, multinational firms usually just report organic sales growth, territory by territory, *before* exchange movements, that is, in local currency terms. The trouble is, this throws out the baby with the bath water. If exchange rate movements are added back, they have to be replaced with something better. The right procedure is to deduct the difference between local and home country inflation from territory organic sales growth, or at least to benchmark local sales growth against local inflation.

---

2   Even if there were absolute and persistent differences in purchasing power between currencies, consolidated accounting might still deliver reliable, inflation-consistent sales data if *relative* PPP held, so that exchange rate movements correctly measured differences in inflation rates. But, again, this cannot be relied upon. Nominal interest rates are the product of real interest rates and expected inflation. If interest rate parity holds but purchasing power parity does not hold, then real interest rates must be diverging internationally. This, and the fact that exchange rate movements reflect expected rather than realised inflation mean that consolidated sales cannot be relied upon to provide an inflation-consistent measure of sales..

REVIEW

- Sales are the usual measure of the size of the firm, and the usual basis for measuring growth.

- In this chapter we looked at the way firms report their growth, and the drivers of growth. We saw that GAAP requires segment disclosure by activities and markets, but little more. Disclosure of other important dimensions of growth – whether growth is organic or from acquisition; volume or price-driven, and real or inflationary – remains voluntary, and must be interpreted with care.

- We need to consider how to define and therefore measure 'organic growth'; the acquisitions and divestments of one year become incorporated into organic growth in future years. Organic growth can be further split into its component elements of unit price growth, mix growth and volume growth. Price changes may increase sales without requiring extra capital, thereby enhancing margin and asset turn. Volume growth may increase sales, but not margin, unless there are also economies of scale

- Growth is unlikely to be valuable when it is simply due to inflation. We examined the impact of inflation, and the circumstances when indexing the data can be helpful in analysis.

- There may be international differences in inflation that affect the reported growth of firms operating globally and we need to consider the extent to which exchange rate movements have compensated for this in a world where purchasing power parity may not hold in the short run. Large firms sometimes disclose additional information about growth, segments and foreign exchange movements; but segment information reported in local currency needs to be benchmarked against local inflation.

Part 4

Accounting analysis

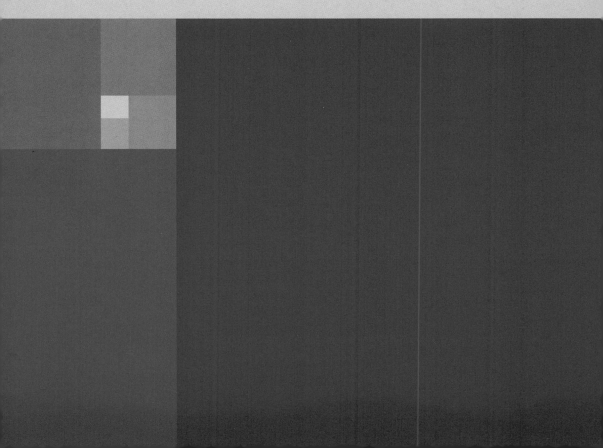

Chapter 11

Assets

This chapter discusses asset recognition and, in particular, the treatment of intangible assets. For GAAP, a necessary condition for recognising an asset in the balance sheet is that the future benefits can be measured reliably. This turns out to be tough on home-grown intangible assets, and their exclusion is the principal reason that balance sheets are incomplete in assets. Though assets such as brands, patents, organisational competencies and know-how may be the most valuable assets many firms have, GAAP generally requires the costs of creating them to be expensed as they are incurred. But if an intangible asset was purchased rather than home-grown, as commonly happens in a takeover, GAAP requires it to be recognised in the balance sheet. The treatment of intangibles is closely linked to that of takeovers, so we also discuss the accounting treatment of takeovers at this point.

From a GAAP perspective, the other key issue for asset recognition is the property rights question: does the firm own the asset? We postpone the ownership question to Chapter 13 because it is best discussed in tandem with the recognition of liabilities.

THE GAAP APPROACH TO ASSET RECOGNITION

We would like the balance sheet to provide a complete list of a firm's assets. The problem for GAAP is that a balance sheet is black and white, but in an uncertain world the value of an asset depends on future events, so it would sometimes be fairer to say 'if this happens, there is a valuable asset, whereas if that happens the asset will be worth less, or worth nothing.' GAAP deals with the ambiguity of the real world by setting tests for an asset to be recognised in the balance sheet.

GAAP: Tests for asset recognition

An *asset* is a resource that is expected to give economic benefits in the future. To be recognised in a balance sheet the future benefits must be probable, and it must be possible to measure the benefits reliably. The asset must be the result of past transactions or events and the firm must enjoy the risks and rewards of ownership of the asset.
[Reference: Con6, IAS16, IAS38]

Example: Alpha Inc

We asked Alpha Inc what they think their main assets are. They mentioned the following:

- Alpha have $50m deposited with the central bank.
- Alpha own the freehold of their headquarters building in San Francisco.
- Alpha have sunk $100m into researching a ground-breaking industrial coatings technology.
- Alpha have a very strong reputation for quality and many of their customers have been with them for ten years or more.
- Alf Alpha built the firm from nothing. He is the CEO and still holds 30% of the firm's shares, and he is a much admired entrepreneur. He is also very well connected politically and delivers a steady flow of profitable government contracts.

Clearly, Alpha's central bank deposit is a riskless asset. They also own the freehold in San Francisco. A commercial building is a low-risk asset, but it is not riskless – there is economic risk, its location could become undesirable, and there is some earthquake risk, though Alpha have insured against this. GAAP is happy for these assets to be recognised in the balance sheet. Alpha are excited about their new industrial coatings technology, but GAAP would respond 'show us the evidence that it will generate income in the future, that is, prove that an asset actually exists.' At present, Alpha cannot do that. You would imagine Alpha could make a stronger case for claiming that their brand is a valuable asset. After all, there is a demonstrable track record of the strength of Alpha's consumer franchise. But in this case also, GAAP is unconvinced. Arguably Alpha's most valuable asset is Alf himself. Assuming his health holds up (Alpha have taken out 'key-man' insurance on his life), Alf should continue to deliver. Of course, Alpha do not own Alf; in fact Alf owns Alpha, which in terms of ensuring his commitment is pretty much the same thing. But Alpha cannot put Alf in their balance sheet.

GAAP does not particularly discriminate against intangible assets, but the asset recognition tests, particularly the 'reliability' test, turn out to be tough on internally generated intangibles. For unique assets, by definition, there is no active secondary market and this makes it hard for firms to demonstrate the value of their intangibles. The paradox of intangibles is that when they are valuable they are valuable because they are unique or differentiated, but this is what stops GAAP allowing them into the balance sheet. The singularity of intangibles is their fortune but, as far as accounting goes, it is also their downfall. In general, GAAP requires firms to expense those expenditures that build intangibles, such as advertising and promotion, training, IT costs and, with some exceptions, research and development expenditures (R&D). For firms that have lots of intangibles this generates a very incomplete balance sheet, as the Singapore Airlines case demonstrates.

However, if a firm buys an asset in an external transaction the asset is recorded in the balance sheet at its cost, whether it is tangible or intangible. Often the transaction that brings intangibles is the purchase of another firm, and intangible assets are just part of a bundle of assets and liabilities that are acquired. In this case 'purchase accounting' is used to allocate the overall consideration for the takeover to individual assets and liabilities. It might seem odd that GAAP always accepts a transaction price as the basis for asset recognition even though the trade may have been a one-off and the price based on an estimate. GAAP polices the risk that misvaluation and over-payment will get into balance sheets in this way by rigorously enforcing tests for asset impairment thereafter, as we see in Chapter 14.

Though this is the status quo, the exclusion of internally generated intangibles from the balance sheet remains controversial and it could be that the treatment of intangibles under GAAP will evolve in the future. Baruch Lev has argued that, though we may accept that intangibles have a high degree of uncertainty attached to them, once that uncertainty is significantly resolved, capitalisation should be allowed according to agreed tests. This is essentially the approach of the IFRS standard (IAS38) described later.

The effect of expensing intangibles on return on capital

If a firm is spending money on something that creates an asset, perhaps R&D, and is forced to expense it, what is the effect on the income statement, the balance sheet, and on return on capital? The effect on the balance sheet is always to understate assets and equity – an asset has been omitted. In the case of the income statement it is not quite so clear-cut. Expensing reduces income, on the other hand if the expenditure had been capitalised as an asset, the firm would have to amortise that asset. In steady-state these would cancel out. But, assuming the firm is growing expensing intangibles tends to understate income each year because the amortisation of earlier expenditure is usually exceeded by the current year's expenditure. The balance-sheet effect tends to dominate the income effect, so, as a general rule, expensing intangibles flatters return on capital. We will assess the impact of this at Glaxo, a case we examine later in the chapter. However, the following example illustrates the point.

Example: Celebrity Zoo

Zap! Media and Pow! Productions are independent TV production companies. Pow! puts $5m of cash, funded from an equity issue, into an operation to develop its new reality game show format, *Celebrity Zoo*. The development is done in the first year and the format is expected to have a five-year life. Profits from cable subscriptions and advertising revenues, less production costs, should be $2m per year in the first year and for the next four years. Zap! has similar expectations of its new format, *Footballer Opera*. Zap! gets another house to develop the concept and it buys a five-year exclusive licence from the developer for $5m. Pow! expenses the $5m costs, immediately while Zap! can recognise the license as an intangible asset in the balance sheet and amortises it over five years at $1m per annum. Neither firm has any debt. Their results over the five years are described in Table 1 and we calculate their return on average capital employed, which since they have no debt is the same as return on equity.

Table 1 Expensing intangibles (figures in $m)

Year	Pow! 1 start	1 end	2	3	4	5	Zap! 1 start	1 end	2	3	4	5
Income statement												
Income		2	2	2	2	2		2	2	2	2	2
Development		-5										
Amortisation								-1	-1	-1	-1	-1
EBIT		**-3**	**2**	**2**	**2**	**2**		**1**	**1**	**1**	**1**	**1**
Balance sheet												
Cash	5	2	4	6	8	10	5	2	4	6	8	10
Licence - cost								5	5	5	5	5
Licence - accumulated amortisation								-1	-2	-3	-4	-5
Assets	**5**	**2**	**4**	**6**	**8**	**10**	**5**	**6**	**7**	**8**	**9**	**10**
Share capital	5	5	5	5	5	5	5	5	5	5	5	5
Retained earnings		-3	-1	1	3	5		1	2	3	4	5
Equity	**5**	**2**	**4**	**6**	**8**	**10**	**5**	**6**	**7**	**8**	**9**	**10**
ROCE		**-86%**	**67%**	**40%**	**29%**	**22%**		**18%**	**15%**	**13%**	**12%**	**11%**

Comparing Pow! to Zap! we can see that the effect of expensing intangibles on the balance sheet is that equity is understated every year until the asset is fully consumed. The effect on the income statement is a disproportionate reduction in earnings during development, but higher earnings thereafter. As a result, after the first year, the effect of expensing on return on capital is doubly flattering.

In the case of Zap! and Pow! the investment in the new format was a 'one-off'. In steady state, if both firms continued to develop, or license, a similar format every year then income would be the same under either treatment. Pow! would spend $5m on developing a new format each year while Zap! would have five licences running at any point, requiring ($1m × 5 =) $5m of amortisation each year. But even if earnings are equalised in steady state, the balance sheet of the firm that expenses intangibles remains incomplete, overstating return on capital.

In reality, firms that invest in intangibles tend to continue to invest but also they tend to grow, if only as a result of inflation. As a result, expensing tends to understate income each year because the $ value of the amortisation of earlier investments lags behind the $ value of this year's expenditure.

Case: Singapore Airlines

Civil aviation has long been an extremely difficult business in which to make money and few traditional full-service airlines consistently earn their cost of capital. The terrorist attacks in September 2001 and the SARS epidemic in Asia worsened the economics of airlines yet further. Singapore Airlines is one of the best performers. In 2000, for instance, its return on (average) shareholders' equity was 16.9%.

If one was asked for a list of the key strategic assets for an airline – the assets that enable an airline like Singapore to earn a superior return – the list would mostly contain intangibles:
- *Landing slots and routes* Singapore Airlines profits from having both its domestic base and a dominant position in Singapore, which is a thriving modern economy but also a well-placed hub on the long-haul route between Asia and Europe.
- *Brand and reputation* For an airline, the key ingredients of reputation are safety and service quality, and airlines try to exploit this through loyalty and frequent-flyer programmes. Singapore frequently wins awards for its service quality and has a successful frequent-flyer programme.
- *Alliances* Some airlines have profited from forming global alliances with other airlines. Singapore is a member of the successful Star alliance.
- *Planes?* Planes, which are a tangible asset, would probably not be on the list. Singapore flies the same mix of Boeings and Airbuses as most other airlines, so its planes are presumably not a differentiator.

Here is a summary of the asset side of Singapore's 2004 balance sheet ($m)

Table 2 Singapore's assets (figures in $m)

Aircraft, etc	12,465
Land, buildings, other long-term assets	3,100
Investments in other firms	1,302
Goodwill	1
Cash	1,519
Other current assets	1,603
TOTAL ASSETS	**19,990**

Singapore's balance sheet looks much like the balance sheet of any airline. The main asset in the balance sheet is planes. (Note that, as with most airlines, some of the planes that Singapore uses are held off the balance sheet on operating leases – 19 out of Singapore's fleet of 108 in 2004.) None of the key intangibles are in the balance sheet. Landing slots are assets that can be bought and sold and can be very valuable. When an airline has bought some slots in a transaction these are recognised in the balance sheet. But mostly, and in Singapore's case entirely, the slots that airlines use are the ones they were endowed with. They were not paid for, so they do not find their way into the balance sheet.

THE NATURE OF INTANGIBLES

The term 'intangible asset' is used in accounting to describe assets that lack physical substance. Clearly intangibles are a rather disparate group. Some are discrete assets that have a contractual basis, have property rights that are protected in law, and are sometimes traded separately between firms. These include:

– *intellectual property* assets such as copyrights, publishing rights and patents;
– *market-based assets* such as brand names, trademarks, and customer lists.

At the other end of the spectrum are aspects of a firm that are diffuse and embedded within it, and are hard to imagine existing separately from the firm. These include:

– *reputation*;
– *relationships*, alliances and networks;
– *information systems* and IT infrastructure;
– *human and organisational capital*, capabilities, knowledge and know-how.

The value of intangibles

Intangibles are potentially valuable and, when a firm is earning a superior return on capital, its competitive advantage can usually be traced to the possession of valuable intangibles. In fact, it may be helpful to see 'intangibles' as a vocabulary; as the way we explain why a firm has competitive advantage.

A key characteristic of intangibles is their *singularity*: the fact that each one is different and unique. This is a necessary condition for any asset to be a source of differentiation. Owning an asset only confers competitive advantage if your competitor does not have a similar asset and cannot get one. So assets that are *commodities*, that is, are identical and are in competitive supply, cannot confer competitive advantage. If one airline is doing better than another this cannot be because it is flying Boeing 737s, because 737s are in abundant supply and more can be produced, so the other airline can have 737s if it wants them. One 737 is fundamentally like another, but the Kit-Kat brand is quite different from the Mars Bar brand and each is unique.

Not all unique intangibles create value. There are many firms with well-known brands that do not manage to earn a superior return with them. Conversely, not all tangible assets are commodities. A trophy hotel with a unique location, like the Ritz in Paris, has intangible value in this respect.

Not all intangibles are singular. IT systems are intangible assets; they can be extremely costly and these costs are typically expensed rather than being capitalised as assets, and no modern firm can survive without its IT system. But this does not mean that IT systems are singular or value-creating assets. Major banks have spent billions of dollars on their back-office systems. Each system looks and feels different because it was bespoke rather than bought off the shelf. But to a large extent they have the same functionality and they represent the cost of staying in the game rather than a source of competitive advantage.

Case: IT at American Airlines, Dell, Wal-Mart, Tesco

There are many examples of firms that have successfully used IT to create competitive advantage. An early example of the ability of information systems to create competitive advantage was American Airlines' SABRE reservation system, which went live in 1964. This was a civilian application of the SAGE resource coordination system built for the US military. In the decade after 1995, Michael Dell built a dominant position in the global PC market using sophisticated logistical control systems linked to on line selling to achieve a mix of low cost and speed of fulfilment that no-one else could match at the time. In the US and the UK, respectively, Wal-Mart and Tesco built dominant market positions using management information systems that enabled them to achieve significantly lower inventory-related costs than rivals. In all of these cases others could replicate the technology, but it was costly and took time, enabling these firms to keep ahead of the competition by continuous innovation, or letting them secure their advantage with other intangibles, perhaps brand or organisational capabilities.

Another reason why some intangibles become very valuable is that they display increasing returns to scale. In some cases, network effects are the source of the increasing returns to scale and this creates a barrier to entry for competitors. eBay is an example of this – the more people who are using an on line auction site, the more attractive it is to use. Intangible assets like intellectual property and brands display increasing returns to scale as a result of scalability – the marginal cost of exploiting them is relatively low, and they have no capacity limit. You may invest $1bn to build the world's best automobile factory, but once the factory reaches capacity there is plenty of room in the market-place for the output from the world's second-best automobile factory. By contrast, if several pharmaceuticals firms are each investing $1bn in the race to develop an anti-ulcer treatment, the drug that has small performance advantages over its rivals, or the drug that simply gets to the market first, may take the whole market. With no alternative uses for the asset, the second-best patent may then have little value, though its development may have generated some knowledge that can be used for other things.

The risk of intangibles

It is easy to see why some intangibles become very valuable, but the corollary is that investments in intangibles may be more risky than investments in tangibles. This is the 'winner-take-all' nature of markets with increasing returns to scale. It is a world in which firms have to make large bets on uncertain outcomes. Legal advances are giving better protection to some intangible assets, reducing the uncertainty associated with their ownership. For patents and copyrights the law gives lengthy protection from trespassers – for instance, for 15 to 20 years for patents and for 60 or 70 years after the author's death for creative copyrights. But in general, a feature of intangibles is the difficulty in fully enforcing property rights. It is harder to prevent people copying an idea than it is to prevent people entering a building. A consequence of the difficulty in establishing property rights over intangibles, and of their singularity, is the lack of active secondary markets for these assets.

RESEARCH AND DEVELOPMENT

GAAP: Treatment of R&D

Research and development is often thought of as the most 'tangible' of intangibles. The GAAP treatment of R&D provides the template for the accounting treatment of other intangibles unless they have their own rules. Although the intellectual property created by R&D can comprise a valuable and long-lived asset, its treatment under GAAP is restrictive.

US GAAP (FAS142) insists that all R&D be expensed. US GAAP makes an exception for software development costs associated with software that is to be resold or, in some circumstances, used internally. These costs must be capitalised once technological feasibility has been established. IFRS (IAS38) requires firms to distinguish research expenditure from development expenditure. Research expenditure has to be expensed. Development expenditure is also expensed, but is capitalised if the firm can demonstrate *all* of the following:

- That the asset can feasibly be completed, that resources exist to complete it, and that the firm intends to complete it.
- That subsequent development expenditure can be reliably measured.
- That the intangible will generate future economic benefits, and that either there is an external market for the intangible or it will be used internally.

Although IFRS appears to be much more permissive than US GAAP in allowing the capitalisation of development expenditure, the fairly demanding tests mean that the effect of IAS 38 has been significant in one or two sectors thus far. One of these is the auto industry, as Peugeot Citroen demonstrates.
[References: FAS142, IAS38]

Case: Development costs at PSA Peugeot Citroen

In 2005, PSA Peugeot Citroen reported under IFRS for the first time, restating its 2004 comparatives. It implemented IAS 38, which permits development expenditure to be recognized as an intangible asset in the balance sheet when it meets certain criteria. Peugeot capitalises development expenditure on vehicles and mechanical parts incurred between the styling decision, or project launch for mechanical parts, and the start-up of pre-series production. The assets are usually amortised over up to seven years for vehicles and over ten years for mechanical parts. Peugeot's total R&D costs for 2005 were €2,151m, of which it capitalized €856m on this basis. The amounts were similar in 2004. The income statement impact was offset by amortisation of development costs of €594m in 2005, and €504m in 2004. The net effect was to increase the consolidated earnings before tax of Peugeot Citroen's manufacturing and sales division by €262m, or 39.7 %, in 2005 and €381m (24.7%) in 2004.

The effect of capitalising R&D

To explore the effects of the non-recognition of internally generated intangibles in the balance sheet, and to see what an analyst who wanted to reverse the GAAP treatment of internally generated intangibles would have to do, we will use R&D in the pharmaceuticals sector as a case study. Few industries spend more on R&D than pharmaceuticals. For decades, many of the world's leading drug firms have delivered very high returns on capital, raising the interesting question, has this sector sustained a remarkably high level of value creation, or does GAAP expensing of R&D lead us to measure the return incorrectly?

Case: Glaxo

Glaxo Wellcome merged with SmithKline Beecham to form GlaxoSmithKline in 2000. For clarity, we will focus on Glaxo prior to 2000. Glaxo's history during the decades prior to 2000 was of strong organic growth with one major acquisition, of Wellcome Laboratories in 1995. Glaxo has spent up to 15% of sales revenue on R&D over the years. Table 3 shows Glaxo's financials in summary from 1990 to 1999 and calculates ROCE using the numbers as published. Even at its lowest, in the middle of this period, Glaxo's ROCE was still between 55% and 60%.

To reverse the expensing of R&D, the analyst has to add back the R&D expense to operating profit, creating an R&D intangible asset in the balance sheet instead. This asset is then amortised over some period of years. The boxed section of Table 3 makes these adjustments. The base case uses a 25% per annum reducing-balance amortisation, which has the effect of writing the asset down to 10% of its initial value after eight years.

Table 3 Glaxo: capitalising the R&D

AS PUBLISHED	1990	1991	1992	1993	1994	1995	1996	1997	1998	1999
Sales	3,179	3,397	4,096	4,930	5,656	7,638	8,341	7,980	7,983	8,490
R&D	420	475	595	739	858	1,130	1,161	1,148	1,163	1,269
R&D as a % of sales	13.2%	14.0%	14.5%	15.0%	15.2%	14.8%	13.9%	14.4%	14.6%	14.9%
EBIT	1,037	1,116	1,310	1,545	1,699	2,459	3,150	2,807	2,762	2,667
Capital employed	1,682	2,164	2,393	2,969	3,058	3,417	3,250	3,237	4,032	4,789
Average capital employed	1,438	1,923	2,279	2,681	3,014	3,238	3,334	3,244	3,635	4,411
ROCE	72%	58%	57%	58%	56%	76%	94%	87%	76%	60%
EBIT margin	33%	33%	32%	31%	30%	32%	38%	35%	35%	31%
Asset turn	2.2	1.8	1.8	1.8	1.9	2.4	2.5	2.5	2.2	1.9
Wellcome assets contribution					653					
R&D Asset (opening)	702	946	1,185	1,484	1,852	2,900	3,305	3,640	3,878	4,071
Amortisation rate 25%	-175	-237	-296	-371	-463	-725	-826	-910	-969	-1018
Additions – R&D expense	420	475	595	739	858	1,130	1,161	1,148	1,163	1,269
R&D Asset (closing)	946	1,185	1,484	1,852	2,900	3,305	3,640	3,878	4,071	4,323
REVISED										
EBIT	1,282	1,354	1,609	1,913	2,094	2,864	3,485	3,045	2,956	2,918
Capital employed	2,628	3,349	3,877	4,821	5,958	6,722	6,890	7,115	8,103	9,112
EBIT margin	40%	40%	39%	39%	37%	37%	42%	38%	37%	34%
Asset turn	1.4	1.1	1.1	1.1	1.0	1.2	1.2	1.1	1.0	1.0
ROCE	57%	45%	45%	44%	39%	45%	51%	43%	39%	34%
With other amortisation rates										
ROCE rate 5%	52%	43%	41%	41%	35%	40%	43%	36%	31%	27%
ROCE rate 15%	55%	44%	43%	42%	37%	43%	47%	40%	35%	30%
ROCE rate 35%	58%	46%	46%	45%	40%	47%	55%	47%	43%	37%

The effect of capitalising R&D on capital employed is always to make it larger – an asset is being included in the balance sheet that was not there before. But the effect on EBIT depends on whether amortisation exceeds expense. In steady state, R&D expense and R&D amortisation will be the same. But assuming there is some growth in R&D expenditure, even if only due to inflation, the expense will run ahead of the amortisation. In this case, capitalisation will increase EBIT. Net, the effect of capitalising R&D expenditure is typically to reduce measured return on capital because the 'asset turn' effect of the larger capital employed exceeds the 'margin effect' of enhanced EBIT. This is the case for Glaxo, where the adjusted ROCE is below the reported ROCE by 20%, and in some years by more.

The mechanics of capitalising R&D are straightforward, but it is challenging to ensure that the exercise is meaningful. These are some of the things that require care.

- *Asset life* What is an appropriate economic life, that is, rate of amortisation, for the intellectual property created by R&D? The base case above uses 25% per annum reducing-balance amortisation, which has the effect of writing the asset down to 10% of its initial value after eight years. At the bottom of Table 3 we show the effect of using different rates, from 5%, which might be too optimistic, to 35%, which must be too conservative. The effect is not great; the return is not very sensitive to the rate of amortisation.

- *Back history* Amortisation will be understated, and the effects of capitalisation exaggerated, until an equilibrium stock of R&D has been reached. This will take some years – the assumed life of the asset, in fact. In practice analysts are frequently careless about this. In preparing Table 3 we started the simulation with an assumed stock of R&D asset in 1976 and ran the simulation from then to build the balance sheet stock.

- *Acquisitions* Acquisitions raise a similar issue. In 1995 Glaxo bought Wellcome, which itself had a large stock of internally generated R&D off its balance sheet. Nowadays, purchase accounting of an acquisition would ensure that a fair estimate of the value of the R&D intangible was recorded in the balance sheet, but in 1995 this was not required, so the analyst needs a similar back history for the acquired firm so as to generate an estimate of its R&D stock. We estimated that Wellcome brought £653m of R&D intangible.

- *Full-cost* Should we capitalise *all* the R&D? The experience of drug firms is that only a small percentage of laboratory compounds reach the market. But so long as the overall activity is profitable, deprival value thinking argues for full-cost accounting, that is capitalising all the R&D, as we will see in Chapter 14.

Exhibit: Intangibles, goodwill and the price to book ratio

Price to book ratios rose steeply around the world from the mid 1970s. In the US, the aggregate price to book ratio rose from around one in 1974 to four by 1999 (Figure 1). Though share prices halved after 2000, the price to book remained at historically high levels.

This rise is often attributed to intangibles. The argument is that the denominator of the price to book ratio is becoming more incomplete, due to the growing proportion of off-balance sheet (essentially intangible) assets to on-balance sheet (essentially tangible) assets. It is true that some new and very valuable intangibles have emerged since the 1970s, notably those intangibles associated with IT. The IT industry itself has created a number of firms like Microsoft and Oracle with very high market capitalisations and negligible book assets. However, most of those IT giants are listed in the US, but rising price to book ratios have been a global phenomenon. On the other hand, key intangibles like brands and intellectual property have differentiated successful firms since capitalism began. So while intangibles might be part of the price to book story it is unlikely that they are all of it. The problem may lie in price rather as much as book. Firms may have been relatively undervalued in the 1970s and overvalued in the 1990s.

Figure 1 Aggregate US price to book ratio

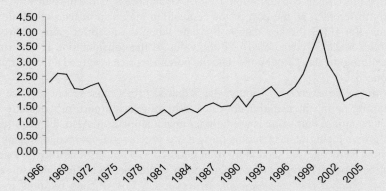

Whether or not unrecognised intangibles explain what happened to price to book ratios, there is no doubt that the price to book ratio triggered the debate on accounting for intangibles and goodwill. This debate started when price to book was continuing to rise, having broken through unity in the early 1980s. Firms saw their book equity apparently shrinking relative to market capitalisation. They were concerned that this might constrain their ability to borrow if investors were measuring borrowing capacity in terms of a gearing ratio calculated on book equity.

The price to book ratio intrudes into accounting most dramatically when there is a takeover. The goodwill component of takeovers has grown since the mid-1980s and goodwill is now a major component of many deals. This is no surprise, because goodwill is just the accounting manifestation of the price to book ratio. When one firm purchases another firm the price it pays is based on the target's market capitalisation but, in accounting terms, what it gets in exchange is based on the target identifiable assets. The difference is accounted for as goodwill. Consider Z Co. Like many firms, Z's price to book ratio was well below unity in the seventies. To be precise, it was 0.6 in 1975, meaning that 100 of Z's assets were trading on the stock market for 60. Suppose you have to pay a 'takeover premium' of 30%, then to purchase Z in 1975 would cost (60 + 30% =) 78, which is less than the 100 of assets in its balance sheet. By 1987 Z's price to book ratio had risen to 1.8, so to acquire it would cost you (180 + 30% =) 234; in other words, more than half the purchase consideration would potentially be for goodwill. Of course, the acquirer is required to revalue the target's book assets on acquisition, thus reducing the apparent goodwill. Also, the acquirer is now encouraged to recognise any acquired intangibles, further reducing the residual goodwill. Nonetheless, goodwill has been a very large component of many takeovers since the 1980s.

PURCHASE ACCOUNTING OF ACQUISITIONS

When a firm acquires another firm it is acquiring a bundle of assets and liabilities in one transaction. The task of the accountant is to identify the individual assets and liabilities that were acquired and attribute a cost to them so that they can be recorded in the balance sheet. GAAP requires the technique called *purchase accounting* to be used for this.

The steps in drawing up the post-acquisition balance sheet using purchase accounting are as follows:

1 ***Determining the cost of the acquisition*** The acquirer records the 'fair value' of the consideration paid. When a firm buys something for cash the price is clear, but in an acquisition some or all of the consideration may consist of shares. The acquirer has to record any shares it issues at their market value on the date of the acquisition. In other words, it records both the par value of shares issued and any associated share premium, as if it had made an issue of shares for cash on the day of the acquisition and used this cash as consideration. US GAAP and IFRS define the date of acquisition slightly differently, so the cost of the acquisition may also differ slightly in the two systems. For IFRS the key date is the date when the acquirer gains control of the acquiree's assets. Under US GAAP the value of the consideration is determined by prices during the days around the date the purchase price is agreed and the transaction announced.

2 ***The 'fair value exercise'*** Though the acquired firm's most recent balance sheet is the starting point, the acquirer does not follow the acquired firm's existing balance sheet accounting. Fair value is used, rather than historic cost. Also, the acquired firm's home-grown intangibles, including those it was precluded from recognising by GAAP, must now be recognised separately from goodwills so long as it represents legal rights or can be separately disposed of, licensed or exchanged. This includes so-called *in-process research and development*. However US GAAP then requires in-process R&D to be immediately expensed. GAAP is relaxed about recognising intangibles that came in a takeover because they would, anyhow, sit in the balance sheet as part of goodwill and be subject to similar impairment tests. So the acquirer effectively takes a blank piece of paper and records all acquired assets and liabilities, including intangible assets and contingent liabilities, at their fair value, which is the price the acquirer would have paid for them individually in an arm's-length transaction in the open market on the date of the acquisition.

3 ***Goodwill*** If the value of the consideration is greater than the fair value of the identifiable assets acquired, including the intangibles, the acquirer records the difference in the balance sheet as the asset, *goodwill*. Goodwill is essentially the residual asset.

There is also an income statement effect.

4 ***Pre-acquisition profits*** The acquirer includes in the income statement only the post-acquisition results of the acquired firm. The logic of purchase accounting is that the acquirer effectively buys a bundle of net assets. In consequence, the acquired firm has no history or pre-acquisition profits from the acquirer's perspective.

Purchase accounting is also known as *acquisition accounting*. The words *takeover* and *merger* are frequently used for acquisition. There is a simple worked example of the operation of purchase accounting, BS Group, at the end of the chapter. AOL's acquisition of Time Warner in 2001, is a rather dramatic actual case.

Case: AOL's acquisition of Time Warner

AOL acquired Time Warner on 11 January 2001. The merger combined the leading US internet service provider, with more than 20m subscribers, and the world's largest media conglomerate, Time Warner, the parent firm of Warner Brothers Studios, HBO, CNN, Warner Music, and Time magazine. Steve Case, AOL chairman and CEO, said '*this is a historic merger. AOL-Time Warner will offer an incomparable portfolio of global brands that encompass the full spectrum of media and content.*' In his view, the merger would increase the combined firm's growth rate significantly, while yielding an immediate $1bn per annum of synergies.

The value of the purchase consideration was $146.6bn, made up of common stock, $135.3bn, preferred stock and other, $1.4bn, stock options, $9.8bn, costs etc., $.2bn. Time Warner's pre-bid market capitalisation was $83bn. Although Time Warner would initially provide two-thirds of the combined firm's earnings, AOL's much higher market capitalisation meant that the new firm would be 55% owned by AOL shareholders. According to AOL's subsequent SEC filing (8-K/A, filed 30 March 2001) the fair value table was as follows:

Table 4 Time Warner fair value table (figures in $m)

	Book	Adjustments	Fair value
Tangible assets	26,265	4,135	30,400
Intangible assets	25,936	-25,936	
Liabilities	-42,240	-16,852	-59,092
Time Warner net assets	**9,961**	**-38,653**	**-28,692**
Film & television libraries		*2,600*	
Music catalogue & copyrights		*2,500*	
Cable television and sports franchises		*31,700*	
Brands and trademarks		*10,000*	
Goodwill and other intangibles		*128,163*	175,313
Consideration			**146,621**

At the time of acquisition, Time Warner's net assets were $9.961bn, but this included $25.94bn of goodwill and intangibles that were a legacy of its own acquisitions. Eliminating these in order to reappraise them in the fair value exercise, AOL paid $146.6bn and received -$28.7bn of tangible and financial net assets in exchange. This $175.3bn gap was attributed at the AOL acquisition to various identified intangibles, the principal one being cable TV and franchises which was given a value of $31.7bn. Nonetheless, the lion's share, $128.5bn, was recorded as goodwill and other intangibles.

Pooling

When two firms are combined, the presumption is that one firm has 'acquired' the other, that is, gained control of it. If so, that the acquirer should use purchase accounting to record the transaction. However, in a merger of equals there is no dominant party and it is unreasonable to talk in terms of an acquirer. In this case an accounting method known as *posting pooling of interests* was traditionally used. Pooling is also called *merger accounting* and *uniting of interests*.

GAAP struggled over decades to devise tests that would prevent firms dressing acquisitions up as mergers to take advantage of the favourable accounting. Eventually, though true mergers of equals are occasionally encountered, both US GAAP and IFRS outlawed pooling altogether. But pooling still needs to be understood, both because it helps explain purchase accounting, and because there is an enduring legacy of pooled transactions in many balance sheets, and also because pooling is still used in some jurisdictions. [References: FAS141, IFRS3]

In pooling:
1 There is no 'consideration'. However it is common to use one or other of the combining firms as the holding company and this will lead to new shares being issued; any shares that are issued are shown at their par value.
2 The assets of the two firms are combined at their existing book values – there is no 'acquired' firm so that neither firm's assets have to be revalued to fair values. No previously unrecorded intangibles are recognised.
3 No goodwill is recognised from the transaction. Any difference between net assets brought into the group balance sheet and shares issued is written off to reserves.
4 In the year of merger, the full year's results of both firms are included in income.

Purchase accounting and pooling give very different results. The accepted wisdom is that pooling is more flattering, principally because it avoids a charge against earnings for the amortisation or impairment of goodwill and also avoids the increased charges for consuming assets that have been revalued to fair values. Acquirers dislike these charges because they believe that markets value them on the basis of earnings in an uncritical way. An additional attraction of pooling for acquirers was that it permitted the inclusion in full of both firms' earnings in the year of the merger.

Case: The SmithKline Beecham merger

Though 'true mergers' are quite rare, the 1989 merger between Beecham of the UK, and SmithKline Beechman of the US, was one. The firms were of similar size, the group retained listings in both the UK and the US, and management went to great lengths to ensure equality of treatment of the two workforces, with parity extending right up to the composition of the main board. The consideration was structured so that the two groups of shareholders were left with similar stakes in the equity of the new firm. The new group put its headquarters in Brentford, England and produced its first annual report in December 1989 under UK GAAP, which treated the transaction as a pooling. Because of the US listing, SmithKline Beecham was also required to report a reconciliation to US GAAP.

SKB's 1989 balance sheet in its UK GAAP and US GAAP versions is summarised below.

Table 5 SmithKline Beecham's balance sheet

		UK GAAP	US GAAP
Fixed assets		1,555	1,555
Revaluation			-156
Intangibles			754
Goodwill	Old Beecham goodwill		461
	On SKB		2,665
Current assets		2,191	2,191
Creditors	Loan	1,983	1,983
	Other	2,039	1,942
EQUITY		**-276**	**3,545**

The US SEC deemed the transaction to be a purchase of SmithKline by Beecham. There were various differences between US GAAP and UK GAAP at that time, but in this case the dominant issue is the restatement as purchase accounting. Book equity is almost £4bn higher in the US, because the US balance sheet records nearly £4bn of goodwill and intangibles. Though there are other compensating items, the US profit figure is correspondingly reduced by £88m due to amortisation of the goodwill and intangibles, and by a further £144m which was earned by SmithKline before the date of the merger and must therefore be excluded in acquisition accounting as pre-acquisition profit.

The impact of the choice of accounting method can be seen by calculating SmithKline Beecham's return on equity using (for convenience) 1989 year-end figures. Under US GAAP, SKB had earnings of £87m and shareholders' equity of £3,545m giving it a return on equity under purchase accounting of a modest 2.5%. By contrast, SKB's UK GAAP earnings were £130 million and its shareholders' equity was -£297m, so that under pooling the return on equity appears to be infinite, or rather it cannot sensibly be calculated since the equity is negative. Recall that this is the same transaction recorded under two different systems.

GOODWILL AND INTANGIBLES IN FINANCIAL ANALYSIS

It has been common practice amongst analysts to do two things.
- To reverse the expensing of R&D and to capitalise an R&D intangible asset instead.
- To reinstate goodwill in the balance sheet where it has been impaired or amortised, or reserve accounted, or where pooling has been used.

Outside analysts do not usually attempt to capitalise any other intangibles, but firms themselves sometimes attempt a more comprehensive reworking of GAAP when they calculate internal performance metrics. For instance, in their management accounts, some branded-goods firms capitalise brand-building expenditure and amortise it over the expected life of the brand.

The financial analysis strategy depends on the objective. If the analyst needs a measure of return on capital that can be reliably compared to the cost of capital – a 'value metric' – then this requires a complete balance sheet valued at current values. This means capitalising all missing intangibles. If the analyst is doing comparative analysis and simply wants a profitability measure that reliably ranks similar firms and provides a good starting point for forensic financial analysis, this is less demanding.

Capitalising R&D

We used the pharmaceutical industry as a case study to demonstrate how we would set about capitalising R&D. There were several lessons from this.
- To do the job thoroughly requires some care and a long run of data, and it brings its own complications and raises some difficult conceptual issues.
- The bias caused by expensing a valuable intangible is a function of the firm's growth rate and the size of the expenditure in question. Between firms that spend much the same proportion of sales revenue on R&D and have similar growth rates, capitalisation is unlikely to add much insight in a cross-sectional comparison.
- In the case of Glaxo we had good data about expenditure on R&D, but a feature of some home-grown intangibles is that it is often quite hard to know what they cost because they are built continuously over a very long period, and also because their costs may be hard to identify. For example, branded-goods firms now keep close track of brand-building costs, brand by brand. But some of the most successful brands are upwards of 50 or a 100 years old and have been subject to investment throughout that period. And it would be difficult to attribute a cost to higher-level brands such as the firm's own reputation.
- One reason for the popularity of capitalising R&D is that the data is easy to get – GAAP requires firms to disclose their R&D expenditure. There is a danger of tokenism in the ritual capitalisation of R&D expenditure but no other intangibles. This may move the balance sheet in the direction of completeness, but it will not get all the way there.
- The analyst cannot avoid thinking about value, and whether the R&D is actually creating an asset. As the Apple case demonstrates, GAAP conservatism will sometimes be the appropriate treatment.

Case: Apple Computer

In its golden period in the late 1980s Apple Computer enjoyed 25% annual sales growth, a market share of over 30%, and had a return on capital of over 100%. Its superior performance was directly attributable to the customer appeal of its operating system with a graphical interface. Apple spent an increasing proportion of its growing sales revenue on R&D, which was 8.6% of sales by 1990. By 1996 Apple's fortunes had reversed. Its revenues fell by 11% in that year, its global market share was in single figures and falling, and it reported a large operating loss. Management's strategy was to seek to build new sources of competitive advantage through research and development, and Apple continued to spend 6% of revenues on R&D. The equity market did not share management's optimism and Apple's market capitalisation fell 60% during financial year 1996. Though we might have been happy to capitalise Apple's R&D in the late 1980s, would we be so sure that its R&D was creating a valuable asset in 1996?

Goodwill

Goodwill raises similar issues. The argument for showing goodwill in the balance sheet is that it may be proxying unidentified intangibles or undervalued tangibles. If purchased goodwill is an asset whose value will be maintained or grow, then to carry it unamortised in the balance sheet will come closer to replacement cost. But a blanket policy of capitalisation of all purchased goodwill ignores strong evidence from research that many companies overpay in acquisitions and, as goodwill is the marginal asset, they are overpaying for goodwill.

Our view is that although there may still be a case for reinstating past goodwill or estimating the goodwill in pooled acquisitions, current GAAP makes further goodwill adjustments by the analyst unnecessary. As we see in Chapter 14, GAAP now requires firms to carry goodwill gross and to subject it to an annual impairment review. The impairment review is much the same valuation exercise as an analyst would undertake.

An argument sometimes used for capitalising intangibles is that investors should be able to expect a return on all the capital that they have invested in the firm in the past, and capitalising goodwill challenges management to provide a return. However, it makes no sense to deny that capital can be lost. We want managers to make a fair return on the assets they actually control, and we should recognise losses as they arise. As in the Apple example, some development expenditure is lost and in this case capitalisation prevents profits and losses being attributed to the right periods.

For a value metric the balance sheet needs to be complete in goodwill, so long as it is not overvalued, because this catches all the intangibles that were acquired. But in a comparison between firms, some of which may have grown organically, goodwill is best excluded. It destroys comparability through time and with organically grown firms. For comparison of operating performance it is better simply to track a bundle of operating assets.

REVIEW

- In this chapter we looked at the recognition of assets in financial statements, with a particular focus on intangible assets.

- GAAP demands that an asset be recognised only when: it results from past transactions or events; when it is probable that future economic benefits will be realised; and when the amount is capable of reliable measurement. The effect of these tests is that intangible assets when acquired externally will be recognised, but internally-generated intangibles are usually excluded from the balance sheet.

- Intangibles range in specificity from those with a contractual basis, such as patents, to those that are rather diffuse and embedded in the firm, such as reputation and organisational competences.

- A firm's competitive advantage can usually be ascribed to the extent to which it possesses unique intangibles. Intangibles can be very valuable indeed when they are scalable, the marginal cost of exploiting them is low and they have no capacity limit.

- But the 'winner-takes-all' feature means investment in intangibles may be much more risky than in tangible assets. Also intangibles are characterised by legal difficulties in fully enforcing property rights and by a lack of active secondary markets.

- Expensing the investment in intangibles means that income is understated in the short run, and assets and equity are understated. On balance, the effect is to flatter return on capital. This understatement of balance sheets may also partly explain the global phenomenon of rising price-to-book ratios.

- We examined the different effects of purchase accounting, which recognises acquired intangibles and goodwill as the residual asset, and pooling.

- Particularly when comparing return on capital to the cost of capital, it may be desirable to capitalise R&D and reinstate goodwill in the balance sheet in order to make the balance sheet more complete. But there is a danger of tokenism, and that R&D will be capitalised and other intangibles overlooked. The capitalisation of gross goodwill is problematic if the firm has overpaid. We should trust the impairment exercise to measure this overpayment.

- If we want comparability with firms that have grown organically, then it may be more helpful to omit acquired intangibles, and compare firms on the basis of tangible and financial assets.

ANNEX BS Group – an example of purchase accounting

Big and Small's balance sheets (in $m) are shown below. Big purchases all 4m of Small's $1 shares in exchange for 25m of its own $1 shares.

Table 6 Big and Small;s balance sheets (figures in $m)

	Big	Small
Cash	15	5
Receivables	30	14
Inventory	20	8
PP&E	50	8
TOTAL ASSETS	**115**	**35**
Payables	10	10
Bank loan		15
Shareholders' funds:		
Issued share capital	65	4
Other reserves	40	6
TOTAL L&SF	**115**	**35**

1 Since Big's shares were trading at 240¢ on the day the acquisition was completed, the fair value of the consideration is (25m × 240¢ =) $60m. Big's new share capital is its original share capital, 65, plus the par value of the new shares issued for the takeover, 25. The remainder of the 60 of consideration will be recorded as share premium. This is calculated as $35m, which is 25m shares times the excess of the issue price over the par value of each share, (240 - 100 =) 140¢.

2 Big reviews Small's net assets to produce a 'fair value table'.
   – It finds that 2m of the receivables should be classified as doubtful, while the inventory, which is on the books at 8m, would cost 9m to replace.
   – Real estate carried at 8m in the balance sheet has a market value of 20m.
   – An important motive for acquiring Small was to gain control of a patent it had developed, which Big values at 20m.

Table 7 Small's fair value table

	Book	Adjustments	Fair value
Cash	5		5
Receivables	14	-2	12
Inventory	8	1	9
Patent		20	20
PP&E	8	12	20
Payables	-25		-25
Net assets acquired	**10**	**31**	**41**
		Goodwill	19
Consideration			**60**

3 The fair value exercise values Small's identified net assets at 41m. Since Big paid 60m, the goodwill in the transaction is 19m.

4 Big has a profit of \$10m in the year to 31 December, and Small has a profit of \$6m. If the acquisition is completed on July 1st, Big's reported profit for the year will be ($10 + 0.5 \times 6 =$) \$13m.

This is how the new BS Group balance sheet looks after the acquisition:

Table 8 BS Group balance sheet

	Big's existing	Acquisition	New
Cash	15	5	20
Receivables	30	12	42
Inventory	20	9	29
Patent		20	20
Goodwill		19	19
PP&E	50	20	70
TOTAL ASSETS	**115**		**200**
Payables	10	10	20
Bank loan		15	15
Shareholders' funds:			
Issued share capital	65	25	90
Share premium		35	35
Other reserves	40		40
TOTAL L&SF	**115**		**200**

Chapter 12

Liabilities

W e want a firm's balance sheet to record all of its liabilities. But as with assets, the challenge for accounting is the indeterminacy of the world. Some liabilities are contingent on uncertain future events, so that at the date of the balance sheet it is unclear how big the liability is and even whether it exists at all. This cannot easily be represented in the black and white world of accounting. We discuss how GAAP deals with this indeterminacy and we examine some of the most important classes of liability for firms, including tax liabilities and pension liabilities.

THE GAAP APPROACH TO LIABILITY RECOGNITION

Given its assets, if a firm recognises a liability that it had not recognised before, this must be at the expense of shareholders. The firm increases liabilities and correspondingly reduces equity. We call this 'pure liability recognition'.

GAAP: Tests for liability recognition

In the language of GAAP, a *liability* measures an expected outflow of resources or sacrifice of economic benefits. The tests for recognising a liability in the balance sheet are the mirror of those for an asset. A liability is recognised in the balance sheet when the outflow of resources is probable and it can be reliably measured, and the obligation resulted from past events. Both US GAAP and IFRS generally require liabilities to be discounted.

The key issue in deciding whether a firm should recognise a liability in the balance sheet is the balance of probability. A liability must be recognised in the balance sheet if it will probably crystallise. IFRS sees 'probable' as more likely than not, while US GAAP sets a higher hurdle.

Example: Beta Corporation

– Beta Corporation has bought $5m of goods from a supplier on two months' credit.
– Beta has a $10m bank loan maturing in five years.
– Beta has a liability to provide pensions and healthcare benefits for its past and current employees.
– Beta makes durable goods such as kitchen appliances. Customers have a statutory right to return faulty appliances for up to a year after the sale, and some customers have bought extended warranties for three years.
– A competitor firm is suing Beta over a patent infringement.

Many or most of a firm's liabilities are determinate – the firm clearly has a liability of known magnitude and there is no need for a debate. Beta's trade payables and bank loan are of this sort. But sometimes matters are not so clear-cut – the firm has a liability but is not sure how big it will be. The ultimate size of Beta's employee liabilities will depend on a number of factors, including the incidence of illness amongst the employees, and their life expectancy, over many years into the future. Beta's product liability will depend on the quality and reliability of its current generation of products, and the proportion of dissatisfied customers who take the trouble to return their products. When a firm has a liability but is uncertain of its size, as in the case of Beta's employee and product liabilities, it has to estimate these liabilities and recognise that amount in the balance sheet. Accountants use the word *provision* for an estimated liability.

Sometimes it is uncertain whether a firm has a liability at all. A potential liability that is possible, but is more than a remote possibility, and is not probable enough to meet the tests for balance-sheet recognition, is known as a *contingency*. Beta's lawsuit is of this sort. GAAP requires the disclosure of contingencies in footnotes to the accounts.

An interesting, and dramatic, example of provisioning in action is the provisions that nuclear power generators such as EDF must make for decommissioning.

Case: EDF's nuclear decommissioning costs

EDF Group is a multinational energy group based in France. Alongside its conventional power-generation capability, it has the world's largest nuclear power-generation fleet. 87% of its French power generation is nuclear, and EDF accounted for 17.2% of global nuclear capacity in June 2005. In late 2005, EDF made a public issue of shares to French retail investors and to the international market, including a sale of shares by the French state, and the following data are taken from the 27 October 2005 offer document. Highly summarised, here is EDF's balance sheet for the half-year to 30 June 2005, which was produced for the first time under IFRS.

Table 1 EDF's balance sheet (figures in €bn)

PP&E	98.3	includes 17.1 for the nuclear fleet
Cash and financial assets	21.8	includes 3.6 of 'dedicated assets'
Other	35.0	
TOTAL ASSETS	**155.1**	
Equity	12.1	
Provisions	46.2	includes 27.3 for nuclear decommissioning
Other	96.8	
TOTAL L&SF	**155.1**	

Within the PP&E of 98.3 is 17.1 for the nuclear fleet, which is the gross cost of the assets, 44.8, less the accumulated depreciation to date, 27.7. EDF tells us that the average age of its French pressurised water reactors (PWR) is 19 years. If these comprise all its nuclear assets, and if depreciation is straight-line, we can estimate the remaining life in accounting terms. Say the full service life is n. So far, 19/n of the life has been consumed, or 27.7/44.8 of their cost. So n = 19×(44.8/27.7), which is approximately 30 years, leaving around 11 years of book life. In fact, EDF say they hope to extend the PWR lifespan beyond 40 years, then start replacing them with the new European pressurised reactors (EPRs) after 2020.

While depreciation accounts for the consumption of the book asset, the future cost of today's nuclear activities is accounted for by making a provision for decommissioning, which is carried as a liability in the balance sheet rather than deducted from the assets. Though the nuclear fleet is currently in the balance sheet at €17.1bn, the future costs of decommissioning are expected to be some €53bn: in excess of €28bn for reprocessing, storage and disposal of nuclear fuel, and €24.5bn for decommissioning and disposal of the core. GAAP allows firms to show the *present value* of a liability. EDF recognised €27.3bn as a provision, or around 50% of the estimated actual future costs, having discounted them at a 5% discount rate.

The creation of a provision is the recognition of an external claim on the firm's assets that, other things equal, comes out of equity's claim. Even discounted, the nuclear decommissioning provision is very large, and this perhaps explains EDF's equity/total assets ratio, which, at 7.8%, is very low for an industrial firm. The provision is obviously matched by assets in the general sense that 'assets equal claims' in a balance sheet. But that does not guarantee that there will be cash to pay the decommissioning costs when the time comes. So EDF has started to build a dedicated portfolio of financial assets for this. It contributed €3.6bn this year, and will do the same each year in the future.

Liabilities must be unavoidable

GAAP does not want firms to understate their liabilities, but it does not want them overstated either. Overstating liabilities is distortive since it means depressing the current period's income and inflating income in some future period, when it is decided that the provision is no longer needed. Here are some other examples of provisioning practices that have been common in the past:

- The incoming CEO of an ailing firm makes large provisions for the costs of future reorganisation. This is colloquially known as 'taking a big bath'. The CEO believes that this will come at little cost in terms of market perceptions because investors were hungry for new management and welcomed the provision as a signal of intentions.
- An acquisition is accompanied by a large reorganisation provision. The creation of the provision just got lost amongst the balance sheet charges in a takeover and its accounting effect is to increase goodwill on acquisition rather than being charged against income.

In both cases, future profits would be enhanced either because the provision would absorb future costs or, if the costs did not materialise, the provision could be written back to income.

GAAP now requires that there must be an 'obligation resulting from past events' before a liability can be recognised. An 'obligation' is something that is unavoidable. GAAP requires a restructuring plan to be under way or restructuring to be unavoidable, rather than just intended, before a provision can be made. GAAP does not allow provisions to be made for liabilities that may be avoided by future actions, so in the Beta example, Beta must recognise its liability for healthcare benefits for past and current employees, but not provide for the healthcare liabilities of future employees it has not yet hired. [References: Con6, IAS32, IAS39]

In the remainder of this chapter we focus on two classes of liability that are large, and challenging for firms to estimate: employee benefits and tax liabilities.

PENSIONS

Wages and salaries are largely paid as they accrue. But if the firm has agreed to provide its employees with a pension or with healthcare benefits into retirement, current employment brings deferred remuneration and a commitment to incur costs long into the future. These are potentially large liabilities that should be recognised in the balance sheet – they relate to past events and they are almost certain to crystallise, though they are hard to estimate. Pension liabilities are enormous for some firms; GM was reported to have a net liability of $37.76bn in 2004 that added $1,500 to the cost of each vehicle produced. Generous corporate pension provision tends to be a feature of high-wage economies, and so has become a source of competitive disadvantage for some nations.

If the pension scheme is *defined contribution*, then the pensioners simply receive whatever income the pension assets can generate – the employee takes the asset risk. But *defined benefit (DB)* schemes promise the employee a certain pension, usually based on final salary and possibly indexed to protect it against subsequent inflation. The size of the liability now becomes a function of the employee's future career path and their longevity after retirement. If Fred has just joined a defined-benefit scheme at 25, and people of his generation are living to 80, then the pension liability to him is contingent on events up to 55 years in the future. If the firm invests in assets to meet this liability, the adequacy of these assets requires a forecast of investment returns over the same period. So a firm's net pension asset or liability, its surplus or deficit, is the difference between two, frequently large, uncertain numbers. The surplus or deficit is inevitably sensitive to small changes in assumptions, so firms are very vulnerable to accusations of misaccounting in this area. Obviously we need to be vigilant, but we should also recognise that accounting for defined-benefit pensions is the toughest accounting challenge that firms face.

A pension scheme creates a liability for the firm to pay its employees a pension on retirement. If the scheme is *unfunded* the firm simply makes full provision in the balance sheet for the future cost of the pension as the rights accrue during employment. Unfunded schemes remain common in Germany, and for healthcare in the US, and because no assets are earmarked the liability frequently becomes the largest single item in the balance sheets of these firms. If the scheme is *funded* the firm creates a separate legal entity to pay the pension and contributes the assets needed to meet the future pension liabilities, which puts those pension assets off the firm's balance sheet. In this case, if the scheme is funded, the fund is likely to have recourse to the firm in order to make up any shortfall if the assets prove insufficient to meet the liability. If the fund is in deficit, or *underfunded*, this is then a liability of the firm. On the other hand, if the fund is in surplus and its assets exceed its liabilities this is an asset of the firm that it can recover by taking a contribution holiday in future years.

Pensions concepts and vocabulary

The *projected benefit obligation (PBO)* is the present value of the expected pension and this is a function of a number of factors, most of which are uncertain. The PBO relating to a particular employee depends on the employee's years of service to date.

Assuming a final salary scheme, the PBO depends on the projected final salary, which will depend in turn on anticipated salary inflation and the probability of the employee quitting or retiring early or, conversely, being promoted to a higher grade. The PBO is then a function of the employee's expected longevity after retirement. These factors all determine the cash outflows that will be required to service the pension. Finally, the PBO depends on the rate used to discount these projected outflows. The accumulated benefit obligation (ABO) makes the same calculation using today's salary. The scheme deficit or surplus is then the difference between the PBO and the value of the fund assets.

Example: Fred's pension

Fred has just joined the pension scheme, which offers a pension of a week's salary per year of service, based on final salary. Fred is 25, and is expected to retire at 60 and die at 80. His current salary is €500 per week and his projected salary on retirement is €1,250 per week. The discount rate is 6%.

At the end of year 1, Fred has qualified for a pension of one week's (projected final) salary, that is, €1,250. So the firm's expected liability is to pay an annuity of €1,250 from his retirement to his death, which is for (80 − 60 =) 20 years. But this will not start for (60 − 25 =) 35 years. So the PBO at the end of year 1 is the present value of a 20-year, €1,250 annuity, discounted for 35 years. The 20-year, 6% annuity factor is 11.47, so the annuity is worth (1,250 × 11.47 =) €14,338; discounted for 35 years at 6%, that is worth (14,338 × .130 =) €1,865.

The *current service cost* is the increment in PBO that arises as a result of the current year's service. In Fred's case, in year 1, this is just €1,865.

Even if no other assumptions change, one year later the PBO will have increased because retirement is one year closer. This increase is the *interest cost* and is found as the opening PBO times the discount rate. But assuming there are pension assets, as there would be in a funded scheme, the interest cost is offset by the *expected return on plan assets*. The difference between the interest cost and the expected return on plan assets is often called the *net investment return*. In Fred's case, the year 2 interest cost is (1,865 × 6% =) €112 so that, at the end of year 2, the PBO of Fred's first year of service is (1,865 + 112 =) €1,977. Suppose Fred's scheme has €900 of assets in it at the start of the year, and the assets are expected to earn a rate of return of 8%, and thus to return (900 × 8% =) €72, then the net investment return is (72 - 112 =) -30.

The service cost, and (because it is based on *expected* asset returns) the net investment return, are both fairly predictable and well behaved. But there are other factors that can affect the value of the PBO and the value of the plan assets and that can bring significant volatility, period by period. Their effects are grouped together as *actuarial gains and losses*. They include changes in PBO due to changes in 'actuarial' assumptions – rates of salary growth, quit rates, retirement dates, assumptions about longevity and mortality, and the discount rate. They also include changes in the value of plan assets due to differences between expected asset returns and the actual return achieved on the assets in the period.

Finally, *prior service costs* are changes in PBO resulting from changes to the plan rules, rather than changes of actuarial assumption. Suppose in year 2, Fred's expected final salary is revised to €1,500. From year 2 onward, the service cost is calculated on this basis, but we need to revise the PBO from year 1. Viewed from year 2, the firm owes Fred a 20-year, €1,500 annuity, deliverable in 34 years. The PBO of that is $1,500 \times 11.47 \times .130 = €2,237$. Currently we are carrying a PBO of €1,977 for Fred's year 1 service, so the actuarial loss is $(2,237 - 1,977 =) €260$. Suppose Fred's expected final salary remained €1,250, but new scheme rules gave 120% of final salary, leading to the same pension. Then, instead of an actuarial loss, we would show a prior service cost of €260.

GAAP: Pension accounting

Income statement

The term 'pension cost' is a catch-all for all the income effects of pensions. The components of the *pension cost* are the change in the PBO and the actual return on plan assets. The change in the PBO is the service cost, the interest cost, the actuarial loss (gain) and the prior service cost. The actual return on plan assets is the change in fair value of plan assets less contributions in the period.

GAAP requires firms to charge immediately in the income statement the actual service cost, and the net investment return (interest cost less the expected return on plan assets). All the amounts charged to the income statement are charged to EBIT under US GAAP, but the net investment return component may be shown as financial income or cost under IFRS.

Prior service costs are spread over the vesting period under IFRS and over the active life of existing employees under US GAAP. GAAP also requires the firm to charge the actuarial gain or loss, smoothed over the expected service life of current employees (IFRS), or over 5 years (US GAAP). However, in either case, this is only done for amounts outside a 10% 'corridor', that is, accounting for variances of more that 10% of the greater of the PBO or the value of plan assets at the beginning of the year. By using the corridor method, GAAP allows firms to ignore relatively small swings in the value of pension liabilities and plan assets that would otherwise cause volatility in income. Alternatively, IFRS allows immediate recognition of all actuarial gains and losses, but in other comprehensive income.

Balance sheet

GAAP requires the firm to discount its pension liabilities at an interest rate based on high-quality corporate bonds to calculate the PBO. If such a bond yield is not readily available, IFRS requires a government bond yield. Plan assets should be valued at market values or discounted cash flows if market values are not readily available. The difference between the fair value of assets and the PBO is often known as the 'net funding position'. This will be disclosed in the notes, but will differ from the net surplus of deficit in the balance sheet if, as described above, the firm is smoothing rather than immediately recognising some of the changes in funding position. US GAAP is now considering requiring fund assets and liabilities to be 'marked to market', taking the annual change to income.
[References IAS 19, FAS 87, 88]

One consolation for a firm with a pension deficit is that when it makes the necessary contributions to eliminate the deficit, these are tax deductible. So firms record a deferred tax asset (liability) that partly offsets the pension deficit (surplus).

How to treat pensions in financial analysis

There are two issues to consider when thinking about how to treat a firm's pension liabilities in financial analysis. The first question is whether the firm's balance sheet correctly values the pension liability and the plan assets, and so fully recognises the pension surplus or deficit. The question is whether, for pensions, the balance sheet is complete and at current value. The second question is a philosophical one. Are pension deficits (surpluses) part of capital employed, or are they operating liabilities (assets) that should be deducted (added) to find net operating assets?

Challenging the balance sheet

Challenging pension valuations is tough, from outside the firm. GAAP tries to equip users of the financial statements to challenge the valuations by requiring the firm to disclose much more data than in the past about the actuarial assumptions being used – mortality assumptions, discount rates, smoothing policies and so forth. The actuarial assumptions that relate to the firm's employee profile are idiosyncratic and particularly hard to challenge. But given the very long time horizons, valuations are highly sensitive to assumed discount rates and to assumed rates of return on plan assets and these are, to an extent, comparable between firms. Some investment banks and financial analysis houses devote considerable resources to re-estimating firms' pension valuations on this basis. For instance, most firms have a strong bias towards equities in their pension fund assets, though the pension liabilities are debt-like. The assets are likely to have a higher expected return than the riskless interest rate used for discounting the liabilities. As a result, even if a firm has a significant funding deficit, its 'net investment return' may be closer to parity. Some analysts rework the accounting on the assumption the plan is invested in riskless assets.

Even when we may not be in a position to rework the firm's pension valuation, it is important to read the actuarial assumptions that lie behind it, in order to assess their reasonableness, and whether they appear aggressive or conservative. More straightforwardly, there may be a discrepancy between the funding position described in the notes and the surplus or deficit in the balance sheet. This arises when the pension fund has experienced a significant actuarial gain or loss that, as permitted by GAAP, it is spreading over a number of years. For analysis, we should consider adjusting the balance sheet asset or liability immediately to reflect this.

Is a pension deficit operating or financial?

Given the balance-sheet treatment, the income effects – the pension cost – are reported under GAAP variously within operating profit, financial costs, or as a reserve movement in other comprehensive income.

The question is where *should* they be shown? This depends whether we view the balance sheet deficit or surplus as an operating, or a financing, asset or liability. Some analysts argue strongly that the decision to run a pensions deficit, that is, to have an underfunded pension scheme, is a financing decision and should be analysed accordingly. After all, it is argued, the firm could have raised the capital to fund its scheme fully, and by not doing so it is using the deficit as a source of finance. We are agnostic on this. Certainly, few firms who are struggling with large pension deficits probably feel as though they have made a financing choice, but that is not the point.

The debate about whether pension liabilities should be treated as financing or operating takes us back to the logic of capital employed. Any liability provides us with financing, and we recognise that financing effect equally by including it in capital employed or by netting it against operating assets. The idea of capital employed is to measure the finance provided by external, debt or equity, investors who have identifiable costs of capital against which we can benchmark the return on capital. Ultimately, how broad or narrow a definition of capital employed we use is a pragmatic choice – we should get the same insight about performance. But what is crucial, is consistency between the numerator and the denominator.

The pension deficit as an operating liability

Simplest is to treat the pension deficit or surplus as an operating liability. If capital employed is calculated as shareholders' funds plus net debt then, by default, the pension liability and any deferred tax are correctly treated as netted against net operating assets.

In this case all income-statement pension costs should be charged against EBIT. US GAAP does this. Under IFRS, the net investment return may be in financing income/expense, below EBIT. It needs reclassifying above the line.

Additionally, for balance-sheet completeness, we might deduct any unrecognised deficit (add any surplus) from net operating assets, and for income completeness, add any associated income or expense into comprehensive income.

The pension deficit as a financing liability

Otherwise, the pension surplus/deficit net of tax is included in capital employed.

EBIT should include the service cost and net interest paid should include the net investment return. IFRS allows this treatment, so may not need adjustment. The net investment return will need to be added back to EBIT, and to net interest paid under US GAAP.

Additionally, for balance sheet completeness, we might add any unrecognised deficit (deduct any surplus) from net operating assets, and for income completeness, add any associated income or expense into comprehensive income.

Case: Peugeot Citroen

Peugeot Citroen reported under IFRS in 2005. At December 31 2005, the present value of projected benefit obligations (PBO) amounted to €4.1bn, while the fair value of plan assets was €3.0bn – an underfunding of €1.1bn. Since Peugeot Citroen only had a negligible unrecognised actuarial loss. €1.1bn is also the deficit recognised in the balance sheet, so in Peugeot's case no further adjustment is required. Peugeot discloses that the expected return on plan assets is 2% higher than the discount rate used for liabilities.

Peugeot Citroen credited SG&A with €62m on account of pensions in 2005 – the service cost of – €91m was more than offset by some special items including an insurance credit. It charged a net investment return of -€19m (which was expected return on plan assets, 168, less interest cost, 187) to 'other income and (expenses), net'. We would include this -€19m in EBIT under the 'operating' approach and in net interest paid under the 'financing' approach described above.

Healthcare benefits

Corporate provision of healthcare benefits post-retirement is a particularly US practice. American Airways is a typical example of the scale of the impact on equity of large US firms when healthcare provisioning was required.

Case: American Airlines

On January 1 1992, American Airlines adopted FAS 106, 'Employers' Accounting for Postretirement Benefits Other Than Pensions', which requires that the expected cost of post-retirement benefits such as health-care and life insurance are accrued during the years of employment. AA recorded a one-time charge of $917m pre tax ($595m after tax) as the cumulative effect of accounting change. At December 31 1992 these other post-retirement benefits increased total projected benefit obligations by 29% to $4.4bn and shifted the AA employee benefits fund from over funded (net assets of $347m) to under funded (net liabilities of $570m) resulting in a fall in shareholders' funds by 21% to $3.3bn.

TAX ASSETS AND LIABILITIES

Governments take a very large proportion of the income of firms – internationally, most corporate tax rates currently lie between 30% and 40%. This makes tax the largest single cost for many firms, along with labour. And the complex operation of the tax system means that this year's activities can have significant tax effects long into the future, requiring tax liabilities and tax assets to be recognised in the balance sheet.

Imagine a world in which governments simply applied the corporate tax rate to a firm's earnings before tax, then required the firm to pay the tax in full during the year, or, if the firm made a loss, paid the firm an immediate subsidy at the same rate. If tax systems worked that way, taxes would be immediate and proportionate, so that the firm's effective tax rate would be the statutory corporate tax rate. There would be no effects outside the year being taxed, so no impact on the balance sheet. Sadly, tax systems do not work that way.

Two minor departures from this simple ideal relate to payment lags and 'disallowables'. Some part of the year's tax, perhaps a final instalment, is typically paid after the year end. This becomes tax payable in current liabilities in the year-end balance sheet. The tax authorities use GAAP principles to measure income, so when they are computing the firm's tax they start from earnings before tax in the income statement. But they then make two types of adjustments to get to *taxable profit*. A feature of most tax codes is that certain expenditure is disallowed for tax by the tax authorities; entertainment expenditure is a favourite. *Disallowables* of this sort are annoying, and they affect the effective tax rate, but have no balance-sheet effects.

Example: PartyCo

PartyCo's accounting earnings before tax is $1,000 but this is after charging $400 of expenditure on entertaining customers. Since this is disallowable for tax, PartyCo's taxable profit is $1,400 and if the corporate tax rate is 30%, the tax charge for the year is (= 1,400 × 30%) $420 .PartyCo has an effective tax rate of (= 420/1,000) 42% .

The two features of tax systems that have a major impact on balance sheets are 'timing differences' and the treatment of tax losses.

Deferred tax accounting

The tax authorities disallow certain expenditure when calculating taxable profit. But a second type of adjustment that the tax authorities make is much more disruptive. These adjustments arise when the tax authorities and the firm apply accrual accounting differently to the same set of facts. Viewed over time, accounting profit and taxable profit will equalise, but year by year the effective tax rate differs from the statutory rate. One option would be to ignore this discrepancy, but GAAP requires firms to bring the tax charge into line with accounting profit for all timing differences by using a 'tax equalisation' account called a 'deferred tax provision'. A persistent, though usually small-scale difference between tax and accounting arises because tax authorities use cash rather than accrual accounting for some revenue and expense items. For instance, some tax systems insist on taxing interest on a cash basis.

Depreciation is a much more substantial source of timing differences. Some tax authorities replace the firm's depreciation schedule with their own schedule when calculating taxable profit. The tax authorities may just share the general mistrust of depreciation, or their motive may be to use the tax system to encourage certain behaviour. For example, governments are keen to encourage industrial R&D, so they may offer immediate expensing of R&D-related investment in plant and machinery. Effectively, the government is offering 100% depreciation of these assets in the first year but, of course, none thereafter. The benefit is that the firm gets the tax savings earlier.

Example: ResearchCo

ResearchCo have spent €800 on a digital scanner. They are depreciating it 25% per year, straight-line, over four years, giving earnings before tax of €1,000 per year. The tax rules allow them to expense the scanner 100% in the year of purchase. The corporate tax rate is 35%. As it stands, this would generate the following profile of earnings:

Table 2 ResearchCo's earnings

	Earnings before tax a	Accounting depreciation b	Tax depreciation c	Taxable profit d=a+b-c	Tax e=dx35%	Effective rate e/a	Earnings after tax a-e
Year 1	1,000	200	800	400	140	14%	860
Year 2	1,000	200	0	1,200	420	42%	580
Year 3	1,000	200	0	1,200	420	42%	580
Year 4	1,000	200	0	1,200	420	42%	580
Totals	4,000	800	800	4,000	1,400	35%	2,600

For instance in year 1, ResearchCo has earnings before tax and after accounting depreciation of €1,000. The tax authorities add back the accounting depreciation of (€800 × 25% =) €200, but deduct the full €800 of expenditure, to get taxable profit of (€1,000 + €200 - €800 =) €400. So, in that year, ResearchCo's tax would be just (€400 × 35% =) €140 on accounting earnings of €1,000. This gives an effective rate of (€140/€1,000 =) 14%, and earnings after tax of (€1,000 - €140 =) €860. But in subsequent years the same process gives an effective tax rate of 42%, and earnings after tax of €580. The accounting depreciation is added back, but there is no tax depreciation. If ResearchCo's tax had been based on accounting profit it would have been (€1,000 × 35% =) €350 every year, giving earnings after tax of €650. The tax and accounting profit come to the same total over time, but year by year they do not. The first year is particularly misleading, as earnings after tax are inflated to €860 by the low tax charge.

The accounting solution is to equalise the tax by opening a *deferred tax* account. In year 1, ResearchCo has an actual tax charge of €140 and charges profit with an additional €210 of deferred tax that it puts into a deferred tax liability account. Effectively, the firm is recognising a future liability of €210 for tax. In year 2, ResearchCo does the reverse; its actual charge is €420, but it offsets this by drawing €70 from the deferred tax account. The impact of deferred tax accounting on the income statement and balance sheet over the four years is as follows:

Table 3 ResearchCo's income statement and balance sheet

		Income statement			Balance sheet
	Earnings before tax	Actual tax	Deferred tax charge	Reported tax	Deferred tax liability
Year 1	1,000	140	210	350	210
Year 2	1,000	420	-70	350	140
Year 3	1,000	420	-70	350	70
Year 4	1,000	420	-70	350	0
Totals		1,400	0	1,400	

The effect of deferred tax accounting is to match the tax to the accounting income, to give a smoother, and more representative, tax charge and after-tax income number. It 'equalises' the tax each year, hence a deferred tax account is sometimes known as a *tax equalisation* account.

GAAP: Deferred tax

Accelerated tax depreciation gives a reduced tax bill in early years that is exactly balanced by higher tax in later years. In the language of deferred tax, the timing differences were *fully reversing*. However, it is easy to imagine a world in which they might not reverse or, rather, would not appear to reverse. For instance, if the firm is continually growing and investing – buying a scanner or some similar kit each year – the reversal of the tax depreciation on earlier investments may be offset by accelerated depreciation on later investments. On this basis, firms have argued vehemently that they should not have to make a provision for deferred tax. However, GAAP says that this reasoning is flawed. It would be one thing to argue that it is improbable that the tax liability arising from past events will crystallise. But these firms are trying to offset a certain tax liability from an unavoidable past event with an uncertain tax benefit from an avoidable future event.

Under both US GAAP and IFRS firms provide in full for deferred tax on timing differences. The tax provision is based on existing rather than potential tax rates. Also, deferred tax assets and liabilities should not, in general, be netted off. If assets are revalued, which is not permitted under US GAAP, the tax that would be payable if they were sold at this valuation must be separately recognised in equity shareholders' funds. The provision for deferred tax is charged in the income statement alongside the actual tax for the year. Firms have to show a reconciliation of actual taxes to the tax that would be payable based on accounting profit.
[References: FAS109, IAS12]

Tax adjustments such as replacing accounting depreciation with tax depreciation add complexity to accounting. Accounting's response – deferred tax accounting – adds more complexity. If the tax authorities' motive is a mistrust of accountants, the alternative would be to trust the firm and its auditors, reporting under GAAP, to ensure that depreciation charges are reasonable. After all, the tax authorities are happy to accept GAAP numbers elsewhere. If the motive is to use the tax system to encourage investment, unfortunately research provides little evidence that such tax incentives work. Firms seem to do what they were going to do anyway, and take the tax subsidy as a windfall. Given the shortage of evidence that adjusting profits for tax has any economic benefits, the tax authorities should perhaps just use GAAP earnings as the tax base.

Tax losses and tax assets

The other major reason tax impacts the balance sheet is the treatment of taxable losses. Sometimes firms make taxable losses. They may have accounting losses, or tax adjustments like accelerated tax depreciation may turn an accounting profit into a taxable loss. If the tax system were symmetrical the tax authorities would need to pay the firm a proportion of its losses when it made a loss, just as they take a proportion of its profits. Governments do not do this; but they cannot simply ignore losses and only tax profits.

Example: Volatile Inc

Volatile makes profits of 60 one year and losses of 40 the next, and the tax rate is 30%. In any two-year period Volatile earns 60 - 40 = 20. But if the government just taxes profits and ignores losses Volatile pays 30% × 60 = 18 of tax, which relative to the 20 of income amounts to a 90% effective tax rate.

The compromise is to allow firms to use tax losses to reclaim tax paid on profits of earlier years *(tax loss carry back)*, and to use the remaining tax loss to offset taxable profits in future years *(tax loss carry forward)*. All tax jurisdictions allow carry-forward, though for widely differing numbers of years, and some allow limited carry-back. Table 4 is a (much) simplified snapshot of the rules in some countries as of 2004. It shows how many years losses may be carried forward and, if permitted, back. Note that in countries that allow relatively long carry-forward there are usually limitations on the ability to transfer the loss if there is a change of ownership of the firm.

Table 4 International corporate tax-loss regimes

	Forward	Back		Forward	Back
Australia	∞	no	Netherlands	∞	3
Belgium	∞	no	Norway	10	2
Canada	7	3	Russia	10	no
Finland	10	no	Spain	15	no
France	∞	3	Switzerland	7	no
Germany	∞	1	Turkey	5	no
Italy	5	no	UK	∞	1
Japan	5	no	USA	20	2

Example: LossCo

LossCo has taxable profits this year of $15m and the corporate tax rate is 30%, so it is liable to pay ($15m × 30% =) $4.5m of tax. But LossCo is carrying forward a taxable loss of $10m that can be offset against this year's profit, and this reduces the tax payable to (($15m - $10m) × 30% =) $1.5m. The value of the tax loss is the $3m current tax saved, which is the tax loss times the tax rate. The value of the tax loss used immediately is its maximum value. Suppose LossCo knows that it will be able to use the loss and save $3m of tax, but not for five years. The value of the tax loss today is the present value of the expected tax saving. LossCo's cost of capital is 10%, so the value is ($3m/(1.1)^5 =) $1.86m. If it is uncertain whether there will be sufficient future profits to absorb the loss, the value of the tax loss is further reduced. If there is a time limit on loss carry-forward and no chance of recovery within that period, then the loss becomes worthless.

GAAP: Tax losses

Carried-forward tax losses become valuable assets, but GAAP used not to allow firms to recognise the asset associated with a carried-forward tax loss in the balance sheet. The basic asset recognition test, that an asset is only recognised if it represents probable future economic benefits, would have meant demonstrating with high likelihood that there would be sufficient taxable profits in the future to utilise the tax loss. This was too tough a test, and the omission of tax losses became a serious source of balance sheet incompleteness for firms with troubled histories that were carrying large tax losses forward. In response, US GAAP required firms to recognise tax assets in full. It achieves this by relaxing the test for an asset. Tax assets are recognised if it is 'more likely than not' (rather than probable) that the benefits will be realised. The same standard also required firms to recognise their deferred tax liabilities in full. On the other hand, IFRS maintains the requirement for probable economic benefits, so firms reporting under IFRS may have valuable tax losses that are unrecognised in the balance sheet.
[References : FAS109, IAS12]

REVIEW

- In this chapter we looked at the recognition of liabilities in financial statements.

- As with assets, the size and even the existence of some liabilities may be uncertain, and the challenge for GAAP is to reflect the ambiguity of the real world in the black and white world of accounting.

- For liability recognition GAAP requires that the outflow of resources must be probable, there must be a defined obligation that arises from prior not future events, and the amount must be capable of reliable measurement.

- If a liability is probable, it is included in the balance sheet as a 'provision'; if it is less certain but nevertheless likely to occur, it is included in the notes to the accounts as a 'contingency' so has no impact on the income statement or balance sheet.

- We looked at pension liabilities in some detail. We need to understand the nature of the pension scheme and of any the obligations to employees. There are two main issues for financial analysis. The first is, does the balance sheet correctly recognise the scheme surplus of deficit? The second is, are pension deficits financing or operating liabilities? The answer to the first question will indicate whether we need to adjust the balance sheet and recognise a corresponding income effect. The answer to the second question, requires us to rearrange the IFRS and US GAAP income components accordingly.

- Deferred tax is an adjustment firms make to take account of differences between the accounting treatment of income and expenditure, and the treatment for tax. The deferred tax account is effectively a tax equalisation account. The recognition of deferred tax assets and liabilities will be determined by the probability that the economic benefit or loss will occur. Common sources of tax timing differences are the treatment of depreciation, and the carry forward of tax losses.

Chapter 13

Asset/liability netting

L iabilities are frequently linked to assets, so asset and liability recognition go hand in hand. When GAAP determines that a firm does not own an asset, the effect is that neither the liability nor the asset are recognised in the balance sheet. This chapter examines how firms do this, including receivables financing and operating leasing. We also examine the rules for accounting for subsidiaries, since the use of 'equity accounting' instead of consolidation for an investment in another firm has the same effect of netting liabilities against assets.

THE GAAP APPROACH TO ASSET/LIABILITY NETTING

The last two chapters discussed 'pure' asset recognition and liability recognition where, in each case, the impact was on equity. The accounting we discuss in this chapter does not affect equity. Often, liabilities are linked to assets, for instance, a loan is raised to finance the purchase of an asset and is secured on the asset, or some assets and liabilities are bundled together within a legal entity. When assets and liabilities are linked, GAAP looks at the ownership of the asset. The liability is only recognised in the balance sheet if the asset is recognised, and the asset is only recognised if the firm owns it. So if GAAP decides a firm does not own some assets, this reduces liabilities too. Effectively the liabilities are netted off against the assets. This transforms the look of the balance sheet and, since the liabilities are usually debt finance, the firm's capital structure and gearing look much healthier. For this reason, *netting* is one of the most controversial areas of accounting.

Some vocabulary

Asset financing describes an arrangement where debt is raised to finance a particular asset or class of assets, and is secured on those assets. In terms of the amounts involved, leasing of long-term assets is the most important form of asset financing, followed by financing of receivables. When a firm contracts so that neither the asset nor the associated financing are recognised on its balance sheet, this is called *off-balance-sheet financing*. A leasing contract of this sort is called *operating leasing*. When assets and liabilities are already on the balance sheet but the firm contracts with a third party to remove them, this is called asset/liability *derecognition* or *defeasance*. In this case the firm is essentially selling the asset. *Securitisation* is a technique with similar effects[1].

Determining ownership

In this chapter we describe three important contexts where netting arises. Two are forms of asset financing – receivables financing, and the operating leasing of long-term assets. The third is accounting for subsidiaries and associates. Though these may seem quite different in nature, they all pose the same challenge. GAAP's general approach is to determine the ownership of an asset by asking who is taking the risks and rewards of ownership. But in a world of complex contracting there may be no easy answer because the risks and rewards of ownership may be *shared* between different parties.

Take the case of leasing. A firm needs to use a long-term asset, a building or a machine, and wants the bank to fund this by buying the asset and leasing it to the firm. The asset is multi-faceted and long-lived, so the contract will have to be complex. Apart from the terms of the borrowing, the contract will need to determine who is responsible for maintaining and insuring the asset, how long the lease is expected to run and whether it can be terminated early, whether the firm may buy the asset from the bank and on what terms, and so on and so forth. Though the contract may share the risks and rewards between the firm and the bank in a complex way, GAAP faces its familiar problem of representing complex reality in the black-and-white world of the balance sheet. GAAP

---

1   *Securitisation* is an arrangement which is popular with banks themselves. Though individual financial assets such as credit-card receivables or mortgage accounts may have credit risk, in aggregate they form a low-risk asset with predictable returns. The bank puts its receivables into a pool and either sells the portfolio to an investor or sells shares in the portfolio as tradeable securities.

has to decide whether in substance the firm is, or isn't, the owner. If this sounds like a hopeless task, it is. GAAP has found it hard to police leasing from the asset side, and a lot of leased assets remain off the balance sheet under operating leases. These leases usually commit the firm to make payments for years ahead; that is, they create a liability. Operating lease liabilities pass with flying colours all of the tests for a liability that were described in the last chapter – they are large, certain and easy to measure. But because GAAP focuses on the asset ownership, the liability does not get recognised. As a result, it is standard practice for analysts to capitalise operating leases, using publicly available data, and we discuss the mechanics of this later.

The sharing problem can also arise dramatically when subsidiaries are not fully owned. If a firm owns some shares in another entity the key issue is the proportion of ownership. If the firm effectively controls the other firm, which in the simplest case means owning more than 50% of its ordinary shares, then its assets and liabilities are added in full to the parent's balance sheet. But if ownership is below that level, *equity accounting* is used and the effect is just the same as derecognition under asset financing – the underlying liabilities are netted against the assets.

Firms sometimes sell assets – for example, a portfolio of receivables – and perhaps use the proceeds to pay down debt. A firm is perfectly entitled to do this, but GAAP's question will now be, has the asset *actually* been sold? In particular, does the firm retain any residual risk?

Separation of the existence and ownership issues

To be recognised in the balance sheet, a firm needs to demonstrate both that an asset exists, and that it owns the asset. In practice these two questions neatly separate themselves. The ownership question that we are discussing in this chapter tends to arise with tangible and financial assets. The question of whether an asset actually exists tends to relate to intangibles, as we saw in Chapter 11. It is helpful to understand why there is this separation.

Firms like to play down the amount of their debt, while fully stating their equity. In economies with well-developed legal systems it is straightforward to borrow against tangible or financial assets. In an economy with a sophisticated capital market, a further step is to write a more complex contract, with the lender taking ownership of the asset, so that the asset and, more interestingly, the debt are off the firm's balance sheet. The accounting tension is then between the firm, which wants to show that it does not own an asset and does not have the borrowing, and GAAP which says that, in substance, it does. The tension for intangibles is the other way round. The difficulty in reliably demonstrating the value of intangible assets means that it is still uncommon for a firm to borrow directly against intangibles. Intangibles therefore tend to be equity financed. Firms want to record their intangibles and to show the corresponding equity. But the same unreliability makes GAAP reluctant to allow it.

GAAP: Offsetting assets and liabilities

This chapter focuses on some contractual arrangements that have the effect of concealing debt through netting. In each case, GAAP has developed specific rules. But there are other temptations to 'net', particularly when the firm has assets and liabilities involving the same third party or 'counterparty'. For example, we have a loan of $10m from Z bank, but we also have $3m on deposit at Z bank. Why not just show a liability of $7m in the balance sheet? We have a deferred tax liability of yen ¥20m but we also have some carried forward tax losses that give us a deferred tax asset of ¥25m. Why not just show a deferred tax asset of ¥5m?

Netting one number off against another always means a loss of information. Except when netting is specifically permitted by a standard, GAAP now says that financial liabilities and financial assets can only be netted in the balance sheet when offset is legally enforceable, and there is an intention to settle in that way. For many European banks, in particular, the introduction of IFRS in 2005 had a significant effect. IAS 32, *Financial instruments: disclosure and presentation*, required them to 'un-net' some assets and liabilities they had traditionally shown net, including deferred tax. The gross presentation affects total assets, and total liabilities and shareholders ' funds, but not net assets or equity. Some banks found their total assets increasing by 20% or more due to the stricter netting rules.
[References: FAS133, 139, IAS32]

RECEIVABLES FINANCING

If a firm wants to borrow against its receivables it can arrange *invoice discounting,* which is equivalent to the 'bill discounting' long used in international trade, or *factoring.* The finance house advances some money immediately, say 80% of the face value. The balance is paid to the firm when the customer finally pays, less finance charges and an administration charge. Most factors and invoice discounters are bank subsidiaries; the cost of capital is related to the bank's lending rate and they apply typical bank lending criteria.

What distinguishes a factoring agreement is that the firm also outsources some of its accounting and credit-related activities to the bank. The factor may provide sales-ledger services such as keeping accounting records and chasing receivables for payment. This is likely to appeal to firms that are too small for it to be economic to have a sales-ledger function, or firms that are growing fast and want to avoid the disruption of reorganising the sales-ledger function. The factor may undertake functions such as the approval and checking of credit applications. The factor may bring scale economies to the credit management process; it will bring objectivity to the credit decision because it will not be influenced by having to make a sale; it may have good access to credit databases and employ skilled credit analysts, and so forth.

Finally, the factor or invoice discounter may accept the risk of the receivable defaulting. Credit insurance is attractive to small firms that cannot withstand the default of a major customer. The key issue is 'recourse'. If the finance house has agreed to take the loss in the event that the receivable defaults, the arrangement is *non-recourse*. If the finance house can recover the outstanding amount from the firm, it is *recourse*.

Lack of data makes international comparisons difficult, but factoring and invoice discounting appears to be widely used. For instance, in France over 30% of small and medium-sized entities use receivables financing. In the UK, according to the industry trade association, some £149bn of receivables were asset-financed in 2005. The great majority was invoice discounting with recourse, and £18bn was factoring; and £16.5bn was non-recourse and therefore off the balance sheet.

GAAP: Financial asset derecognition

Recourse is key to the accounting treatment when finance is raised against financial assets. In a non-recourse arrangement the firm can then derecognise the asset and the related borrowing. It has effectively sold the asset, because the finance house has agreed to take the risks and rewards of ownership. GAAP allows derecognition of some or all of a financial asset if substantially all the risks and rewards of ownership have been transferred, or control has been transferred. But, unless this condition is met, the financing is shown as debt, within liabilities. So the treatment is binary: the asset is either in or out of the balance sheet.
[Reference: IAS39, FAS140]

A trade receivable is a simple current asset, so if the firm sells such an asset to a bank and uses the proceeds to pay off debt, then the balance-sheet treatment should be straightforward. But even in this case there is potential for ambiguity. If the customer defaults and the bank takes the loss, the receivable was clearly sold. If the bank has recourse to the firm to recover the money, then clearly the receivable was not sold. However, a contract may have been written in which in certain situations the bank will take the loss and in others not. UK GAAP, under accounting standard FRS5, used to offer an intermediate treatment in such a case. Under FRS5, if there was 'partial recourse', firms could use the so-called 'linked presentation'. Both the receivable and the loan had to be disclosed, but the loan was deducted from the receivable within current assets. One firm to take advantage of this was WPP.

Case: Receivables financing at WPP

WPP is one of the world's largest communications groups, parent company to many of the world's best known agencies, including JWT, Ogilvy and Mather, Y&R, and Hill and Knowlton. In its 2004 and 2005 balance sheets, WPP reported the following within current assets:

Table 1 WPP's current assets excerpt (figures in £m)

	2004	2005
Trade and other receivables	2,541.5	4,795.5
Trade receivables within working capital facility		
Gross receivables	545.7	
Non-returnable proceeds	-261.0	
	284.7	0.0

Evidently in 2004 WPP had borrowed 261.0 against the security of a portfolio of 545.7 of its trade receivables. The arrangement was 'partial recourse' in the sense that if the cash from the 545.7 of receivables was insufficient to repay the 261.0 of financing, the bank would have no further call on WPP. That event would apparently require more than half of the receivables to default. The probability of this is vanishingly small in any setting, and particularly so at WPP, whose clients include many large and illustrious blue-chip corporations. Nonetheless, WPP was able to use the 'linked presentation', which meant that 261.0 of borrowing was netted against current assets rather than being reported as debt within liabilities.

GAAP now enforces a 'binary' rule for derecognising financial assets, and IFRS (IAS32, IAS39) does not permit linked presentation. Like other quoted European firms, WPP adopted IFRS from 1 January 2005, and they tell us that the drawdown on the facility was transferred to debt on that date. Without the favourable accounting treatment this method of borrowing possibly may have lost its attraction to WPP, and they tell us that the receivables financing arrangement was cancelled altogether in August 2005. As a result there is no corresponding item in the 2005 report.

The WPP case gives a glimpse into the book-keeping associated with derecognising a financial asset. The problem with financial asset derecognition is that it is opaque from outside. It leads to lower balance-sheet receivables and current assets, and we may misinterpret this in ratio analysis as signalling better operating efficiency or credit control. The reader of the financial statements needs to be alive to the possibility that the firm has simply sold some financial assets.

LEASING

When a lease contract transfers the risks and rewards of ownership to the firm[2], this is known as a *finance lease* or *capital lease*. *Hire purchase* is a similar contractual form to finance leasing. Under a *hire purchase* contract the bank buys an asset on behalf of the customer, who pays for it in instalments. The bank retains ownership until the final instalment is paid. Since the intention is purchase by the firm, hire purchase contracts are treated as finance leases for accounting. A lease that is not a finance lease is an *operating* lease. Passing across the threshold between a finance lease and an operating lease radically changes the look of the financial statements, though the substance is little changed. In particular, the liability to make minimum lease payments disappears from the balance sheet.

GAAP: Lessee accounting

Identifying a finance lease

A lease is an operating lease unless it is identified as a finance lease. GAAP has evolved a number of tests to decide whether the firm is taking the risks and rewards of ownership. Any one of the following implies a finance lease:
- The present value of the minimum contracted lease payments is substantially all of the fair value of the asset (US GAAP sets a 90% threshold).
- The lease term is the majority of the asset's life (US GAAP sets a 75% threshold).

---

2   For convenience throughout this section we call the lessee the 'firm' and the lessor the 'bank'. In practice, lessors are not all banks. Some of the largest leasing firms are subsidiaries of major industrial firms.

- Ownership is transferred to the firm, or the firm may purchase the asset on very favourable terms, at the end of the lease.

IFRS puts greater emphasis on the substance of the transaction. Any one of the following may also indicate a finance lease under IFRS:

- The asset is specialised to the lessee.
- The lessee bears the lessor's losses on cancellation.
- The lessee takes any capital gains and losses on the asset.
- The lease may continue at below market rental after the minimum term.

Accounting

For an operating lease, the firm must disclose the current period's lease payment, the minimum lease payments (MLP) for each of the next five years and the total thereafter. A firm and a bank can agree any schedule of lease payments they like, including, perhaps a payment holiday at the beginning and a larger 'balloon' payment at the end. So that users of financial statements are not misled by low lease payments in early years, GAAP requires the firm to recognise the rental expense on a straight-line basis, that is, in equal instalments throughout the life of the lease.

For a finance lease, the firm recognises both the asset and the implied liability in the balance sheet. The value of the asset and liability at inception are calculated as the present value of the future minimum lease payments (MLPs) under the lease. The present value is calculated using either the rate implicit in the contract or the firm's marginal borrowing rate (IFRS prefers the former and US GAAP the latter). The asset depreciates over its useful life, or over the lease term if this is shorter, and if the firm is not certain to take ownership of the asset at the end.
[Reference: SFAS13, IAS17]

A simple example of finance lease accounting follows.

Example: Joseph

Joseph has taken a five-year finance lease on a wedge grinder. The MLPs are $100 per annum and the marginal cost of debt in the lease is 5%. The accounting effects are shown in Table 2:

Table 2 Joseph's accounting

Year		1	2	3	4	5
MLPs		-100.0	-100.	-100.0	-100.0	-100.0
Income statement						
Lease amortisation		-86.6	-86.6	-86.6	-86.6	-86.6
Interest charge		-21.6	-17.7	-13.6	-9.3	-4.7
		-108.2	**-104.3**	**-100.2**	**-95.9**	**-91.3**
Balance sheet						
Lease asset	432.9	346.4	259.8	173.2	86.6	0.0
Cash	0.0	-100	-200	-300	-400	-500.0
	432.9	**246.4**	**59.8**	**-126.8**	**-313.4**	**-500.0**
Lease liability	432.9	354.6	272.3	185.9	95.2	0.0
Retained earnings	0.0	-108.2	-212.6	-312.8	-408.6	-500.0
	432.9	**246.4**	**59.8**	**-126.8**	**-313.4**	**-500.0**

At inception, the lease asset and liability are recorded at $432.9, which is the present value of the five MLPs of $100, discounted at 5%. Over the life of the lease the asset is depreciated on a straight-line basis. On the income statement there are two entries: the annual depreciation charge and an interest payment. Since the lease is of five years' duration the annual depreciation charge is ($432.9/5 =) $86.6. The interest payment is computed as the lease liability outstanding at the start of each year times the cost of debt. So the interest payment in year one is $21.6, which is the opening lease liability multiplied by 5%. Each year the lease liability is written down by an amount equal to the annual cash payment (the actual cash payment made to the lessor) less the interest element. In year one the lease liability reduces by $78.4, which is the cash payment of $100 made to the lessor, net of the $21.6 interest payment. 'Cash' in the balance sheet decreases each year by the annual cash payment. Note that each year the lease liability is equal to the present value of the remaining MLPs. Thus in year three there remain two payments of $100 whose present value, discounted at 5%, is $185.9. Note also that in consequence the value of the lease asset and of the lease liability diverge quite markedly over their lifetime.

Capitalising operating leases from outside

Because operating leases are sizeable liabilities for many firms, it is common practice to complete the balance sheet by capitalizing them.

A finance lease is accounted like an owned asset, bought with debt finance. Compared to this, operating lease accounting has three effects on the financial statements. The asset, and the equivalent loan, are missing from the balance sheet, so:

a) *the balance sheet is incomplete* in assets and liabilities. Had the asset been owned, depreciation would have been charged against EBIT and the interest on the loan charged as part of net interest paid. When the asset is operating leased, both of these are bundled within the lease rental, which is charged against EBIT. As a result,

b) *interest is misclassified* as a cost within EBIT,

c) the timing of depreciation is different period by period, though it equalises over the whole life of the lease. By default, depreciation is the operating lease rental minus the interest element, which is unlikely to be the depreciation schedule the firm would have chosen for the owned asset. As a result, the value at which the asset is carried in the balance sheet, which is its depreciated cost, will also have a different profile through time, though it will eventually converge to the same value.

To capitalise a firm's operating leases, the outsider has to try and recreate the full picture on the basis of what can be spied through the keyhole of operating lease disclosures. They would like to do what the internal accountant does when they capitalise a finance lease. But the internal accountant has full information and the lease contract in front of them. For operating leases only a summarised schedule of minimum lease payments is disclosed, and this is in aggregate across all the firm's leases, and the contractual cost of borrowing for these leases is not disclosed. So estimation is required. We need to guard against the fallacy of spurious precision, which is always a tempting refuge in financial analysis. The approach we will adopt is to adjust for the first two effects of operating lease accounting, a) balance sheet incompleteness, and b) interest misclassification, but make no attempt to adjust for c) the depreciation schedule.

The steps are as follows:

1 *Profile the minimum lease payments* Estimate a plausible schedule of minimum lease payments based on the firm's operating lease disclosures. This means making some assumption about the distribution of MLPs when we do not have full disclosure. For instance, the analyst might assume that payments decline in later years at the same rate as they decay in the first five years. Operating lease payments tend to include amounts for maintenance, taxes and insurance. These are not financing costs and therefore it is theoretically incorrect to include them in the PV calculation. However, there is usually inadequate disclosure to identify these amounts.

2 *Interest rate* For the operating lease interest rate we use an estimate of the firm's long-term borrowing rate. Firms frequently disclose this, otherwise it can be estimated as a marginal rate based on current market conditions by taking the current yield on 10-year government bonds plus an estimate of the firm's debt premium.

Some analysts suggest measuring the operating lease borrowing rate by estimating the implied interest rate in the firm's capitalised finance leases, if it has them. For example, for its finance leases the firm reports the first period's MLP and that period's capital repayment, so the difference must be the interest. We know the capital sum outstanding, and if we make an assumption about the timing of the rental payment we can calculate the implied interest rate. Unfortunately, while backing the interest rate out of finance leases is an enjoyable piece of detective work, it falls into the category of 'spurious precision'. Even if the firm has finance leased assets they may be different in type, located in different countries, and be of different vintages. Crucially, the finance leases are likely to be different in risk to operating leases, which is why they are finance leases not operating leases. The lessor accepts the asset risk in an operating lease and seeks compensation for that. Obviously a simple 'vanilla' long-term borrowing rate for the firm doesn't capture any of this either, but it has the virtue of simplicity and transparency.

3 ***Adjustments*** Use the estimated profile of MLPs and the interest rate to calculate the following adjustments:
   - Discount the future MLPs, *excluding* the current period's payment, to provide an estimate of the debt in operating leases at the end of the year. This is added to capital employed and to net assets at the *end* of the financial year to complete the balance sheet.
   - Make a similar estimate of the debt outstanding at the *beginning* of the year by discounting MLPs *including* the current period's payment. Applying the cost of debt to that, estimate the interest due during the year. This is added to EBIT and to interest paid to correct the interest misclassification.

In the balance sheet the asset is simply set equal to the liability each year. In consequence, in the income statement the sum of the annual depreciation and interest payment equals the annual cash rental payment under operating leasing. We are forcing the depreciation of the asset each year to equal the repayment of the loan. Doing this, rather than trying to reprofile the depreciation each year, makes life much simpler. It leaves earnings, and retained earnings, the same as in the published, 'operating leasing', statements. This also means we will not worry about re-estimating the corporation charge as if the firm had received a different profile of tax-depreciation allowances.

On the website of the book we work an example called Repono that is based on a real firm who gave us access to their management accounts. Repono is an interesting case because while they report their assets as operating leases in their GAAP accounts, they treat the assets as finance leases for internal accounting. So we can compare the two results, and we can see how close an outsider's attempt to capitalise the operating leases, using the approach described in the text, gets to the correct figures. The outsider's estimates of the lease liability in the closing balance sheet, and of the interest charge, necessarily are made with error. But comparison with the full-capitalisation financial statements suggests that this gives a tolerable approximation, at least in Repono's case. Certainly, capitalising the operating leases in this way pushes the balance sheet most of the way towards completeness with respect to these assets.

Case : WPP's operating leases

WPP's 2005 annual report disclosed that they had a charge for operating lease payments of 272.6 (all figures £m) in 2005. Minimum lease payments over the next five years would be 231.8, 202.2, 176.4, 156.5 and 112.9. A further 360.0 would be payable beyond 5 years. We note that each year from 2005 to 2010, the lease payment has been around 85% of the previous year. We use this as a rule of thumb for spreading the 360, and this gives us the schedule on the left of Table 3, with 51.2 as the balance in 2015. Elsewhere WPP disclose that their average cost of long-term debt is 6.1%. We elect to use this as the discount rate for the leases.

Table 3 WPP's operating lease schedule (figures in £m)

MLP's	Ref.		Capitalisation	Ref.	
2005	c	272.6	Cost of debt	a	6.1%
2006		231.8	PV starting	b	1,182.8
2007		202.2	PV ending	f	982.4
2008		176.4	Interest	d=a*b	72.2
2009		156.5	Remainder	c-d	200.4
2010		112.9			
2011, estimated		96.4	Net debt adjustment		
2012		82.3	In current liabilities		218.5
2013		70.2	In long term liabilities		763.9
2014		59.9			
2015		51.2			

Discounting the full schedule of lease payments at 6.1% gives a present value of 1,182.8. This is the value of the outstanding lease liability at the *beginning* of 2005. We use this to calculate the adjustment to EBIT. WPP paid 272.6 in 2005, but (1,182.8 × 6.1% =) 72.2 of this was accrued interest. We add this to EBIT and to net interest paid, leaving the remainder (272.6 - 72.2 =) 200.4 where it is, as 'depreciation' of the leased assets. If we discount the lease schedule again, but this time ignoring the 2005 payment, the present value is 982.4. This is the lease asset/lease liability that we add to the end-2005 balance sheet. To assess the scale of the adjustment, WPP's reported (pre-adjustment) tangible assets were 333.8, out of total assets of 11,317.7. Of course these figures are purely estimates based on published data; as outsiders we do not know whether they are accurate. These estimates have the following effect on WPP's ratios. Capitalising operating leases has countervailing effects on margin and asset turn, leaving ROCE pretty much unchanged (ROCE is pre-tax; WPP report that their WACC is 7.8% in 2005). The principal effect is on gearing.

Table 4 WPP's ratios

	Unadjusted	Adjusted
ROCE	15.5%	15.4%
EBIT margin	13.1%	16.2%
Asset turn	1.2	1.0
Gearing	16.7%	30.9%

The debate about operating leasing

We described in Chapter 9 the ambivalence towards borrowing that is deep in the psyche of firms – debt finance is nice to have, but you would rather not appear to have any. Off-balance sheet financing permits firms to borrow and get the tax benefits, without appearing to borrow. Though GAAP tries to police operating leasing from the asset side of the balance sheet, it takes a 'liability-side' view of firms' motives for leasing. It believes that off-balance sheet financing is primarily motivated by a desire to reduce balance sheet debt, so GAAP strives to limit it. Most practising analysts capitalise operating leases on the grounds that the commitment to minimum lease payments is a real liability. Critics of operating lease accounting invariably use airlines as an example. Take a bunch of airlines at random and though they are all in the same business, they will display wide variation in the proportion of their fleets that are on the balance sheet (owned, or finance leased) or off the balance sheet (operating leased). This is prima facie evidence, it is argued, of the abuse of operating leases. In fact, US GAAP and IFRS have reduced the use of operating leasing by airlines somewhat, but it is still significant.

Case: Operating leasing by airlines

Here is the number of planes on operating leases as a proportion of the their fleets for some major carriers in recent years:

	Year	Proportion
Southwest	2005	84/445 = 19%
Singapore	2005	22/114 = 19%
Lufthansa	2005	71/432 = 16%
Air France/KLM	2004	220/568 = 39%
American	2004	27/286 = 9%

Airlines demonstrate the challenge for GAAP. Airlines form alliances which enable them to share resources with other airlines. When they 'code share' they are effectively delivering their service using another airline's planes. Some airlines write franchise contracts with other, usually smaller, carriers to fly certain routes for them. To the passenger, the franchiser is indistinguishable from the airline. Operating leasing is just one of a number of contractual relationships that airlines have with a network of firms, and limiting its use may encourage airlines to migrate to arrangements such as franchising.

The competitive modern economy forces firms to be increasingly clear about the sources and nature of their competitive advantage; about which assets are 'strategic' and which are commodities that can safely be owned by others. So firms tend to take an 'asset-side' view and present operating leasing as a business model choice. They argue that the assets involved are non-strategic and they emphasise the flexibility that operating leases give.

The economic case for leasing is very strong. The exhibit, *The economic case for leasing,* describes some of the literature. Economic theory provides convincing reasons why firms should lease their assets, and in certain situations should use flexible arrangements like operating leases. But the argument is not about whether firms should lease, but about how they should account for leasing. A non-cancellable operating lease involves a financial commitment that can stretch way into the future and is identical in substance to debt, and it makes no sense to exclude these liabilities from the balance sheet. GAAP has worked hard to discipline operating leasing, but it uses an asset-side notion – effective ownership – to achieve a liability-side result. Even when a firm takes a short-term lease it is buying an asset, which is the right to use a building or a machine for part of its life, that is a lease.

CONSOLIDATION AND EQUITY ACCOUNTING

Accounting has three ways of treating an investment in another firm, depending on the degree of ownership and control.

- The income statement and balance sheet of a subsidiary are consolidated, added line by line, into those of the parent to produce group accounts.
- Substantial investments in other firms that fall short of being subsidiaries are known as associated firms and they are 'equity accounted'. Under equity accounting the balance sheet shows the firm's share of the net worth of the associate, and the income statement shows its share of the associate's income.
- If a firm owns a relatively small proportion of the shares of another firm then this is accounted as an investment. It is carried in the balance sheet at cost and any dividends received are shown as 'other income' in the income statement.

The crucial threshold is the one between consolidation and equity accounting. The use of equity accounting allows the firm to net liabilities against assets. The 'net' treatment

Exhibit: The economic case for leasing

Economists argue that a valuable function of asset financing lies in its ability to resolve potential 'agency costs', which are the costs that arise because there is a separation between the people who own the firm and the people who manage it. When investors have difficulty in monitoring and controlling how their money is used, other assets may be substituted for planned investment or the money may not be spent on assets at all, resulting in underinvestment. Asset financing resolves these problems. Theory predicts that leasing is more likely to occur if its assets are non-specialised; if a firm is going to lease, it is more likely to lease its generic assets. The more sensitive an asset's value is to use and maintenance, the more likely it is to be owned. Also, economies of scale may enable the bank to buy the asset more cheaply, and to provide servicing and maintenance more economically than the firm could. The bank may have better access to second-hand markets. The cumulative savings associated with the bank's asset market expertise will be greater, the more frequently the asset needs to be transacted. So assets that are not expected to be used for their whole life are likely to be leased. S. A. Sharpe and H. H Nguyen (Capital market imperfection and the incentive to lease, *Journal of Financial Economics*, 1995) find strong evidence that US firms that are likely to face higher financial costs are more likely to lease. They also find that small firms are more likely to use operating leases, which they explain both in terms of the higher financing costs faced by small firms, but also in terms of other size related factors. They also find evidence that financially constrained firms finance a greater share of their on-balance sheet assets using capital leases.

Theory predicts that smaller firms, and firms that are financially distressed and are already highly geared, are more likely to lease. By increasing the amount of debt-like finance available to the firm, correspondingly less equity is required. This is particularly valuable to the principal of a smaller enterprise, since it relaxes the constraint on him achieving his optimal portfolio diversification, and so reduces his cost of capital.

There can be a strong tax argument for leasing. For instance, the firm that pays little or no corporation tax may be unable to enjoy the available tax depreciation allowances associated with asset investment. Leasing can restore the incentives to invest by transferring the tax allowance to a bank, that has sufficient taxable capacity to enjoy it. The bank then returns the tax allowance to the firm through the lease payment schedule, restoring the incentive structure intended by the tax system.

in equity accounting is radically different in appearance to the 'gross' treatment under consolidation and, if the underlying firm is highly geared, it is much more flattering.

GAAP: Consolidation and equity accounting

Consolidation based on control

Traditionally, the criterion for classifying an investment was the percentage of voting shares owned. Ownership of over 50% of the voting shares defined a subsidiary; of between 20% and 50%, an associate and below 20%, an investment.

At first sight, '% of voting shares owned' looks like the right basis for classification. Indeed, in the great majority of cases, parents do own 100% of their subsidiary's shares. But firms that wanted to avoid consolidation found it very easy to structure so that, while the *substance* was that they enjoyed the benefits of owning a subsidiary, the legal *form* was that they had less than 50% of the voting shares. One structure might be as follows: a trusted partner, perhaps a bank, would own the majority of the shares but the firm would have the right to appoint the board of directors, the firm could take pre-emptive rights, perhaps using call options, to ensure it captured the value in any assets created by the subsidiary, and so forth.

More robust tests for a subsidiary look at effective control and the substance rather than the form of the relationship. Substance-based tests were introduced in Europe in the European Seventh Directive, enacted in 1983. However, the US still relied principally on the 'traditional' test of a subsidiary until reform following the Enron scandal in 2000.

Under IFRS, a firm is a subsidiary when the parent company has the power to control its financial and operating policies. Control is presumed where the subsidiary behaves as though it were a subsidiary or where the parent controls the voting rights or has decision-making power, or the rights to capture most of the benefits, or is exposed to most of the risks from the subsidiary.

US GAAP has twin tests. A firm is consolidated when either the traditional model requires it; that is, the parent has a majority of the voting rights. Consolidation is also required for an entity that is a so-called *variable interest entity* (VIE) and the parent is entitled to receive the majority of the expected gains or losses from the entity.

GAAP for equity accounting

GAAP requires a firm to account for another firm as an *associate* when it has 'significant interest' in it and holds shares with a view to benefiting in the long term, not just from resale. This reflects the power to influence but not to control. The traditional measure, ownership of 20% or more of the voting shares, remains the principal evidence of an associate. Further evidence would be a seat on the board. US GAAP requires associates' income to be reported net of tax. US GAAP requires some underlying detail of income and assets to reported for significant associates.
[References: IAS28, FAS94]

A *joint venture* is a hybrid between a subsidiary and associate, and arises when the firm has joint control, shares control of some other firm or activity. Joint ventures are usually equity accounted, with some additional disclosures. But IFRS also permits proportionate consolidation, which is line-by-line inclusion, like full consolidation, but just of the proportion of assets, liabilities, revenue and costs owned.

An associate or associated entity is also known as a *related* firm. While the firm's investment in an associate falls below the level needed for control, in a joint venture the firm shares control with others. The word *alliance* is used broadly for any of these relationships. A s*pecial-purpose vehicle* (SPV) or *special-purpose entity* (SPE) is a firm created to support a particular transaction or set of transactions and structured to qualify for equity accounting.

Equity accounting and consolidation compared

Equity accounting	Consolidation
Measure fair value of associate's assets and liabilities, record the firm's share of the net assets of the associate as one figure under 'investments'.	Include 100% of the subsidiary's assets and liabilities item by item.
Record goodwill on a proportionate basis and include in the investment figure.	Record goodwill separately.
Record the firm's share of the associate's after-tax earnings in the income statement.	Include 100% of the components of the subsidiary's income statement, item by item.
	If firm does not own 100% show the proportion not owned as 'minority interest' in the balance sheet and in the income statement.

The power of equity accounting

GAAP sets a threshold for an investment in another firm. On one side of this line the firm must be consolidated but, below it, the liabilities of the firm may be netted against its assets so that it is 'equity accounted'. The difference in result between these two treatments can be dramatic.

Example: X Co

Nenor Inc and its bankers, Complicit Partners, each invest $3m of equity in a new firm, X Co, which then borrows $94m from Willing Bank. X Co thus has $100m of cash that it invests in industrial assets. Nenor owns exactly half the shares in X Co, which is now a very highly geared business with debt/capital employed of 94%. If Nenor has to consolidate X Co, the effect on Nenor's balance sheet will be as in the first column in Table 6. Nenor takes in the whole of the assets and the debt, and accounts for the half of the shares owned by Complicit as a minority interest of $3m. So the highly geared structure flows directly into Nenor's balance sheet. But if X Co is deemed not to be a subsidiary, so that if Nenor can equity account its investment, the result is the second column. All we see is the investment of $3m.

Table 6 Nenor's balance sheet

	Consolidated	Equity accounting
Assets	100	-
Investment	-	3
	100	**3**
Debt	94	-
Minority	3	-
Equity	3	3
	100	**3**

This effect, of netting liabilities against assets to report an innocent looking net asset, is the dangerous consequence of equity accounting. As it happens, the structure described in the X Co example is pretty much the same as the one used by Enron for its famous Jedi subsidiary. This simply exploited US GAAP at that time. US GAAP still mainly relied on the traditional test for consolidation, based on majority share ownership. Further, an EITF ruling had established that SPEs could be equity-accounted so long as a third party held 50% of the voting shares, representing 3% of the total assets of the firm.

The Enron case is described in more detail below. In a sense, Enron is a very unrepresentative case that emerged from a failure of financial governance on a grand scale that is very rare. But for us here, Enron is a just reminder of the importance of consolidation. Almost everything Enron did was dependent on being able to use equity accounting. The power of equity accounting extends beyond taking debt off the balance sheet. When a subsidiary is equity accounted there is a presumption that it is an independent entity and that transactions with it are at 'arm's length'. So if the equity accounted-firm is truly controlled by the parent, this creates enormous potential for manufacturing profits.

The great majority of subsidiaries are fully consolidated. But occasionally firms will seek to exploit equity accounting where it is inappropriate, and GAAP has had to work hard at policing the boundary between a subsidiary and an associate. In Europe, the shift to more robust tests based on the substance of the relationship took place in the 1980s. In the US, this took much longer to come. Consolidated accounting is essential to understanding economic reality. It is therefore extraordinary how late many countries were to adopt group accounting.

Case: Enron

Enron's announcement in late October 2001 of a $1.2bn charge for losses in LJM1, an off-balance sheet equity fund, triggered a plunge in stock price. LJM1 was one of a complex web of affiliates created by Enron, with the apparent motive of parking currently underperforming assets off the balance sheet, thus flattering earnings and reducing reported debt. This stock price fall through 2001 was unfortunate for Enron, since it had used its own equity to capitalise some of these vehicles. This, and the ensuing collapse in investor confidence, led to its bankruptcy on 2 December 2001. After its failure, it became clear that Enron had been engaging in a number of very aggressive accounting practices, both to conceal balance sheet debt and to flatter income. The necessary framework for this was the creation of numerous off-balance sheet SPEs that were effectively controlled by Enron, although equity-accounted. These vehicles were very highly geared and, since they were equity-accounted entities, this debt was not consolidated into Enron's balance sheet.

But the SPE structure also underpinned the income accounting practices. Long-term contracts with SPEs were 'marked to market' and the value added taken to income immediately. FASB 133 permitted derivatives to be marked to model, as did EITF 98-10 for energy-trading contracts. Future revenues were compounded to an up-front value. For instance, JEDI, which subsequently became the most discussed of the SPEs, agreed to pay Enron a management fee. 80% of this was made a 'required payment' to June 2003, and so taken as revenue. Using borrowed money, the SPEs bought assets from Enron for cash and at favourable prices, generating profits on disposal that could be taken as income by Enron.

Entity versus equity

One challenge for an accounting model based on property rights occurs when the firm shares ownership of an asset with another firm. If the firm does not control the other entity, it simply shows as an asset in its balance sheet the proportion of the underlying net assets that it owns. Proportionate, is a literal application of the property rights principle. If the firm controls the other entity, say it owns 75% of the shares, a case could again be made for consolidating 75% of its assets and liabilities on a line-by-line basis. This method used to be common, particularly in Europe, and is called *proportionate consolidation*. However GAAP now usually requires full consolidation of any entity the firm controls; in other words, the firm records 100% of the underlying assets and liabilities even if it only owns 75% of them. The corrective is the 'minority interest' liability, which identifies the amount of the net assets recorded in the consolidation balance sheet that belong to third-party shareholders.

The logic of full consolidation is that the balance sheet records the net assets that the firm controls rather than those it owns. So, strictly, full consolidation is a breach of property rights accounting in that the balance sheet is *over* complete. However, full consolidation is consistent with the entity view that we take when calculating measures such as return on capital employed. Moreover the minority interest correction works well and enables us to switch to an equity view when that is needed.

Nonetheless, full consolidation can raise complications, for instance, when the firm acquires a subsidiary in steps with the result that there is a sharp discontinuity when control is achieved. And occasionally it raises strong passions amongst people who believe financial statements should be prepared from a shareholders', that is an equity, perspective. Such a debate erupted in late 2005 when GAAP proposed that consolidated balance sheets should be made more complete by including the goodwill associated with the minority interest as well as the firm's own goodwill.

REVIEW

- In this chapter we looked at off-balance sheet financing, in particular operating leasing and receivables financing, and at the accounting treatment of subsidiaries and associates. These arrangements all have the effect of netting liabilities against assets, transforming the appearance of the balance sheet, and reducing the firm's apparent borrowing.

- When assets and liabilities are linked, GAAP focuses on the assets and whether the firm owns them.

- Receivables financing may be simple invoice discounting, or provide more substantial sales ledger services, in the case of factoring. If the receivables financing is 'non-recourse' the receivables are taken off the balance sheet'; current assets and debt are correspondingly lower.

- Operating leases are leases accounted under GAAP so that neither asset nor liability is included on the balance sheet. This is a consequence of GAAP focusing on asset ownership, even though operating leases create liabilities that can be very large.

- The consequences of the accounting treatment of leases as operating leases rather than owned assets are that the balance sheet is incomplete, and interest payments are misclassified as charges within EBIT. Finally, depreciation, and thus earnings, differs period by period.

- In response, analysts often capitalise operating leases and we looked at the techniques of capitalisation.

- There are three methods of accounting for investments in other firms, but the key margin is the one between a subsidiary and an associate. Consolidation records a subsidiary's assets and liabilities and income statement, line by line. Equity accounting shows the parent's interest in the net assets of the associate. The effect is a netting of the assets and liabilities of the associate, with potentially misleading results.

- The traditional test for a subsidiary was 'percentage of voting shares held': an investment was a subsidiary when there was over 50% holding, and an associate otherwise. GAAP has worked hard to police this margin, and now focuses on the substance of the relationship, and whether the parent has effective control.

Chapter 14

Balance sheet valuation

If balance sheets were to measure the opportunity cost of the firm's capital stock, we would want firms to carry assets and liabilities at their current values, revaluing them upwards and downwards as appropriate. That way, the income that comes from rising and falling asset values will also be recognised in a timely way. This is not what GAAP does. Broadly, balance sheets record assets and liabilities at historic cost – if assets become worth less than cost they are written down or 'impaired', but if they become worth more they are left at cost. US GAAP insists on historic cost. IFRS permits fixed assets and intangibles to be revalued, though revaluation is uncommon. Also GAAP requires 'fair valuation' of some financial assets and liabilities. The result is that financial statements give us a cocktail that has a base of historic costs with some current value mixed in.

THE GAAP APPROACH TO BALANCE SHEET VALUATION

Broadly, the valuation of assets and liabilities depends on the type – whether they are tangible, intangible or financial – and on whether they are held for use, that is, expected to be held to maturity, or are held for sale. But before discussing the GAAP rules, we need to assemble some vocabulary.

Some vocabulary

The question 'what is the current value of an asset?' has at least three answers, each describing a different aspect of the asset's value. The first two are market prices: the asset's buying price and selling price in the market. *Replacement Cost (RC)* is the current cost of acquiring the asset in the market place. *Realisable Value (RV)* is the expected proceeds from selling the asset, net of the costs of selling. The third, *economic value (EV)* is the present value of the expected stream of income from the asset.

Valuation is an area that is rife with vocabulary variants. Many people, including US GAAP, refer to current value as *fair value*. IFRS uses 'fair value' for realisable value, which US GAAP tends to call *market value*. Economic value is sometimes known as *value in use*, and the higher of economic value and realisable value is sometimes called the *recoverable amount*. The term *mark-to-market accounting* is commonly used both to refer to the process of revaluation to realisable value, but also for current value accounting more generally.

GAAP: Valuation of tangible and intangible assets

Assets are initially recorded in the balance sheet at what they cost – at their historic cost. The cost of a long-term asset must be written down systematically to the expected residual value at the end of the asset's useful life, unless the firm claims that the asset has an indefinite life. This process is called 'depreciation' for tangible assets, and 'amortisation' for intangible or financial assets. The exception is goodwill, which GAAP does not allow to be amortised.

The most accurate way to figure out how much of the firm's assets had been consumed in a period would be to revalue every asset at the end of every period; the change in value would measure the assets' true *economic depreciation*. Revaluing each asset every year would be prohibitively costly and accounting depreciation is best seen as an efficient rule of thumb for achieving the same thing.

Assets are revalued downwards, that is, subject to *impairment*, if their value falls permanently below their carrying amount in the balance sheet.

Current assets such as inventory are held for sale. Hence they are reviewed for impairment annually, and are carried at the lower of cost and market value. Market value is normally measured by realisable value, but US GAAP uses replacement cost if it is lower than realisable value. Normally, long-term assets are held for use, but if the firm decides to dispose of a long-term asset it becomes an asset held for sale. It is then treated like inventory, and valued at the lower of cost and realisable value.

Upward revaluation

US GAAP prohibits upward revaluation of assets. IFRS gives firms the option of current value for tangible assets, though in practice this option is not often used by firms. If an asset is revalued upward under IFRS, all assets in the same class must be revalued, so firms cannot cherry-pick which assets they revalue; also, values must be kept up to date. In principle, IFRS also permits intangibles to be revalued upward but only if there is a 'readily ascertainable market value'. In practice, this is unlikely to be possible since active secondary markets are rarely available for intangibles.

If an asset is revalued under IFRS, the gain on revaluation is 'reserve accounted'[1]. The gain is unrealised and is not part of earnings. A revaluation reserve is created in shareholders' funds and is credited with the revaluation surplus, which is therefore part of other comprehensive income. Correspondingly, if a revalued asset is impaired the impairment charge is taken first against the revaluation reserve, and only against earnings when the revaluation reserve for that asset is exhausted.

There are some special cases. GAAP says that certain non-financial assets must be carried at current value and revalued upwards as well as downwards. Principally this applies to commodity-type assets held for trading, such as precious metals and minerals. IFRS requires current value to be used for 'biological' or agricultural assets (IAS41).
[References: FAS143, IAS36, 38, 41]

GAAP: Valuation of financial assets

Financial assets are cash, or assets that will be settled in cash or in the form of another financial asset, or that are shares in another firm. Financial assets such as loans or receivables are valued in the same way as non-financial assets, depending on whether they are current or long-term. Long-term loans and receivables that are held to maturity are valued at amortised cost. Current trade receivables are valued at the lower of cost and realisable value, through the process of providing for bad and doubtful debts.

Two important groups of financial assets are carried at current value. Financial assets held for trading are held to generate profit from short-term price fluctuations and are carried at fair value. Surpluses and deficits on revaluation are passed through the income statement, so to this extent earnings includes realised and unrealised gains and losses. Available-for-sale financial assets include all other financial assets including equities and are valued at fair value. For these assets, revaluation is recognised in shareholders' equity, and so movements are part of other comprehensive income. These gains or losses are put through the income statement when they are realised or when the asset is impaired.
[References: FAS133, IAS39]

---

1   But if a firm elects to revalue investment properties, any gains or losses must be taken to the income statement, (IAS25, 40). Investment properties are property assets held for rental and capital appreciation, rather than as productive assets. So, for example, a property is not an investment property if, say, the owner provides significant services to the occupants, as in a hotel. US GAAP does not have the concept of an investment property.

OPPORTUNITY COST VALUATION

If balance sheets were to have the data integrity of a carefully constructed investment analysis, they would need to carry assets and liabilities at current values, and in fact would need to use a particular measure of current value in order to measure the opportunity cost of each balance sheet component. This would generally be its replacement cost, but might be economic value or realisable value in certain circumstances. In this section we explain what opportunity cost valuation would mean, and why GAAP does not do it.

The relationship between RC, RV and EV

Investment and disinvestment decisions are all about the interplay between EV, RC and RV. The net present value (NPV) of an investment in an asset is the increase in the investor's wealth as a result of making the investment, which is the present value of the expected stream of income that will result from having the asset, EV, less the cost of the asset. If we are investing, the cost of the asset is the cost of acquiring the asset, RC, so NPV = EV - RC. But if we already own the asset and are wondering whether it is worth keeping, we are making a disinvestment decision. Now the cost of the asset is its realisable value, RV, because that is what we forego if we keep it, so NPV = EV - RV.

In general the replacement cost of an asset must exceed its realisable value by some margin. Otherwise, we could all make money by simply buying assets and immediately reselling them. Of course, sometimes these opportunities do arise and 'arbitrageurs' do earn money by buying and selling. Their actions restore the normal state of affairs.

The margin between RC and RV is known as the *spread,* and in financial markets as the *bid-ask spread.* For actively traded assets the sources of the spread are the costs of holding inventory, and transactions costs, including the costs of market intermediaries, are the source of the spread. In markets for actively traded shares, the spread may only be a percent or two. In some financial markets the spread is much smaller still. But in markets for tangible assets like vehicles or workshop machinery, the spread can become sizeable even when the markets are active.

Case: The market for Fiat Puntos

Consider the market for second-hand cars like the Fiat Punto 1.2 litre three door hatchback. This is a popular model, with thousands changing hands each year, and it is in a highly contested segment of the market so there are plenty of close substitutes to choose from. There are publications that report current car prices in great detail. Open one of these magazines in early 2006 and you would find that a 2001 Punto (price new, €10,600) with 40,000 miles on the clock would cost €3,395 (=RC) from a dealer, though the dealer would pay you €2,590 (=RV) for the same car. So in this active market there is apparently a 24% spread between RC and RV. This spread is somewhat reduced by the dealer's implied warranty.

When a market is inactive and assets are thinly traded, the gap between RC and RV can widen dramatically, and the realisable value for an asset that has few if any alternative uses can fall far below replacement cost. Indeed, if there are decommissioning costs the realisable value could be negative.

Case: EDF's nuclear decommisioning costs

The extreme case of decommisioning costs in the modern world are the costs associated with nuclear plant. We looked at EDF's balance sheet in Chapter 12. The physical assets were being conventionally depreciated on the asset side of the balance sheet, and had a net book value of €17bn in 2005. But the other side of the balance sheet EDF recognised a potential decommisioning liability of €53bn, discounted to €27bn.

Deprival value

Whenever we use an asset we forego the opportunity to use it for something else. The *opportunity cost* of an asset is its value in the next best use. A helpful way to get at the opportunity cost of an asset is to ask what loss a firm would suffer if it were deprived of the asset. This is called the *deprival value* of the asset.

In most cases, the opportunity cost of an asset is its replacement cost because, normally, a firm owns an asset because it is worth having, so if it is deprived of the asset, the firm wants to replace it. RV and EV enter the picture because sometimes the firm has an asset that would not be worth replacing but nonetheless has some value. This leaves two choices – the firm can keep the asset and capture its economic value, or it can sell it. It is the better of these two opportunities, known as the 'recoverable amount', that measures the extent of the firm's loss if it is deprived of the asset. So EV, RC and RV can each measure the opportunity cost of an asset in certain circumstances. Tthe deprival value of an asset is the lower of the replacement cost of the asset on the one hand, and the greater of its realisable value and its economic value on the other, as depicted in Figure 1.

Figure 1 Deprival value

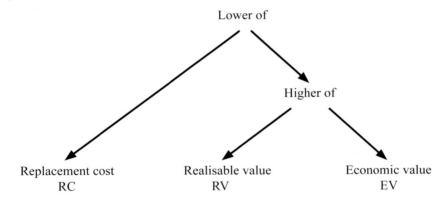

Replacement cost
RC

Realisable value
RV

Economic value
EV

Example: Gomez Garment

The Gomez Garment Manufacturing Co used a computer-controlled cutting table that has just been destroyed in a fire. Gomez reckons he could have sold the table for $30,000 though it would cost $40,000 to replace. Imagine three different worlds in which the economic value of the machine to Gomez was, in turn, $60,000, $35,000 or $20,000. What is the deprival value in each case, and what is the intuition of this in terms of the logic of investment and disinvestment?

Suppose the cutting table is expected to generate a stream of income with a present value of $60,000. The table has a positive (investment) net present value of $60,000 - $40,000 = $20,000. If deprived of the table, Gomez would want to replace it and the deprival value is the cost of the replacement, which is $40,000. On the other hand, suppose the EV of the table has fallen below RC. With hindsight Gomez now regrets having bought the table, but there are two things Gomez can do – use the table or sell it. The value to Gomez of having the table is the higher of the economic value and the realisable value. If the EV were $20,000, Gomez would have been better off selling the table for $30,000, and probably planned to do so. So by being deprived of the table, Gomez has lost the opportunity to sell it and the deprival value is $30,000. If the EV were $35,000, it was still not worth replacing the table, but since Gomez already had the table, it was better off keeping it. The value of using it, $35,000, compares favourably with the realisable value, $30,000. In this case the deprival value is $35,000.

Deprival value thinking contains an important lesson here. A big gap can open up between the RC and the RV of illiquid assets, and EV can easily fall into the gap. So we sometimes find firms legitimately continuing to use assets even though, measured against replacement cost or even historic cost, they earn a return below the cost of capital. With hindsight the firm should not have bought the assets, but now it has them they are better kept than sold.

Table 1 Summary of Gomez's position

EV	Deprival value		Invest?	Disinvest?
$60,000	$40,000	= RC	yes	no
$35,000	$35,000	= EV	no	no
$20,000	$30,000	= RV	no	yes

Measuring current value in practice

We will see later in the chapter that determining the historic cost of an asset is not always straightforward, but cost is usually knowable. If the balance sheet were to measure opportunity cost, the firm's assets and liabilities would need to be regularly revalued to current values. In practice, this raises a number of challenges:

– **Costs of estimation** Current values require estimation and this can be costly. Asset values can be subjective. Economic value depends on expectations of future income. Although replacement cost and realisable value are market prices, they may also require estimation, particularly if assets are relatively thinly traded. For example, the realisable value attainable in a fire sale may be significantly lower than the price obtainable in normal markets. The appropriate replacement cost is not generally the price of a new asset, rather the cost of an asset of similar vintage, which is sometimes known as depreciated replacement cost. Anyhow, frequently, technological change means that the firm would not replace with identical assets.

– **The aggregation issue** The replacement cost of assets measured individually is likely to be different from the replacement cost of the firm as a whole, that is, the investment that would be needed to recreate the firm just as it is today. Similarly, looking at realisable value, we might ask what the firm's assets would fetch if they were sold individually, but in practice when a firm is liquidated business units are often sold as going concerns and at a valuation well above asset value. The reason a business has a value as a going concern that is higher than the value of its individual assets is that these are glued together by intangibles – organisational competences, reputation, goodwill and so forth – so the challenge of revaluation links back to the issue of completeness and to missing intangibles.

– *The effect on income* The accounting identity tells us that changes in the valuation of assets and liabilities flow directly into accounting income. It also tells us that this income effect is just about timing – how you value the balance sheet determines *when* gains and losses will be recognised. Current value accounting raises difficult questions about the nature of income. If the firm has assets whose market prices are volatile, for example inventories of commodities or financial assets, revaluing them to current value each year will generate volatile income. If the firm has long-term assets whose value is rising, then revaluing them each year generates accounting income which is unrealised.

The preference for historic cost

The history of GAAP is characterised by an extreme reluctance to require firms to carry their assets at current values. The aversion to the upward revaluation of long-term assets in US GAAP dates back to the Great Crash of 1929. There was a view that asset revaluations in balance sheets had fuelled the stock market in the 1920s and when the US Securities and Exchange Commission (SEC) was created in the aftermath, historic-cost accounting was one of its founding tenets. Revaluation was allowed by national GAAP in a number of European countries, but in countries like France revaluation surpluses were potentially taxable, which provided a disincentive to revalue. Instead, infrequent, compulsory and usually tax-exempt revaluations were carried out. The UK and Holland were countries where economic theory was influential in the design of GAAP. Revaluation was permitted and revaluation of tangible fixed assets was widespread in these countries. Their influence carried through into IFRS when it was created. The influence of economic theory persists in UK government accounting, which uses deprival value for balance sheet accounting .

Nowadays, even though IFRS permits firms to revalue, relatively few firms do it. Firms claim to dislike upward revaluation because it is costly and because they find historic-cost accounting much simpler. GAAP is concerned that the estimation inherent in revaluation brings subjectivity and opens up the possibility of manipulation. In fact, as we see later, historic cost with impairment gives us a conservative version of the deprival value rule. So the sceptic might say that GAAP is happy to trust estimates of current value when they bring bad news, in the context of impairment, but not when they bring good news!

The distortion caused by historic-cost accounting depends on the rate of inflation. The exhibit, *Some inflation history*, reports US inflation experience over the last three centuries. Most developed economies would show a similar inflation profile. The deflation of the late eighteenth century was so persistent that it prompted widespread concern that historic cost balance sheets were *over*stating the value of some firms' assets at that time. The twentieth century, and especially the second half of the twentieth century, was a period of sustained systemic inflation. But even at annual inflation levels of 10% to

20% in the late 1970s and early 1980s, the major economies were reluctant to require financial statements to be carried of current values. Both the US (FAS33, 1979) and the UK (SSAP16, 1980) required firms to show current value accounting numbers. In the UK, these were based on deprival principles, as supplementary disclosures to the historic cost accounts. By the mid-1980s inflation had abated and the mandatory GAAP current value disclosures were abandoned. FAS33 was replaced by voluntary disclosure under FA589 (1986). SSAP16 was made voluntary in 1985 and subsequently withdrawn.

Of course at very high levels of inflation historic-cost accounting becomes meaningless, and there is no alternative to adjusting accounting number for inflation. Economies are usually defined as *hyperinflationary* when they have 100% inflation over a three-year period. In these conditions GAAP requires the balance sheet and income to be fully indexed.

Exhibit: Some inflation history

The table below reports US consumer price inflation for the last three centuries. It shows the average yearly inflation in each decade, and the change in prices over the whole decade. The bottom row does the same for the whole century.

US inflation (by decade starting in...)

	Yearly	Cumulative		Yearly	Cumulative		Yearly	Cumulative
1700	-0.8%	-7.3%	1800	0.0%	0.0%	1900	0.9%	9.0%
1710	-0.8%	-7.9%	1810	0.3%	3.4%	1910	6.6%	89.9%
1720	-0.2%	-2.4%	1820	-3.1%	-26.8%	1920	-0.1%	-1.0%
1730	-2.5%	-22.5%	1830	0.0%	0.0%	1930	-2.1%	-19.0%
1740	3.1%	35.5%	1840	-1.9%	-17.9%	1940	5.6%	71.7%
1750	1.7%	17.9%	1850	0.8%	8.7%	1950	2.0%	22.1%
1760	-0.6%	-6.1%	1860	5.1%	64.0%	1960	2.3%	25.9%
1770	4.7%	58.1%	1870	-3.1%	-26.8%	1970	7.1%	98.2%
1780	-3.2%	-27.9%	1880	-0.8%	-7.5%	1980	5.5%	70.9%
1790	3.4%	39.6%	1890	-1.0%	-9.9%	1990	3.0%	34.3%
1700s	**0.4%**	**54.2%**	**1800s**	**-0.4%**	**-32.4%**	**1900s**	**3.0%**	**1,892.4%**

In the eighteenth and nineteenth centuries, rates of inflation varied widely, interspersed with periods of deflation. Prices would rise strongly in one decade, often associated with war, and fall in another. Overall, US prices rose 54.2% in the eighteenth century and fell 32.4% in the nineteenth century. Allowing for the different base, this fall and rise were just about identical. A typical item costing $1 in 1700 cost $1.54 in 1800 and (1.54 × (1 - .32) =) $1.04 in 1900, though there were perhaps not many people still alive to remark on it. Anyhow, though this long-term price stability is arithmetically neat, its social welfare consequences were not neat. The deflationary periods that were the corrective to wartime inflation often would have brought widespread poverty and hardship.

It was the twentieth century that was the century of inflation. Prices rose by 1,892% over the twentieth century as a whole. The war decades experienced high levels of inflation but, in contrast to the past, this was not corrected by subsequent deflation, except for the partial reversal of the 1930s. Inflation then became systemic in the second half of the 20th century. Aided by the Vietnam war, and the oil price shock of 1974, the 1970s experienced an average annual rate of inflation of 7.1%. Overall, prices rose 98%, that is, doubled, in the 1970s, and rose by 71% in the 1980s. Such is the power of compounding that even when an annual rate of inflation looks modest, if it is sustained and with no offsetting periods of deflation, the cumulative effect soon becomes significant.

The inflation of the 1970s triggered almost immediate reform of corporate tax codes as it became apparent that the statutory tax rate applied to historic cost profits was generating punitive effective tax rates, because historic cost accounting significantly understated the cost of replacing fixed assets and inventory. So, for example, the UK started to allow firms to deduct 100% of their investment in plant and machinery in the year of purchase, and the inflationary increase in their holdings of inventory. The effect of the latter is to allow LIFO for calculating income, while recording the balance sheet at FIFO.

THE COST OF FIXED ASSETS

To record an asset in the balance sheet you need to know what it cost. This is not always as straightforward as it sounds since there may be many costs associated with commissioning an asset. The question is, which costs can be capitalised as part of the cost of the asset in the balance sheet, and which must be charged against profit as expenses? The GAAP principle is that all costs directly attributable to bringing a tangible asset to a productive state are included in its cost.

Example: Monet Inc

Monet have just bought a new lathe and
- they have the bill from the manufacturer for $50,000,
- a $2,000 haulage bill for delivering it, and
- a builder's bill for $3,000 for adapting the workshop to hold it.
- The machine is digitally controlled and Monet bought the software separately at a cost of $6,000.
- They spent $3,000 retraining the workforce to use the new technology.

It would be hard for Monet to prove that the benefits of the training were entirely specific to the machine, so these costs would be expensed. But the other costs are legitimately part of the cost of the machine and Monet records a long-term asset of $61,000 (= $50,000 + $2,000 + $3,000 + $6,000) under 'plant and equipment' in the balance sheet.

The principle that costs incurred in bringing an asset to a productive state are included in its cost has a number of specific applications.
- *Capitalised interest* GAAP says that financing costs that are necessarily incurred during the construction of a tangible fixed asset can be capitalised as part of its cost. Indeed, under US GAAP capitalisation is mandatory in these circumstances.
- *Software* In the same spirit, firms are allowed to capitalise the cost of software as part of the cost of the related hardware when it is attributable to bringing the asset into use. In the Monet example there was software of this sort.
- *Startup costs* GAAP now prohibits what used to be a popular accounting ploy of arguing that operating costs incurred in the early days of an asset's life should also be capitalised as an asset. For example, a new restaurant is loss-making for the first year or two until it develops its reputation. In the past, some firms would have capitalised those early losses as the intangible asset 'startup costs'. GAAP now says that necessary costs incurred in the commissioning period in preparing an asset for use can be capitalised as part of the cost of a tangible fixed asset. But operating costs incurred in the startup period when assets are functioning but there is insufficient demand, or they are not functioning at full capacity, must be expensed as they are incurred.

Joint costs and exploration costs

When an asset is developed in-house – when it is 'home-grown' or 'internally generated', rather than being acquired complete from a third party – the process of its creation is usually spread over time, and the challenge for the accounting system is to identify the relevant costs, especially where there are joint costs.

As we saw, pharmaceutical firms are generally not allowed to capitalise the cost of their R&D assets under GAAP. But if they want to measure asset costs for internal performance measurement, identifying the cost of individual drugs can be difficult. Drugs emerge out of programmes of research; several drugs may emerge from the same programme. Also many are abandoned or fail along the way, but the expenditure on these failed drugs may yield valuable learning as part of the continuing programme of research.

Successful efforts and full cost

Sometimes there is 'exploration' involved in developing an asset and the outcome is uncertain. Suppose you have to drill twenty bores to find one oil well, and it costs $5m to drill each bore. What is the cost of an oil well – is it the cost of the successful one, $5m, or the cost of the whole venture, $100m? Under *full-cost* accounting the exploration firm would capitalise all the costs of exploration as the cost of the oil well. Under *successful-efforts* accounting, only the costs of the successful bore are capitalised. So applying successful-efforts accounting in the present example, the cost of the asset in the balance sheet would be $5m and the remaining $95m would be expensed as incurred. What is the right treatment in principle? Deprival value thinking argues for full-cost, which is the expected or 'ex ante' replacement cost of the oil well. In the present example this would be the cost of drilling 20 holes.

The 'successful-efforts/full-cost' issue sounds rather specific to oil and gas, but it would apply in any setting where acquiring an asset involves exploration with an uncertain outcome. In the tangible world this obviously includes mining and natural resources. In the intangibles world, it includes the creation of intellectual property in a 'hit-based' market – technological research such as pharmaceutical R&D, creative products such as music, film, and games, and so forth. However, as we saw, the generally conservative attitude of GAAP towards intangibles means that the accounting choice does not surface there, because capitalisation would not usually be allowed either way. In other words, GAAP does not even allow successful efforts accounting for these intangibles. This has been a long-running discussion for GAAP has developed a standard to deal specifically with this issue in the oil and gas industry, and it permits either treatment.

THE COST OF INVENTORY

The word 'inventory' evokes a picture of physical things – a stockroom containing bins full of components. In accounting, inventory simply describes costs that are incurred in the provision of goods or services for resale, but that are not yet billed to the customer. So inventory may or may not be tangible. For instance:

- In a manufacturing firm that buys physical inputs and adds value to them there are three types of inventory, raw materials purchased from outside, which become work in progress as value is added to them, and finished goods when the firm has finished adding value to them.
- A retailer that does not add value is likely just to have one class of inventory: goods purchased and waiting for resale.
- A pure service business that has no physical inputs but only adds value may just have work in progress. For instance, in an advertising agency there are probably no tangible inputs, but the agency may have incurred significant time-related costs working on a campaign that is not yet finished and billed.

Added value

When a firm builds or adds value to inventory, what is the appropriate amount of cost to charge to the asset? How much cost may the firm capitalise in connection with the inventory? GAAP says that direct costs may be included, and a 'fair' proportion of indirect cost or overhead, based on normal capacity. In other words, if the factory is partly idle, factory overhead must be expensed rather than being dumped into inventory.

Example: Joe's Printworks

Joe's Printworks costs $10,000 a week to run on a fully costed basis, including labour, power and so forth, rent and the depreciation of the presses. The business is going through a lean spell. In the final week of the year Joe is working at just 25% of capacity and has two books in press, *Financial Statements* and *Plastering for Beginners*. These two books are work in progress in Joe's year-end inventory, and he plans to include $5,000 factory costs in the carrying value of each book, that is, he wants to split the full cost of the week, $10,000, between them. GAAP won't let him. He can attribute $1,250 of overhead to each book, but he must charge the remaining $7,500 against profit.

Original cost

The second issue, which is peculiar to inventory, is how to determine the original cost of raw materials and components. This can have a big impact on the balance sheet and on income in certain industries. When a firm uses a lot of identical components, keeping individual records of the cost of each item may be prohibitively costly. Airbus buys the wings for its jumbo jets from the aerospace manufacturer, BAE Systems. Each wing costs many millions of euros, so Airbus will be happy to track the cost of each one. But think of General Motors and think of a bin full of wheel-nuts in the stockroom. GM might use millions of identical wheel-nuts each year, and each vehicle has thousands of such components. So for items like this, at the end of the year the firm does a stock check to see how many items it has in inventory, then uses a rule of thumb to decide their cost. These are the most common rules of thumb:

- **FIFO (first in, first out)** The inventory contains the most recently bought items, so inventory is valued at current prices.
- **LIFO (last in, first out)** The inventory contains the original items and most recently bought items were used. So inventory is valued at original prices.
- *Average cost* The inventory is representative of the whole year's purchases, and is valued at average prices for the period.

To see the effect of this choice we need to recall the 'accounting identity'. Other things equal, every extra $1 of asset in the ending balance sheet is $1 extra of income. In the case of inventory, this is given effect through the calculation of 'cost of sales'. The accountant calculates the cost of sales in the year as purchases in the year, less inventory building:

$$Cost\ of\ sales = Purchases + Opening\ inventory - Closing\ inventory$$

An increase in closing inventory reduces cost of sales, and increases gross profit by the same amount.

Example: Dimitri

Dimitri buys 1,000 items of component-x each month. At the annual stock check on 31 December the storeman finds they have 2,000 of component-x in inventory, as they had last year. Having been $2 for as long as anyone could remember, the price of component-x went up three times during the year, to $2.90 on 1 April, to $3.00 on 1 May, and to $3.10 on 1 December. Dimitri's opening inventory was (2,000 × $2.0 =) $4,000. Purchases in the year were (3,000 × $2.0 + 1,000 × $2.9 + 7,000 × £3.0 + 1,000 × $3.1 =) $33,000. Dimitri's sales were $38,000.

How will the closing inventory be valued?
- Using FIFO, the cost of the inventory is November and December's purchases, (1,000 @ $3.0 +1,000 @ $3.1 =) $6,100
- Using LIFO, the cost of the closing inventory is the same as the cost of the opening inventory, $4,000.
- The average cost could be calculated in several ways. Suppose we calculate it as expenditure on purchases in the year, $33,000, divided by the number bought, 12,000. The average cost per unit is ($33,000/12,000 =) $2.75 and the value of the closing inventory is (2,000 × $2.75 =) $5,500.

These three valuation bases generate the following profit numbers:

Table 2 Dimitri's profits

	Sales	Purchases	Opening inventory	Closing inventory	Cost of sales	Gross profit
FIFO	**38,000**	33,000	4,000	- 6,100	**30,900**	**7,100**
LIFO	**38,000**	33,000	4,000	- 4,000	**33,000**	**5,000**
Average cost	**38,000**	33,000	4,000	- 5,500	**31,500**	**6,500**

With positive inflation, LIFO shows the lowest closing balance sheet value and therefore the lowest profit. That is, it charges most cost against the profit of the year and leaves least to carry forward in the balance sheet. This is why LIFO is unpopular with tax authorities in most jurisdictions. But LIFO is accepted for tax in the US, and in consequence LIFO valuation of inventory is common amongst US firms .

GAAP: Inventory valuation

US GAAP and IFRS say the following on the valuation of inventory. Inventory is valued at the lower of cost and realisable value. FIFO and average cost are the normal methods. Under IFRS, LIFO is not permitted. US GAAP requires that the accounts treatment should follow the tax treatment. If the firm uses LIFO for reporting, the SEC requires disclosure of the reconciliation to the current cost of inventory, showing the difference as a 'LIFO allowance'. There are detailed differences between IFRS and US GAAP in the definition of costs that can flow into inventory valuation; what was referred to as the 'costs of added value' earlier. IFRS has extensive guidance on cost that may be included in inventory.
[References: ARB43, IAS2]

Case: LIFO at Tiffany

In 2005, Tiffany states that the US company and the overseas branches (excluding Japan) value inventories on a LIFO basis, whereas the overseas subsidiaries and Japan use an average cost method. LIFO-based inventories represented 66% of Tiffany's net inventories. In 2004, using LIFO decreased earnings per diluted share by $0.05 (from $2.05 to $2.00), but no figure is given in 2005. In 2005, Tiffany discloses that whereas reported net inventory was $1,057.2m, the current cost would have been $1,121.3m, a difference of $64.0m. For comparison, Tiffany's EBIT was $494.1m. For a firm that holds a year's cost of sales in stock, as does Tiffany, a small percentage difference in the inventory and cost of sales has a significant impact on EBIT.

DEPRECIATION

Suppose an asset costs C and the firm estimates that its useful life will be n years and that its *residual value*, which is the realisable value of the asset at the end, will be V. Then over its useful life the firm will consume $C - V$ of the asset's value and must choose a *depreciation schedule*, which is a rule or algorithm for allocating this consumption to each year. The simplest depreciation schedule is *straight-line depreciation*, which spreads the consumption in equal parts each year:

$$Annual\ straight\text{-}line\ depreciation = (C - V)/n$$

Straight-line depreciation is by far the most commonly used in practice. The main alternatives to straight-line depreciation are *accelerated* or front-end loaded depreciation schedules, which give a higher charge in earlier years. Possible arguments for doing this are that:

Exhibit: Depreciation – some history

Vitruvius (Marcus Vitruvius Pollio) was a Roman architect, engineer and writer. He lived from the first century BC to the early first century AD and began work at the time of Julius Caesar. He is the author of the earliest surviving architecture text and is usually identified as the first person to talk about depreciation, 'the price of the passing of each year' (*pretia praeteritorum annorum singulorum*). Based on the assumption that a masonry wall will last 80 years he said that, when valuing a masonry wall, 1/80 of its cost should be deducted for each year it has stood. A generation later, the Roman agricultural writer Columella estimated the profits from wine growing and, in a modern way, compared the rate of return to investing money at 6% interest. However it seems he ignored both depreciation and labour costs.

During the English industrial revolution in the late eighteenth century, depreciation was well understood by 'scientific' managers. In the 1790s the Boulton and Watt Soho foundry charged 5% depreciation on buildings and 8% on steam engines. In 1772, Josiah Wedgwood, concerned about declining profitability in his factory, attempted to introduce a total costing system reflecting both depreciation and the interest on capital. But many businesses were extraordinarily profitable in the early days of industrial capitalism – for instance, the cost of sinking a coal mine could be recovered in a few months. So very conservative accounting was also common. For example the Dowlais Iron Company, which grew by 1842 to have the largest ironworks in the world, expensed all its capital expenditure along the way. If a business was profitable enough for 100% depreciation to be absorbed comfortably, this was attractive to managers because it discouraged investors' claims for dividend payments and conserved capital.

The industrial revolution needed relatively little outside capital. However it was followed by the era of large 'joint stock' companies. They used the stock markets, which had hitherto traded government securities, to fund the construction of utilities and, in particular, railways. Many of these businesses were extraordinarily *unprofitable*. It has been estimated that English railway firms' return on capital was rarely above 6% in the mid-1800s and that, prior to 1850, their asset turn never exceeded 0.08. Government bonds were paying around 5% at that time. All profits were distributed by railway companies and the challenge was to show enough profit. In consequence, railway companies omitted to charge depreciation on their railway infrastructure. (see John R. Edwards, *A History of Financial Accounting*, Routledge, 1989)

- it smooths the total cost of ownership over time, since maintenance costs tend to increase in later years,
- it provides some hedge against the risk of technological obsolescence by writing the asset off quickly,
- it better proxies the way that the market values of assets tend to decay,
- it brings tax advantages in jurisdictions where the tax authorities accept accelerated depreciation when measuring taxable profit.

Popular accelerated schedules include reducing- or declining-balance depreciation, double-declining balance depreciation, and sum-of-the-digits depreciation. There are obviously many different depreciation schedules that could be used, and GAAP is fairly tolerant so long as the method has an economic rationale and reflects the pattern of consumption of the benefits the asset will yield. Whatever schedule is used, annual depreciation is very sensitive to n and V.

Appreciating assets and decommisioning costs

Though the visible effect of depreciation is to write down the value of an asset, this is not strictly the way the book-keeping works. The asset is kept in the books at its cost, and a 'depreciation reserve' is accumulated. When the balance sheet is drawn up the accumulated depreciation reserve is netted off against the cost of the asset, so that long-term assets are presented as being at 'net book value'.

If V is greater than C the asset is *appreciating* rather than depreciating or, put another way, it has an indefinite life. Examples are buildings like hotels or pubs that are maintained to a high standard. Brands are an example from the intangible domain – when carefully managed and supported with advertising, some brands appear to have an indefinite life and to continue to grow in value. A basic GAAP principle is that all assets other than land must be depreciated, but GAAP can hardly force firms to depreciate assets for which V is expected to exceed C. GAAP disciplines claims that an asset has an indefinite life by requiring the firm to submit the asset to an annual impairment review instead.

At the other extreme, V may be negative and in some cases it may be enormously negative. This happens when an asset not only has no alternative uses at the end of its life but requires decommissioning, perhaps for environmental clean-up reasons. The EDF case, earlier in the chapter, was an instance of this.

Depreciation is a real cost

Depreciation is probably the most misunderstood number in accounting. Any depreciation schedule is somewhat simplistic, and requires the accountant to make a judgement about the useful life of the asset and its ultimate value. In fact this is the whole point about depreciation. Accounting depreciation is an efficient system that avoids the prohibitive costs of revaluing all assets annually to measure their economic depreciation.

Nonetheless people latch on to the subjectivity, and on to the fact that depreciation relates to expenditure that may have taken place a long time in the past. All of this tempts them to conclude that depreciation is not a real cost at all and is 'just book-keeping'.

Some history is helpful here. As the exhibit, *Depreciation – some history* reports, the idea of depreciation has long been used and people have always found it easy to ignore depreciation when it suited them, which was usually when they were unprofitable.

At least in the old days people did not try to justify what they were doing but, more recently, ignoring depreciation has been sanctified as part of the cult of EBITDA. As we saw in Chapter 8, EBITDA is EBIT with depreciation and amortisation added back. Its popularity as a measure grew in the late nineties when, coincidentally, there were many highly-rated but unprofitable technology businesses on the market. Used with care, EBITDA can be a useful way of isolating a certain subset of costs when comparing a group of similar firms. But it tends to be justified with the argument that, by omitting depreciation and amortisation, EBITDA represents a better measure of profit, one that better approximates cash flow. This is nonsense. Depreciation is a very real cost. It is the cost of consuming productive capacity. For some capital-intensive firms, depreciation is the largest cost they have. By omitting depreciation we mis-measure income and cannot judge economic performance.

On the whole, it makes sense to trust firms to choose sensible depreciation schedules, and to rely on GAAP and on the auditor. But, as always, we need to be vigilant. If a firm's depreciation seems inappropriately liberal or conservative, the solution is to recalculate it on a more appropriate basis.

Case: Airlines

In capital-intensive businesses depreciation can be a very large number and the discretion management have in choosing n and V seems to offer scope for manipulating earnings. In the airline industry, we have seen great divergence in the depreciation policy applied to the same aeroplanes, both across airlines and over time. The airline industry is one in which many carriers have had great difficulty in sustaining an adequate return on capital. Moreover, the scale of investment in aeroplanes means that depreciation policies can have large effects on earnings.

IMPAIRMENT

Revaluation is a costly exercise. Nonetheless, GAAP sometimes requires revaluation in order to see whether assets have *lost* value, that is, whether they are impaired. Such a revaluation is called an impairment review.

GAAP: Asset impairment

Each year, the firm must check if there is any indication that the value of long-term assets that are being depreciated has fallen below their carrying value in the balance sheet. If there is an indication of impairment, then the asset must be subjected to a full impairment review. US GAAP uses a specific quantitative test for possible impairment – impairment is indicated if the (undiscounted) sum of the expected future cash flows from the asset is below its carrying value. Any long-term assets that the firm is not depreciating or amortising, because they are claimed to have an indefinite life, must have a full impairment review each year. Goodwill is a special case. GAAP specifically does not allow goodwill to be amortised, so it must have a full impairment review each year.

Under IFRS, full impairment review is conducted by measuring an asset's economic value and its realisable value. If the higher of these two (that IFRS calls the 'recoverable amount') is below the amount at which the asset is being carried in the balance sheet, the carrying value has to be written down to this level, that is, to the recoverable amount. Figure 2 summarises this. GAAP is giving us a conservative version of deprival value, with historic cost rather than replacement cost as the upper bound[2].

Under US GAAP, the full impairment renew is similar, but involves a comparison of the carrying value to 'fair value', which is *either* realisable value or economic value. [References: IAS36, FAS144]

Figure 2 Historic cost with impairment

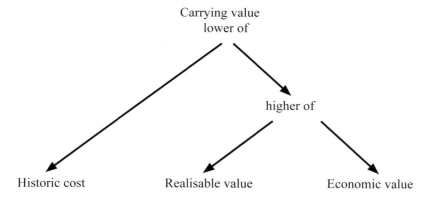

2   Of course, those firms who have taken advantage of the revaluation option under IFRS will be carrying their long-term assets at fair value, so for them this comes closer to deprival value.

The impairment write-down is charged in the income statement. If the value of an impaired asset subsequently recovers, US GAAP does not allow the impairment to be reversed. IFRS requires the impairment to be reversed, and if the impairment was charged in the income statement, the reversal is taken as a credit in the income statement. When an asset is impaired that had been upwardly revalued under IFRS, the impairment is initially charged to the revaluation reserve in the balance sheet and only against income when this is exhausted.

Impairment of goodwill and purchased intangibles

In general, an asset is reviewed for impairment by measuring its economic value and its realisable value. However, the general approach to impairment will not work with goodwill because its value cannot be measured directly. Goodwill is a residual; it drops out of the 'purchase accounting' of an acquisition, as the difference between the cost of the acquisition and the fair value of the identifiable assets acquired.

So to review goodwill for impairment, GAAP requires the firm to rerun the purchase accounting exercise but with a current estimate of the value of the acquired firm. The firm estimates the economic value of the business unit to which the goodwill relates. If the economic value is less than the carrying value of the business unit's identifiable tangible and intangible assets including goodwill, the goodwill is presumed to be impaired by that amount. Once the goodwill is exhausted, the impairment is taken against the remaining assets. In other words, each year after an acquisition, GAAP says 'never mind what you paid, what would be a fair price now for that business unit? And what would the implication be for the value of the goodwill?'

A number of research studies over many years has shown that, more often than not, an acquirer's share price falls following an acquisition. This suggests that acquirers tend to overpay. They may have overestimated the synergies that could be achieved; underestimated the costs of combining the two firms; or simply got carried away in the bidding. Either way, they paid too much for what they got. Since goodwill is the residual, if a firm overpays, by definition, it is overpaying for goodwill. The goodwill impairment regime described above was implemented in the late nineties. Prior to that, acquirers amortised goodwill relatively slowly or, in some jurisdictions, could simply lose the goodwill by 'reserve accounting' it. That is, acquirers were allowed to write goodwill off immediately to reserves.

The new regime is much more rigorous and tries to get acquirers to measure the overpayment and write it directly off against income. This has already had some dramatic consequences; for example, in unravelling the effects of takeovers consummated at very high prices during the stock market bubble of the late nineties. This is demonstrated by the AOL case described below.

Case: AOL

Chapter 11 described AOL's acquisition of Time Warner in January 2001, and how this $146bn transaction led to the recognition of some $175bn of goodwill and intangibles in AOL Time Warner's balance sheet. In 2002, AOL Time Warner was forced to write off more than half of this goodwill and intangibles. As a result they reported a net loss of $98.6bn in the year 2002,

This is now in the record books as the largest loss in corporate history; a record that, like Bob Beamon's long-jump record, could take a long time to be beaten.

As shown in the income statement below, the write-off shows up in two places. In January 2002, AOL Time Warner adopted FAS 142, which requires that all existing goodwill must be assigned to reporting units, including the reporting units of the acquirer. As a result, a portion of the goodwill generated in the merger was reallocated to the AOL segment. Upon adoption of FAS 142, AOL Time Warner recorded a charge of $54bn to reduce the carrying amount of goodwill, which was recorded as a 'cumulative effect of accounting change'. Additionally, the annual impairment review for goodwill and intangible assets during the fourth quarter of 2002 resulted in a further charge of $45bn, giving total goodwill impairment during 2002 of around $100bn. $33bn related to the AOL segment, basically due to the continued decline in the online advertising market, and another $33bn to the Cable segment, which reflected market conditions, as evidenced by the decline in the stock prices of comparable cable television companies. The rest of the impairment charge related to segments such as Networks and Publishing.

Table 3 AOL Time Warner 2002 Income Statement summarised (figures in $m)

Sales	40,961
Cost of sales	-24,315
SG&A, other	-10,251
Goodwill/intangibles amortisation and impairment	*-46,270*
Operating loss	**-39,875**
Interest, other	-4,446
Tax	-140
Cumulative effect of accounting change	*-54,235*
Net income	**-98,696**

Impairment of goodwill and intangibles is essentially done by writing them down to their estimated economic value. A firm's market capitalisation is the market's estimate of its economic value. So for a merger like AOL Time Warner we would expect a close parallel between the accounting and what was happening to the share price. When the deal was announced on 10 January 2000, the market reaction was negative and AOL's share price fell 12% on the day of the announcement, and 20% over the next 30 days (while the S&P 500 fell 2.8%). Despite a recovery by the end of March 2000, the stock significantly underperformed the market thereafter. From the beginning of 2000 to the end of 2002, AOL Time Warners's market capitalisation fell by approximately $100bn.

THE HISTORIC COST BIAS

Holland and the UK are good places to observe the impact of revaluing long-term assets. In both countries economic theory was influential in the development of GAAPs, and they permitted upward revaluation. Many firms took advantage of this; in particular, revaluing real estate.

Case: Young's brewery

Young & Co's Brewery is a family-run brewing firm that is listed on the Alternative Investment Market of the London Stock Exchange. In 2004, Young's was still brewing beer on the same site, in Wandsworth, London, that it had acquired in 1831 for £140,000. Then, Wandsworth was a small riverside community; it is now a busy urban suburb of London. In addition, Young's has retained a vertically integrated structure, selling its products through an estate of over 200 pubs that it has acquired over the same period. Many of these pubs are valuable properties, located in the extremely prosperous south-east of the UK.

Table 4 shows Young's results for the period 1995 to 2002. Like many UK brewing firms, Young's started to revalue its real estate around 1980, updating the valuation every five years, and most recently in 1997. Until the late 90s, the accounting regime was relatively benign; brewing firms did not depreciate their pubs, but did not have to submit them to an annual impairment either. Since 1998, GAAP required non-depreciated assets to be reviewed for impairment annually, and many revaluing firms, including Young's, decided to freeze their valuations at that point and not update them going forward. So, going forward, these valuations will become increasingly out of date. If the firm does not revalue annually, the revaluation reserve naturally declines anyhow between revaluations, as the firm removes the reserve relating to individual assets that it sells each year, passing any surplus through the income statement as a realised gain.

Table 4 Young's results (figures in £m)

	1995	1996	1997	1998	1999	2000	2001	2002
PP&E	131.5	130.8	138.6	139.5	140.3	146.3	154.9	162.3
Total assets	**161.5**	**161.0**	**170.3**	**174.7**	**182.8**	**189.6**	**201.1**	**212.3**
Equity shareholders' funds	116.7	118.2	127.1	129.1	132.0	134.3	138.3	141.8
includes revaluation reserve	*85.9*	*85.5*	*92.6*	*92.2*	*91.6*	*91.5*	*88.5*	*88.6*
Net debt and preference shares	30.9	28.3	28.5	28.7	27.8	31.1	38.9	46.2
Capital employed	**147.5**	**146.5**	**155.6**	**157.8**	**159.8**	**165.4**	**177.2**	**188.0**
cost of equity, estimated	*12.8%*	*12.4%*	*11.9%*	*10.2%*	*8.9%*	*9.6%*	*9.1%*	*9.6%*
Return on equity, reported	3.1%	2.9%	3.1%	3.4%	3.9%	4.5%	5.5%	4.3%
Return on equity, ex revaluation	12.0%	10.7%	11.2%	12.2%	13.1%	14.5%	16.1%	11.8%
WACC, estimated	*10.5%*	*10.6%*	*10.2%*	*8.7%*	*7.6%*	*8.0%*	*7.4%*	*7.7%*
After-tax ROCE, reported	3.7%	3.5%	3.6%	3.9%	4.3%	4.8%	5.5%	4.5%
After-tax ROCE, ex revaluation	8.9%	8.4%	8.7%	9.4%	10.1%	11.0%	11.7%	8.8%

By 2000, Young's had total assets of £189.6m, of which £146.3m was PP&E, which, in turn, reflected the cumulative effect of revaluation of £91.5m. Like many such brewing firms, Young's has not been very profitable. As a guide, the table estimates Young's cost of capital, assuming a 5% equity risk premium. Against that benchmark, both return on equity and after-tax ROCE are below their respective costs of capital.

How would Young's have looked if it had not revalued? That is, how would a similar firm to Young's look in most other countries? We see this by simply removing the revaluation reserve from capital employed. On that basis, both measures of return are comfortably above the cost of capital.

The extent to which the user of financial statements needs to worry about the historic cost bias in accounting depends on inflation rates, obviously, but also on the sector and on the business model that individual firms are using. The historic cost bias is still significant for firms from high inflation settings. In many economies, inflation rates are currently quite low. But even at relatively low rates of inflation the gulf between historic cost and replacement cost can become significant. Clearly that problem is most marked in sectors that use significant amounts of long-lived tangible fixed assets. But for firms that are in a low capital intensity business, or have outsourced the assets they need, there will be no issue. If we are looking at a century-old manufacturing firm that operates on a town-centre site, we will be vigilant for understated assets. If we are looking at Microsoft, or Google, we are going to lose no sleep about the historic cost bias in its fixed assets.

REVIEW

- In this chapter we considered how assets and liabilities are valued in balance sheets.

- If principle we want the balance sheet to measure the current value of the firm's assets, which might be their replacement cost, realisable value, or economic value in different circumstances. The deprival value rule explains how these combine to measure the opportunity cost of an asset.

- In practice, measuring assets at current value is difficult. Regular and universal remeasurement would be costly and subjective, and raises issues in deciding how far to aggregate assets. Finally, current value accounting can make income more volatile. For these reasons, GAAP accounting remains dominantly historic cost, with some current value mixed in.

- Upward revaluation of long-term assets is allowed by IFRS, though remains uncommon. Some classes of non-financial assets held for trading must be revalued to market values, and financial assets if they are held-for-trading or available-for-sale assets

- The cost of an asset must include all costs incurred in bringing it to a productive state. Inventory may include a proportion of overheads; fixed assets may also include some capitalised expenditure.

- Though GAAP does not require upward revaluation of operating assets, it does require downward revaluation or 'impairment' when current value falls below carrying value. Current assets are tested for impairment annually, and are carried at the lower of cost and market value. Long-term assets are subject to an impairment check, and if there is evidence of impairment, to a full impairment review. Goodwill is must be reviewed annually for impairment.

- Depreciation and amortisation are best seen as efficient rules of thumb to measure the consumption or economic depreciation of assets.

- If a firm is carrying fixed assets it has owned for many years the use of historic cost has a marked effect on its ROCE, and this is accentuated in periods of high inflation.

Chapter 15

Income

Income measurement is essentially about timing and since firms have some discretion over the recognition of revenues and costs, to an extent, they can choose when income is recognised. We have already had most of the discussion we need of cost recognition in Chapters 11 and 12, where we saw that GAAP now polices provisioning and cost capitalisation quite closely. In this chapter we focus on GAAP's approach to revenue recognition. We also discuss how the outsider can detect aggressive income recognition practices by firms.

How the income statement is presented can be as important as how income is measured. We have seen that the income statement does not report the comprehensive income of the firm; some gains and losses are taken directly to reserves in the balance sheet. In addition, firms may emphasise some components of income while classifying others as exceptional or transitory. In recent years some firms have taken this further by producing a 'pro-forma' version of key numbers alongside the GAAP numbers.

GAAP APPROACH TO COST RECOGNITION

A firm's income in a period is the increase in shareholders' funds in the balance sheet, adjusted for exchanges with shareholders. So the approach to income measurement that comes from economic theory emphasises assets. This is the approach that this book has taken and it leads to a focus on the integrity of the balance sheet – on whether the balance sheet is complete in assets and liabilities, and on how they are valued. By contrast, an 'income statement' approach to income measurement starts by calculating the firm's revenue in the period, then matches the costs that were needed to earn that revenue. Of course, these are two sides of the same coin. Postponing the recognition of a cost, or anticipating a revenue, creates an asset in the balance sheet. Anticipating a cost or postponing revenue creates a liability. So the balance sheet approach and the income statement approach should give the same answer.

GAAP uses both languages, but has increasingly shifted towards an emphasis on the balance sheet. Its concern is that, unconstrained, matching costs and revenues gives firms too much discretion. So GAAP has got tougher, particularly on cost capitalisation, and says you cannot carry a cost forward unless you can provide convincing evidence that an asset has been created. Indeed, some people argue that GAAP is now too conservative on the cost side, particularly when it restricts the ability of firms to recognise their home-grown intangible assets. In terms of cost recognition, we have already covered the relevant GAAP in Chapters 11 and 12 and just review the issues below.

Cost capitalisation

GAAP requires that, with a few exceptions, expenditures that create intangibles must be expensed as they are incurred. This includes what are, for many firms, major expense categories such as the research and development expenditure that builds intellectual property, the advertising and promotion that builds brand equity, and the training that builds human and organisational competences. As we become increasingly aware of the importance of intangibles in the modern economy this 'bias to conservatism' in GAAP has become controversial. It is argued that intangibles are assets and that expenditure on building them should be capitalised. Otherwise earnings are artificially depressed in the years in which investment in intangibles occurs.

Provisioning

If expenditure expected to be incurred in the future should more rightly be treated as a cost of the current period this is achieved by *provisioning*. So provisioning is, in a sense, the opposite of cost capitalisation. The accountant charges a cost to the income statement in the current period and recognises a corresponding liability in the balance sheet that absorbs the expenditure when it eventually arises. The write-down of assets is also usually done through provisions, for example the provision for impairment, for bad and doubtful debts, for slow-moving inventory. The asset continues to be carried in the books at cost, but a provision is created as an estimate of the part of the cost which will be unrecoverable. This provision is offset against the asset in the balance sheet.

Example: Serge's time share

Serge had net proceeds this year of €20m from building and selling a holiday time-share development. The trouble is, it has not got a roof. His lawyers reckon they can hold off purchasers' claims that it should have had a roof for another two years, but Serge will eventually have to put a roof on and this will cost €5m. Let's assume Serge likes to do his accounting properly, even though he is not so careful about his building. He should make a provision for the eventual cost of the roof in order to show the correct profit on the timeshare now, which is €15m. The book-keeping to charge €5m against income now, and to record a corresponding liability of €5m in the balance sheet. This liability is carried in the balance sheet for the next two years and absorbs the expense when it eventually occurs.

Table 1 Serge's provision (figures in €m)

Year	1	2	3
INCOME STATEMENT (extract)			
Net proceeds	20	-	-
Cost			-5
Provision	-5	-	5
Profit	**15**	**-**	**-**
BALANCE SHEET (extract)			
Change in provision	5		-5
Provision	**5**	**5**	**-**

Serge was an example of a provision that helped tell the correct story of the profitability of his venture – as it stood, the revenue happened to precede the cost, so the provision brought the cost forward to match the revenue. Firms are not always looking to flatter earnings; they may want to consistently understate earnings to create reserves against a rainy day. Broadly defined, the mechanism of conservative accounting is provisioning. The accountant accounts creatively by recording liabilities at more than their value, and by recording assets below their value. For instance, on the asset side this means over-depreciating fixed assets, over-providing for bad and doubtful debts, and the aggressive write-down of inventory on the grounds that it is obsolete or slow-moving. This reduces the need for similar charges in future periods, or reduces the carrying value of the assets when they are consumed; both flatter later earnings. On the liabilities side this means recording liabilities – for tax, for reorganisation and for other contingencies that are too pessimistic. To the extent that these liabilities are not subsequently needed they can be released back to earnings. Understating current profits in this way creates 'hidden reserves'.

Case: Daimler-Benz

It is not possible to report conservative earnings for ever. Conservative accounting is a preparation for a rainy day. Following Daimler-Benz's listing in New York in 1993 its accounts prepared under German GAAP had to be restated under US GAAP and, famously, a DM615m profit was translated into a DM1,839m loss. This seemed to contradict the notion that German accounting was particularly conservative. In fact Daimler had used the fruits of previous conservative accounting in the form of accumulated provisions to offset a trading loss in 1993. The conversion to US GAAP forced it to unwind the large write-back of provisions that had been used to achieve this. Daimler's reconciliation to US GAAP in 1993 showed:

Table 2 Daimler-Benz (figures in DM)

Earnings per German GAAP	**615**
Reversal of transfer from provisions	-4,262
Deferred tax	2,627
Other	-819
Earnings per US GAAP	**-1,839**

Big bath accounting

A firm takes a *big bath* when it takes a big one-time charge against profit by writing down assets, or by creating provisions to absorb the future costs of reorganising the business. For example, it was not uncommon for the new management team taking over an underperforming firm to take a big bath. We should be wary of big baths because they play on investors' psychology. Though it may lead to the firm reporting a current loss, the effect on the share price might be positive if the market applauds the tough medicine and sees it as a signal of a change in management style. Indeed, if the market is in the mood for bad news why not pile it on and create an unnecessarily large provision? This could be written back to income in future periods, or used to absorb future costs that would have been incurred anyhow. We saw in Chapter 12 that GAAP is keen to discourage excess conservatism in provisioning. GAAP now requires future costs to be unavoidable, or the reorganisation to be already scheduled, before a provision may be made.

REVENUE RECOGNITION

Most of the time revenue recognition should be uncontroversial. When a firm sells tins of beans or any good or service for immediate delivery it should be pretty clear what its revenue is in each period. The problems arise when delivery spreads over several periods. In industries such as construction, where jobs can take a number of years to complete, GAAP allows the firm to recognise some revenue, and therefore take some profit, along the way, on the basis of independent certification of the work completed in each period. We start by describing the accounting for these well-behaved cases.

GAAP: Revenue recognition

For practical purposes the everyday notion of revenue serves fine: a firm's revenue is the value of the goods and services it has delivered. GAAP's definitions are less intuitive. IFRS talks about a 'gross inflow of economic benefits arising from operations'. US GAAP does not have a separate standard on revenue recognition, but in its concept statement it emphasises 'actual or potential cash flow as a result of operations'.

Though the revenue recognition rules are differently worded in IFRS and US GAAP, in substance they are the same. IFRS requires that revenue should be recognised when: there are probable economic benefits to the seller; when the amount of revenue – and, if relevant, of costs and the stage of completion – can be measured reliably; when there is transfer of the risks and rewards of ownership; when no managerial involvement or effective control are retained. US GAAP has specific revenue recognition guidance in a number of places. US GAAP emphasises that revenue should be realised. SEC rules for SEC-registered firms requires that: the price is fixed or determinable; collectability is reasonably assured; persuasive evidence of an arrangement exists; delivery has occurred or services have been rendered.
[References: IAS18, SFAC6]

Delivery

The accounting effect of selling goods is that inventory, measured at cost, leaves the balance sheet and an asset is created in the form of a receivable (or cash, if the customer has paid cash) for the sales value of the goods[1]. *Delivery* is the key event – the firm can record revenue when it has delivered the corresponding good or service. On delivery, title in the goods passes to the customer. If a customer cancels an order before it has been delivered, the firm could sue them for the consequential loss, which is any irrecoverable costs it has incurred. But once delivery has taken place the firm can sue the customer for the agreed price, which is cost plus profit, that is, revenue. Precisely what constitutes delivery is a complex issue in law, but delivery usually means physical transfer of possession. Delivery can take place even if the goods remain in the warehouse so long as the customer accepts title to them.

An important issue in practice is *returns*. You delivered the goods and thought you had sold them, but they came back later because they were faulty. If they are returned after the end of the period, there is a risk of revenue being overstated in the current period. In industries where this is significant firms have to estimate the returns and create a provision to cover the cost. The amount credited to the provision is deducted from revenues. For instance, car manufacturers maintain a reserve in the balance sheet to provide for the rectification under warranty of faults in the cars they have sold. Airlines with frequent-flyer programmes have a similar issue – they sell tickets this year that entitle the customer to frequent-flyer miles. This year's revenues will be overstated unless they make some provision for the expected costs of redeeming the frequent-flyer miles.

Staged delivery

Sometimes, delivery spreads over more than one period; delivery is staged or piecemeal. Suppose a construction firm is building a bridge that will take three years to complete. GAAP provides clear guidance on how revenue and profit can be recognised for long-term contracts of this sort. Independent experts – architects or civil engineers in the case of a bridge – certify the value of the work completed in the period, and the builder can recognise that proportion of the revenue. The difference between that revenue and the

---

1   If this is unclear, it may be wise to revisit Chapter 2 before continuing.

costs attributable to the period's work is the profit that can be recognised in the period, less a provision for any anticipated losses in future periods.

GAAP: Long-term construction contracts

The dominant method for valuing long-term contracts under IFRS and US GAAP is the 'percentage of completion' method. Under this method, cost, revenue and therefore profit is recognised by reference to the stage of completion of the job. The potential danger in the piecemeal delivery approach is clear. A construction job is not really delivered until it is completed. If you asked a builder to put a bridge across the Pacific and they abandoned it 10 miles from America, the fact that the bridge was 99.9% complete would not be much of a consolation to you. For this reason GAAP requires firms to implement the standard conservatively. In practice firms just recognise a proportion, say 75%, of the certified revenue to keep something in reserve against contingencies. If a loss is expected overall, the loss is recognised immediately.

The percentage of completion method works when progress is reliably measurable. Otherwise, US GAAP requires the 'completed contract' method to be used, under which revenue is only recognised when the contract is essentially complete. When progress cannot be reliably assessed, IFRS applies the 'zero-profit' method which allows the recognition as revenue of those costs that are expected to be recovered.
[References: IAS11, 18]

Example: BridgeCo

BridgeCo has a contract to build a bridge, over three years, at a total value of €10m. Independent surveyors certify the work each year and the client makes a progress payment of 90% of the certified value. Put another way, the client withholds a 10% 'retention'. The client pays the remaining balance at the end of year four. BridgeCo's policy is to recognise 80% of the 90% progress payment as revenue each year.

Though the long-term-contract GAAP was developed for activities such as construction and heavy engineering, activities like bespoke software contracting have similar economics. A software house may be contracted to build a back-office system for a bank. This could take a year or two to develop and another year or two for implementation and testing. In the early days of the software industry there were controversial examples of companies recognising revenues in full on contracting. GAAP now applies similar principles to long-term construction accounting, to these firms.

Case: MicroStrategy Inc

MicroStrategy was incorporated in Delaware in 1989 and had its initial public offering in 1998. It is a global business intelligence software provider with revenues mainly coming from product licences, fees for maintenance, technical support and training, and consulting and development services. MicroStrategy's shares dropped from $260 to close at $86 when, on 20 March, 2000, it announced that it would restate its results for the years 1998 and 1999. When, a few weeks later, the firm announced it would also restate 1997, the shares fell to $33. Reported revenues for the three years had been $365m. Restatements reduced these by around $66m, with $54m of this relating to 1999. The main adjustment was for premature recognition of revenue, where the firm had sold a licence for software but significant future services or products were still to be provided. Other restatements resulted from deals in which the firm had not properly executed contracts in the year in which revenue was recorded. For example, the SEC found that to achieve the desired quarterly results, MicroStrategy held over contracts that had been signed by customers but had not yet been signed by the firm. After the close of the quarter when it had decided upon the desired financial result, the unsigned contracts were distributed, signed and given an 'effective date.' GAAP requires the signature of both the firm and the customer before recognising revenue.

Detaching revenue from activity

The approach that GAAP uses for long-term construction contracts is attractive because revenue recognition follows the underlying productive activity – there is matching of revenue to costs, with a bias to conservatism. But suppose a firm has written an enforceable long-term contract with its customer, so that the customer is committed to pay or, even better, the customer has already paid up front. In this case the firm may argue that an asset has been created in the form of a receivable which is not contingent on performance or further delivery, so the revenue is realised and the firm should be allowed to recognise the contracted revenue immediately.

Franchise fees

Franchising is a frequently used arrangement in the distribution of goods and services. For example, in the fast-food industry an independent firm (the franchisee) contracts to assume the firm's trade name and livery and distribute its products for an agreed number of years. The firm typically receives an annual fee or royalty based on the francisee's sales. The firm may also sell product to the franchisee, earning a margin on the sale. This income is well behaved in the sense that it reflects the underlying economic activity, which is the franchisee's sales, period by period. But franchise agreements also involve an 'up-front fee' or contract-signing fee and these up-front fees can be sizeable.

Example: BurgerCo

Suppose BurgerCo receives an up-front franchise fee of €1m for one of its outlets and the franchise agreement is for 10 years. How should it recognise the revenue? One treatment would be to spread the revenue over the 10 years of the contract. The accounting would be for BurgerCo to record the €1m receivable as an asset in the balance sheet, and at the same time record €1m as a *deferred revenue* liability. It would then transfer €100,000 from deferred revenue to the income statement each year.

In practice, so long as the up-front fee is not contingent on future events, that is, it is non-returnable or 'non-recourse', BurgerCo is likely to take the whole fee as revenue in the year of signing. BurgerCo will argue that the delivery under the contract, the extent to which taking the revenue up front is in conflict with the principle of spreading the revenue in proportion to underlying activity depends on what the franchisee is getting. Some of it might be for immediate delivery of goods like shop fittings. Often, there is a promise of future delivery in the form of continuing management support and advice. But, mostly, the up-front fee is a payment for the right to use an asset – the firm's brand. But this is not a one-time transfer; so, while the franchisee may not be able to recover its fee, there is an implied commitment to maintain the brand by advertising and in other ways and, at the very minimum, an implied commitment that the firm continue to exist.

Case: McDonalds

From McDonalds' 2005 annual report: 'Initial fees are recognized upon opening of a restaurant, which is when the Company has performed substantially all initial services required by the franchise agreement.'

Whatever the rights and wrongs of immediate recognition of up-front fees as revenue, the analyst will have to be careful if franchise fees are significant since the franchisor's revenue growth and profit margin will be flattered in the years in which it sells a lot of franchises. If the payments under a contract are not certain, then an asset does not exist and revenue should not be recognised.

Case: Queen's Moat Houses

Queen's Moat Houses was a large UK-based hotel group that fell into financial distress in 1993. Amongst other things, the firm had written incentive contracts with many of its hotel managers under which the managers made a commitment to achieve certain revenues and profits during the next few years and were allowed to keep the surplus above this level. QMH had been recognising these promised amounts as revenues at the time of signing, despite there being no certainty that the hotel managers would be able to make the payments. Indeed, one reason for QMH's failure was that some hotel managers defaulted during the economic downturn of the early nineties.

DETECTING ROGUE ACCOUNTING

In everyday language, we talk about *creative accounting* or *rogue accounting* when people or organisations use accounting to paint a false economic picture. Sometimes this is simply aggressive – stretching what is permissible under GAAP to the limit; occasionally it is fraudulent – through negligence or criminality, the accounting is in breach of GAAP. Particularly when there has been a run of major accounting scandals, people start to accuse GAAP of being too 'soft' and allowing firms too many choices. Of course, flexibility in the rules governing the measurement of assets and liabilities is essential given the rich variety of business types and the necessarily judgemental nature of accounting. And inevitably weaknesses in GAAP emerge and need fixing as the world changes and as firms innovate.

So there is flexibility in GAAP, and this creates scope for firms to boost earnings, perhaps to meet analysts' expectations, or so that the CEO gets his or her bonus. The snag is, it catches up with you sooner or later. The relentless logic of the 'accounting identity' says that every \$1 extra of overstated income is got by overstating closing net assets, so is stolen from the income of future years. For that reason, significantly overstating income is unattractive to healthy firms. Almost always, the firms that are seriously challenging GAAP in this way are firms in trouble. So while rogue accounting undermines people's confidence in GAAP, it is exceptional. Most firms do not have these incentives and they are more concerned to smooth the profit stream through time, perhaps with a bias to conservatism in order to keep something in reserve. AOL in 1995 was a case in which there were quite strong incentives for managers to boost income at the time.

Case: AOL

At the end of the twentieth century, fast-growing high-tech companies, including the 'dot-coms', were some of the most aggressive in accounting. These companies were not making profits and frequently had few revenues either. Investors were struggling to justify sky-high share prices and were trying to decide who would be the winners and losers. In this environment, there was a strong incentive for firms to be the first in their sector to report a profit.

In 1995 AOL reported an operating profit of $23m. It got a good deal of acclaim for being the 'first to profit' in its sector. However it did this by capitalising $130m of costs, which was almost all of its R&D and marketing (customer-acquisition cost); these are probably the two main cost categories for a firm like this. AOL's policy was then to amortise the R&D asset over five years, and the marketing asset over two years. So the cost postponement was quite short-term, but given AOL's high growth rate this was sufficient to show a profit in 1995. AOL reversed the capitalisation of customer acquisition costs in 1996, taking a charge of $385m. AOL still carried a R&D asset but by 2000 this was $100m out of total assets of $5,348m.

We need to be on the look out for accounting that is aggressive within the rules, and for outright non-compliance. It is not always easy or even possible to see this at the time, particularly in cases where fraud. We depend heavily on the robustness of GAAP and the integrity of the auditors in enforcing it. But the user of the financial statements needs to be vigilant. There are two places to look, in particular, for evidence of income manipulation.

Watch the balance sheet

The accounting identity always holds. Other things equal, a dollar more income means a dollar more net assets at the end of the year. Postponing the recognition of a cost by capitalising it creates an asset; anticipating revenue means creating a receivable to balance it. On the other hand, depressing earnings by anticipating a cost involves the creation of a provision; postponing revenue means creating a deferred revenue liability. So even if our reading of the income statement does not raise suspicions, reading the balance sheet and routinely calculating the asset turn ratios may reveal something. Users of financial statements who are fixated on earnings and only really look at the income statement – a group that includes many professional equity analysts, apparently – are at risk. Readers of this book, with its emphasis on the balance sheet, stand a better chance. AOL's cost capitalisation in 1995, though subsequently viewed as audacious by the SEC, was easy to spot since two new categories of intangible asset appeared in the balance sheet.

Though creative accounting always has a balance sheet effect, the problem is that the effect may be too small relative to other balance sheet magnitudes, or is masked by other changes, so that the signal is lost.

Case: Queen's Moat Houses

The failure of Queen's Moat Houses in 1993 became one of the biggest accounting scandals of the early nineties. When new management took over they revealed a catalogue of accounting practices over many years, designed to flatter income. We noted on the previous page that QMH had been anticipating revenues. They had also been capitalising costs, including bonuses, interest costs, and acquisition and start-up costs. Most impressively, while QMH did not charge depreciation on its hotels, it capitalised the costs of maintaining them. Though this continued for some years, the markets were apparently unaware of the scale of the rogue accounting until after the firm's failure. The problem was that while, year by year, QMH was perhaps capitalising (£) millions or tens of millions of expenses within hotel fixed assets, it was acquiring hotels worth hundreds of millions and selling others, while at the same time revaluing the hotel estate annually. Without detailed disclosure, the reader would have little chance of detecting the effects of capitalisation in the balance sheet aggregates.

Nonetheless, while not giving determinate answers, the financial ratios should have raised questions for users of the financial statements to take to management. Over the period from 1983 to 1991, QMH's asset turn halved, from 0.54 to 0.27. Margins gradually increased and, though the European hotel industry was moving into a downturn and other groups were reporting falling margins, EBIT margin jumped from 23% in 1989 to 28% and 27% in 1990 and 1991, respectively. Average receivables/sales jumped from 21% in 1989 to 27% and 25% – there could be several explanations for this, including aggressive revenue recognition.

Watch the effective tax rate

In some jurisdictions, a major disadvantage of boosting income by creative accounting is that you end up paying more tax; a real and expensive consequence of a cosmetic benefit. Many European countries have operated tax systems where income is taxed as reported, and this has created an incentive to understate profits in those jurisdictions.

However, elsewhere and notably in the US, the UK and other so-called 'common law' countries, tax reporting and financial reporting are independent. The tax authorities start from the reported income statement, then override it with their own measurement rules where necessary. The tax authorities by default use GAAP accounting, so if this gives a lower income number, the lower income is what they tax. In consequence, firms that have been aggressively boosting income may have effective tax rates that are below the statutory tax rate.

Example: CreativeCo

CreativeCo reports earnings before tax of $200. The statutory tax rate is 30%. The tax authorities send in Diana, their investigating accountant, who discovers that Creative has been significantly overstating profits by anticipating revenues and capitalising costs. In other words, they are recording income that is not yet taxable, and capitalising costs that could have been charged as expenses for tax. Diana concludes that, correctly measured, CreativeCo's taxable income is $80 and she assesses them for $(80 \times 30\% =)$ $24 of corporate tax on that basis. So CreativeCo's income statement shows: earnings before tax, $200, tax payable, $24, giving an effective tax rate of $(24/200 =)$ 12%.

Firms do not disclose their taxable income, but in a simple case like this it is easily deduced by multiplying reported pre-tax earnings by the ratio of the effective tax rate to the statutory tax rate, as $(200 \times 12\%/30\% =)$ 80. In this case, also, the ratio of the statutory tax rate to the effective tax rate gives us an index of the degree of over-statement of profits, $(30\%/12\% =)$ 2.5 times.

Cases: Queen's Moat Houses, Enron

Not infrequently, firms that have subsequently been found to have inflated profits have had low effective tax rates. The arithmetic mean ratio of the statutory to the effective tax rate at QMH over the decade prior to its failure was 2.48 times. Enron paid zero tax in the five years before its failure.

So is a low effective tax rate always a signal of creative accounting? Of course not. It may simply reflect excellent tax management by the firm. It frequently reflects a favourable tax regime for certain types of firm or activity. As always in forensic financial analysis, we are making a conjecture, and there are competing hypotheses. The low effective tax rate simply raises a question we need answering. GAAP now requires firms to provide in full for deferred tax, and to provide a reconciliation of their effective tax rate to the statutory corporate tax rate.

STOCK OPTIONS

A share option or stock option gives the owner of the option the right to buy a share in the firm at a set price, the exercise price, at any time during some agreed exercise period in the future. Share options are widely used for pay, and especially for executive pay. In the US in particular, options now represent the largest single component of executive pay.

Example: Scoop S.A.

Scoop inhabits the very simplest of worlds. The market understands that there are just two possible and discrete futures: either Scoop will be awarded a once-in-a–lifetime contract in six months time, or it will not, and there is a 50% chance of each outcome. With the contract the firm is worth (at present value) $4 per share; without it, $2. Rationally-valued, the shares are valued today at their expected value, which is the weighted-average ($4 × .5 + $2 × .5 =) $3. Scoop grants Lara, an employee, an option to buy a share in six months time at an exercise price of $3. What is that option worth today?

In accounting language, the difference between the share price when an option is awarded, and the exercise price of the option, is called the *intrinsic value* of the option. The intrinsic value in the case of Scoop's option grant is clearly ($3 - $3 =) precisely zero. When the underlying share price is below the exercise price, an option is 'out of the money'. When the share price is above the exercise price, an option is 'in the money'. In the language of options, Lara's option was granted 'at the money'. If the goal of granting stock options is to motivate employees to grow the stock price then for optimal incentives employee options should be granted at the money or thereabouts, that is at zero intrinsic value, and rebased down if the stock price falls.

The value of an employee stock option

Clearly, the intrinsic value of an option is not what the option is actually worth. The value of an option comes from its optionality – if the share price rises above the exercise price, the owner exercises the option, if it falls below the exercise price, the owner just tears the option up. On the day the option is granted, Lara foresees two payoffs. If Scoop gets the contract, the shares are worth $4, Lara exercises her option for $3, and makes a $1 gain. If Scoop does not get the contract, Lara just walks away from the option. So the value of the option is the expected value of the payoffs, which is ($1 × .5 + $0 × .5 =) $0.5.

Because of this asymmetry in payoffs, a firm that is riskier in the sense of having a higher variance of future outcomes, has a more valuable option other things equal. There is another firm, Risky Scoop Inc that also has a $3 share price, reflecting the market's belief that Risky Scoop will be worth $1 with the contract and $5 without. The payoff to an at-the-money option in this case is $2 with the contract and $0 without, so the option is worth ($2 × .5 + $0 × .5 =) $1.

For convenience, we described Scoop's share price as having just two possible outcomes. In reality, the future distribution of a firm's share price is a continuous density function and the model that is almost universally used to value stock options in this case is the Black-Scholes model, after economists Myron Scholes and Fischer Black. Black-Scholes is also commonly used to find the fair value of the options that firms grant to employees. Black-Scholes was developed to value traded options, and it assumes that investors are fully diversified and trade in liquid markets, so it probably overstates the value of stock options to the employee. Employees cannot sell, cannot short-sell, and are likely to be very under-diversified and over-weight in to their own firm's shares, especially since their human capital is also invested there. But the accounting task is to measure the opportunity cost of the options to the firm, rather than the value of the options to the employee. The analogy is with the company car scheme. Lara is now a director and gets a $100,000 Mercedes with the job. She is a woman of modest tastes and would, in fact, have been equally happy with a $40,000 Toyota, but from an accounting perspective this is irrelevant; her car cost $100,000.

GAAP: employee stock options

GAAP requires (since mid-2005 in the US and January 2006 under IFRS) share-based payment transactions with employees, such as stock options, to be measured at fair value and charged as compensation expense. The charge is spread over the *vesting period,* which is the period before the employee becomes unconditionally entitled to the option or shares. In employee stock option schemes this is typically three years or more.

Previously, GAAP based the recognition of employee stock options on intrinsic value rather than fair value. If options were granted at, or out of the money, they did not have to be recognised in the income statement. As a result, income statements understated the cost of remuneration. In some firms, where senior management were energetically using stock options to expropriate the wealth of outside shareholders, the understatement was enormous. GAAP's blind spot was partly a result of strong corporate lobbying. Partly, it reflected genuine confusion about whether granting options was a real cost. Benefits-in-kind always seem slightly nebulous but the way to clarify thinking is to insert a cash step – imagine the firm had to buy the options for cash on the open market, then give them to employees. They are clearly a cost.

In the US, the mismeasurement of income has been exacerbated by the fact that firms receive a tax deduction equal to the gain recognised by employees on the exercise of

their non-qualified stock options. So, especially when share prices are rising, many firms with active option schemes have been reporting much-reduced tax bills.
[References: FAS123, IAS19]

Case: Tiffany

In its 2005 SEC filing, Tiffany records the costs of stock options in accordance with FAS 123, Tiffany using the Black-Scholes valuation method. The stock compensation expense charged against income in 2005 was $22.1m and there is a corresponding credit to 'additional paid-in capital' in shareholders' equity. Since this is a non-cash charge, there is a corresponding adjusting item in the operating activities section of the cash flow statement. Tiffany shows a deferred tax asset of $9.3m relating to stock options. The same amount is reflected as a reduction in the tax charge in the income statement.

Tiffany also report a $6.7m credit to additional paid-in capital for the exercise of stock options during the year, representing 482,000 shares, adding $4,000 to the par value of common stock in the balance sheet. $6.7m is also reported as proceeds from exercise of stock options in the cash flow statement. There is a $3.8m credit to additional paid-in capital for the tax benefit from the exercise of stock options. Tiffany explains in the Notes that it has $64m of unrecognised compensation expense, which will be charged to the income statement over the vesting period of approximately 3 years. At the end of 2005 Tiffany had 13.5m stock options outstanding, compared to 144.5m issued shares.

Case: Publicis

In its 2005 financial statements Publicis notes that personnel expenses includes a charge for €20m in respect of stock option plans. The fair value of options granted is recognised over the vesting period, as determined by an independent expert using Black-Scholes. €20m is also credited to 'reserves and retained earnings' in shareholders' equity and adjusted as a non-cash charge in the operating activities section of the cash flow.

Publicis provides descriptions of the various plans it has in place in Note 28 to the accounts. It had 11.4 million options outstanding at the end of 2005, compared to 184 million issued shares. The disclosure includes not only numbers of options granted, exercised and lapsed for the 17 different tranches that Publicis has granted that are still active, and also the underlying assumptions for the fair value calculation.

PRESENTATION

The way in which earnings are presented can be as important as the way they are measured. In a sense it is more important: the accounting identity always holds, so more income recognised today is less income later on; but if the reader simply ignores a cost or a component of income, that never gets reversed. Sometimes it can be useful to separate out the transitory components of income, to help identify core or sustainable income for forecasting, or when comparing a group of firms in an industry. But for a value metric, we always want complete income. There are a number of ways in which the reader of the income statement may be led to use an incomplete measure of income.

Comprehensive income

One source of incompleteness in earnings follows from the operation of GAAP itself. Some changes in shareholders' equity are excluded from earnings and must be included to give comprehensive income. The following items are recorded as 'other comprehensive income' under GAAP:

– Revaluation surpluses on revaluations of long-term assets (only under IFRS).
– Revaluation surpluses/deficits from fair valuation of 'available-for-sale' securities, and certain financial instruments that are hedges; reserve accounted under both US GAAP and IFRS.
– Differences on foreign exchange translation.
– Cumulative effects of changes in accounting policy.

The list is quite short, nonetheless other comprehensive income can be significant. In Chapter 3 we studied four firms: Tiffany, Odfjell, Asahi and Publicis. They are not necessarily a representative sample, but for three of them other comprehensive income was around 30% of earnings, positive or negative.

Exceptionals and extraordinaries

If firms face pressure to produce steady growth in earnings, they tend to draw attention away from the bottom-line earnings to other income numbers. For example, a bad performance in a division which is then sold off may be de-emphasised by stressing profit on continuing operations'. Other words like 'sustainable profit' or 'core profit' may be used. 'Extraordinary items' are profits and losses that relate to events that are significant but infrequent and unusual, and are shown at the bottom of the income statement net of tax, below earnings. The idea is to exclude items that are non-recurring and non-sustainable from the earnings figure. US GAAP now polices extraordinaries very tightly, and they are now very rare under US GAAP. IFRS prohibits extraordinary items. As a result, the pressure has moved up the income statement to 'exceptionals'. GAAP does not use the term 'exceptional item' as such, but both IFRS and US GAAP actively require separate disclosure of items where their size or nature makes this necessary in order to explain performance.

Pro-forma earnings

Firms sometimes present some income numbers in press releases or elsewhere in a 'non-GAAP' way, perhaps excluding exceptionals or excluding amortisation and impairment of goodwill. The term *pro forma accounting* is used to describe non-GAAP presentations of income. Firms are perfectly entitled to do this so long as they are also filing GAAP numbers. Pro forma disclosures can be very useful in focusing attention on important issues or to help comparisons with prior years or to emphasise the results of core operations. The trouble is, pro forma financial information can also be used to mislead when it is being presented in a way that obscures the GAAP results.

The US SEC had become concerned about misuse of pro forma accounting and warned firms that to do so could be considered fraudulent. It now requires US public firms that release pro forma measures to include a reconciliation of the pro forma data to the most directly comparable GAAP measure. One case cited by the SEC was Trump.

Case: Trump Hotels and Casino Resorts

The SEC alleged that Trump Hotels issued a press release announcing positive results for its third quarter earnings in 1999 using a pro-forma net income figure that differed from GAAP net income. The press release stated that the results excluded a one-time charge, but failed to mention the inclusion of a one-time gain of $17.2 million. This created the impression that Trump had exceeded earnings expectations when net earnings were actually lower than analysts' forecasts. On November 4 1999, Trump Hotels filed its quarterly report which disclosed the one-time gain.

The presentation of costs and revenues

With no effect on the bottom line, firms may seek to present the component costs and revenues more flatteringly, in various ways. As we saw in Chapter 3, GAAP does not regulate the categorisation of costs and revenues very closely. Presentational games became more common during the 'dot-com bubble'. We discussed one in Chapter 7, which was the classification of costs so as to flatter gross margin.

The novelty of the late nineties was that many newborn and still loss-making firms were going straight to a full quotation on public capital markets. Absent earnings, analysts started to value these firms on a multiple of revenues; a practice with little economic logic. This created an incentive for firms to boost revenues. Rebates, discounts, and sales incentives, conventionally deducted from sales, might be shown as marketing expenditure. Firms with an online presence would barter or swap advertising with each other, crediting this as a sale at full value, and recording the equivalent cost as marketing expenditure. Agency businesses might be tempted to record the gross value of transactions, rather than their commission, as sales.

Example: Agent.com

Agent.com was a US firm selling holidays and travel tickets online. Its annual numbers were:

Revenue	**$152m**
Product costs	-$134m
	$18m
Other costs	-$120m
Operating result	-$102m

In GAAP [SAB101] the test is who is the 'merchant of record'; who bears the risks and rewards of ownership? If Agent is the principal in the transaction, buying in the holidays and adding value to them , before reselling them as its product, then it is entitled to report as it did. If Agent is reselling other people's products as an agent, then its revenue is its commission, which is $18m.

REVIEW

- The capitalisation of expenditure has the effect of deferring the recognition of costs in the income statement. Provisioning is a means of bringing forward costs. 'Big bath' accounting is tempting, particularly to new management as it flatters income in later years, but GAAP now polices excess provisioning.

- Though GAAP has got tougher on cost capitalisation, it struggles with revenue recognition. When there have been high-profile corporate failures, management frequently turn out to have been stretching the revenue-measurement rules beyond acceptable limits.

- When accounting for long-term construction contracts, GAAP allows firms to recognise a proportion of the certified value of work completed to date, and this provides a benchmark for revenue recognition when delivery spans multiple periods. Though in principle, delivery is the key event for determining revenue recognition, we need to be alert for mechanisms that allow firms to recognise revenue on contracting.

- Rogue accounting undermines people's confidence in GAAP, but it is exceptional. Most firms do not have these incentives, and are more concerned to smooth the profit stream through time, perhaps with a bias to conservatism in order to keep something in reserve.

- The presentation of income may be as important as income measurement. There are various ways in which we may collect an incomplete picture of a firm's income. The income statement is incomplete to the extent that firms have other comprehensive income. The classification of items as 'exceptional' or 'extraordinary' and the use of pro-forma accounting can tempt us to treat some items as one-off, and not representative of the firm's on-going performance.

- In order to understand how differences in policy may impair comparability between firms, and to be alert to the occasional extreme cases of rogue accounting, we need to understand where there is latitude in GAAP. Though rogue accounting can be hard to identify at the time, it invariably has a balance sheet effect, and it may depress the effective tax rate.

Appendix

Financial arithmetic

This appendix describes some of the financial arithmetic that we use in accounting and in analysis of financial statements.

PRESENT VALUES AND FUTURE VALUES

Investments have returns that spread through time. Suppose these returns are cash flows, or are streams of returns that can be expressed as cash flows. We assume that people value a dollar today more highly than a dollar received in the future, so money has a 'time-value'. *Discounted cash flow (DCF)* is the technique that is used to quantify the time-value of the money.

If $100 is invested today, that we will refer to as time 0, at 10% per annum interest, then one year later the investor will have $100 \times (1 + .10) = 110. If he leaves the capital and interest to earn interest for another year he will have by the end of the second year:

$100 \times (1 + 0.10)$
= $100 \times (1 + 0.10) \times (1 + 0.10)$
= $100 \times (1 + 0.10)^2$
= 121

This process of reinvesting capital and interest to earn interest for another period is called *compounding*. The outcome of this process is the *future value (FV)* of the initial amount. Using symbols, if PV is the *present value*, that is, the initial outlay which is compounded at the rate of interest, r, for n time-periods, then

$$FV = PV \times (1 + r)^n$$

We will assume in this discussion that interest is paid annually, in other words we assume *annual compounding*. In practice examples are commonly found of semi-annual compounding (banks often pay interest twice a year) right down to daily, or even finer, compounding. The formula holds in all cases provided r is the semi-annual, daily, or whatever rate of interest, and n is the number of half-years, days, etc.

Example: Schlomo

Your friend Schlomo approaches you and says: 'My father is giving me $50,000 in two years' time. The trouble is I want to sail round the world now. If you'll just lend me the $50,000, I'll return it when I get back in two years.'

Does this seem a good deal to you? Probably not. For one thing Schlomo might easily perish along the way, or decide to linger somewhere nice instead of coming back. But, ignoring the risks, by lending the money you are prevented from investing it and earning a return. The opportunity cost of the loan is the return you could earn elsewhere. You decide to calculate the amount you would need in two years to compensate for the loss of $50,000 now, the future value of the $50,000. You discover you could invest at 7%, so $FV = $50,000 \times (1+.07)^2 = $57,245$

Clearly $57,245 in two years is equivalent in value to $50,000 now. If the going rate of interest is 7%, no one would accept less than $50,000 now for $57,245 in two years, and no one would offer more.

Having established the link between a present sum and a future sum, the logic can be reversed to find the present value of a known future amount. If we know FV, and wish to find PV we can arrange the formula.

$$PV = \frac{FV}{(1 + r)^n}$$

Example: Jamila

Jamila wants to have $1,000 in three years time. She can invest at a return of 9%. How much does she need to invest now? To solve this problem we find the PV of $1,000 received in three years' time where,

$$PV = \frac{1,000}{(1 + .09)^3} = \frac{1,000}{1.295} = \$772.18$$

You can confirm that $772.18 compounded at 9% for three years yields $1,000.

The % rate used for discounting, 9% in the previous example, is commonly called the *discount rate*. The procedure we just adopted was unwieldy in one respect. $1,000 was multiplied by $1/(1 + .09)^3$, which is called the *discount factor*, and which had to be calculated. Tables of these factors, already calculated, are called discount tables, or present value tables, and they give the PV of $1 received after n years at interest rate r.

Annuities

The same sum received regularly for a number of periods is known as an *annuity*. Suppose one wants to find the present value of an equal sum of $200 received each year for the next five years, discounting at 10%. This could be calculated as follows:

Year	1	2	3	4	5	Total
Cash ($)	200	200	200	200	200	
10% discount factors	.909	.826	.751	.683	.621	
Present values	182	165	150	137	124	**$758**

This is correct, but it would have been quicker to sum the discount factors to get an 'annuity factor', then multiply the $200 by the annuity factor, saving computations. Again, 'annuity tables' do this for you. The 10%, five-year annuity factor is 3.791 (0.909 + 0.826 + 0.751 + 0.683 + 0.621 = 3.790; there is a small rounding difference) so the present value of the annuity is $200 × 3.791 = $758.

If an annuity factor is wanted for a run of equal cash flows, but starting some time in the future, this can be found by combining annuity factors. Suppose we wish to find the present value of a five-year annuity of $300 to be received from the 12th year from now to the 16th, with a 10% discount rate:

16 year, 10% annuity factor	7.824
Subtract the 11 year, 10% annuity factor	(6.495)
12 to 16 year factor	1.329

So the present value is $300 × 1.329 = 398.7.

NET PRESENT VALUE AND INTERNAL RATE OF RETURN

Investments have returns that spread through time in the form of a stream of cash flows. Capital has a time-value because it has an opportunity cost, which is the return the investor can get from alternative investments. The purpose of DCF analysis is to incorporate this opportunity cost of capital into the analysis. This is why it is cash flows, rather than, say, profit flows, that are traditionally used in valuation. It is upon payment and receipt of cash that the financing clock starts and stops ticking.

Net present value

In investment analysis we want to find the present value of the whole bundle of cash flows, positive and negative, which result from making an investment. The term *net present value (NPV)* is used for this. Suppose C_t is the cash flow (+ or -) in period t, and r is the required rate of return, which is the investors' opportunity cost of capital, the return they could get on the best alternative investment, then:

$$NPV = \sum_{t=0}^{n} \frac{C_t}{(1 + r)^t}$$

People sometimes present this expression in a slightly different way, to reflect the fact that investments typically require an investment or outflow of cash, I, at the beginning, which is time t = 0.

$$NPV = \sum_{t=1}^{n} \frac{C_t}{(1 + r)^t} - I$$

The first term on the right of this expression is often called the *economic value (EV)* of the asset or investment. It is the value of the expected future cash flows, once the investment has been made. Hence the *net* present value is the difference between the economic value and the required investment, NPV = EV - I. The NPV measures the amount of cash the owners could immediately withdraw as a result of the investment; in other words, it is the immediate increase in the owners' wealth associated with making the investment.

Internal rate of return

The *internal rate of return (IRR)* measures the yield or return from a set of cash flows in percentage terms. The IRR is the discount rate that makes the NPV of the cash flows equal zero. Mathematically, it is R in the following formula, where C_t is cash flow in period t and n is the life of the project.

$$NPV = \sum_{t=0}^{n} \frac{C_t}{(1 + R)^t} = 0$$

Consider the project that comprises an initial outlay of $12,500 followed by four annual receipts of $4,000, that is, a four-year annuity of $4,000. We find the IRR by repeatedly solving with different discount rates in order to find one that gives a zero NPV. Try 8% first. The four-year 8% annuity factor is 3.312, so NPV = (4,000 × 3.312 =) 13,248 - 12,500 = $748. Discounting at 8% gives an NPV of +$748, so a higher rate is needed to reduce the contribution of the future inflows. 10% gives an NPV of +$180. 12% gives an NPV of -$352. Hence the IRR is between 10% and 12%. We could roughly identify it by 'interpolating' between 10% and 12% linearly. The interval between 10% and 12%, which is 2%, represents a range of ($180 + $352 =) $532 of value. So the discount rate that gives zero NPV is approximately 10% + 2% × 180/532 = 10.7%. The precise method for finding IRR is an iterative process. It involves converging on a solution by informed trial and error. In fact, there is no other way of finding the IRR. Manual solution of IRR is rather time-consuming, but the task is the sort that computers enjoy.

In summary, the relationship between the IRR and the NPV of an investment is as follows: NPV is the investment's value using the cost of capital as the discount rate. IRR is the discount rate that makes an investment's NPV zero.

Using Excel

Nowadays we pretty much always use spreadsheet software such as Excel to do financial arithmetic. To find NPV in Excel, we enter into a blank cell $= NPV (r;C_1...C_n)$. r is the discount rate, or the cell address where the discount rate is located. $C_1...C_n$ is the series of cash flows separated by commas, or the range address where the series of cash flows is located. Excel assumes that the first cash flow in the series is one period ahead, so if there is a C_0, say an initial investment, it has to be added separately. The C_0 is already at today's value, so does not need discounting. So the complete expression for NPV in Excel is $=NPV(r;C_1...C_n) + C_0$.

We could use the NPV command in Excel to get a discount factor, if we wanted to. So, in the Jamilla example we wanted the 3-year, 9% discount factor. Typing $= NPV(9\%,0,0,1)$ would return .77218.

To find an IRR in Excel we enter $= IRR(C_0...C_n, guess)$. In this case the first cash flow is the current (usually negative) cash flow. Also, Excel invites you to submit a 'guess' as to the solution, to help the iterative process along. The guess is optional; if it is omitted, Excel assumes it is 10%.

PERPETUITIES

One expression that is extremely useful in practice is the expression for the present value of a *perpetuity*, which is a periodic amount received for ever. The general DCF formula for the value today, V, of a series of cash flows, C_t, running from today until infinity (∞) is :

$$V = \sum_{t=0}^{\infty} \frac{C_t}{(1 + r)^t}$$

If we are willing to assume that the cash flow grows at a constant annual rate, g%, and so long as the growth rate g is less than r, this simplifies to:

$$V = C_1/(r - g)$$

This expression says that the value of a growing perpetuity is the year 1 cash flow divided by the difference between the discount rate and the growth rate. If there is no growth, that is, if the cash flow is a flat annuity, the expression simplifies further:

$$V = C/g$$

So the value of an annuity of $10 a year for ever, when the interest rate is 5%, is ($10/5% =) $200. This is completely intuitive because, put the other way round, it simply says that $200 invested at 5% would pay $10 per year.

Financial assets like bonds may promise a simple profile of future cash flows of this sort, but the income from investments in operating assets and in firms never turn out this way. The reason these perpetuity formulas are so useful in practice is that, *in advance*, predicting constant growth is often the best we can do. A widely-used application is the *Gordon growth model*, named after the financial economist Myron Gordon. In this case, if the cash flow is a dividend, *Dividend*, expected to grow at g% per year, and the discount rate is the cost of equity capital, r_e, then the value of a share, V, is:

$$V = Dividend_1/(r_e - g)$$

Financial arithmetic

Derivation

$$V = \sum_{t=0}^{\infty} \frac{Dividend_0 \, (1 + g)^t}{(1 + r_e)^t}$$

expanding,

1.
$$V = \frac{Dividend_0 \, (1 + g)}{(1 + r_e)} + \frac{Dividend_0 \, (1 + g)^2}{(1 + r_e)^2} \, \ldots \ldots + \frac{Dividend_0 \, (1 + g)^{\infty}}{(1 + r_e)^{\infty}}$$

Multiplying throughout by:
$$\frac{1 + r_e}{1 + g}$$

2.
$$V = Dividend_0 + \frac{Dividend_0 \, (1 + g)}{(1 + r_e)} \, \ldots \ldots + \frac{Dividend_0 \, (1 + g)^{\infty}}{(1 + r_e)^{\infty}}$$

Subtracting 1 from 2:

$$V \, \frac{(1 + r_e)}{(1 + g)} - V = Dividend_0 - \frac{Dividend_0 \, (1 + g)^{\infty}}{(1 + r_e)^{\infty}}$$

Assuming $r_e > g$, the final term vanishes, so

$$V \, \frac{(1 + r_e)}{(1 + g)} - V = Dividend_0$$

$$V \, \frac{(1 + r_e) + (1 + g)}{(1 + g)} = Dividend_0$$

$$V \, (r_e - g) = Dividend_0 \, (1 + g)$$

Since

$$Dividend_0 \, (1 + g) = Dividend_1$$

$$V = \frac{Dividend_1}{(r_e - g)}$$

ECONOMIC PROFIT VALUATION

So far we have talked about the value of an investment in terms of discounting future cash flows. It turns out that you can get the same answer by discounting a stream of earnings or, to be precise, discounting future economic profit. The general valuation formula on the previous page found the value of a share, or the whole firm, as the present value of its expected dividends. Equivalently, the value of the firm to its shareholders is the present value of future economic profits, discounted at the same cost of capital, plus today's shareholders funds, E. Using a simple perpetuity approach:

$$V = E + \frac{Income - E \times r_e}{r_e - g}$$

This is an important result. It can be a useful alternative to valuing cash flows in practice. More fundamentally, it helps us understand accounting. It reminds us of the fundamental logic of accounting, described by the accounting identity, in which earnings and cash flow are hard-wired to each other through the balance sheet. We show how the economic profit valuation formula is derived below. The intuition is simple. According to the accounting identity, *dividend = income - increase in assets*. So if we take the dividend valuation model and replace *dividend* by *income - increase in assets* we must get the same result.

Derivation

Though the logic is simple, the derivation will seem a little tortuous because we first need to manipulate the accounting identity to get it into the most useful shape.

Income – E $\times$ r_e is economic profit, because the cost of capital, r_e, times shareholders' funds, E, is the capital change. The intuition of the economic profit valuation model is that the value of an asset or a firm is the book value of the assets, plus the present value of the expected stream of income over and above the normal return, r_e, on those book assets.

The accounting identity

The version of the accounting identity we met in Chapter 4 said:

Accounting income = Dividend + Increase in shareholders' funds

If we call accounting income just *income*, and shareholders' funds, *E*, and rearrange:

Dividend = Income - Increase in E

It is going to be helpful to develop this idea of the 'increase in shareholder's funds' further. Firstly, the increase in E is simply the proportion of income that the firm reinvests, rather than pays out as dividend. Call the reinvestment rate, i, then the accounting identity becomes:

$$Dividend = Income\ (1- i)$$

We can relate reinvestment to the firm's growth rate, g. Assuming i is a constant proportion, then the growth rate of income and growth rate in dividend are the same thing. The rate of growth in the firm's income will be a function of the percentage, i, of its income it reinvests to build E, and the return it gets on that reinvestment. Assume the return on the extra E, is the firm's return on equity ratio, ROE, which is $income/E$. So $g = i \times ROE$, and thus $i = g/ROE$.

Using this insight, we can reexpress the accounting identity as:

$$Dividend = Income\ (1- \frac{g}{ROE})$$

Example: Growth Inc

To see the link between reinvestment, growth and the return on equity, consider a simple example. Imagine a firm which reinvests 30% of its income its each year to grow, and which has a ROE of 15%. In year one its income is $1,000. It invests $300, leaving $700 for dividend. It earns a return of 15% on its $300 investment, generating incremental income next year of $45. So year two income is $1,045 (= year one income of $1,000 + incremental income of $45). Again, it invests 30% of this amount, leaving $731.5 for dividend. Income from year one to year two has grown by 4.5%, which is the reinvestment rate of 30% × the ROE of 15%.

The valuation formula

For convenience, we can work with the simplified version of the dividend valuation model, the Gordon growth model, that we met in the last section. To simplify still further we will drop the time subscript from *Dividend*.

$$V = \frac{Dividend}{r_e - g}$$

Substituting from the accounting identity,

$$V = \frac{Income\ (1 - \frac{g}{ROE})}{r_e - g}$$

Since *Income* = $ROE \times E$, we can restate value as:

$$V = E \times \frac{ROE\ (1- \frac{g}{ROE})}{r_e - g}$$

This simplifies to:
$$V = E \times \frac{ROE - g}{r_e - g}$$

Add and subtract $r_e - g$ in the numerator:
$$V = E \times \frac{(ROE - g) + (r_e - g) - (r_e - g)}{r_e - g}$$

Split the right hand side of the equation:
$$V = \frac{E \times (r_e - g)}{r_e - g} + \frac{E \times [(ROE - g) - (r_e - g)]}{r_e - g}$$

Simplifying:
$$V = E + \frac{E \times (ROE - r_e)}{r_e - g}$$

Since ROE is *Income/E*, $E \times (ROE - r_e) = Income - E \times r_e$

So
$$V = E + \frac{Income - E \times r_e}{r_e - g}$$

Entity-level economic profit valuation

We derived the economic profit valuation model in terms of shareholders. We get exactly the same result if we work at the entity level and substitute:
– *operating free cash flow* for shareholders' cash flow (*Dividend*)
– *EBIAT* (sometimes called *NOPAT*) for *income*
– *WACC* for equity required return (r_e)
– *capital employed* for shareholders' funds (*E*).

Then,
$$V = capital\ employed + \frac{EBIAT - capital\ employed \times WACC}{WACC - g}$$

Glossary of terms

This glossary collects and defines the financial and accounting vocabulary used in this book.

A

Accelerated depreciation   A depreciation schedule that charges relatively higher depreciation in earlier years

Accounting identity   Mathematical identity that describes the logic of accounting; Accounting income = Dividend + Increase in shareholders' funds

Accounting income   Income measured by the accounting identity

Accounting model   Set of rules that determine what assets and liabilities are recognised in the balance sheet, and at what values

Accounts payable   Trade payables

Accounts receivable   Trade receivables

Accrual   An estimate of a liability known to exist at the balance sheet date but for which no invoice has been received

Accrual accounting   The accounting method used by firms, in which accounting records the creation, and consumption or discharge, of assets and claims

Acid test ratio   Similar to the 'current ratio' but excludes inventory from the numerator

Acquisition accounting   Purchase accounting

Acquisition growth   Growth achieved by buying other businesses, in contrast to 'organic growth'

Alliance   Word used broadly for a group of associated or related firms

Amortisation   The accounting method used to measure the consumption of intangible or financial assets

Annuity   A fixed sum paid annually

Appreciating asset   An asset that is expected to increase in value, rather than depreciating

Asset   A resource that is expected to produce economic benefits in the future

Asset financing   Arrangement where debt is raised to finance a particular asset or class of assets and is secured on those assets

Asset turn, asset turnover   Ratio of sales to net operating assets, or equivalently, to capital employed

Associate, associated firm	A firm in which there is a substantial investment, but which falls below the threshold for consolidation
Average cost	In the context of inventory valuation, a rule of thumb that assumes the items in inventory were purchased at average prices, of the year, or of goods consumed

B

Balance sheet	Consists of two lists that must be equal in total: a list of the firm's assets and a list of the claims upon those assets
Best-efforts accounting	Successful-efforts accounting
Bid-ask spread	The margin between the buying and selling price in financial markets
Book	Used as an adjective to mean 'using balance sheet data'
Book equity	Equity shareholders' funds in the balance sheet
Business model	Term used in this book to refer to the particular way resources have been configured, given the choice of business

C

Capital employed	The finance the firm has raised from investors; shareholders' funds plus net debt
Capital expenditure, 'capex'	Investment in long-term assets
Capital lease	Finance lease
Capitalisation	Treatment of expenditure as an asset in the balance sheet, rather than charging it as an expense, against profit
Cash accounting	An accounting model that only recognises transactions in the financial statemenst when cash has been received or paid
Cash equivalents	Financial assets such as Treasury bills that are highly liquid and can be converted into cash without notice
Cash flow identity	The expression describing the relationship between the cash flow, income statement and the balance sheet; Cash flow = Income - Change in balance sheet
Cash flow return on investment (CFROI)	A proprietary return on capial measure that makes a number of adjustments to the accounting data
Cash from financing	Net flow of cash derived from equity shareholders and debt holders
Cash from operations	Cash flow derived from the business activities of the firm, as distinct from its investing and financing activities
Cash interest cover	Interest cover ratio calculated with cash flow in the numerator, commonly proxied by EBITDA, and cash net interest paid in the denominator

Glossary

Clean-surplus income	Comprehensive income
Common shareholders	Ordinary shareholders
Common shares, common stock	Ordinary shares
Company, corporation	An entity that has a legal identity separate from that of its members, referred to as a 'firm' in this book
Compound growth rate	Average growth rate over a number of periods, calculated using the geometric mean
Comprehensive income	The total accounting income of shareholders, including income recognised in the income statement and income taken straight to reserves in the balance sheet
Conservatism	Practice in accounting of understating assets while fully-stating liabilities, thus recognising losses earlier and gains later than otherwise
Consolidated financial statements	Group accounts
Consolidation	The process of preparing consolidated financial statements
Contingency	A potential liability that is not probable enough to meet the tests for balance sheet recognition, but is more than a remote possibility
Cost of capital	The return required by the firm's investors, that is thus the firm's cost of capital
Cost of sales, cost of goods sold, COGS	The costs incurred in acquiring goods and bringing them to a saleable condition
Creative accounting	Accounting that paints a false picture of economic reality
Credit	A reduction in an asset or an increase in a claim
Credit analysis	Financial analysis that focuses on the probability that a firm will default on its liabilities
Credit rating	Standardised score, published by a credit rating agency, indicating the firm's estimated probability of default
Credit risk	The risk that creditors will not recover their money
Current asset	An asset that is expected to be liquidated within one year
Current liability	A liability expected to be discharged within one year
Current ratio	Ratio of the current assets of the firm to its current liabilities.
Current value	The current value of an asset to the firm; measured as replacement cost, realisable value or economic value, in different contexts

D

Debit	An increase in an asset or a reduction in a claim
Debt	Borrowing, including short- and long-term borrowing
Debt capital	The funds provided by lenders
Debt ratio	Gearing ratio
Debt servicing	Interest payments and contractual repayments of principal
Debt to equity ratio	Ratio of, net or gross, debt to equity shareholders' funds
Defeasance	Derecognition
Deferred tax provision	A tax equalisation account created to recognise the future impact of timing differences between accounting profit and taxable profit
Defined benefit	Pension scheme that promises the employee a certain pension, typically based on their final salary
Defined contribution	Pension scheme where the pensioner receives whatever income the assets contributed can generate, and where there is no further recourse to the firm
Delivery	The completion of a service or physical transfer of goods, which is evidence that title has passed and revenue can be recognised
Depreciation	The accounting method used to measure the consumption of tangible long-term assets
Depreciation schedule	The profile of the depreciation of an asset through time
Deprival value	The loss a firm would suffer if it were deprived of an asset; measured as the lower of replacement cost, on the one hand, and the higher of realisable value and economic value, on the other
Derecognition	An arrangement where a firm has an asset and the related liability on its balance sheet, but recontracts in order to remove them
Deverticalising	Exiting some activities to focus on other activities in the value chain; the reverse of vertical integration
Direct cash flow	A method of presenting cash flow under which the cash flow statement shows the net cost effect of a transaction or event
Discounted cash flow	Valuation method in which future cash flows are converted to present values by discounting
Disallowable	Expenditure charged in the income statement that is disallowed for tax
Dividend	A distribution by a firm to its shareholders

E

Earnings	The income available for ordinary shareholders after all other claims have been met, which is recognised in the income statement
Earnings before interest and after tax (EBIAT)	EBIT less the tax on EBIT
Earnings before interest and tax (EBIT)	Income from all sources, principally from operations, that is available to pay tax and for investors
Earnings per share (EPS)	Earnings divided by the average number of ordinary shares outstanding in the year
EBIT margin	The ratio of EBIT to sales
EBITDA	Earnings before interest, tax, depreciation and amortisation
Economic depreciation	The actual change in the value of a depreciating asset in a period
Economic profit	Earnings measured after making a charge for all of the capital the firm is using
Economic value (EV)	The present value of the expected stream of income from an asset
Economic value added (EVA)	Term for economic profit used by consulting firms, especially when accounting adjustments are made to the underlying data
Economies of scale	Efficiency gains reflected in a reduction in the average cost of production when output is increased
Effective tax rate	The percentage of tax actually payable on earnings before tax
Enterprise price to book	The price to book ratio measured at the entity-level rather than at the equity-level
Enterprise value	Capital employed measured using market values rather than book figures: the value of shareholders' funds plus the value of net debt
Enterprise level	Entity level
Entity level	Analysis conducted, or a financial ratio measured, at the level of the whole business, that is, at the level of operating assets, however financed; contrast with 'equity level'
Equity	The balance sheet claim of the firm's own shareholders; the share capital and reserves of a firm
Equity free cash flow	Residual cash flow after debt servicing

Equity method	Method used to incorporate the results of an associate firm. The balance sheet shows the firm's share of the net assets of the associate firm, and the income statement shows its share of the associate's profit or loss
Equity to total assets ratio	Proportion of the firm's total assets funded by equity
Equity, equity capital	The funds provided by ordinary shareholders
Exceptional items, exceptionals	Items of income or expense that, whilst arising in the normal course of business, are significant enough to merit separate disclosure
Extraordinary items	Items of income or expense that do not arise in the ordinary course of business of the firm

F

Factoring	An arrangement in which a bank advances finance against receivables, whilst also providing credit management services
Fair value	The amount for which an asset or liability can be exchanged in an arms' length transaction; synonymous with current value in US parlance, and with realisable value under IFRS
Finance lease	A lease contract under which the lessee bears effectively all the risks and rewards of ownership, and thus recognises the asset and associated liability in the balance sheet
Financial asset	Cash, or a claim that is denominated in money terms
Financial leverage	The degree to which the firm is debt financed
Firm	General term used in this book for an incorporated business entity
First in, first out (FIFO)	A rule of thumb for inventory valuation that assumes the items in inventory are the ones most recently purchased
Fixed asset	Long-term asset
Fixed cost	Cost that is invariant as sales change in the short run
Foreign exchange gains and losses	The differences that arise when assets and liabilities, and revenues and costs, denominated in one currency are translated into the home currency
Full cost accounting	In relation to mining/exploration firms, accounting system where all the costs of exploration are capitalised, in contrast to 'succesful efforts' accounting
Fully reversing	In the context of deferred tax accounting, an adjustment to accounting profits that has an equal and opposite adjustment in future years
Fully-diluted earnings per share	Earnings per share calculated as though all outstanding options were exercised.

Funded pension scheme	A pension scheme where the employer creates a separate fund and contributes the assets needed to meet the future pension liabilities

G

GAAP	Generally accepted accounting principles
Gearing, book gearing	The proportion of debt in capital employed in balance sheet terms
Going-concern	A firm that is solvent and is expected to continue in operation for at least a year
Goodwill	The residual asset recorded in purchase accounting an acquisition, measured as the difference between the fair value of the consideration for the acquisition, and the fair value of the identified assets and liabilities acquired
Gross margin	The ratio of gross profit to sales
Gross profit	The difference between sales and cost of sales
Group	A parent firm and its subsidiaries
Group accounts	The financial statements of a group of companies, obtained by line-by-line addition of the assets, liabilities, income and expenses of the parent and its subsidiaries

H

Hire purchase	A finance-lease type arrangement that gives the lessee the tax benefits of ownership by deeming the transaction a purchase in which the purchaser obtains immediate possession of the goods, but obtains ownership only upon payment of agreed instalments
Historic cost	The original purchase cost of an asset
Holding company	Parent
Hyper-inflation	Endemic high inflation; inflation of at least 100% over a three-year period

I

Impairment	Reduction in the amount at which an asset is carried in the balance sheet, when its value falls permanently below its carrying amount
Income	A general term for a flow that increases assets
Income statement	A statement explaining how a business earned its income during a period
Incorporation	Process of registering a company or corporation

Indirect cash flow	A method of describing cash flow under which the statement shows the inocme and balance sheet components separately
In-process R&D	Acquired intellectual property associated with on-going research and development
Intangible assets	Fixed assets that have no physical substance
Interest cover	Ratio of EBIT to net interest
Interest rate parity	A world in which changes in exchange rates accurately reflect differences in interest rates
Interest tax shelter	The tax that the firm saves because interest is deductible for tax
Internal rate of return (IRR)	The average return implied by a series of cash flows; found as the discount rate at which the present value of future cash inflows and outflows from an investment is zero
Intrinsic value	The difference between the value of the underlying share when an option is granted, and the exercise price of the option
Inventory	The stock of raw materials, partly-completed goods or work-in-progress, and finished goods
Inventory days	The ratio of inventory to sales, multiplied by 365
Investment accounting model	The accounting model that would generate reliable period-by period measures of investment return
Investment-grade	Firm or bond with a credit rating of BBB/Baa or above
Invoice discounting	An arrangement in which a bank advances finance against receivables
Irredeemable preference share	Preference shares that are not repaid after a fixed term

J

Joint-venture	Arrangement where the firm shares control of an entity or activity with others

L

Last in, first out (LIFO)	A rule of thumb for inventory valuation that assumes the items in inventory are the ones purchased first
Leverage ratio	Gearing ratio
Liability	An obligation to transfer economic benefits, generally cash; an expected outflow of resources
Like-for-like growth	In retail, growth achieved from existing retail space

Limited liability	A legal structure in which the owners of a firm are not liable for its debts beyond the capital that they have contributed
Liquidity ratio	Solvency ratio
Long-term accrual	Spreading expense over a number of periods, through mechanisms such as depreciation
Long-term asset	An asset neld for use rather than resale, not expected to be liquidated within one year
Long-term liability	An amount owed to a third party, expected to be discharged in more than a year

M

Maintenance capex	The capital expenditure required to maintain operating capacity at its current level
Margin	Ratio of profit to sales
Market gearing	The gearing ratio calculated using the market values of debt and of equity instead of book figures
Market value	General term for current value; US GAAP term for realisable value
Market value added (MVA)	A firm-level proxy for NPV, used by some consulting firms, measured as the difference between market capitalisation and book equity
Mark-to-market accounting	Revaluation of financial asses and liabilities; term also used for current value accounting more generally
Matching concept	The principle that the revenue for a particular period is matched with the expenditure incurred to achieve it
Merger accounting	Pooling
Merger, merger of equals	Combination of two firms when neither is dominant or controls the other
Minority interest, minorities	The stake of third-party shareholders in a subsidiary that has been fully consolidated

N

Net assets	In this book, used as shorthand for 'net operating assets'
Net current assets	Current assets less current liabilities
Net income	Earnings
Net interest paid	The amount of interest paid by a firm, less interest received
Net margin	Sometimes used to describe the ratio of earnings to sales
Net operating assets	The firm's operating assets, less its non-financing liabilities

Net operating profit after tax (NOPAT)	Earnings before interest and after tax
Net operating profit less adjusted taxes (NOPLAT)	Earnings before interest and after tax
Net present value (NPV)	The value created by an investment; measured as the present value of future cash flows, less the origninal investment
Net worth	US term for shareholders' funds, and sometimes for net assets
Nominal growth	Growth in the value of sales, including inflation
Nominal value	Par value of a share
Non-cash charges	Expenses charged against income that have no associated cash flow; for example, depreciation and amortisation
Non-cumulative preference share	If the firm passes a dividend, the dividend is not carried forward as a liability to future periods
Non-financial data	Firm data not recorded in the accounting system
Non-recourse	In relation to an arrangement such as a loan secured on a financial asset, the lender cannot recover the outstanding amount from the firm in the event that the debtor defaults

O

Off-balance-sheet financing	Structuring so that neither an asset nor the associated debt appear on the balance sheet
Operating cash flow	Cash from operations
Operating free cash flow	Cash flow after investment in long-term assets, which is available for investors
Operating lease	A lease contract under which the bank retains the 'asset risk' and thus is deemed to be the owner of the asset
Operating leverage	The ratio of fixed to total cost
Operating margin	The ratio of operating profit to sales
Operating profit	The surplus generated by a firm from its operations
Opportunity cost	In relation to an asset, its value in its best alternative use, which is therefore the benefit foregone from employing it in its current use
Ordinary share	One unit of ownership in a firm
Ordinary shareholders	The investors who own the firm and who have the residual claim on its assets
Organic growth	Growth that arises naturally from existing activities, and perhaps from using existing capacity

Other income	Income from non-operating sources
Outsourcing	Using other firms to provide support activities
Overdraft	A negative balance on a chequing account

P

Paid-in share capital	Amounts raised by the firm by issuing ordinary shares; sum of par value and share premium
Par value	The unit value in which a firm's shares are denominated, according to a firm's statutes
Parent	A firm that owns one or more other firms in a group
Participating	In the context of preference shares, an arrangement where the investor gets to share in any profits above a certain level, in addition to the contractual preference dividend
Partnership	More than one person, trading together as an unincorporated entity
Payables days	The ratio of payables to sales, multiplied by 365
Perpetuity	A regular payment, expected to be received forever
Pooling of interests	Technique to account for the merger of two firms, when neither is dominant nor acquires the other, as distinct from purchase accounting
Preference shares	Hybrid financing instruments with some attributes of equity and some attributes of debt
Prepayment	A payment made for goods or services in advance of their receipt
Price to book ratio	Ratio of a firm's market capitalisation to its book equity
Price/earnings ratio	Ratio of a firm's share price to its earnings per share
Primary activities	In the context of the value chain, the sequence of discrete productive activities
Profit	A general term for income; income from trading or operations, or gains on the sale of assets
Profit and loss account	Income statement
Profit margin	General term for margin
Profit or loss on disposal	Difference between the disposal proceeds from an asset and its carrying value in the balance sheet; final adjustment to depreciation when the true terminal value of the asset is known
Profitability equation	The equation that expresses the insight that any return on capital measure is the product of margin, which is proft/sales, and asset turn, which is sales/assets

Property rights	Legally enforceable ownership claims
Property, plant and equipment (PP&E)	Tangible fixed assets; the land, buildings and equipment used by the business
Provision	The balance sheet record of a liability of uncertain amount or timing
Purchase accounting	Technique to record the acquisition by one firm of another
Purchasing power parity (PPP)	Describes a world in which the same sum, converted to the currency of another country, will buy the same bundle of goods and services in that country

Q

Quick ratio	Acid test ratio

R

Real growth	Growth adjusted for inflation
Realisable value (RV), net realisable value (NRV)	The proceeds of selling an asset, net of the costs of selling
Realised income	Income realised in cash or in the form of assets that are reasonably certain to be converted into cash
Receivables days	The ratio of average receivables to sales, multiplied by 365
Recognition	General term to describe the inclusion of an item or reflection of an event in the financial statements
Recourse	In relation to an arrangement such as a loan secured on a financial asset, the lender can recover the outstanding amount from the firm in the event that the debtor defaults
Recoverable amount	The higher of economic value and realisable value
Related firm	A general term for an associate
Replacement cost (RC)	The current cost of acquiring an asset, or replacing a liability, in the market place
Reserve accounting	Recognition of income as a movements in shareholders' funds in the balance sheet, rather than in the income statement
Residual income	Traditional term for economic profit
Residual value	The expected proceeds from selling an asset at the end of its useful life
Retained earnings; retained profits	The firm's earnings available for distribution, less any amounts already distributed
Return on capital	Generic term for any measure of the return that a firm earns on investors' capital

Return on capital employed (ROCE)	The financial ratio that measures the return that the firm has earned on its capital employed, which is the capital raised from all its investors; entity return on capital
Return on equity (ROE)	The financial ratio that measures the return on the capital provided by the firm's equity shareholders
Return on invested capital (ROIC)	Commonly used measure of entity return
Return on net assets (RONA)	The financial ratio that measures the return that the firm has earned on its net assets; equivalent to ROCE
Return on sales	Margin
Return on total assets	Ratio of EBIT, or earnings, to total assets; sometimes used as a measure of return on capital
Return spread	Difference between the IRR and the cost of capital
Revaluation reserve	The reserve that records the surplus arising when a firm revalues its assets
Revenue	Sales
Rogue accounting	Creative accounting

S

Sales	Value of goods and services sold in the period
Sales, general and administration costs (SG&A)	Term used in this book for all remaining costs, when the firm has identified its cost of sales
Securitisation	An arrangement whereby a firm pools a group of similar financial assets and sells shares in the resulting portfolio
Semi-fixed costs	Costs that are part fixed and part variable with sales
Share premium	The amount payable by shareholders to the firm for shares issued for cash, in excess of the par value
Shareholders' equity	Equity
Shareholders' funds	The balance sheet claim of all shareholders, that is, equity plus non-equity shareholders such as minorities and preference shares
Short-term accrual	Recognition of income or expense where the related cash flow takes place in an adjacent period
Sole trader	An individual trading as an unincorporated business
Solvency ratio	Ratio that measure the ability of a firm to meet its immediate liabilities from its liquid assets
Special-purpose entity (SPE)	Special-purpose vehicle

Special-purpose vehicle (SPV)	A firm created to support a particular transaction or set of transactions, usually structured to qualify for equity accounting
Spread	The margin between the buying and selling price of an asset
Statutory tax rate	The rate at which tax is charged on taxable income; usually describes the rate in the jurisdiction in which the firm reports
Stock	Inventory; the US term for ordinary shares
Stock option	The right to buy shares in a firm
Stock return	The return from holding a share during a period; measured as dividend per share plus capital gain, divided by opening share price
Straight-line depreciation	Method of depreciation that spreads the consumption of the asset equally in each period
Subsidiary	A firm that is owned or effectively owned, so that its accounts are consolidated by the parent firm
Successful-efforts accounting	In relation to mining/exploration firms, a treatment in which only the costs associated with successful exploration are capitalised in the balance sheet
Support functions	In the context of the value chain, service functions that support the firm's primary activities

T

Tangible assets	Assets that have physical substance, for example property, plant and equipment
Tax equalisation account	A deferred tax provision designed to spread tax charges through time
Tax loss	Taxable loss, calculated according to the rules of the tax authority
Tax loss carry back	The use of tax losses to reclaim tax paid on income of earlier years
Tax loss carry forward	The use of tax losses to offset taxable profits in future years
Taxable profit	Income calculated according to the rules of the tax authority, as a basis for taxation; usually measured by making adjustments to accounting profit
Total recognised gains and losses	Comprehensive income
Total shareholder return (TSR)	Stock return
Trade payables, trade creditors	Amounts owing to suppliers

Trade receivables, trade debtors	Amounts owing from customers
Trading profit	Operating profit
Transaction	An exchange of assets and claims with third parties, including receipts and payments of cash
Treasury stock	Shares that have been repurchased by the firm and are held for reissue
Turnover	Sales

U

Unbundling	The term used in this book for deverticalising
Unconsolidated entities	A firm not included in the consolidated financial statements, perhaps because it is an associate rather than a subsidiary
Underfunded	A pension scheme which has insufficient assets to meet the expected laibilities
Unfunded pension scheme	A pension scheme that relies on assets in the firm's balance sheet to pay the pension when the time comes
Uniting of interests	Pooling

V

Value added	Difference between the value of sales and the cost of the material inputs used to produce the sales
Value chain	Representation of productive activity as a sequence of primary activities, with support functions that service all parts of the chain of primary activities
Value creation	Used in finance to describe the creation of wealth through activity that earns a return greater than the investors' required return
Value in use	Economic value
Value metric	An accounting-derived number used to signal value creation or value destruction
Value retention	Sustained value creation by protecting the competitive advantage associated with innovation
Variable cost	Cost that varies with sales in the short run
Variable interest entity (VIE)	In US GAAP and in the context of consolidation, a firm in which we do not have the majority of the voting rights but are entitled to receive the majority of the gains and losses
Vertical integration	Undertaking a sequence of primary activities within a single firm

Vesting period	In the context of stock options, the number of years before the employee becomes unconditionally entitled to the option or shares.

W

Weighted average cost of capital (WACC)	The average of the cost of debt capital and the cost of equity capital, weighted in the proportions of the market gearing ratio
Work in progress, work in process	The stock of partly-completed goods or services
Working capital	Inventory plus trade receivables less trade payables; more broadly, current assets less current liabilities

Y

Yield	General term for a percentage return on an investment

Glossary of financial ratios

Measures of return on capital

$$\text{Return on equity} = \frac{\text{Earnings}}{\text{Average equity shareholders' funds}}$$

EBIT = Earnings before interest and tax

Capital employed = Shareholders' funds + net debt (= debt - cash)

$$\text{Return on capital employed (ROCE)} = \frac{\text{EBIT}}{\text{Average capital employed}}$$

$$\text{Return on net assets (RONA)} = \frac{\text{EBIT}}{\text{Average net operating assets}}$$

Earnings before interest, after tax, EBIAT = EBIT - Tax on EBIT

$$\text{After tax ROCE} = \frac{\text{EBIAT}}{\text{Average capital employed}}$$

The profitability equation

$$\frac{\text{EBIT}}{\text{Average capital employed}} = \frac{\text{EBIT}}{\text{Sales}} \times \frac{\text{Sales}}{\text{Average capital employed}}$$

or,   ROCE   =   'EBIT margin'   ×   'Asset turn'

$$\text{Receivables days} = \frac{\text{Average receivables} \times 365}{\text{Sales}}$$

Net credit given = (Receivables - Payables) × 365/sales

Working capital days = (Receivables + Inventory - Payables) × 365/sales

Economic profit

WACC = Weighted average cost of capital

Capital charge = Average capital employed × WACC

Economic profit = EBIAT - Capital charge

Market-based measures

Earnings = Dividend + Closing shareholders' funds - Opening shareholders' funds

$$Stock\ return = \frac{Dividend + Change\ in\ market\ capitalisation}{Opening\ market\ capitalisation}$$

$$Price\ to\ book = \frac{Market\ capitalisation}{Equity\ shareholders'\ funds}$$

Enterprise value = market capitalisation + value of debt - cash

$$Enterprise\ price\ to\ book = \frac{Enterprise\ value}{Capital\ employed}$$

Asset cover

$$Equity\ to\ total\ assets\ ratio = \frac{Equity}{Total\ assets} = 1 - \frac{Total\ liabilities}{Total\ assets}$$

$$Current\ ratio = \frac{Current\ assets}{Current\ liabilities}$$

$$Acid\ test\ ratio = \frac{Current\ assets\ less\ inventory}{Current\ liabilities}$$

Financial leverage

$$Book\ gearing\ =\ \frac{Net\ debt}{Capital\ employed}$$

$$Debt\ to\ equity\ ratio\ =\ \frac{Debt}{Equity}$$

$$Interest\ cover\ =\ \frac{EBIT}{Net\ interest\ payable}$$

$$Cash\ interest\ cover\ =\ \frac{EBITDA}{Cash\ net\ interest\ paid}$$

Index